EVANGELICAL TRUTH
Practical Sermons for the Christian Home

EVANGELICAL TRUTH
Practical Sermons for the Christian Home

Archibald Alexander

Solid Ground Christian Books
Birmingham, Alabama
2004

SOLID GROUND CHRISTIAN BOOKS
PO Box 660132, Vestavia Hills, AL 35266
205-443-0311
sgcb@charter.net
http://www.solid-ground-books.com

EVANGELICAL TRUTH:
Practical Sermons for the Christian Home

by Archibald Alexander (1772-1851)

From the 1850 edition by Presbyterian Board of Publication, Philadelphia, PA

Published by Solid Ground Christian Books

Classic Reprints Series

First printing of paperback edition October 2004

ISBN: 1-932474-54-4

Manufactured in the United States of America

CONTENTS.

	PAGE
SERMON I.—Obedience to Christ gives Assurance of the Truth of his Doctrines. John vii. 17.	7
SERMON II.—The Knowledge of Sin by the Law. Rom. iii. 20.	25
SERMON III.—The First and Greatest Commandment. Mark xii. 29, 30.	44
SERMON IV.—The Second like unto the First. Mark xii. 31.	54
SERMON V.—The Name Jesus. Matt. i. 21.	68
SERMON VI.—The Incarnation. Luke ii. 13, 14.	76
SERMON VII.—Christ's Gift of Himself for our Redemption. Titus ii. 14.	91
SERMON VIII.—The New Creation. Gal. vi. 15.	106
SERMON IX.—Repentance and Forgiveness the Gift of our exalted Saviour. Acts v. 31.	126
SERMON X.—Receiving Christ by Faith. John i. 12.	140
SERMON XI.—Privileges of the Sons of God. John i. 12, 13.	151
SERMON XII.—Deceitfulness of the Heart. Jer. xvii. 9.	161
SERMON XIII.—Wickedness of the Heart. Jer. xvii. 9.	171
SERMON XIV.—Christ our Wisdom, Righteousness, Sanctification, and Redemption. 1 Cor. i. 30.	195
SERMON XV.—The one Thing needful. Luke x. 42.	208
SERMON XVI.—The Love of Christ. Ephes. v. 2.	220
SERMON XVII.—Love to Christ. John xxi. 17.	229

CONTENTS.

PAGE

SERMON XVIII.—Keeping alive the Love of God. Jude 21. - 246
SERMON XIX.—Strength Renewed by Waiting on the Lord. Isa. xl. 31. - - - - - - - - 268
SERMON XX.—The true Israelite. John i. 47. - - - 275
SERMON XXI.—God to be glorified by those bought with a Price. 1 Cor. vi. 19, 20. - - - - - - 291
SERMON XXII.—The Way in which God leads his People. Isa. xlii. 16. - - - - - - - - 308
SERMON XXIII.—Not slothful, but Followers of the Saints by Faith. Heb. vi. 12. - - - - - - - 333
SERMON XXIV.—Christ the Believer's Refuge and Consolation. Heb. vi. 18. - - - - - - - - 355
SERMON XXV.—Returning to our first Love. Rev. ii. 4, 5. 372
SERMON XXVI.—The Blessedness of trusting in God. Psa. ii. 13. - - - - - - - - - 391
SERMON XXVII.—Faith's Victory over the World. 1 John v. 4. 407
SERMON XXVIII.—The Benefits of Affliction. Psa. cxix. 71. 424
SERMON XXIX.—Excellency of the Knowledge of Christ. Phil. iii. 8. - - - - - - - - - 437
SERMON XXX.—Holding forth the Word of Life. Phil. ii. 16. 447
SERMON XXXI.—The house of God desirable. Psa. lxxxiv. 1, 2. 458
SERMON XXXII.—The Misery of impenitent Sinners. Acts viii. 23. - - - - - - - - - 480
SERMON XXXIII.—Spiritual Worship. Phil. iii. 3. - - 496
SERMON XXXIV.—The Difficulty of knowing our Faults. Psa. xix. 12. - - - - - - - - 514
SERMON XXXV.—God's Grace sufficient. 2 Cor. xii. 9. - 533
SERMON XXXVI.—The dying Martyr's Prayer. Acts vii. 59. 543
SERMON XXXVII.—Christ's gracious Invitation. Matt. xi. 28. 558

PREFACE.

SEVERAL years have elapsed since the author promised to a few friends, that, if life and health should be continued, he would endeavour to prepare a volume of sermons on practical subjects, to be circulated by the Presbyterian Board of Publication. Incessant occupation in professional duties, occasioned the postponement of the fulfilment of this promise from time to time; until recently, when he was informed that the Board of Publication were desirous to put such a volume into circulation; especially for the benefit of families who were deprived of the opportunity of attending on the preaching of the gospel.

At first it occurred to him, that for the purposes of the Board, such a volume had better be composed of a collection of sermons contributed by different ministers of our church. But upon reflection, he was persuaded that it would be found difficult to get the proper persons to furnish discourses on the topics which might be prescribed. And he has observed, that when the sermons of several persons are included in the same volume, there is a disposition in many readers to make invidious comparisons between the authors; and while some discourses are highly valued, others are neglected. Upon the whole, it seems best that every author should make his own book; and to obtain a desirable variety, more volumes of sermons than one should be put into circulation.

The author being aware that books of sermons are not in as much demand as publications of another kind, would not have consented that the Board of Publication should run the risk of an edition of this volume; but this objection was obviated by the generous proposal of the friends referred to above, to bear the whole expense of stereotyping the work.

PREFACE.

In considering what subjects ought to be treated in such a volume, it struck the writer forcibly, that besides the usual evangelical topics, the duties arising out of the several domestic relations should have a place in a work intended especially for the use of families. And in pursuance of this idea, he commenced the preparation of sermons on the duties of husbands and wives, parents and children, masters and servants; but he had not proceeded far, until he found that to do justice to this subject would require a volume by itself; and such a volume he is of opinion is a real *desideratum* in our church. If the author were not so far advanced in years, as to render the undertaking new works presumptuous, he might make an attempt to supply the want which exists. But he feels that he must shortly relinquish, not only his pen, but all earthly labours; and, therefore, he leaves this work to be performed by some other person.

As to the character of the sermons now presented to the public, the reader must judge for himself; but the author would inform him that he must not look for any abstruse disquisitions, eloquent descriptions, or startling novelties in this volume. The sermons contain what the author believes to be evangelical truth, in the exhibition of which, his aim has been to render the gospel perspicuous to persons of common understanding. He has, therefore, adopted a style as plain and simple as he could. The sermons are short, and on an average, may be read in fifteen or twenty minutes. And as this is probably the author's last literary work, it is his earnest desire and prayer, that it may be useful in promoting evangelical and experimental religion when his head shall lie beneath the clods of the valley! He invites other Christians to unite with him in this prayer, for the success of the volume now given to the Christian community.

There is nothing in these sermons which will be found offensive to the lovers of evangelical truth in other denominations. The author, in a long life, has found that real Christians agree much more perfectly in experimental religion, than they do in speculative points; and it is his belief, that a more intimate acquaintance among Christians of different denominations would have a happy tendency to unite them more closely in the bonds of brotherly love. May the time soon come when all the disciples of Christ shall form one great brotherhood under the name of CHRISTIANS! A. A.

PRACTICAL SERMONS.

SERMON I.

OBEDIENCE TO CHRIST GIVES ASSURANCE OF THE TRUTH OF HIS DOCTRINES.

If any man will do his will, he shall know of the doctrine whether it be of God.—JOHN vii. 17.

THE truth of the Gospel is established by two kinds of evidence; external and internal. The former is historical, and depends on the testimony of men to the miracles which have been wrought in confirmation of the Christian religion, and the fulfilment of prophecies, which furnish conclusive evidence of the truth of any doctrine. The nature of this kind of proof is very obvious. If God, by the exertion of his power, in a miraculous way, gives attestation to the declarations of any person, then we know that that person speaks the truth; for God, we are sure, will not give his attestation to an impostor, or to that which is false. Persons, however, may be well acquainted with this species of evidence, and yet may not know any tittle of the truths contained in the Bible, or may entertain very erroneous ideas of the nature of the truths revealed. Thus, in fact, we find men who have examined the external evidences of Christianity, and have been by this means fully convinced of its truth, differing entirely in their views of the doc trines of revelation. In this, there is nothing unaccountable, as this kind of evidence does not bring before the mind the truths revealed, but is external to them; and while two men are equally convinced that the Christian religion is from God, on account of the miracles performed, the record of which has come down to us, well attested; and on account of the numerous prophecies which have been exactly fulfilled; they may nevertheless interpret the Bible on very different principles, and in consequence arrive at very different conclusions. Or, the one may attentively study the contents of the Bible; while the other pays no serious attention to the subject, and remains ignorant of the true system of doctrines taught in this book.

But, in regard to the internal evidence of Christianity, the case is different. The evidence here arises from a view of the truth itself; and can only be fully appreciated by a mind under divine illumination. This evidence may indeed be rendered convincing to any rational mind not under the influence of strong prejudice, by an exhibition of the perfection of the theory of theology and morality which the Bible contains. It can easily be shown, that this theory is far more perfect, than that of any of the heathen sages; and yet the writers were destitute of human learning, and unaided, were utterly incapable of producing such admirable works. By an argument of this kind, Soame Jenyns has demonstrated the truth of Christianity. This mode of reasoning can be appreciated by every rational mind; but there is another species of internal evidence, which is perceived and felt only by such as enjoy the illumination of the Holy Spirit. This arises from a view of the truth itself—from a discernment of its beauty and glory; and also from a consciousness of its salutary effects on the heart. This is the kind of evidence on which saving faith is founded. It is a kind of evidence which can be appreciated by the weak and unlearned, as readily as by the greatest scholars and philosophers. In regard to it, all stand upon a level; or, rather, the simple and unlearned possess the advantage; for the pride of reason and of human science stands very much in the way of the exercise of faith. In accordance with this, our Saviour says, "I thank thee, O Father! because thou hast hid these things from the wise and prudent, and hast revealed them unto babes." For it is an established rule in God's government, to resist the proud, and to cast contempt on the wisdom of this world. As saith the Scripture, "God hath chosen the foolish things of the world to confound the wise, and the weak things of the world to confound the things which are mighty."

Many suppose, that plain unlettered Christians, who know little or nothing of history, and are therefor unable to appreciate the force of the external evidence in favour of Christianity, have no rational foundation for their faith; but merely receive the Scriptures, because they have heard, from their parents and teachers, that they are the word of God. That many in christendom have no better foundation for their faith than this, is readily admitted: but the real Christian, whose mind has been enlightened by the Spirit of God, believes the Scriptures to be the word of God on the best and highest evidence, on the testimony of God himself; for when the truth is apprehended in its spiritual nature, by a divine light shining upon it, it manifests itself to be the word of God; because it bears the impress of God on its face. A blind man may be fully convinced that the sun exists, because thousands testify to the fact; and because, though he does not see this great luminary of day, he feels warmth from its rays; so, men blind to spiritual things may be fully and rationally convinced that Christ was a divine teacher, and the Son of God, by many conclusive arguments. But as the blind man remains ignorant of the visible appearance of the sun, which is perceived by every child who has eyes; so unrenewed men—men destitute of spiritual life, however intellectual and learned, remain blind to the true nature of spiritual objects. The humblest, weakest believer, possesses a better knowledge of the true character of Christ than can be attained by any exercise of reason. This is humbling to human pride, and men of the world are disposed to disbelieve the statement; but its truth is proved by the effects produced by the different kinds of knowledge. "By their fruits ye shall know them." Speculative or natural knowledge, not penetrating into the true excellence of the truths believed, but resting on the external evidences and systematic relations of the truth, exercises but a small influence on the heart and affections; whereas spiritual, or saving knowledge, by which the beauty and glory of divine things are apprehended, has the immediate effect of exciting the affections and emotions, in a way corresponding with the nature of the objects perceived: so that under the influence of new and holy feelings, the purpose of the heart to honour, worship, and obey God, is formed, and this purpose becomes habitual; and the clearer the soul's views of divine things, the firmer and stronger this purpose becomes. The person thus enlightened and affected, is renewed—converted—and all his pursuits, his hopes and fears, his joys and sorrows, are different from what they were before. "Old things are done away, and all things become new."

From what has been said, we may learn the true import of the text, "If any man will do his will, he shall know of the doctrine, whether it be of God;" which may be thus paraphrased. If any man possess that state of mind which will prompt and lead him to choose the service of God, and determine to obey Him, he will be at no loss respecting the truth of my doctrine; for he will have such a view of the excellency of the truth which I deliver and will possess such a conviction of his own sinful and helpless condition, that he will, at once, be persuaded of the divine origin of the plan of redemption, from its perfect adaptation to his own urgent wants. And if he obtains such a view of the purity and perfection of the commandments of God as to delight in the law of God, after the inner man, and to resolve to render universal obedience, he will entertain no doubt about the truth of my precepts; which are nothing else than an exposition and application of the law of God, and whosoever does the will of God from the heart, will experience a pleasure, so pure and-soul satisfying, that he will be sure it must proceed from the eternal fountain of felicity; according to that of the Psalmist, "In keeping thy commandments there is a great reward;" and according to the words of Christ, "my yoke is easy and my burden is light;" and of the apostle John, "his commandments are not grievous."

Suppose a man to be brought to the fixed purpose, to obey the will of God, and to proceed daily in his service, delighted with the law in all its precepts, such a person will experience great peace of mind, and the joy arising from the exercise of holy affections will have an internal evidence of the truth of religion, which no unregenerate man can possess, or well conceive of, for such affections and such obedience are contrary to the bent and inclination of his soul, and he can scarcely believe that there can be a real pleasure in those exercises for which he has no taste. He may, indeed, admit, that if there exists a strong relish for such pursuits, there may be pleasure; but he is apt to be incredulous about the existence of an ardent love of the service of God. For the most part, he views religion to be a constraint, which men place on themselves, and that it is a yoke hard to be borne.

A number of persons brought up in a dark cave, into which the rays of the sun never entered, if brought out, when this luminary was shining in its brightness, would need no arguments to prove its existence; they would have the evidence in themselves, in the shining of the light into their eyes, or, if placed where they could not see the sun, yet, where there was a reflection of his rays, they would need no other evidence of its existence.

Christians are described as persons brought from darkness to "marvelous light;" as being "light in the Lord." Now, if this divine and spiritual light has shined into their hearts, to give them the light of the knowledge of the glory of God, in the face of Jesus Christ, will they be at any loss to know, whence this divine light proceeds? Can they ascribe these new views to any other source, than to the "Father of lights, from whom cometh down every good gift and every perfect gift?" When the mind is in a right state; that is, when it is freed from the blindness of nature, and has the eyes of the understanding opened, the light of the glorious gospel will shine into such a regenerated mind, revealing to it the beauties of holiness, and causing it to rejoice in the glory of God. To such an one Christ appears lovely—the chief among ten thousands, and he becomes the jewel of their hearts. Idols are at once cast away, and he as their rightful King is enthroned in their affections. If believers doubt of their own sincerity, yet they do not and cannot doubt of Christ's excellency and suitableness. His doctrines they humbly receive, and found their hopes of salvation on his faithful word alone. The doctrine of Christ is not merely what as a Prophet he taught; but it is also the doctrine which respects himself. Christ himself is the centre—the substance of Christian doctrine. His divinity—his incarnation—his holy life and miraculous works—his sufferings and humiliation—his crucifixion as an atonement for sin—his resurrection, ascension, and glorification—these truths which relate to Christ's person and work, are known to be divine, by every one who is truly enlightened by the Spirit of God. Every one who does the will of the Father in heaven is thus enlightened, and receives, simply and cordially, the whole doctrine of Christ as far as he is instructed in the Holy Scriptures. He has received an unction which teaches him all these things; that is, a spiritual illumination; so that without the authority of any man or any church, he knows by an internal evidence, that these doctrines which relate to Christ, are true; and that they came from God. To know the truth, to embrace it cordially, to love it sincerely, and to be moulded into a conformity with it, is that which constitutes any one a true Christian. Error never can supply the place of truth. As well might you expect the body to be nourished by poisons as the soul by error. Truth is sometimes mixed with error, in doctrines taught to the people; and if the errors are not fundamental, the truth which accompanies them may prove nourishing; but its efficacy will always be hindered or impaired by error, in proportion to its magnitude and prevalence in the system. In order to salvation, Christ's doctrine must be known and cordially embraced. All the children of God are taught by him. "Ye shall know the truth," says Christ, "and the truth shall make you free." Apostasy is nothing else but a denial of, and departure from, the truth, once professed. Those judicially abandoned of God, and given up to believe a lie that they might be damned, are such as "received not the love of the truth, that they might be saved."

Christ declares, "I am the way, the truth, and the life." All truth as well as life, dwells in him as in its fountain. And every obedient believer is made to know something of the excellence of the truth; so that he can say with Paul, "I count all things but loss, for the excellency of the knowledge of Christ."

Every true believer has the witness in himself. He needs no external evidence to convince him of the truth of the gospel. As he needs no proof that the sun exists and is the source of light when it shines into his eyes; so when the light of the glorious gospel of Jesus Christ who is the image of God, shines into his heart, he knows that this spiritual light proceeds from the Sun of righteousness.

Thus, every true Christian, however weak and unlearned, has a solid and rational foundation for his faith; and there is no other foundation on which a saving faith can rest. Many beheld the wonderful miracles wrought by Jesus Christ, who remained his enemies; and many now believe without a doubt, that these miracles were wrought, on the testimony of eye witnesses, and from the effects produced by Christianity on the state of the world; and they have no doubt, but that many prophecies are proved to be from God, because they have been exactly and literally fulfilled; and yet these persons remain under the predominant influence of the love of the world. "No man," says John, "can say that Jesus is the Christ, but by the Holy Ghost.

In all countries, and in all religions, the mass of the people have a traditional faith. They believe as they have been instructed, and seldom doubt of the truth of their religion, which, however, they receive implicitly, without any examination. The majority in christendom receive the Christian religion on no better evidence, for although it is attended with convincing evidences of its divine origin, with these they are not acquainted. But let us suppose a person to have grown to manhood, with no other than this traditional faith, and then to be brought under a deep conviction that he is a sinner, and that he can do nothing to remove the sentence of condemnation under which he lies, or to restore to purity and perfection his corrupt nature. To such a convicted sinner, the most important inquiry is, "What must I do to be saved?" He hears the gospel. He learns that by believing on Christ, the Son of God, he may obtain everlasting life. At first, the news seems to be too good to be true. He fears that there is some mistake in the matter. But now the Spirit of God enlightens his mind to understand the gospel method of salvation. He sees that the atonement of Christ is sufficient to satisfy all the demands of law and justice. He sees that the door of reconciliation is set wide open, and that he is invited and entreated to be reconciled unto God; and that the greatness and number of his sins are no barrier to the free exercise of mercy. And he not only sees and believes, that Christ is in all respects, a suitable

Saviour, just such an one as he needs; but he beholds a divine glory shining in the face of Jesus Christ, by which he is so attracted, and his thoughts so occupied, that he forgets himself. He is absorbed in the contemplation of the wisdom, the love, the justice, and faithfulness of God, as these attributes shine in the work of redemption. Under these believing views, his affections are strongly moved. He feels springing up in his heart a love to God in Christ, such as he never felt to any other; and his soul is ravished with a peculiar joy, which, as to kind or degree, cannot be described. At this moment, he gives himself away to God. He has a fixed purpose formed in his heart, to honour and obey his Lord and Master, come what will. Has this person no rational evidence of the truth of the Christian religion? There may be a question, whether this evidence ought to be denominated *rational;* for although it is such as does and ought to satisfy the rational mind, it is an evidence not owing to the deductions of reason, or any logical process, but it arises from the supreme excellence of divine truth revealed to the soul, by the illumination of the Holy Spirit. This man knows now certainly, that the doctrine of the gospel is of God. This is the divine anointing, which if a man possess, he needs no one to witness to him, that Jesus Christ is the Son of God, and the Saviour of the lost; for the evidence is complete, and this faith which he exercises in Christ, as thus exhibited, is "the faith of God's elect." But all do not attain to those clear spiritual discoveries which have been described. Some have but dim views of divine truth, and their faith is in proportion weak; but in the use of appointed means it gains strength, and that which was feeble in the beginning, will grow up to maturity. Few of those who are favoured with bright spiritual discoveries of the glory of Christ, at first, continue to enjoy these clear views, long at a time. The blessed vision passes away. They fall back, if not into distressing darkness, yet into an obscure twilight. This is necessary, lest they should conclude that these spiritual views were their own and depended on themselves; and as spiritual pride is apt to rise and swell, in consequence of the delightful exercises of mind, which the soul enjoys, it is expedient that God should withdraw from the soul those views, in a measure, and leave it to feel its own weakness and unworthiness. When the soul is made to see something of the depth of its depravity, and to feel sin, on account of its turpitude, to be a burden, this very conviction furnishes a strong evidence of the divine authority of the word; for it is by the law, as revealed in the Holy Scriptures, that this knowledge often is acquired. That sin does really partake of the evil which is seen in it, the enlightened soul can no more doubt, than it can of its own existence. But if this conviction be true and correct, then certainly, the word which has produced it, must be the word of God. No word of man could ever thus affect the conscience, and search out the secret faults of the heart. The effect of the truth on an awakened conscience is wonderful. It "divides between the soul and the spirit, and is a discerner of the thoughts and intents of the heart." When the faithful preaching of the gospel is heard by one, just beginning seriously to consider his ways, it often appears to him that the preacher has the power of searching the heart; or that some one has communicated to him information respecting his character. All deep conviction of sin, therefore, furnishes a direct proof of the truth of the word. And when we consider how completely the feeling of guilt and condemnation is removed by faith in Christ, and what secret peace takes possession of the mind, we are sure that words which can produce such an effect, must be from God; for where else do we find such effects produced? Whatever others may think, the believer himself cannot doubt, that views which have so suddenly charmed away his grief, must be from God. There is no change in nature more remarkable, than that produced on the feelings of a convicted and distressed sinner, by the simple exercise of faith in Christ. It is a change from overwhelming sorrow, to joy unspeakable; from darkness to marvelous light—from condemnation to reconciliation—from enmity to friendship; in short, from death to life. The enlightened and renewed man has then, the very best evidence of the truth of Christ's doctrine, an evidence which no other can possess, until enlightened by the same Spirit. And now, suppose the person thus renewed by the grace of God, never to have heard or known any thing of the external evidences of Christianity; even if he were to suppose that the gospel was of modern origin, yet he would cleave to it, as having undoubted evidence of being the word of God. And when the children of God fall into darkness, and are sorely buffeted by Satan, and have skeptical thoughts injected into their minds, their deliverance does not come from reasoning, and reading books on the evidences of Christianity, but by the shining of the truth itself into the heart. One ray from the Sun of righteousness will scatter a darkness which has long been oppressive; and one gracious promise applied, and sealed on the heart, will bring peace, when all other resources fail.

Let those who are slow to believe these things, contemplate the patience, the courage, the joy and triumph of the martyrs of Jesus, in the early times of the gospel. Whence this superhuman contempt of torture and of death? Whence the elevated joy, experienced by some in the midst of racks and flames? It was the sight of such effects as these, which multiplied converts to Christianity, at a time, when the very name was punished with a cruel death. And these effects of the gospel have not entirely ceased, even in our day. Even converts lately called out of a savage state, especially in the island of Madagascar, have manifested a Christian fortitude and cheerful resignation to cruel sufferings for the sake of Christ, which does not fall below the same traits in the early martyrs. And how often have those who have had much experience about the beds of dying saints, been filled with wonder and gratitude, at the power of the word of God, when accompanied by his Spirit, to support and console the departing spirit, even when the body was racked with excruciating pain! The evidence, arising from such scenes, is often not only convincing but overwhelming. Often have I wished, when witnessing such scenes, that infidels could be present to see the wonderful efficacy of the gospel, in giving peace and joy to persons in the agonies of death*.

From what has been said, we may derive the following inferences.

1. That unrenewed men, who are not taught of God, however they may by learning and the exercise of reason arrive at the conclusion that the Holy Scriptures are given by inspiration, and contain a true revelation of the will of God; yet never can attain to a true, saving faith; for "we are saved by grace, through faith, and that not of ourselves, it is the gift of God." And we see the reason why a merely rational, or historical faith does not work by love, nor produce any radical change in the character; because by it, however clear and strong, the excellence and beauty and glory of Christ and divine things are not revealed to the mind. The

---

* The writer has now in his recollection, the case of an obscure young woman, whose habits of reserve and modesty were such, that very few persons knew any thing of her religious exercises, until she was laid on the bed of death. Though poor, and obscure, she was not ignorant nor uncultivated; far from it. She had a mind of uncommon intelligence, which, by reading, she had stored with knowledge, especially religious knowledge. The Bible was her daily companion—the Bible was the source of all her comfort. And the doctrines of Christianity she understood not only theoretically, but experimentally. She had felt their power. She had daily proof of their efficacy to support the soul under peculiar trials. Though her pastor, the writer had known nothing of the elevation and fervency of her piety, until called to visit her in her last sickness, when, instead of giving instruction and comfort to the dying saint, he felt it to be one of the highest privileges he ever enjoyed, to witness the heavenly serenity of her countenance, and to hear the expressions of faith and hope which flowed from her lips.

blind man may be as fully convinced of the existence of the rainbow as any other person, and may assent to the fact that what are called colours are exhibited in this phenomenon; but he is incapable of those emotions which are produced in the minds of those who can see, by this sublime and beautiful arch in the heavens. And in this case, we see, that there may be a certain conviction of a truth, when the evidence which produces it, does not present to the mind, the true nature of that truth. Just so it is, in regard to spiritual things; persons who are blind to their nature may, by conclusive arguments and testimony, be convinced of their reality.

2. We learn also, that where there is a sincere love of truth, and a pious disposition to be conformed to the will of God, both by believing what his word declares, and doing what it commands, there is a true faith, and hence it may be inferred that the person possessing such a state of mind, in regard to the truths of the Bible, has been enlightened by the Spirit of God. A ray from Christ, who is "the light of the world," has shined into his heart, to give him the knowledge of the glory of God in the face of Jesus Christ. True knowledge and pious affections are inseparably conjoined; the one cannot exist without the other. The views of the understanding and the purposes of the heart, from the constitution of the mind, must be in coincidence. But the affections and volitions of the heart, are not in coincidence with the mere speculative convictions of the understanding, for reasons already given. Hence we see clearly the true ground of difference between a dead and a living

faith; it is owing entirely to the different kinds of evidence on which they are respectively founded. In the one case, the evidence though convincing, does not afford to the mind a view of the real nature of the truths believed, in the other, the evidence is the excellence and spiritual beauty of the objects of faith. In the one case the evidence is external to the truth; in the other, it is the internal shining of the truth into the mind.

3. Finally, when faith is weak, the true method of strengthening it, is not to be found in logical reasoning, but in divine illumination. There are doubts, which may be removed by a careful and impartial investigation of the evidences of divine revelation; but this may be effected, without any real increase of true faith; this can only be invigorated by the same efficient Agent, by whom it was first produced. All the most vigorous efforts of human reason, in the most gifted minds, can never produce one spiritual idea. This dependence of the soul on God for every step of progress in the divine life, is beautifully illustrated in the prophet Isaiah, "He giveth power to the faint, and to them that have no might he increaseth strength. Even the youths shall faint and be weary; and the young men shall utterly fall. But they that wait upon the Lord shall renew their strength; they shall mount up with wings as eagles, they shall run and not be weary, they shall walk and not faint." Let all then who wish to know whether the doctrines of Christ are true, pray for the illumination of the Holy Spirit; let them get their minds into that state which is favourable for the clear discovery of

the truth, and they will find, that as the light of the sun needs no witnesses to testify of its existence, when it shines into the eyes; so, when obstructions are removed, and the intellect is prepared to receive spiritual ideas, the light of truth shining into the mind, carries its own evidence with it. The man thus enlightened, has no need that any one should testify to him of the truth; for he perceives the light, and tastes the sweetness of the truth, as it is in Jesus. The more the believer grows in grace, the firmer and more efficacious will be his faith. And as the Spirit is given in answer to prayer, freely, we should unceasingly cry to God for this richest, this sum, of all spiritual blessings. The indwelling of the Spirit is the rich fountain of life, from which all holy acts and spiritual exercises and enjoyments proceed.*

* In accordance with the sentiments and reasonings in the preceding discourse, are the facts in the case. Converts among the heathen, in whom the moral change is so remarkable, are not convinced of the truth of the gospel by being made acquainted with its external evidences, of which they are as yet incapable, but by its internal light and power by which their consciences are awakened, and the demerit of sin, and the efficacy of the promises of the gospel to relieve and compose their troubled minds, are felt. And, among men of strong and highly cultivated minds, more have been converted from infidelity, by reading the Scriptures, than by studying the external evidences. This is said to have been the fact in regard to those two eminent men, Saome Jenyns, and Gilbert West, who have written so ably in defence of Christianity. Striking examples of the same kind have been observed by the writer.

SERMON II.

THE KNOWLEDGE OF SIN BY THE LAW.

For by the law is the knowledge of sin.—Rom. iii. 20.

THE Jews, and particularly the Pharisees, prided themselves on the high privileges they enjoyed, as being the chosen people of God, sealed with his seal, the objects of a special providence, and the descendants of Abraham, the friend of God. They seem, therefore, to have entertained the flattering opinion, that they were in a safe state, and that the threatenings contained in the Scriptures did not relate to them, but to the heathen, and apostates. The apostle in this epistle, takes great pains to convince them of their error; and after having proved, by a reference to known facts, the desperate wickedness of the heathen, proceeds to show, by irrefragable arguments, that the Jew was really in no safer condition than the Gentile; that both were naturally under condemnation; that all had sinned, and come short of the glory of God. He insists upon it, that the curses denounced against sinners, in the written law, related rather to the Jews, than to the Gentiles; "for," says he, "what the law saith, it saith to them that are under the law; that every mouth may be stopped, and all the world may become guilty before God." The necessary inference from this universality of sin and guilt is, that by the deeds of the law no flesh can be justified in the sight of God: for the evident reason, that "by the law is the knowledge of sin." That law which convinces of sin, must of necessity condemn, but cannot justify. A sentence of justification is grounded on the fact, that the law has been perfectly obeyed, or has been fully satisfied. But if every man may be convicted of sin by the law, then, evidently, the impossibility of being justified by the deeds of the law, that is, by our own obedience to the law, is manifest.

Our object, in the following discourse, is to make some observations on the nature of the law—and to consider the import of the declaration, that "by the law is the knowledge of sin."

Another apostle gives us a comprehensive definition of sin, which coincides exactly with the import of our text. "*Sin*," says he, "*is the transgression of the law.*" By transgression here, we should understand every want of conformity to the law, for this is the true meaning of the original term here used.

The definition, therefore, includes sins of omission, as well as of commission. Sin has no existence but in relation to the law; for, as the apostle reasons, "where there is no law, there is no transgression." The law may be compared to a straight rule. Sin is the deviation from this rule, and the enormity of the sin may be measured by the degree of obliquity in any act. Laws are of different kinds, according to the nature of the subject regulated. The universe is under law, for the Creator is a God of order; and acts uniformly in the government of his creatures, when they are placed in the same circumstances. But our inquiry, at present, relates to the law given to man, as an accountable moral agent. This law was originally written on the human heart, where vestiges of it are still discernible. It has, therefore, been called, the law of nature. But as through the prevalence of ignorance and error, this law has been greatly defaced in all men, and in the minds of some, almost obliterated; it pleased God to make a full revelation of it, comprehending all moral duty, under two great commandments, enjoining love to God and our neighbour; and to show how these general precepts were to be carried out in their application to practice, ten commandments were engraven by the finger of God, on two tables of stone. These summarily comprehend the whole duty of man.

But as the spiritual and perfect nature of the law was misapprehended by the Jews, and many of the precepts set aside by the false glosses of the Scribes and Pharisees, our blessed Lord, in his public discourses, gave the true interpretation of the law, and repudiated the erroneous opinions of moral duty, which had been long inculcated on the people, by their teachers. Many, in our day, also, entertain very inadequate ideas of the nature and obligations of the law. By some it is believed and taught, that the strictness of the moral law is now relaxed, and that a milder and more indulgent rule of life, has succeeded to the law given to our first parents, while in a state of innocence. But no conclusion is more certain from both reason and Scripture, than the indispensable, immutable nature of the law. As it arises from the nature of God, and the relation of man to him; and is really, a transcript, as far as it goes, of the moral attributes of God, it never can be relaxed, nor undergo any change in its principles. As God is infinitely holy, he never can require less holiness in his creatures, than they are capable of. The idea of bringing down the law to adapt it to the ability of fallen man is absurd; for on that principle, the more any man was under the dominion of sin, the less would the law require of him. This principle would go far to nullify the law altogether, and render it utterly impossible to ascertain precisely what it requires. It is a sound principle, that any inability arising from a depraved nature, has no tendency to alter the demands of the law. The law, therefore, ever remains the same, to the man in innocence—to the man under sin—to the man partially sanctified, and to the saint in heaven. It is the standard of human perfection, and its moral obligation can never cease.

Antinomians hold, that in consequence of Christ's perfect obedience, the law has no demands on those in whose place he obeyed. They pretend, therefore, that the moral law is not obligatory on Christians, to whom the righteousness of Christ is imputed. This is a gross abuse of a cardinal doctrine. And if the thing were true, it would be no privilege, but a real detriment to the believer; for he finds that the keeping of the commandments of God, even in this world, is attended with a great reward.

Others, again, entertain the opinion that the law was altered and improved by our Lord; and they refer to the sermon on the mount. But the alteration is not in the law itself, but in the interpretation of the law; the erroneous opinions respecting some things were set aside, in that discourse. But our Lord, when he lays down the precepts of the law, gives us precisely the great principles of duty which are found in the law of Moses. God is the same from everlasting to everlasting, and his law must be the same.

The law of God is not an arbitrary rule, but, as was said, is founded on the nature of man, and the relation in which he stands to God, and his fellow creatures. Reason dictates, that a rational, choosing agent, should employ all his faculties, and direct all his actions, to the glory of his Creator; and as this end can in no other way be attained, than by obeying the will of God, therefore, the manifestation of the divine will must be the law of all rational creatures. And as to the measure of obedience required, it is evident, that there can be no limit to its perfection, except that which necessarily arises from the limited nature of the faculties of creatures. The idea intended to be communicated is, that all the faculties and affections of every rational creature, are reasonably put into requisition, to glorify the Creator. It cannot be supposed, that any thing less than entire devotedness to the will of God should be required; or when required, that there should not be a moral obligation on the creature to obey.

That the law of God requires perfect obedience is self-evident; for what is perfect obedience but that which the law demands? To suppose that any law could be satisfied by an imperfect obedience, involves the absurdity, that the law requires something which it does not require. It may, perhaps, appear to a mind alienated from God, to be a hardship, to be under obligation to love and serve God continually, to the full extent of its powers. But if the mind were renewed, and the law and service of God were found to be the happiness and delight of the soul, then it would no longer appear to be a hardship to be required to love God with all the heart. No man will complain of that which is necessary to his highest felicity. But if something less than the entire heart were required, we might ask, how much less? And if not required to serve God, all our time, what proportion should be devoted to his service? But, if it should be alleged, that uniform perfection of obedience ought not to be insisted on, since man is a fallible, erring creature; but that there ought to be some indulgence granted to the frailties of human nature, I would reply, that if any indulgence to sin be allowed, there can be no limit fixed to which it should be extended. Such a principle would destroy the obligation of the moral law. There ought to be no indulgence allowed to that which deforms the image of God in man, and which tends to destroy or lessen his own happiness. Again, these frailties belong not to our nature, as it came perfect from the hand of the Creator, but belong to our sinful nature, to which a holy law can show no indulgence. And, as before intimated, our happiness is intimately connected with universal obedience. No creature can render to God as much love and reverence as he deserves. If the capacity of any such being were enlarged a hundred, or a thousand fold, the obligation to exercise all his powers in loving and serving God, would be as complete as to serve him with the ability which he now possesses.

Since then we are capable of paying so small a part of what we owe to our Creator, is it not most ungrateful, as well as unreasonable, to wish to detract from his service any part of what we are capable of rendering? Would not this be the worst kind of robbery, even the robbery of God? Such murmurings against the demands of the law, are after all, founded on some undefined notion, that there is some injustice in the case; as if it would be a privilege and an increase of desirable liberty, if we were not under this obligation, to render perfect obedience, at all times. Now, although this is the language of a depraved heart, yet it can easily be demonstrated, that the idea is not consonant to the truth; and that the law of God is not only holy and just, but wise and good, and the very best and happiest rule under which the creature could be placed.

The ground of difficulty is in our depraved nature, which has lost all relish for the service of God. The mind of man must be active, and no species of action is in itself so morally excellent, and accompanied with so much pleasure, as the love and service of God. And to a soul rightly constituted, the most intense exercise of holy affection is so far from being felt as a burden or task, that it affords the sweetest pleasure of which we ever partake. If the heart were right, even as God made it, there would be no difficulty experienced in complying with the command to love the Lord our God, with all our heart, mind and strength. And the same may be said respecting the love of our neighbour. It is our sinful selfishness which renders this duty difficult, and causes some to think that the command to love our neighbour as ourselves is not only unreasonable, but impossible.

To be perfectly obedient to the commandments of God is to be completely happy. Surely, no one ought to complain of being required to pursue his own greatest happiness. The angels in heaven are happy, because they are holy, and always employed in holy exercises and duties. From what has been said, the truth of the apostle's declaration is evident, that "the law of God is holy, and the commandment holy, just and good."

The proposition contained in our text, that "by the law is the knowledge of sin," is so evident from the definition of sin, given by the apostle John, that there does not appear to be any necessity for further demonstration of its truth. All that will be requisite, in regard to this point, will be to make a practical use and application of the evident truth.

If our actions had always been conformable to the precepts of God, the closest application of the law would produce no conviction of sin. And that such perfection of obedience is possible to human nature is manifest, by the example of Christ, who possessed all the faculties and appetites which are the constituents of human nature; and was in all points tempted as we are; and yet "he knew no sin," though he knew the law perfectly. He could appeal to his bitterest enemies and say, "which of you convinceth me of sin?" He continued from the beginning to the end of his life, "holy, harmless, undefiled and separate from sinners, and no guile was found in his mouth." From this perfect example it is manifest, that the law of God is perfectly adapted to human nature, and that it may be constantly obeyed by the faculties which we possess, were it not for sin which dwelleth in us.

If the moral law is the measure of our duty, then just so far as man has deviated from this perfect rule, just so far the law shows that he is a sinner. And, whereas the law demands a positive compliance with its requisitions, as well as prohibits the doing of certain acts, it follows, that there are sins of omission as well as sins of commission. And, indeed, as love is the main thing which the law requires, the defect of this holy affection is the evil fountain from which all other sins take their rise. Sins of commission could never be committed until there is some defect in the strength and constancy of this holy principle. Human nature may be compared to a complicated machine, which has within it, powerful springs which keep it in operation. But such a machine requires a balance or regulator, which may preserve all the parts in their proper places, and give due energy and direction to every part. If the balance wheel, be taken away, the machine loses none of its power, but its action becomes irregular, and no longer subserves the purpose for which it was put in motion. It moves, it may be, more rapidly than before, but to its own ruin. So it is with man. He is an agent, possessing active powers, and a variety of appetites, affections, and passions, which require to be regulated, and properly directed; otherwise, their most powerful action will be of a ruinous character. Now if it be asked, what was made the regulating principle in man, to which all his powers should be subservient? Two things are necessary to give harmony and a right direction to the complex faculties and affections of man. The first is, light; the second, love. Or, to speak more correctly, an enlightened conscience, and uniform and constant love to God. But when sin was introduced, the mind was blinded, conscience misdirected, and the love of God in the soul was extinct. The man however, still remains a moral agent, and an accountable creature; otherwise, he would be incapable of sinning.

Although the mind of man has fallen into an awful state of blindness, and disorder, yet conscience is not obliterated: as far as it has light, it still remonstrates against the commission of sin, and utters its voice of condemnation, when sin has been committed Happily, some actions are intuitively seen to be morally wrong, and by no sophistry can the soul be persuaded to approve them. But in regard to a large part of sinful acts, or omissions, most men remain ignorant of them, because they know not the extent and spirituality of the law. This is remarkably the case in regard to the affections and purposes of the heart, in which sin has its origin, and its essence. And mere theoretical knowledge of the law is not sufficient: many by means of a good religious education, possess this; and yet feel no deep conviction of the depth and turpitude of the sin of their hearts. It requires the convincing light of the Holy Spirit to shine in upon the conscience, and to cause the mind to view itself, as it were in the mirror of God's holy law. This conviction by the law, is the common preparatory work, before mercy is bestowed. "The whole need not a physician, but they who are sick." It is unnecessary to perplex ourselves with doubts about our spiritual condition, because we may not have had, in our experience, as distinct a work of the law, as some others. If we are true Christians, we do now possess such a spiritual knowledge of the law, that we are daily convinced of our want of conformity to it, and do see and feel something of the odious nature of the sin which dwells within us. Now, this is the only kind of conviction, which is essential to true religion. The greatest degree of mere legal conviction is no evidence of a renewed mind. The devils and impenitent sinners will all have this kind of conviction, at the day of judgment, and to all eternity. If, therefore, we have been led to see and feel the intrinsic evil of sin, we need not be troubled because we cannot distinctly trace, in our experience, what is commonly called a law work; for, though conviction of sin by the Holy Spirit, is essential to a true Christian, yet this is always included in true repentance; repentance, indeed, founded on just views of the turpitude of sin, as seen by the light of the Spirit, in the mirror of God's holy law. This conviction of sin increases in the mind of the true believer, in proportion to his growth in grace. The more eminent any man is in piety, the deeper will be his sense of the inward defilement of sin, and the greater his self-abhorrence on account of it, according to that of Job "I have heard of thee by the hearing of the ear, but now mine eye seeth thee, wherefore I abhor myself, and repent in dust and ashes."

They who dream of a perfection in this life, which leads them to think, that they are free from all sin, evidently have not the same kind of religion as the patriarch Job, who is declared to have been "a perfect and upright man." Such are evidently ignorant of the purity and spirituality of the law of God; or ignorant of the true state of their own hearts. Whoever obtains a spiritual view of the law, will possess by the law, a right knowledge of sin. There is no better evidence of an enlightened mind, and renewed heart, than just views and feelings in regard to our own sins; and especially, the sins of the heart. It seems, at first view, wonderful, that any person should be so blinded as to think and say, in the face of express declarations of Scripture to the contrary, that he has no sin. But there are many blinding influences which operate on the human heart, which itself is declared to be "deceitful above all things." And among these none is more efficient than spiritual pride. The selfish heart rejoices and glories in the idea of its own superiority to others; and under this illusion, with avidity admits the persuasion, that all its iniquities are purged, and that it needs no further purification; and is henceforth free from the necessity of mortifying the deeds of the body, and crucifying the flesh with its affections and lusts; and from the necessity of asking for the pardon of daily sins.

That the majority of men possess very inadequate ideas of the evil of sin, is evident from their contentment under its defilement. Many are not only contented to remain under the power of sin, but they embrace the odious monster with a wonderful avidity, and repel every attempt to deliver them from this mortal and evil disease. Even those who, for the sake of reputation, maintain an exterior free from gross transgressions, do often, cherish in their hearts ideas, desires, and purposes, which contain the very essence of iniquity; and yet they seem to have no discernment of the hateful nature of the lusts of the flesh and of the spirit, which they cherish in their hearts. They appear to be satisfied, like the Pharisee of old, if they can keep the outside of the cup and platter clean. How little the real evil of sin is perceived, even by professors of Christianity is manifest, from the little concern which they feel to be cleansed from all filthiness of the flesh and spirit. They do not groan as did the apostle Paul, under a painful sense of indwelling sin, but are very much at ease in Zion. If, indeed, under the power of temptation, they are guilty of some overt act of transgression, they are often deeply wounded, and discover much concern and sorrow for what they have done. But it is an evidence, that this concern, for the most part, springs from a selfish principle, that sins of greater turpitude are committed in the spirit, in the imaginations and desires of the heart, for which they feel little or no regret. But souls under the sanctifying influence of the Holy Spirit, are led to see that their chief disease is one of the heart; and before God, they mourn daily over their want of holy feelings and emotions, and on account of the many evils which they, by the application of the law, detect in themselves. And from the evil thoughts and desires which often spring up in them, they are convinced that the heart itself, which generates such sinful thoughts, must be desperately wicked. So far indeed, as it has been renewed, there is another principle implanted; but the old man has great strength, and even when it was hoped that particular sins were completely mortified, yet afterwards, under circumstances favourable to their exercise, they sprout anew, and with vigour strive for the mastery. The great business of the Christian is to oppose and mortify these corruptions, which remain after conversion, in the regenerate. Hence there must be a perpetual conflict between the flesh and the Spirit—between the old man and the new. And although the real Christian is often discouraged with his want of success, in this warfare, yet the Captain of salvation has assured him of ultimate victory. None do truly engage in this warfare but such as have been enlightened to see the evil of sin as reflected from the mirror of the holy law. And the more they are convinced of sin, the more do they have recourse to the fountain opened for sin and uncleanness.

The use which we should make of this subject is

1. To endeavour to get clear views of the extent, spirituality, and purity of the moral law, in order that we may know something of the multitude and malignity of our sins. We should, therefore, not only learn the nature of the law as exhibited in the Holy Scriptures, but should with conscientious fidelity and diligence apply the rule to our own hearts and lives, by a frequent and impartial examination of ourselves. Every hour spent in such self-scrutiny will reveal to us evils which before we had not noticed. And no sin can be mortified and subdued, until it is detected, and its evil nature discerned. And, as all true spiritual knowledge is from the Holy Ghost, we should incessantly pray for this inestimable blessing, which Christ has so emphatically taught, will be freely given to every one who asks—that is, who asks with faith and importunity.

2. As the law convicts every man of sin, justification by it is impossible; for even one sin would render it impossible for the transgressor to receive a sentence of acquittal; how much more impossible is it, when our sins are literally innumerable!

The only condition of justification by the law, is perfect obedience, and no such obedience can be rendered by any mere man; but it has been rendered by Christ, in our nature, for he was made under the law, and fulfilled all righteousness. And of this ground of acceptance the sinner is warranted, by the free call of the gospel, to avail himself, by believing with all his heart in the Lord Jesus Christ.

3. If the law discovers sin of every kind to be a base and odious thing, we should be solicitous to be cleansed from its defilement; and, in order to this, should come often to the fountain for sin and uncleanness, opened by the death of Christ; that is, we should by faith apply to the blood of sprinkling, and should seek daily to purify ourselves from all filthiness of the flesh and spirit. We should earnestly and importunately offer up the petition, which Christ offered in his intercessory prayer, "Sanctify us through thy truth, thy word is truth." The word rendered effectual by the Holy Spirit, is the efficient means of cleansing to the souls of believers. We should ply this work every day; for it is carried on by the use of means, and our success in it depends very much on the diligence and fidelity with which we use the means of God's appointment. "Blessed," says Christ "are they that hunger and thirst after righteousness, for they shall be filled. Blessed are the pure in heart, for they shall see God. Be ye holy, for I am holy."

4. A spiritual knowledge of the law is the true source of evangelical repentance. As sin is a disconformity to the law, and its turpitude is seen in this glass, the sight of it will fill the soul with sorrow and compunction, and work such a hatred of sin as will effectually turn away the soul from the abominable thing which God hates. This view of sin, in its deformity and vileness, will also cause the soul not only to mourn, but to be ashamed and con-

founded in the presence of God. And as this quality of baseness and defilement belongs to all sin, true repentance will consist in a hearty aversion to all sin, and a fixed purpose to forsake it, which will show itself by reformation of life.

5. The knowledge of sin, produced by the law, will have a tendency to make the true penitent willing to leave the present state, and forsake the clay tabernacle, as sin cleaves to the soul as long as it remains here, and these vile bodies must be laid in the dust, before they will be purified from the disorder which sin has introduced. As perfection in holiness is the blessedness reserved for the future state of the believer, he will often direct a longing look to those regions of purity, into which neither sin nor sorrow can ever enter. This delightful hope he cherishes, and it leads him, while detained below, to seek for purity. "He," says the apostle John, "that hath this hope in him, purifieth himself, even as He is pure." How sweet the rest, when all contest with sin and temptation shall cease! How glorious the state in which we shall see no longer darkly through a glass, but face to face, and where we shall know even as we are known!

6. The most important benefit of the knowledge of sin, by the law, is, that it shows us our absolute need of a better righteousness than our own, and impels us to look for salvation, to the cross of Christ. The law is a schoolmaster to bring us unto Christ; and, although this had primary reference to the ceremonial law, the moral law is not excluded; but is now made use of to drive sinners to that refuge, which God, in mercy, has prepared

for them. Commonly the first concern of the awakened soul has relation to the law, which he now begins to see to possess a binding obligation, and that he has broken it in innumerable instances, in thought, word and deed. The application of the law to the conscience of an awakened sinner, puts him, at first, on earnest efforts to repair the breach which he has made. He now strives by prayers and tears, and various human devices, to make satisfaction for his sins; but the more he strives to raise himself out of the horrible pit and miry clay, the deeper he sinks, and like a prisoner in a dark deep pit, no effort that he can make, has any tendency to extricate him from his helpless condition. But when having exhausted all his efforts, without success, he is ready to despair of salvation, he hears the voice of a kind Deliverer, inviting him to look unto him and be saved. It is as though one let down a rope to the helpless prisoner. All he has to do is to take fast hold, and he is drawn up and finds himself in safety, and at liberty. So the convinced sinner seizes the invitations of the gospel, with the strong grasp of faith, and behold! he is brought out of darkness into the marvellous light of the gospel, and from a state of condemnation to complete justification. If I now speak to any convinced, discouraged soul, who finds that he can do nothing to remove either the guilt or defilement of sin, I would earnestly and affectionately exhort such to take immediate refuge under the cross. The crucified Redeemer sends forth an influence from this point, which effectually draws the hearts of sinners to himself. "Look unto me and be ye saved, all the ends of the earth, for I am God, and there is none beside me." As Moses lifted up the brazen serpent in the wilderness for the healing of those who were dying by the venemous bite or sting of the fiery serpents; so the Son of Man has been lifted up, that whosoever believeth on him might have everlasting life. All that was required in the former case was to look, and all that is necessary to salvation now is faith, which is nothing else but looking unto Jesus for his help and deliverance.

SERMON III.

THE FIRST AND GREATEST COMMANDMENT.

The first of all the commandments is; Hear, O Israel, the Lord our God is one Lord: and thou shalt love the Lord thy God with all thy heart, and with all thy soul, and with all thy mind, and with all thy strength. This is the first commandment.—MARK xii. 29, 30.

THERE are two reasons why God should be loved with all the heart: the first is his infinite excellence and loveliness in himself; the second, his goodness exercised toward us in creation, providence, and redemption. It should not seem hard to be required to love God with all the heart, soul, mind and strength. This requisition is most reasonable; for God is worthy of our highest and most constant love; and our own happiness also is consulted in this requirement; for the soul can never be completely blessed but in the perfect love of its Maker. But, in our fallen state, we cannot love God with that intensity and constancy which are required in this first commandment. True, in our fallen state we cannot love God at all, by any strength that is in us. But does this prove that it is unreasonable to love God in any degree? If the heart was right in the sight of God, it would be as easy to love God with all the heart, as to love him in the lowest degree; yea, it would be easier; for the soul would be happier in the perfect exercise of love, than in an imperfect exercise of this affection. Again, if God was satisfied with less than perfect love, he would be content that his rational creatures should possess less moral excellence, less of his own image, than they are capable of; yea, he would be satisfied that they should remain in a state of moral depravity; for every defect of perfect love is moral depravity—is sin, that "abominable thing which God hateth." The total want of love to God is the essence and root of all depravity; and just so far as we fall short of that perfect love which this first commandment requires, just so far we are inwardly defiled with sin. But is it reasonable to require of creatures what they have no ability to perform? If they desired with all their heart to do their duty, and yet could not, for want of the proper faculties, then indeed, they would be blameless; no more could be required of them. But what is the sinner's inability? It is not the want of faculties or opportunities. The same faculties and affections with which he so ardently pursues after the world, would be sufficient for the performance of all that is required of him, if he was rightly disposed. But "the carnal mind is enmity against God; is not subject to his law, neither indeed can be." Will the sinner plead this inveterate enmity as his excuse? This is too absurd to be received by any one. Such inability as this is the essence of iniquity. Instead of excusing the sinner, it is the very ground of culpability. External acts are evil as proceeding from such a malign principle. No one truly convinced of sin can ever think of pleading this inability as an apology. If the law had required us to love God with all the powers of the highest angel, who is possessed of faculties which do not belong to human nature, it would have been unreasonable. But his requisition is to love him with all *our* hearts, with all *our* souls, with all *our* minds, with all *our* strength. The law is exactly adapted to our minds. It requires just what our faculties are capable of, when not debilitated by sin. And to holy creatures, the command to love God with all their hearts, cannot appear grievous. The holy angels would not consider it a privilege to be released from the obligation to love God with all their powers. Indeed, holy men upon earth do not view this as a hardship. They have no desire that this first and greatest of all commandments should be annulled or relaxed. They see not only a reasonableness in the requisition, but a divine beauty in conformity to it, which causes them to hunger and thirst after perfect holiness. This then is not an arbitrary appointment, but the law of our nature.

These four things may be distinguished in our love of God. 1. A high esteem of his character, and a complacency in his moral attributes, as exhibited in Holy Scripture. 2. A desire that God should be glorified, and a rejoicing in his greatness, majesty, sovereignty, independence, perfection, and blessedness. 3. Gratitude for his favours and blessings of every kind, conferred upon us. 4. A desire of the greatest possible nearness to God. The soul actuated by love, ardently seeks union with the beloved object, of the closest kind; and communion intimate and reciprocal. Love is impatient of absence, and exerts itself to remove hindrances to a near access to the person beloved. But, as in our present state of ignorance, the soul enjoys only obscure views of God, love is chiefly exercised in desire—desire of clearer knowledge—desire of greater conformity—desire of more intimate communion—desire that God may be glorified. Under each of these heads a great variety of emotions are found in experience to exist, not only different degrees of the same affection, but a variety in kind, according to the view which the rational soul is enabled to take of the attributes, works and dispensations of God. Among these is adoration, accompanied with holy wonder at the incomprehensibility of the great Creator! This emotion, we have reason to think, enters deeply into the worship of the heavenly hosts; especially of those who, like Gabriel, stand in the immediate presence of God. And this view cannot be entertained without a corresponding sense of the creature's littleness and insignificance, and a voluntary self-abasement. The heavenly worshippers are, therefore, represented as veiling their faces, and falling prostrate, and casting their crowns at the feet of the great I AM. And even in the imperfect worship among men, this holy veneration and godly fear is an essential ingredient. The holiest men, as Isaiah, Daniel, John &c., were overwhelmed when the divine majesty was clearly manifested to their view. Some of the divine attributes are adapted to produce the feeling of awe or fear; but others, complacency, or an emotion of elevated delight. Now, as the views which are obtained of the character of God, are commonly complex, the emotions experienced will also be of a mixed nature; the awful or the joyful predominating, according as the one or the other class of divine attributes is presented to the mind.

As our love to creatures includes not only complacency, but benevolence, it may be asked, how we can exercise benevolence to the infinitely glorious and ever blessed God, as he is incapable of receiving any accession to his glory or felicity. The reply to which is, that towards God this affection is exercised in desiring that his glory may be manifested to all intelligent creatures; in rejoicing in the infinitely glorious excellence of his character and in the immeasurable felicity which he possesses in and of himself, and in his immutable independence, and eternal sovereignty over all creatures in the heavens and in the earth.

Some persons, fond of over-refinement in their speculations, have come to the abstract conclusion, that gratitude is no virtue, or no part of a holy character, because, as they allege, it is not a disinterested, but a selfish feeling. Now, whether it be selfish or disinterested, the unsophisticated moral sense of all men has determined, not only that it is a virtuous exercise, but that a large part of holiness in the creature, consists in a flow of gratitude to the Author of all good, for his multiplied and marvellous benefits, freely bestowed. And the Holy Scriptures confirm the dictates of our moral feelings. No iniquity is portrayed in darker colours than ingratitude. "The ox knoweth his owner and the ass his master's crib, but Israel doth not know, my people doth not consider." "Hear, O heavens, and give ear, O earth, for the Lord hath spoken, I have nourished and brought up children, and they have rebelled against me." A large part of the Psalms, given by divine inspiration, is taken up in expressing gratitude to God for his various mercies. Take for example Psa. ciii., "Bless the Lord, O my soul, and all that is within me bless his holy name. Bless the Lord, O my soul, and forget not all his benefits. Who forgiveth all thine iniquities, who healeth all thy diseases. Who redeemeth thy life from destruction; who crowneth thee with loving-kindness, and tender mercies. Who satisfieth thy mouth with good things, so that thy youth is renewed like the eagle's." The expression of gratitude by praise is declared to be not only comely, but the method by which God may be glorified. And it is not confined to the earth, it is the chief employment of heaven. The redeemed of the Lord, who stand on Mount Zion, clothed in white robes, with palms in their hands, cried with a loud voice, saying, "salvation to our God who sitteth upon the throne, and to the Lamb." And the burden of the song of the redeemed, in heaven is, "Unto him that loved us, and washed us from our sins in his own blood, and hath made us kings and priests unto God and his Father; to him be glory and dominion for ever and ever."

But there is no propriety in considering religious gratitude a selfish feeling. We are incapable of a more disinterested affection. It is true, it is occasioned by benefits conferred upon ourselves; but it essentially consists in a desire to make some suitable return for the mercies received. Genuine gratitude would not stop short of a full return, if the thing were possible, but as it is not, it vents itself in praise and thanksgiving. Much of the spirit of true devotion in heaven and in earth consists in the lively exercise of gratitude. And when any are brought under true conviction of sin, no view of their disobedience affects them so deeply and tenderly, as their ingratitude. These are the views which melt the hard heart, and produce genuine contrition of spirit. The inferences which we may draw from what has been said, are,

1. That when all duty to God is expressed by the word love, the term must be understood in a very comprehensive sense, as including a great variety of emotions and affections, all which however, are produced by some just views of the divine character.

2. If this commandment is still in force, and God's moral law never changes, then undoubtedly, all men who ever lived in the world are sinners; for sin is a transgression of the law. All have failed to love God with all the heart and soul and mind and strength.

3. It hence appears, that not only have all men failed to come up to the perfection which this commandment requires; but, by nature, all have utterly and totally come short; for by nature, all men love the creature more than the Creator. "They are lovers of pleasure, more than lovers of God." Indeed, they do not love God at all, but are at en

mity with him. They are "alienated from the life of God, through the ignorance that is in them. There is none that doeth good, no not one. There is no fear of God before their eyes, and the way of peace have they not known. The heart is deceitful above all things and desperately wicked. The carnal mind is enmity against God."

4. We see from a consideration of this subject, that the want of love to God is the corrupt fountain from which all other sins, as so many streams, flow. The first sin, and every other sin have had their source in this defect. All evil actions, even the worst, may be traced up to this corrupt source. As the sum of obedience was love, so the germ of all sin is the defect of this holy principle. And where the defect is total, there is total depravity.

5. From this subject, Christians may learn how much iniquity still remains in their hearts. Just so far as you come short of loving God with all the heart, soul, mind, and strength, just so far are your hearts evil in the sight of God. Here, two things deserve consideration; the first is, that when we do love God, the affection falls very far short of that intensity which this commandment requires. It is cold, and feeble, when it should glow with sacred fire. And again, there is often an interruption of the exercise of our love. We fail in constancy, as well as in intensity. We forget God, or we forget his benefits. The objects of the world, too often steal away our hearts from God. O how little veneration do we feel, when we pronounce the awful name of Jehovah! or when we enter into

his house, and professedly engage in his solemn worship. How little zeal have we for the glory of God! How little delight in contemplating his character! How little gratitude for his marvellous loving-kindness; especially for his redeeming love! When we hold up this mirror before us, how dreadful our deformity! How innumerable our sins! Truly "they are more than the hairs of our head."

6. From this subject, we learn the blindness of those, who depend for salvation on their own goodness of heart, on their innocence of life, on the morality of their conduct; or, on a scrupulous and exact performance of external duties, whether ceremonial or moral.

7. And hence, we see the absolute necessity of a radical change of heart. If the moral image of God in man is defaced, none but God himself can renew us again in this image. In the first creation, it was the noblest production of the Almighty, and in the new creation, God must be the efficient agent. By him alone, can we be "created in Christ Jesus unto good works."

8. But although we see nothing in mere man but disconformity to this holy commandment; yet in Jesus Christ, who was made under the law, we observe obedience to this commandment perfectly exemplified. He obeyed both internally and externally, for "he was holy, harmless, undefiled, and separate from sinners." He never had a thought or desire which in the least deviated from this rule. And this perfect righteousness of our Mediator, was not only for our example, but for our justification, by being made over to us by imputation.

9. "The end of the commandment is charity out of a pure heart." "If ye love me," says Christ, "keep my commandments." "Love," says Paul, "is the fulfilling of the law." As all holy obedience flows from love, and is its natural expression; if we wish to glorify God by doing good works, we must keep ourselves in the love of God, by the Holy Ghost. Good works are the fruits which the Christian must bring forth; but the savour and sweetness of these fruits is nothing else but love to God.

10. Finally, we should be constantly endeavouring to approach nearer and nearer to the perfection which the law requires. We should be engaged daily, in cleansing ourselves from all filthiness of the flesh and spirit, and perfecting holiness in the fear of God. The more conformable we are to this commandment, in heart and life, the greater will be our felicity and glory in the world to come.

SERMON IV.

THE SECOND LIKE UNTO THE FIRST.

And the second is like, namely this, Thou shalt love thy neighbour as thyself.—MARK xii. 31.

IF man had been placed alone upon earth, or so far separated from all other rational creatures that he could have had no knowledge of them, there would have existed no foundation for this commandment. But man was made to live in society, and mutual love is the very cement of society. Men should love one another, because they are all the workmanship of the same almighty hand; because they all partake of the same nature, being the descendants of the same original parents; because they are all subjected to the same evils and infirmities; and because they are all under the same responsibility, and hastening to the same termination of their earthly existence. Originally man was created in the image and likeness of God, in knowledge and true holiness, and this was the foundation of the obligation to exercise mutual esteem and moral complacency. But this likeness to God having been defaced, we cannot be required to love one another with this kind of love, until we are renewed in the spirit of our mind; renewed in knowledge after the image of him that created us. Certainly, God requires no one to approve of that which He disapproves, or to love that which He hates. But the loss of the moral image of God does not release us from the obligation to love one another as the creatures of God, and as proceeding from the same stock. The love of benevolence which regards the happiness of the person beloved, may be exercised to the utmost extent, toward those whose moral character is not amiable. When God is said to love the world of mankind, it cannot be supposed that he approves their sinful character, but that he seeks their best interests—their everlasting welfare. So, when his law requires men to love one another, it must be the love of benevolence which is primarily required, while they remain in an unholy state. But whenever his image is in any degree restored in any of our fallen race, it is evident that we should love them on account of that image, for the same reason that we should love the moral excellence of God himself.

The principal difficulty which has been found in explaining this second commandment is the degree of love which is required of us, toward our neighbour. "THOU SHALT LOVE THY NEIGHBOUR AS THYSELF." Now, to many this seems to be simply impossible. Some expositors have therefore explained the meaning to be, Thou shalt love thy neighbour as truly as thyself, or with the same kind of love. But this cannot be admitted to be the true import of this commandment. For in the first and greatest commandment, the degree in which we should love God is fixed. It must be with all the heart, all the soul, all the mind, and all the strength. If it had only been intended to teach that we should love our neighbour in some degree, there would have been no use in saying "as thyself." And according to this interpretation, the least conceivable degree of love would have answered the demands of the law. Undoubtedly, the commandment should be taken in its plain and obvious meaning. It does require, that we should love our neighbour as much as we love ourselves. And however impossible this may be to fallen man, it would not be so, if he were perfectly holy. First then, whatever of excellence my neighbour may possess, I should have the same esteem for it, as if that excellence belonged to myself. Paul, who is a good expositor of the law, exhorts, "to esteem others better than ourselves." Why should we value moral worth when perceived in our own character, more than when the same is observed in the character of another? And as self-love would lead us, under views of truth, to desire our own moral improvement, so the law of God requires us to seek the moral improvement of our brother, with the same intensity of desire.

Again, we should desire and seek his happiness, as much as we seek our own. Here is the point of difficulty; and to remove it, I would remark, that it is not the instinctive desire of well-being which is implanted in us, and in all living creatures, to which reference is had. This principle of self-preservation is not at all under the control of the will. We can no more divest ourselves of it, than of our existence. No principle of the same kind and strength is implanted in us, in relation to the well-being of others. And no rational, voluntary affection can ever be so strong as to countervail this instinctive desire of the continuance of life and of happiness. This instinctive principle, so deeply inherent in our constitution, is not of a moral nature. It exists in equal strength in the good and the bad, in angels and devils. But, besides this, there is in man a rational regard to his own best interests, leading him to adopt and pursue such measures as appear to him to be best adapted to promote his highest happiness. Now this regard to our own best interests is a duty recognized in this very commandment; for we are required to love our neighbour as *ourselves;* that is, as we love ourselves. The rule of duty prescribed is this: As you will not omit to pay a regard to your own welfare and happiness, for the principle of self-preservation will prompt you to this; so pay the same regard to the welfare and best interests of your neighbour. This kind and degree of affection to one another does not require us to neglect or disregard our own happiness. If I had a disposition to seek my neighbour's happiness as much as I do my own, this would not lessen but increase my personal happiness; for true enjoyment is not so much connected with the exercise of self-love, as with the indulgence of benevolence. But to bring this matter fairly before the moral judgment of our minds, I will suppose this case; that I have it in my power by some act of mine to increase my own happiness, by depriving my neighbour of an equal portion of his, would it be right for me to do so? Every mind of right moral feelings would answer promptly and unhesitatingly, It would not. But why would it not? No reason can be assigned but this, that I am bound by the law of God, to regard the happiness of my neighbour as much as I do my own. If this were not the true principle of duty—if it were lawful for me to love myself more than I love my neighbour, then it would be lawful for me to detract from his happiness to increase my own.

What has been remarked respecting the instinctive principle of self-preservation, is equally applicable to what are called the natural affections, as of parents to their children. These affections are a part of our constitution, and are often exceedingly strong, and intended, like the principle of self-preservation, to secure what could not be so well provided for, by any perfection of reason or conscience. And no love governed by reason and a sense of duty can commonly overcome these strong instinctive affections. They are, however, not so uncontrolable as the principle of self-preservation. These affections belong, not to the class of selfish, but benevolent feelings; and therefore they do not directly serve to illustrate our subject.

Though we are bound by the law of God to desire and seek our neighbour's welfare, as much as our own, it does not follow, that we have as much in our power, in regard to him, as ourselves. Every man, so to speak, is put in charge of himself, but not in the same degree of his brother. We have a power over our own minds, but no direct power over the mind of another. We are ever present with ourselves, but only occasionally with others; therefore we can do much more to promote our own happiness, than the happiness of others. On the same principle, without interfering with this commandment, we have many more duties to perform to our own families and dependents than toward those with whom we do not stand in the same relations. But whenever a case occurs in which I have the same opportunity and ability to advance his welfare as my own, I am bound to have an equal regard to it, and to use the means to promote it, as much as my own, and to avoid every thing which would have a tendency to injure him, as vigilantly, and earnestly, as I would avoid those things which would be injurious to my own interests. And, as was before said, this obligation to love my neighbour as myself cannot injure me, or interfere with the pursuit of my own happiness. There is no collision, nor interference between the selfish and benevolent affection, or rather, the exercise of love to others in the full extent of the commandment, is the most effectual method of promoting my own happiness.

The Jews before our Saviour's time, had a proverbial saying, "thou shalt love thy neighbour, and hate thine enemy." They therefore thought, that they owed no good will or kindness to those whom they reckoned to be enemies. They felt free, therefore, to indulge their hatred toward such, and had reduced it to a law or maxim. But our blessed Lord gave to the commandment of God its true extent and import, teaching that we should love our enemies and do good to them that hate us. On one occasion, a certain scribe thought to puzzle him with this very question, in relation to this commandment, "and who is my neighbour?" which led him to deliver one of the most beautiful, touching, and instructive discourses which is to be found in the New Testament. It is as follows.

"And Jesus answering said, A certain man went down from Jerusalem to Jericho, and fell among thieves, which stripped him of his raiment, and wounded him, and departed, leaving him half dead. And by chance there came down a certain priest that way; and when he saw him, he passed by on the other side. And likewise a Levite, when he was at the place, came and looked on him, and passed by on the other side. But a certain Samaritan, as he journeyed, came where he was: and when he saw him, he had compassion on him, and went to him, and bound up his wounds, pouring in oil and wine, and set him on his own beast, and brought him to an inn, and took care of him. And on the morrow when he departed, he took out two pence, and gave them to the host, and said unto him, Take care of him; and whatsoever thou spendest more, when I come again, I will repay thee. Which now of these three, thinkest thou, was neighbour unto him that fell among the thieves? And he said, He that shewed mercy on him. Then said Jesus unto him, Go, and do thou likewise."

The shortest and most comprehensive commentary ever given of this commandment is that of our Lord, several times repeated; "Whatsoever ye would that men should do unto you, do ye even so to them." This is declared to be "the law and the prophets;" that is, it comprehends all the duties which we owe to our fellow men, inculcated in the law and the prophets. The whole that the law requires of us is, that we love our neighbour as ourselves; and the treatment of our neighbour which this love leads us to observe, is comprehended in the aforesaid precept; for as we never fail in a proper degree of love to ourselves, if we make this the rule of our conduct to our neighbour, we shall then be found fulfilling the law. Self-love always demands of others fully as much as they are bound in duty to do unto us. But may not self-love be excessive and demand too much? then this rule will serve to check the excess and reduce it to what is just and reasonable. Suppose a man should indulge the unreasonable desire that his neighbour should bestow upon him his whole estate. Then by this precept he would be bound to give back the whole to his neighbour. This precept well deserves the appellation of the "golden rule," for while it teaches us the measure of our duty, it provides an effectual guard against the disposition unduly to favour ourselves.

From this subject we learn the true foundation of justice among men. It is the application of this commandment to the common intercourse of society. Whatever in our dealings with men, proceeds from a disposition to give the preference to our own interest, when it comes in competition with that of another, is in violation of this law. We never can innocently aim at making gain by that which will be our neighbour's loss. In barter, or the commutation of articles of value, there should be a disposition to do equal justice; for lawful trade should be mutually profitable to those engaged in it. It is true, my neighbour is the proper judge of what he wants, and of what he will give in exchange for articles which I possess; and if he judges erroneously, we cannot be accountable for it, unless we by our words or actions mislead him; then are we guilty of injustice. All attempts, therefore, to undervalue the articles which he offers in exchange; or to exaggerate the value of our own, so as to bring about an unfair result, is evidently unjust. So also, if I know that his goods are more valuable than he supposes, and acting on my superior information, obtain his property for less than he would have taken for it, had he possessed my information, I do not love my neighbour as myself. I ought not to wish to get possession of my neighbour's property for less than its real value. What this may be, is a matter on which men may differ in opinion. And if men are honest in forming their opinions, there may be nothing wrong. But to put off a defective article without making known its defects, is evidently unjust, as also to put off in trade goods as being of a different kind from what we know they are. If these principles be correct, then you will say, the world is full of injustice. All our shops and markets are scenes of injustice. And it may be asked, if these strict rules are obligatory, who is there, that has clean hands? And what profit would there be in commerce? Lawful commerce was never intended to permit one man to make gain by the loss of others; but I may have articles which

I do not need but which my neighbour wants; so he may have articles which he does not need, but which suit me; or not having such articles himself, he can give me that which will enable me to procure them. And thus lawful commerce is mutually beneficial. But how can a man make his fortune by trade, on these principles? No man has any right to grow rich on the losses of his fellow creatures. He has no right to enrich himself by impoverishing them. But if a merchant takes the pains, and runs the risk of carrying goods to a foreign country, and bringing back in exchange articles which are needed by thousands, they may be willing to allow him for these articles which they need, what will be great gain to him, and at the same time a great convenience to them. There is then cause for honest gain, and such acquisitions are worth possessing; but unjust gain, never. The blessing of God rests upon the one, but his curse upon the other. On this principle the Scriptures so frequently condemn deceitful weights and measures. It is plain, if we love our neighbour as ourselves, we shall be far from plotting against him, from doing violence to him or injuring his reputation, or even wounding his feelings, except for his benefit. It is unnecessary to enumerate the crimes which are in violation of this commandment. They are exceedingly numerous. Our prisons, our courts of justice, and our laws give testimony, that the world is full of crimes forbidden by this precept. Indeed our very locks and bolts, our bonds and mutual covenants, are intended to guard against injustice. Now, let us suppose for a moment, that all men were disposed to love others as themselves, and to do justice to every one, what a change would there be in the condition of the world! Every body would have a sufficiency, and all would be far happier than at present. Some think to excuse themselve for overreaching and taking advantage of the simple, that most others do the same, and they are under the necessity of acting in this manner, in self-defence. If this were a valid apology for the common practices in the commerce of men, it would be sufficient to justify stealing and forgery, and every crime committed against property. No, there is no necessity for any species of dishonesty. The old proverb is true, "Honesty is the best policy."

The duty of charity, or giving, as far as may be in our power, relief to the indigent and distressed, owes its obligation to this command. As the number of those who need relief is so great in every country, if the heart of any one was influenced to the degree it should be, by love to his fellow-men, he would be constantly labouring for their relief. Well, in proportion as we feel good will to men, we shall be disposed to open wide the hand of charity, in giving alms to the poor, and in extending relief to the suffering of all descriptions. It would matter not to what country or sect he belonged, or how degraded and depraved he might be, still he is our *neighbour*, and we are bound to love him as ourselves. The only limit to our acts of kindness and beneficence should be our ability; and we should seek industriously, the means of doing good; and should seek out the most suitable objects of charity, when we can only relieve a part. Our

Lord required some to sell all that they had, and give to the poor. This could never be a duty generally incumbent, for then the giver would become poor and the receivers made rich; on which they would be bound to give all back again; and so there would be nothing but a perpetual change of condition between the rich and the poor. But Christ did command that we should give alms of what we possess. But alms-giving is but a small part of the duties of charity which arise from this commandment, of loving our neighbour. In the description of the day of judgment, given by Christ, in the xxv. of Matthew, we have an emphatical lesson on the importance which on that day will be given to this duty. For the King having separated the righteous and the wicked, as a shepherd separateth the sheep from the goats, and having placed the sheep on his right hand and the goats on the left, will say to them on his right hand, " Come, ye blessed of my Father, inherit the kingdom prepared for you from the foundation of the world: For I was an hungered, and ye gave me meat: I was thirsty, and ye gave me drink: I was a stranger, and ye took me in: Naked, and ye clothed me: I was sick, and ye visited me: I was in prison, and ye came unto me. Then shall the righteous answer him, saying, Lord, when saw we thee an hungered, and fed thee? or thirsty, and gave thee drink? When saw we thee a stranger, and took thee in? or naked, and clothed thee? Or when saw we thee sick, or in prison, and came unto thee? And the King shall answer and say unto them, Verily I say unto you, Inasmuch as ye have done it unto one of the least of these my brethren, ye have done it unto me. Then shall he say also unto them on the left hand, Depart from me, ye cursed, into everlasting fire, prepared for the devil and his angels. For I was an hungered, and ye gave me no meat: I was thirsty, and ye gave me no drink: I was a stranger, and ye took me not in: naked, and ye clothed me not: sick, and in prison, and ye visited me not. Then shall they also answer him, saying, Lord, when saw we thee an hungered, or athirst, or a stranger, or naked, or sick, or in prison, and did not minister unto thee? Then shall he answer them, saying, Verily I say unto you, Inasmuch as ye did it not to one of the least of these, ye did it not to me. And these shall go away into everlasting punishment: but the righteous into life eternal."

But our love must not be confined, nor principally directed to the welfare of the body. The immortal soul chiefly calls for our benevolent exertions. To rescue souls from everlasting ruin, is the noblest charity. And here, what a field of exertion opens to the truly benevolent! The people are perishing for lack of knowledge: will not love to your neighbour impel you to send them the Bible, and to teach them to read it? Will it not make you willing to forego ease and selfish indulgence, that you may have the means of sending the living teacher to instruct the ignorant? But the number who labour under a spiritual dearth is so great, that it is in vain to think of supplying them all; and of what account will be the exertions of an individual, and especially of one poor and destitute of talents? You need not take in the whole field of destitution. Consider what is within your reach. If it be ever so small a spot of earth that you can cultivate, withhold not your hand. "Sow your seed in the morning, and in the evening withhold not your hand." Do what you can and leave it to God to raise up other labourers to supply the fields which you cannot reach. Despise not the day of small things. The word is the seed, and is often prolific, bringing forth an hundred-fold. "The kingdom of heaven is like leaven which a woman took and hid in three measures of meal, till the whole was leavened." And whether your labours for the salvation of souls are successful or not; yet your duty in the case is plain and must be performed. And whether the people be converted by your labours or not, you shall receive your reward. The Lord never forgets "works of faith and labours of love." And as the power of man is able to accomplish nothing in this business without divine aid, O wrestle with God in prayer, day and night, for the outpouring of his Holy Spirit, and for the propagation of the Gospel over the whole world. Give him no rest until he establish and make Jerusalem a praise in all the earth. Say, "For Zion's sake I will not hold my peace, and for Jerusalem's sake I will not be silent, until the righteousness thereof go forth as brightness, and the salvation thereof as a lamp that burneth."

SERMON V.

THE NAME JESUS.

And she shall bring forth a son, and thou shalt call his name JESUS for he shall save his people from their sins.—MATT. i. 21.

NAMES, among the Hebrews, were generally significant. In some instances, on record in the Old Testament, God was pleased to make some change in the names of his servants, as in the case of Abram and Sarai, which, by divine direction, were altered to Abraham and Sarah. And to Jacob the name of Israel was given, after his successful wrestling with the angel. Names, therefore, are not unimportant; and especially, those which have been written in the BOOK OF LIFE, before the foundation of the world.

The name Jesus, in the New Testament, answers to Joshua in the Old; and twice, when Joshua is spoken of, he is called Jesus, in the New Testament, (Acts vii. 45; Heb. iv. 8.) This name also in the Old Testament, is sometime written Jehoshua, and Oshea; but the signification is the same in every case. It means a saviour. It was, therefore, peculiarly suitable to be the name of Messiah. From Josephus, it appears, that it was a name very common among the Jews. There are two eminent persons called by this name in the Old Testament, both of whom may be considered types of Jesus the Saviour. The first was the minister of Moses, who succeeded him as the leader of the tribes of Israel. He had the honour of introducing the people of God into the promised land, a privilege which was denied to Moses, though earnestly desired. Under Joshua as the captain of the armies of Israel the nations of Canaan were subdued, and their country divided as an inheritance among the tribes of Israel. The other distinguished person named Joshua, or Jeshua, was the high priest who with Zerubbabel conducted the Jews from Babylon, after their seventy years' captivity, back into their own country. It is not necessary to dwell upon the points of resemblance between these two eminent persons and the Messiah. The main point is, that both these brought the covenanted people of God from the land of their captivity and bondage, and conducted them to the land which God had promised to Abraham, Isaac, and Jacob, and to their seed; and JESUS, the Saviour, leads all his chosen people from the bondage of sin and captivity of Satan, into the liberty which God gives; and, finally, he will conduct them to those mansions in his Father's house, which he has gone to prepare for them.

The angel said, "thou shalt call his name JESUS, for he shall save his people from their sins." Our attention must first be directed to that state from which Jesus saves his people. It is from SIN. Sin is defined by an apostle to be " the transgression of the law," or, "a want of conformity to the law of God;" as the original term more properly imports. "By the law, then, is the knowledge of sin." The moral law which God has given to man is like himself, "holy, just, and good." It is such a law as must proceed from a Lawgiver who is infinite in every perfection. It is a law wisely suited to the constitution and capacity of the rational creature. It requires nothing but what is connected with the highest dignity and happiness of man. To have required less, would have indicated less wisdom, goodness, and holiness, in the Governor of the universe. The law is perfect; it could not be better or holier than it is. It requires man to love his Creator with all his powers, but it requires no more than the right exercise of the faculties bestowed. The law being a just expression of the moral excellence of the Lawgiver, the transgression of it, or any disconformity to it, must be the opposite of this excellence. This is sin,—the vilest thing in existence. God is the Author of all good; but he is not the Author of sin. He is, indeed, the Author of the free agent; but sin proceeds from the abuse of that liberty which is essential to a free, moral agent. Sin is a most unreasonable thing, for it opposes itself to all that is good. Sin is the height of folly, for it turns away from the only true source of happiness. Sin is odious in its intrinsic nature. It deforms, defiles, and disorders the soul into which it enters. It is the essence of ingratitude, for it returns evil for good. It is rebellion against the most rightful authority. It is the proper cause of all misery, the prolific poisonous seed, which produces a harvest of woes. We can conceive of no evil which is not included in sin. There is nothing else with which we can compare it, to show its evil. The apostle seems to labour for expressions strong enough to represent its evil, and sums up his description, by saying, that it is "exceeding sinful." Now, the law of God denounces a curse against all sin: "cursed is every one that continueth not in all things written in the book of the law to do them." All who have sinned are, therefore, under the curse. And from this no creature can deliver them. All sinners are equally condemned, but all are not condemned to equal punishment. The Lord is just, and will render to every one according to his deserts. But banishment from his presence, is the doom of all sinners. Nothing which the sinner can do, himself, will save him from either the punishment due to sin, or from its inherent defilement. This was the condition of every man of Adam's race; all have sinned, and are under the curse. The Son of God, viewing our unhappy condition, pitied us, and consented to become our Saviour. This required a wonderful humiliation on his part. It required, that he should become man, that he might bring in a justifying righteousness. The demands of justice must be satisfied, and this could only be done by answering all the claims of the law. He must not only become incarnate, but he must place himself under the law, not only to render a perfect obedience to its precepts, but that he might endure its penalty. "When the fulness of time was come, God sent forth his Son, made of a woman, made under the law, to redeem them that were under the law." "Christ hath redeemed us from the curse of the law, being made a curse for us; for it is written, Cursed is every one that hangeth on a tree." By the obedience and death of Christ, a foundation is laid for the gratuitous justification of the believing sinner, however ungodly he may have been. The atonement of Christ is of infinite value, and sufficient to take away the guilt of the most enormous sins. There is, therefore, pardon and peace for every penitent believer. But they who reject the Saviour, or neglect to fly to the hope set before them in the Gospel, must perish. For such there is no escape. There is no other sacrifice for sin. There is no other name by which they can be saved—no other foundation on which they can build. To those who trust in Christ, there is complete safety. To them who are in Christ Jesus there is no condemnation. "Being justified by faith, we have peace with God, through our Lord Jesus Christ." But Jesus not only saves from the curse and condemnation of sin, but from sin itself. There can be no real salvation, which does not deliver from sin's power and pollution in the soul. Sin has in itself so much evil, that it will produce misery, wherever it exists and reigns. Sin and misery are as indissolubly connected as holiness and happiness. The bitterest punishment of the lost will consist in the unrestrained violence of malignant passions, and the remorse which accompanies them. Jesus, therefore, had it as a main object of his coming into our world, " to save his people from sin." This is a work which no creature can perform. It supposes the complete renovation of the inner man. "Verily, verily, I say unto thee, except a man be born again, he cannot see the kingdom of God." This destruction of sin in the soul is the peculiar work of the Holy Spirit, to whom it belongs to enlighten the mind, to purify the heart, and to mortify sin. The word of God, however, is the instrument in the hand of the Spirit by which regeneration and sanctification are effected. "Being born again, not of corruptible seed, but of incorruptible, by the word of God which liveth and abideth forever. Sanctify them through thy truth; thy word is truth." Sin has struck its roots deep in our nature. Nothing short of a divine energy can eradicate the evil. God could, no doubt, sanctify the soul in as short a time as it is regenerated, but it has pleased him to pursue a different course. He chooses to carry on this work gradually, and by making the believer active in using the means of his own sanctification. Upon this plan, the people of God become much better acquainted with the evil of sin, than if they were saved from it at once. And by their various struggles with indwelling sin, they learn more highly to value the pardoning and renewing grace of God. They have, in the course of their pilgrimage much experience of the mercy and faithfulness of God, for it is by his strength they maintain their ground, and gain the victory over sin. Though, while in this world, none are perfectly free from the pollutions of sin; yet the work which grace begins here, will be carried on to perfection; and before the redeemed soul enters heaven, it will be completely purified from all sin; and will be presented without spot or wrinkle, or any such thing. This perfection of holiness, we believe, is attained at death; not that the separation of the soul from the body produces that effect, as some seem to suppose, but that is the time when the Spirit of God completes the work of sanctification.

Christ will not only save the soul from sin, but the body also from that death which is the effect of sin. Salvation will not be complete until the resurrection of the body. Let us then rejoice that a Saviour has been born, that his name is JESUS, and that he will save his people from their sins. This name is precious to the believer. It is like ointment poured forth, a sweet odour which refreshes the fainting heart—a reviving cordial, which raises our courage, and adds new strength to our efforts.

Let us be thankful, that the salvation which Jesus accomplishes is a salvation from sin—a complete deliverance, not only from its curse, but from its defilement. Now we are conscious of much sin within us, so that we are often forced to cry out, "O wretched man that I am, who shall deliver me from the body of this death! But thanks be to God who giveth us the victory." The time is approaching, O believer, when you will be surprised to find that you are free from sin, saved, eternally saved from sin!

INFERENCES.

1. If there is a name given by which sinners may be saved, and if this is the only name; if the

knowledge of this name is necessary to salvation, then it is exceedingly important that this NAME with its divine import and saving power should be made known to all the world. For this end was the Gospel ministry instituted: and all who seek the ministry now, from right motives, have this as their main object, to make known the name of JESUS.

2. But the mere hearing of this name, and obtaining a historical knowledge of the life and death, resurrection and ascension and glorious exaltation of JESUS, is not sufficient for salvation. "Whosoever calleth on this name shall be saved," i. e. whosoever believeth with the heart and confesseth with the mouth, that Jesus is the Christ—the MESSIAH, the SON OF GOD, shall be saved. We must endeavour to bring men to repentance toward God, and to faith in the Lord Jesus Christ.

3. They who would bring others to believe in Jesus, ought to be true believers themselves, as saith the apostle, or rather the psalmist, "I believed, therefore have I spoken. We also believe, and therefore speak." One of the greatest dangers of the Church is an unconverted ministry. If the blind lead the blind both shall fall into the ditch.

SERMON VI.

THE INCARNATION.

> And suddenly there was with the angel, a multitude of the heavenly host, praising God, and saying, Glory to God in the highest, and on earth, peace, good will to men.—Luke ii. 13, 14.

THERE are two memorable occasions, in time past, on which the angels are represented as joining in chorus to praise God in relation to our world. The first was when the corner-stone of the fabric of the universe was laid, and its foundations were fastened. Then " the morning stars sang together, and all the sons of God shouted for joy." The other was at the birth of a Saviour; which is referred to in our text. And we are informed by the sure word of prophecy, that at the overthrow of the spiritual Babylon, and at the marriage of the Lamb, there will be another grand chorus, when a voice coming out of the throne shall say, " Praise our God, all ye his servants, and all ye that fear him, both small and great." " And I heard," says John, " as it were the voice of a great multitude, and as the voice of many waters, and as the voice of mighty thunderings, saying, Alleluia, for the Lord God omnipotent reigneth. Let us be glad and rejoice, and give honour to him, for the marriage of the Lamb is come, and his wife hath made herself ready."

It is exceedingly gratifying to be introduced to some acquaintance with the celestial inhabitants, and to find that they are possessed of feelings very much like our own; except, that they are exempt from all sin and imperfection. It cannot but be very interesting to know, that the angels have a kind and tender feeling towards the children of God; and that they are employed as guardians to watch over them, and as helpers to deliver them from evils which would otherwise overwhelm them. It is wisely ordered, that in their common ministry to the heirs of salvation, the angels act without being seen, and render the most important services to the people of God, without their knowledge. For the visible presence of these holy beings would so overawe us, that we should through fear be unfitted for the common duties of life. For a long period, the visits of angels had scarcely been known in the Church; but when the Son of God was about to be manifested, the angel of the Lord appeared, first, to Zacharias, the father of John the Baptist, when he was wide awake, ministering in the temple, and afterwards to Mary, and to Joseph, her espoused husband. But on the memorable night of the birth of Christ, it pleased God to send his angel, probably Gabriel, to announce the joyful event, to a company of shepherds, who were remaining in the fields near Bethlehem, with their flocks, by night. " Suddenly, the angel of the Lord came upon them, and the glory of the Lord shone round about them, and they were sore afraid." It is not in human nature to look on the face of an angel and not be afraid. Conscious guilt abashes us in the presence of beings so holy and so far superior to us. But these benevolent messengers of God when they appear, do commonly, in the kindest and gentlest manner, allay the fears of those to whom they are sent. In this case, the angel said to the frightened shepherds, "Fear not, for behold I bring unto you glad tidings of great joy which shall be unto all people. For unto you is born, this day, in the city of David, a Saviour, who is Christ the Lord. And this shall be a sign unto you, ye shall find the babe wrapped in swaddling clothes, lying in a manger." Though but one angel appeared at first, to the shepherds, yet he was not alone. This was not an event to be made known by a solitary messenger: it was one which commanded the attention and interested the feelings of all the inhabitants of heaven; and they were filled with gladness at the prospect of such a mighty Deliverer appearing among men. Now "suddenly there was with the angel a multitude of the heavenly host, praising God, and saying, Glory to God in the highest, peace on earth, and good will to men."

The first thing in this divine anthem which demands our attention is, the disposition manifested by these celestial beings. The sentiments of their song are precisely such as we should expect from holy angels: and though the words sung by them, in concert, were few, yet they contain a complete expression of a disposition perfectly holy. They first ascribe all glory to God. This, undoubtedly, is the very essence of a heavenly temper. Whatever tends to the glory of God, will be delightful to the feelings of holy angels. To promote this object, they are ready for every service which may be required of them; and whether it be of an exalted nature, or an humble ministry to sinful men, they are equally prompt in their obedience; for the love of God is the predominant and absorbing passion of their minds. But where there exists supreme love to God, there will be found benevolence to his creatures. The angels rejoice in the birth of a Saviour, because this will restore peace to the earth. The existence of war among the offspring of the same parents, and partakers of the same nature, is itself an awful evidence, that ours is a fallen race. The number of men destroyed in war cannot be calculated; and much of the time and wealth of nations is expended in preparing for and carrying on this most inhuman employment. But the angels considered the birth of a Saviour as connected with permanent and ultimate peace. Let the kingdom of Christ be once fully established in the world, and wars will cease, every where: for whence come wars and fightings? come they not of men's lusts? The spirit of the Gospel is peace—the tendency of the Gospel is to lead men to convert their swords into ploughshares, and their spears into pruning hooks. The heathen had in their pantheon, gods who delighted in war; but our King is THE PRINCE OF PEACE, and the holy angels rejoice in the prospect of peace on earth. And they cherish a hearty good will to men; and because the Gospel breathes such a temper, they rejoiced at its introduction, and now daily rejoice at the conversion of every soul, rescued from the guilt and defilement of sin, and from the dominion of Satan. "There is joy in the presence of the angels of God, over one sinner that repenteth."

We see here, what the temper of heaven is, and what we pray for, when we say, "thy will be done in earth as it is in heaven." The spirit manifested by this great multitude of angels, and which pervades and actuates the whole innumerable company of angels, is the very spirit which should be predominant among men. They should all rejoice in the glory of God, and should breathe peace and good will to men. What a blessed change will it be, when all men, or the most of men, shall be actuated by this spirit! Perhaps we cannot spend our time better, than by contemplating the connection between the birth of a Saviour, and the glory of God, and also the happiness of men.

God is glorified by every thing which makes his glorious attributes more fully known. As he is absolutely and infinitely perfect, nothing can be added to his essential perfection; but by means of his creatures, his attributes may be exhibited; and so far as this is done, God is said to be glorified. And reason and Scripture unite in teaching, that this is the object at which God aims in all his works and dispensations. There can be no higher or nobler object. And rational creatures should make this the supreme object of pursuit also, and should glorify God in every way possible, and with all their powers. How do the heavens declare the glory of God? evidently by showing forth his power, wisdom and goodness. Thus also the earth is said to be full of the glory of God, because his attributes, already mentioned, are conspicuously displayed in every animal and in every vegetable; in the productions of the earth, in the clouds, the rain, the sea, the vines, the fountains of water, in the light, the air, the vicissitude of day and night, in the varying seasons, in seed time, and harvest—in fact, every thing upon earth furnishes evidence of the wisdom and goodness of the Creator. But in the Gospel, God has given a richer and fuller display of his attributes, than in the creation. Here his wisdom is very conspicuous, in the incarnation. The child that was now born, was not a common child—was not a mere human being, but though a perfect man, was the SON OF GOD. In this birth "the Word was made flesh;" "God was made manifest in the flesh." Here we have what may be called the depths of divine wisdom;—Deity united in personal subsistence with humanity; so that, the same who is the Son of God, is also the son of man—God-man; but still so united, that the perfections of deity are not communicated to the human soul, nor the properties of the human soul transferred to the divine nature. By this wise and wonderful constitution of the person of Christ, a foundation is laid for the salvation of sinners, in consistency with the truth and justice of God. Many suppose, that God can save the sinner by a mere act of sovereign power. As to mere power, he could, but where would be his justice? Where would be the honour of his law? To save sinners without an atonement, would be giving such an exhibition of his character, as would encourage his creatures to sin; or at least, remove all terror from the prospect of doing evil. His opposition to sin would not, in that case, be manifest; and so the holiness of his character would be obscured. The difficult problem to be solved was, how God could be just, and yet justify the ungodly. It is only by a person constituted as that of Jesus Christ is, that justice and mercy can be reconciled in the salvation of a sinner. That which is requisite is to satisfy the law and justice of God. Supposing the Ruler of the universe willing to accept of a substitute—a thing which God has made known in the revelation which he has given—here is one perfectly qualified to do and suffer all that is requisite for the honour of God, and for the salvation of the sinner. Though wisdom is gloriously illustrated in the incarnation; love and mercy are not less conspicuous. Indeed, we must consider LOVE as the first mover in this stupendous plan of salvation. Wisdom and power are exerted to open a way in which divine mercy may have a vent. Mercy cannot be exercised at the expense of justice. It is necessary, therefore, that the plan contain a provision for the complete satisfaction of justice. That which would have been pronounced impossible by any creature, however exalted, has been accomplished by the wisdom of God. "O the depth of the riches both of the wisdom and knowledge of God!" But, as was intimated, the whole contrivance was to make a way for the exercise of love and mercy. In the birth of a Saviour, we have the brightest manifestation of the free love of God, of which we can possibly conceive. "God so loved the world as to give his only begotten Son that whosoever believeth in him should not perish, but have everlasting life." "Herein is love, not that we loved God, but that he loved us." "Behold what manner of love the Father hath bestowed upon us, that we should be called the sons of God." "God, who is rich in mercy, for his great love wherewith he loved us." "As Christ also hath loved us and given himself for us." "That ye may be able to comprehend with all saints, what is the breadth and length and depth and height, and to know the love of Christ which passeth knowledge." "Greater love hath no man than this, that a man lay down his life for his friends. But God commendeth his love to us, in that while we were yet enemies, Christ died for us."

That justice is an essential attribute of God reason teaches; and the same is prominently held forth in the Sacred Scriptures. Even in those passages where he reveals his name, as "the Lord, the Lord God, merciful and gracious, slow to anger, keeping mercy for thousands," it is declared, "that he will in no wise clear the guilty." It is unnecessary further to explain how this attribute is gloriously illustrated in the advent of Christ and the plan of salvation: for we have seen already, that the great obstacle which stood in the way of the sinner's salvation, was the inexorable demands of justice, which could not be set aside without satisfaction. And it has already been shown, that the wisdom of the plan consisted in its being so contrived as fully to satisfy the claims of justice, by satisfying the law by the mediation of a competent substitute, or surety. And that this is not an imaginary device, of man's invention, but God's revealed scheme of mercy, will be evident from the citation of a few passages of Scripture. "For he who knew no sin was made sin for us, that we might be made the righteousness of God in him." "For what the law could not do, in that it was weak through the flesh, God sending forth his Son, for sin—condemned sin in the flesh, that the righteousness of the law might be fulfilled in us." "But when the fulness of time was come, God sent forth his Son, made of a woman, made under the law, to redeem them that were under the law." "For it is written, Cursed is every one that continueth not in all things written in the book of the law to do them." "Christ hath redeemed us from the curse of the law, being made a curse for us." "As by the disobedience of one many were made sinners, so by the obedience of one shall many be made righteous."

The truth and faithfulness of God are also rendered most manifest by the birth of a Saviour. For thousands of years, prediction after prediction had been given, as proofs to support the faith of the people of God, that a Messiah, a Prophet, a Priest, like unto Melchisedek, and a King on mount Zion, should be revealed. The time of his arrival had been specified, in several remarkable prophecies, and the fulness of time was come. According to every human prospect, indeed, there seemed little probability of the exact fulfilment of those predictions. The Jewish nation had fallen under the Roman yoke, and the family of David were scattered and impoverished. But God is at no loss to accomplish his purposes, and fulfil his own predictions. When Israel was in Egypt, in bondage, the time of the promise drew nigh, but what appearance of a fulfilment? Yet on the very day on which the four hundred and thirty years of afflictions predicted to Abraham, were expired, on that very day, the whole nation marched out of the land of their bondage. So when Daniel's seventy weeks were coming to an end, the Son of David is born. A holy virgin of the family and lineage of David, accompanied by her espoused husband, is by the Providence of God, brought from Nazareth to Bethlehem. And see how God overrules the hearts of kings to accomplish his purposes. Augustus Cæsar must make a decree requiring every family to repair to its own city, in order to be registered. And here Joseph and Mary, in their deep poverty, are found obeying the imperial edict; and thus, God's word was fulfilled in regard to Bethlehem. "But thou, Bethlehem Ephratah, though thou be little among the thousands of Judah; yet out of thee shall He come forth unto me that is to be Ruler in Israel." But the prophecies not only designated the Messiah by the place of his birth and his descent from the family of David, but as one who was to be born of a virgin. "Behold," says Isaiah, "a virgin shall conceive and bear a son, and shall call his name Immanuel." Such a thing as this was never known from the foundation of the world; but it was literally fulfilled in the case of our Saviour. The evangelist Matthew informs us, "that the birth of Christ was on this wise. When as his mother Mary was espoused to Joseph, before they came together, she was found with child of the Holy Ghost. Then Joseph her husband being a just man, and not willing to make her a public example, was minded to put her away privily. But while he thought on these things, behold the angel of the Lord appeared unto him in a dream, saying, "Joseph, thou son of David, fear not to take unto thee Mary thy wife, for that which is conceived in her is of the Holy Ghost. And she shall bring forth a son, and thou shalt call his name Jesus, for he shall save his people from their sins. Now all this was done that it might be fulfilled which was spoken by the prophet, saying, Behold a virgin shall be with child, and shall bring forth a son, and they shall call his name Immanuel, which being interpreted, is, God with us." Thus God was glorified by the birth of this child, because by this event, the truth and faithfulness of God were clearly manifested. That the birth of Christ was indicative of good will to men needs no further proof, for we have shown that the origin of the whole plan of salvation was love, and good will is only another name for love. If God loved our world, it cannot be disputed that he exercised good will toward men. And that the tendency of the gospel is to bring about universal peace among men, was stated in the beginning of our discourse; but it may be proper and consistent with Scripture usage to give a more extended meaning to the word peace. This is a term, which when used by Christ and his apostles, is rich in import. It is one of those words which are commonly used in benedictions. As when Jesus says, "My peace I leave with you, my peace I give unto you." "These things have I spoken unto you that ye might have peace." "The fruit of the Spirit is love, joy, peace." So Paul's usual salutation runs, "Grace be unto you and peace from God our Father and from our Lord Jesus Christ." And he speaks of "the peace of God which passeth all understanding." Taking this word in the most comprehensive sense, it will include three important blessings. First, peace with God; in order to which, his wrath must be appeased by the blood of Christ. This is nothing else than that perfect reconciliation which is spoken of in Scripture. It is the result of our pardon and justification. "Being justified by faith we have peace with God through our Lord Jesus Christ." Peace with God also includes the slaying of the natural enmity of the human heart, and filling it with love. The second blessing included under this word is, peace of conscience, and tranquillity and harmony in the exercise of the desires and affections of the mind. Sin has produced direful disorder in the exercise of the human powers. Grace restores peace and harmony; and the conscience of the sinner, though it may sleep, though it may be seared, yet never enjoys a solid peace, until sprinkled with the blood of atonement. This is the only balm which can remove the pain of a wounded spirit. The third blessing is peace with our fellow men. Christians must, from the nature of the doctrines which tney believe, and from the dispositions with which they are inspired, be men of peace. Their rule is, as far as in them lies, to live peaceably with all men. And they are ever found to be peace-makers. Nothing more is necessary to produce universal peace, than the general prevalence of the gospel.

We may bring this discourse to a close by a few reflections:

1. It is delightful to the pious mind to know, that although there are so few in this world who engage sincerely in the worship of their Creator; and although by most his authority is despised, and his law trodden under foot; yet there is a world, peopled by an innumerable company of beings far more exalted than man, where all, without exception, esteem it their highest honour and greatest felicity to be constantly employed in the high praises of God, and in executing his commands. It is probable, that while multitudes are employed in ascribing praise and glory to God, others are sent as messengers to declare the will of God, and as ministering servants, to minister unto, and exercise a guardianship over, the people of God, and that, in both these services, they take their turns; so that all enjoy the high privilege of joining in the grand concert of praise around the throne; and all in their turn are required to execute the divine will as angels or messengers.

2. How pleasing is the thought that these celestial beings are lovers of men, and take a lively interest in all our concerns; especially, that they are deeply interested in all that relates to the salvation of God's elect, and cheerfully condescend to attend on such to guard them from evil, and to help them in ways unknown to us.

3 But the service which angels can render to us

is small, compared with the work of redemption wrought by the Son of God. What measure can be assigned to the gratitude due for the birth of a Saviour? And although this glorious event occurred above eighteen centuries since; yet its importance is not in the least diminished. The blessed effects of the incarnation are as great now, as they ever were. Christ, who was born in Bethlehem, is as mighty to save now, as when he died: his precious blood shall never lose its power. And we may have as free access to the Redeemer now, as his immediate disciples had. Faith does not require a visible Saviour for its object; but the blessing is rather on those who have not seen, and yet believed.

4. Let us endeavour to imbibe the Spirit which animated this multitude of the heavenly host, and make it our constant aim to give glory to God in the highest, to seek the peace of the world, and to exercise good-will to men. Let us remember, that we are not our own, but bought with a price, and that we should, therefore, glorify God with our bodies and spirits, which are his. Whether we eat or drink, or whatever we do, we should glorify God; and should let our light so shine, that others seeing our good works, should be led to glorify our Father in heaven.

Let us remember, that time is short; that our opportunities of glorifying God in this world will soon be past. Work then while it is called to-day, for the night cometh on apace when no man can work.

5. The lively remembrance of the Saviour's birth should not be confined to any certain day in the

year, but should call forth our gratitude and praise, every day. We read nothing in the New Testament of setting apart one particular day for the celebration of this great event. The minds of the apostles and primitive disciples, were so imbued with the spirit of the gospel, that they appear to have disregarded those external circumstances and associations, which have since so greatly occupied the thoughts of men. We never find the apostles, when at Jerusalem, visiting holy places, or seeking after relics. No allusion to any such thing is found in the pages of the New Testament. And yet, if we had been informed of the precise time of our Saviour's birth, there would be no harm in paying attention to this anniversary, without superstition. But the day of the year in which Christ was born, is utterly uncertain; and never can be ascertained without divine revelation.

SERMON VII.

CHRIST'S GIFT OF HIMSELF FOR OUR REDEMPTION.

Who gave himself for us that he might redeem us from all iniquity.—
Titus ii. 14.

That Jesus Christ is the person here spoken of, is perfectly evident: but what the true character of Jesus Christ is, is a point disputed, and one of unspeakable importance. No greater difference of opinion can exist, than whether our Saviour is a mere man, or the mighty God. As we embrace the one or the other of these opinions, our whole system of doctrines will be modified. Accordingly, it is found, that all who deny the deity of Christ, reject all the fundamental truths of the Christian religion. The divinity of Christ being a fundamental doctrine, we find the proofs of it every where scattered through the Scriptures.

In the context we have a proof of the doctrine of the most convincing kind. In the verse preceding our text, the apostle Paul, under the inspiration of the Spirit, says, "Looking for that blessed hope, and the glorious appearing of the great God, and our Saviour Jesus Christ; who gave himself for us," &c. Now, the point to be determined is, whether by the terms "the great God and our Saviour Jesus Christ," two persons are intended or only one. If the former, then this text furnishes no evidence of our doctrine; but if both appellations belong to one person, then the doctrine of Christ's supreme Deity is taught in the very strongest terms. In our version, there exists some ambiguity, which does not appear in the original; for according to the established rules of construction in the Greek tongue, where two nouns are connected by a copulative, and the first has the article prefixed, and the other is without it, both must be referred to the same person or thing. That is the fact in this case. Therefore, the Saviour, Jesus Christ, is the great God. Ambiguity would be removed and the true meaning given, if for "and" we substitute "even." Then it will read, "the great God even our Saviour Jesus Christ."

And the same doctrine seems to be clearly indicated by comparing the third and fourth verses of the third chapter of this epistle; for in the former, God is called our Saviour, and in the latter, "the Lord Jesus Christ our Saviour," is the form of expression. We can hardly avoid the conclusion, that in both verses, the same person is called Saviour Moreover, the word *appearing* is never used in reference to the Father, whom no man hath seen or can see, but constantly in relation to the second Person, who was manifest in the flesh.

Having ascertained the character of the person spoken of in our text, we are prepared to consider the gift which he is said to have made, and the end which he had in view in making it: "Who gave himself for us, that he might redeem us from all iniquity."

The value of a gift may be estimated by several considerations, to which your attention is earnestly requested.

1. From the dignity of the person by whom it is bestowed. A ring or medal from a king or queen, or from some other royal personage, is appreciated, not so much by the intrinsic value of the gift itself, as by the condescension manifested by an exalted personage towards one in an inferior condition. But what is the disparity between a king and the meanest of his subjects, compared with that which exists between the infinite God and the greatest of his creatures? That this august Being should with any favour regard such creatures as sinners of the human race, is indeed wonderful. As sings the royal Psalmist, "When I consider thy heavens, the work of thy fingers; the moon and the stars which thou hast ordained; what is man, that thou art mindful of him? and the son of man, that thou visitest him?" A gift from such a Being to such an unworthy creature, deserves to be appreciated very highly.

2. Another consideration proper to be taken into view, in estimating the value of a gift is, the sacrifice at which it is made; or what it costs the donor. God gave us existence by a single act of his will, by the mere word of his power, and bestows upon us the bounties of his providence, without any sacrifice; for giving does not impoverish him. But in man's redemption it was necessary that God should give his own Son. It is written, that "He

spared not his own Son, but gave him up for us all." And of the Son it is said, "He loved us, and gave himself for us, an offering and a sweet smelling sacrifice unto God." No man can give a greater gift than his own life. And this is a gift scarcely to be expected from men. "Scarcely for a righteous man will one die." But death may be endured in very different circumstances. Sometimes it is honourable, and attended with inconsiderable pain; but the death of Christ was both ignominious and excruciating. He died as a criminal. His death was accursed. He suffered with the vilest malefactors, that the impression might be made on the public mind, that he was of the same character. A seditious murderer was preferred before him. He died on the cross, a kind of punishment inflicted on none but slaves and the vilest malefactors. The sufferings of the Son of God were protracted through many hours, and were endured under cruel mockery from men, and under the frowns of the Almighty Father. Indeed, his whole life was a kind of extended martyrdom, for from the beginning, "He was a man of sorrows, and acquainted with grief."

3. Next, let us endeavour to estimate the value of the gift itself. The text says, "He gave *himself* for us." This was the greatest gift which could possibly be made: heaven itself could furnish nothing more valuable than the Son of God. And a second gift equal to it could not be made. It is seldom that men in bestowing gifts, are willing to give themselves. This is not a theme for declamation; but rather for devout and silent wonder. Nothing more astonishing can possibly be conceived,

than that the PRINCE OF LIFE should consent to die for sinners. Angels must have been astounded at the mysterious spectacle. The sun refused to look upon it, and withdrew his rays for several hours at mid-day. The earth trembled, and the rocks were rent, and the veil of the temple, which concealed the most holy place, was rent in twain from the top to the bottom; and the place which for ages had been too sacred for the eyes of men, was now exposed to the gaze of all. What Christ endured in giving himself for us, no tongue can tell, nor heart conceive.

4. But after all, that which chiefly enhances the value of a gift is the motive which impelled the donor to bestow it.

Now, that motive which above every other, stamps a value on a gift, is LOVE. Love may be truly said to be the most excellent thing in the universe. It is that which gives worth to every thing else. The love of rational creatures toward others is the most valuable thing which they have it in their power to bestow. And the richest possession which any creature is capable of receiving, is the love of God. As God is possessed of infinite excellence, he must be a God of love. God loves all his obedient creatures, and his goodness, which is but another name for his love, renders them happy, according to their respective capacities. Such love as this is continually manifested in all the laws by which the natural world is governed, and particularly by the constitutions of all sensitive beings, and the provision which is made for their comfort. But in the gospel we have a new view of this attribute of the divine nature; it is the love of God to sinners, and the wonderful provision for their redemption. "God so loved the world, that he gave his only begotten Son, that whosoever believeth in him should not perish, but have everlasting life."

There is something inexplicable in this whole subject. Among men there must be something amiable in the object beloved; but God fixed his love on sinners, in whom there was no good thing. And it could not be merely because they were creatures, for then sinning angels would have been loved as well as men and before them; but they were not. And the same mystery hangs over another part of divine revelation. It is that the love of God is not exercised indiscriminately toward all the human race, but is specially directed to a chosen people, who by nature are no better than others. Much goodness, in the dispensations of Providence, is manifested to the whole human race; but the unspeakable gift of which we have been treating, is intended for the redemption of the elect; on whose behalf the Father and the Son, with the concurrence of the Holy Spirit, entered into a covenant of peace: which covenant is the foundation of the gospel, with all its privileges and ordinances. But if it be inquired, what induced the adorable Trinity to enter into such an engagement, and to devise a plan of redemption for the recovery of the chosen race, no other answer can be given, than that it was love, unparalleled, incomprehensible love! This was the rich and deep fountain from which all spiritual saving blessings flow: "Who loved us, and gave himself for us:" "Not that we loved God, but that he loved us, and sent his Son to be the propitiation for our sins." The wonderful and mysterious nature of this subject should not prevent our frequent meditation on it; nor does its incomprehensible nature hinder, but rather promote our adoration of the Triune Jehovah. The human mind is constituted by the Creator, so as to experience a sublime delight in the contemplation of an infinite object. That which we can clearly comprehend, must appear too small to be an object of worship and adoration. The soul is not satisfied with finite things, it aspires to something higher and nobler. From this we may infer, that the soul of man was formed for the adoration of an infinite Being.

There is a delightful passage in Paul's epistle to the Ephesians on the incomprehensible nature of the love of Christ. "That he would grant you, according to the riches of his glory, to be strengthened with might by his Spirit; that Christ may dwell in your hearts by faith; that ye, being rooted and grounded in love, may be able to comprehend with all saints, what is the breadth and length, and depth and height; and to know the love of Christ, which passeth knowledge, that ye might be filled with the fulness of God." Although the pious soul ardently desires to comprehend this love, yet as it must for ever "pass knowledge," it would perhaps have been better in our version, to say, "that ye may be able to *apprehend;*" for the original will bear this translation, and it would remove the appearance of contradiction.

5. The excellency of this gift will also be mani-

fest from the benefit which accompanies it. Man was placed in a very necessitous condition. He had fallen into a state of sin and misery, from which he could not deliver himself; nor was it in the power of any creature to afford him any effectual relief. He was bound by a holy law to suffer a dreadful penalty, which could not be set aside, unless an adequate atonement should be made And even if this penalty were removed, he was rendered incapable of the enjoyment of true happiness, by reason of the inherent disorder of his nature; sin having infected all the faculties of his soul, so that nothing truly good is found in any of the children of Adam, in their natural state.

Men are considered in Holy Scripture, as in bondage, under the slavery of sin, and subject to the tyranny of Satan. From this state of thraldom, they can be delivered only by an almighty Redeemer. But power alone is not adequate to the work of redemption. A price—a ransom sufficient to satisfy divine justice must be paid. Silver and gold, and all earthly treasures avail nothing in the redemption of the soul. Blood must be shed, and life sacrificed. But no blood of lambs and bullocks can answer the purpose; such blood was shed in profusion for many ages, but could not take away the guilt of one sin. It answered to represent, typically, and in lively figure, the atonement necessary, and which God had determined should be made. Neither would the blood of prophets and martyrs serve as an adequate atonement. The blood shed and the life given, must be divine. But how can this be? The eternal Son of God offers himself to be the Redeemer, and to pay the price required. "Lo, I come," says he, "in the volume of the book it is written of me, to do thy will, O God: by which will we are sanctified, through the offering of the body of Jesus Christ once for all." "By one offering he hath perfected for ever them that are sanctified."

"Christ our passover is sacrificed for us." He was named JESUS because he should save his people from their sins. "Who gave himself for us, that he might redeem us from all iniquity, and purify to himself a peculiar people, zealous of good works." Salvation from sin is the great object of the sacrifice of the cross. "Without the shedding of blood there was no remission." The removal of the punishment of sin was the direct object of the sacrifice of Christ, when he gave himself for us, and made his soul an offering for sin. But deliverance from guilt is not the whole of redemption. Sin is not only a crime which exposes to punishment, but a disease which disorders the whole soul, and renders it unfit for the service of God, and entirely incapable of the enjoyment of the happiness of heaven. Redemption, therefore, delivers from the defilement of sin. This is effected by the operation of the Holy Spirit, in the regeneration and sanctification of the soul. This work of renovation is carried on by appropriate means, especially by the word, during the whole period of the Christian's pilgrimage. And when the soul is separated from the body, and enters into the eternal world, we believe, that it will at once be delivered from all iniquity. Although this renovation was not the direct object of the atonement; yet this sacrifice was necessary to be made, before the Holy Spirit could be sent to renew the depraved nature of man. The relation in which the sinner stood to the law, as a justly condemned criminal, rendered it altogether unsuitable that he should be visited by this divine Agent.

And it may properly be observed here, that as the work of sanctification is carried on by the truth, perceived by the enlightened soul; so, no view of truth is so important and efficacious in producing holy affections in the believer, as the sacrifice of Christ on the cross. It is the wisdom and power of God to every one that believeth.

When the chosen people of God are freed from all their sins, they will be presented by their Redeemer, before the presence of his Father, "without spot or wrinkle, or any such thing." For having begun this good work, he will not abandon it, but will carry it on to the day of redemption. None of those for whom he gave himself can possibly fail of salvation. He is the SURETY of all such, and bears their names on his breast, as he stands pleading as their Intercessor; for "he is able to save to the uttermost all who come unto God by him; seeing he ever liveth to make intercession for them." By giving himself unto death, he has paid a sufficient ransom for them, and has redeemed them from all iniquity, and purchased them as a peculiar people for himself. And none shall be able to pluck these redeemed ones from his hand. These are the sheep for whom the great Shepherd laid down his life. But, as the work of sanctification is carried on by the use of means, the active diligence of the soul in the use of them is requisite. The Spirit works by setting the soul to work. We are commanded, therefore, "to work out our salvation with fear and trembling, because God worketh in us both to will and to do, of his own good pleasure." Hence, the Scriptures are full of earnest exhortations to Christians, to let their light shine; to cleanse themselves from all filthiness of flesh and spirit; and to perfect holiness in the fear of God.

The sanctification of his people is the great end of the whole mediatorial scheme. God was able, at once, by his power, to render them perfect in holiness. But it was consistent neither with his justice, his truth, nor his wisdom, to suffer sin to go unpunished. God is known to his intelligent creatures by his acts and dispensations If he were to treat the transgressor as the obedient subject, it might be inferred, that he entertained no abhorrence of iniquity. It was necessary, therefore, that the sinner should not be taken into favour, and renewed again in the image of God, unless a satisfactory atonement was made. For God must show himself just, while he justifies the sinner.

This redemption from all iniquity, is not accomplished suddenly, but for wise reasons, the redeemed soul, after its justification and regeneration, (which two benefits are contemporaneous,) is not taken to heaven at once, but left in this world, exposed to various temptations, and in a state of imperfection, so that no man can truly say, "I am free from all sin." The inbred corruptions of the heart are permitted to vex the Christian, and sometimes to overcome him. A perpetual conflict is kept up between the flesh and spirit; that is, between the renovated nature, and the remaining corruptions which are opposed to holiness.

But this work, though imperfect in all during this life, yet is progressive. Believers die daily more and more unto sin, and live unto righteousness. Their growth in grace too, is connected with their own diligent efforts. By an increase of knowledge and of faith, they attain to much higher degrees of holiness, than they possessed at the time of their conversion. One reason of this part of the economy of salvation, is, that they who are redeemed from sin, may more thoroughly understand the great evil of sin, and the utter inability of man to extirpate it from his nature; so that he is more and more convinced that his salvation is all of grace. And by being thus left to struggle with evil, he comes to know experimentally, the unchanging love and faithfulness of a covenant-keeping God. In heaven the gratitude of the saints will be greater, in consequence of their severe trials and temptations in their pilgrimage on earth. When they lay aside their clay tabernacles, and are admitted into the presence of their Saviour, they shall be free from all sin. This completion of the work of sanctification is not produced by death, as some seem to suppose, but by the same divine Agent, who commenced the work. Then will the Saviour redeem his chosen people from all iniquity.

This subject furnishes matter for many interesting reflections, a few of which shall now claim our attention.

1. How glorious is redeeming love and saving grace! "God so loved the world, that he gave his only begotten Son, that whosoever believeth on him, should not perish, but have everlasting life." How wonderful, that the great God our Saviour should give himself for us! Angels may well be astonished, and stoop from their exalted thrones to contemplate this grace, so rich and so unsearchable! And what renders this grace the more surprising is, that it passed by sinning angels—beings of a nobler nature than man's, and was freely extended to our inferior nature. For this discrimination, men have endeavoured to account; but their reasons are futile. It is one of the unsearchable things which are hidden in the depths of the infinite mind of God. The same inscrutable nature belongs to the electing love of God, by which, while one is taken, another is left. "O the depth, both of the wisdom and knowledge of God! his ways are past finding out." The only reason which he assigns for this discrimination is, the "good pleasure of his will." "Even so, Father, for so it seemed good in thy sight. He has mercy on whom he will have mercy, and whom he will he hardeneth." But in all this, God is perfectly just. He will punish no one who does not deserve it. And as a Sovereign, he has a perfect right to do what he will with his own. No sinner has any claim upon his grace, and if he leaves some to their own chosen ways, and renders to them, according to the fruit of their own doings, they have no reason for complaint.

2. The work of redemption is God's most glorious work. Creation sprung up at the word of his

power, but redemption required a sacrifice, the richest and greatest that could be made; a sacrifice which no creature could offer; a ransom not of silver and gold, but of blood—of blood divine. God must become manifest in the flesh. The God-man must make atonement for sin by giving himself—by giving himself to death—to the accursed death of the cross! O what wonders cluster around the cross! God forbid, that we should glory, save in the cross of Christ.

3. The redeemed of the Lord should be careful to carry out the Redeemer's holy purpose, by departing from all iniquity. God is holy, and they should be holy too. Christ came not to be the minister of sin. His name was called JESUS, because he saves his people from their sins. Until we are delivered from our sins, we are not saved. Vain, therefore, is the dream of the antinomian, that Christ has purchased for him a liberty of sinning; or that he can be saved in his sins. For without holiness none shall see the Lord "And the great God, the Saviour, gave himself for us, that he might redeem us from all iniquity, and purify to himself a peculiar people zealous of good works."

4. As it is impossible for the redeemed to make any adequate return for such a glorious and inestimable gift, our gratitude should be fervent and constant. Gratitude is, therefore, the chief duty of redeemed souls. And this feeling should lead those who have been redeemed at such a price, and by such a sacrifice, to express their sense of obligation in unceasing praises, and in acts of obedience to the will of God. The habitual outgoing of the

heart should be, "thanks be to God for his unspeakable gift." We are exhorted evermore to give thanks; and surely there is no subject of thanksgiving comparable to redemption. And the song of praise for redeeming love, which is commenced in the church on earth, will not be terminated at death. No! Then it will be raised to more perfect and elevated strains, when they shall be present with the Lord, and see him in his glory, and when they shall no more see him darkly as through a glass, but "face to face," "and shall know as they are known." When all the ransomed children of God, shall be gathered together from every region under heaven, and shall sit down in the kingdom of heaven, with Abraham, Isaac, and Jacob, and shall surround the throne of God and the Lamb, their song shall ever be, "TO HIM WHO LOVED US, AND WASHED US FROM OUR SINS IN HIS OWN BLOOD."

SERMON VIII.

THE NEW CREATION.

For in Christ Jesus, neither circumcision availeth any thing, nor uncircumcision, but a new creature.—GAL. vi. 15.

THE first dispute which disturbed the peace of the Christian Church related to the point, whether converts from the Gentiles were under obligation to observe the ceremonies of the law of Moses. It was then assumed as an admitted principle, that the Jewish proselytes should continue to render obedience to this law, as before. The controversy, therefore, had relation only to such as were now initiated into the Christian Church from among the Gentiles. When proselytes had been received into the Jewish Church, it was always required that they should be circumcised, and also their children; and these Judaizers, who troubled the primitive churches, believing that all the precepts of the ceremonial law were of perpetual obligation, insisted on the necessity of requiring obedience to this law from all Gentile converts. And not only so, but they taught that such observance was essential to salvation, and thus changed the very nature of the gospel, making salvation to depend on external works. The Galatian churches, which had been gathered by the labours of Paul, were not only troubled with these false teachers, but had been seduced by them from the simplicity of the gospel; and had adopted another system, which Paul denounces as subversive of the gospel, and anathematizes any one, even if he were an angel from heaven, who should have the audacity to preach a doctrine so opposite to the true gospel, which they had received from him, and which had been confirmed among them by miracles, which, by the Holy Spirit, he had wrought among them. This language is very bold and striking, and equally applies to any other false doctrine which tends to the subversion of the gospel. "But though we, or an angel from heaven, preach any other gospel unto you, than that which we have preached, let him be accursed. As we said before, so say I now again, if any man preach any other doctrine than that ye have received, let him be accursed."

But whilst Paul so severely denounced any attempt to introduce any other method of salvation, he was very tolerant in regard to a mere difference of opinion respecting the propriety of observing Jewish rites, which had been enjoined by divine authority, and which they as Jews had always been accustomed to observe. Indeed, he himself conformed to these ceremonies, when it seemed necessary to obviate the prejudices of the Jews; and, in this, became all things to all men. The rule which he laid down for himself and inculcated on others, was, "Let every man be fully persuaded in his own mind," and not to censure or condemn a brother for a different opinion or practice, in regard to these ceremonies. He, therefore, treats this difference as a matter of no real importance. Twice, in this epistle, he declares, that neither circumcision nor uncircumcision availed any thing; but turns the attention of the Galatian Christians to what was essential in religion; which, in the one case, he declares to be "faith working by love," and in the other, which is our text, "the new creature." The import of both passages is the same; for "faith working by love," is the acting of the new creature. Some would render this *a new creation;* but the meaning is the same; for this new creation is the renewal of the soul itself, by which it becomes a new creature.

Our object, in the sequel of this discourse, will be, 1. To take notice of some things which are implied in this doctrine of a new creation: 2. And then to point out some mistakes into which you may be liable to fall; and 3. Finally endeavour to describe some of the traits or lineaments of the renewed man.

The human nature being the subject of this new creation, it is evident, that man must have been created at first, in a state of moral imperfection, or his nature must have deteriorated, since he was made, otherwise there could be no need of a new creation. The first supposition cannot be admitted without casting dishonour upon the character of God, as though he had produced an imperfect work. The alternative must, therefore, be received, namely, that man has fallen from that state of integrity in which he was originally created. And this is the doctrine of Holy Scripture, from the beginning of Genesis to the end of Revelation. God created man "in his own image and after his own likeness," but all, both Jews and Gentiles have sinned, so that "there is none righteous, no, not one." What the prophet says, applies to the whole race, "The heart is deceitful above all things, and desperately wicked." And what Paul says of himself, is equally true of every other man, "For I know, that in me, that is, in my flesh, dwelleth no good thing."

1. The doctrine of "a new creation" implies that the departure of man from God, was not partial but total; for had it been the fact, that man's nature had undergone only some slight or partial deterioration, there would not have been need of "a new creation." Paul, in another epistle, when speaking of this new creature, expresses the greatness of the change in very strong terms: "If any man, says he, be in Christ, he is a new creature; old things are done away, behold, all things are become new." The greatness of the change is also evident from other metaphors employed to set it forth. It is called a "new birth," or being "born again." It is a resurrection from the dead: "And you hath he quickened who were dead in trespasses and sins." And all experience goes to confirm the doctrine of Scripture respecting the total depravity and utter ruin of the human race, in consequence of the introduction of sin into our world. "By one man sin entered into the world, and death by sin; so that death hath passed upon all men, because that all have sinned." Just as far as death reigns, so far does sin exist; for "death is the wages of sin."

2. Another thing implied in the doctrine of a new creation is the necessity of a divine Agency in the change which man undergoes. Creation is a work which can be performed by no other but God. It is by the visible creation that we know that God exists. Man is no more capable of producing the new creation, than of creating a world. This must be evident to every mind. If, then, there is "a new creature," God only can be the author of this change. The apostle Paul confirms this dictate of reason, by an explicit and decisive testimony: "For God who commanded the light to shine out of darkness hath shined in our hearts, to give the light of the knowledge of the glory of God, in the face of Jesus Christ." Again, "For we are his workmanship, created in Christ Jesus unto good works." Accordingly, the new birth is ascribed to God alone. "Who are born, not of blood, nor of the will of the flesh, nor of the will of man, but of God." The attempt to make man a co-operator with God in this work, is as absurd, as to suppose that the dust out of which Adam's body was formed co-operated with the power of God in its creation. In what conceivable way can a soul, dead in sin, co-operate in the production of spiritual life? Talk not of the freedom of the will: the will, as much as any other faculty, is under the influence of depravity. If the will were capable of putting forth one right volition, one holy act, the new creation would be unnecessary; for life, in that case, would have an actual existence in the soul of man. Let it be remembered then, that God is the author of the new creature. The efficiency in this work belongs

entirely to him. There is no divided agency in the work; though means are appointed to be employed, on which it is proper, even for the unregenerate to attend. The efficiency of God in the new creation, no more excludes the use of appropriate means, than his efficiency in the natural world, where second causes are employed, while the efficiency is of God.

II. In the second place, I am to guard you against some mistakes into which you are liable to fall, in relation to this work of almighty power.

1. In the new creation, the substance of the soul is not changed. The soul of man, considered in its essence, needs no change. The essence of the soul is incapable of corruption. As the work of God, it is still "very good," and perfect in its kind. In time of the Reformation, some theologians taught, that the very substance of the soul was converted into sin; but this gross error was promptly rejected by the wise and considerate.

2. Though the new creation be a great change, yet is there no new faculty created. Man, before conversion and afterwards, possesses the same rational faculties, which belong to the constitution of human nature. If a new faculty were bestowed on man, in the new creation, he would then be of another species from what he was before. He would no longer be a mere man; but possessing a new faculty, would differ specifically from those who remain in a state of nature.

3. Neither does this new creation give new strength to the faculties, which belong to human nature. The man of weak understanding is not,

by this change, made to possess a strong mind; the understanding of a child is not at once made to possess the vigour of manhood. Persons constitutionally deficient in quickness of apprehension, in memory, or judgment, remain the same, as it relates to the vigour of their intellect, as before; except that the rational powers, when freed from the misdirection of evil motives, act more correctly. When the mind forms a relish for any particular subject, it manifests a power in understanding that subject, which is peculiar, and which it does not display on other subjects. Hence it is, that pious persons of weak understanding in other matters, often discover much sagacity in religious matters. But this can readily be accounted for, without supposing that the natural faculties are enlarged or strengthened, by regeneration.

4. Again, many persons, when they hear of the greatness of this change, are led to infer, that its greatness must always be manifest to the consciousness of the person who is the subject of it. And hence, real Christians are induced to doubt of the reality of the change experienced by them. But though the change be truly great, as being a transition from death to life; yet the first pulsations of real life may be so feeble, and the actings of the new creature so weak, that it may be, and often is, difficult to ascertain whether a new life has commenced or not. Those who possess the scriptural characteristics of genuine piety, need not be distressed and perplexed, as they often are, because they cannot determine the day and hour of their conversion. Very few can do this; and they who

pretend to be so exact, are often mistaken. That which they experienced, at the time specified, may not have been a genuine exercise of new life, or, if it was, it may have been not the first actings of the new creature, but only a more lively and vigorous exercise of the spiritual nature, than any before experienced. It is not an easy thing for any man to ascertain the precise time of his being "created anew in Christ Jesus;" nor is it a matter of any importance. The great point is, do I possess this new nature? Have I now, habitually, the views, affections, and emotions, the desires and purposes, which are peculiar to the sons of God?

5. One other mistake into which young converts are apt to fall in regard to conversion is, that when this great change is experienced, all sinful thoughts and feelings will be for ever banished from the mind. They entertain the idea, that, so great a change must certainly cleanse the soul from all its defilement; and that no more trouble will be experienced from the corruptions of the heart. Well, the first lively exercises of faith and love in the new convert, seem to favour this anticipation. But after a while, when the soul is involved in darkness, and the flesh lusteth against the Spirit, and a distressing conflict is experienced, the Christian concludes, that all his fondest hopes were fallacious. "Surely," the perplexed soul is ready to say, "I never could have experienced the great change, or I should not be thus infested with evil thoughts, and inbred corruptions. Those that have been renewed have pure hearts, for faith works by love and purifies

the heart. But alas! my heart is full of evil Iniquities, which I supposed to be entirely subdued, show themselves anew; and I now see evils in my heart, which I never thought existed within me before. Surely, I have been awfully deceived in entertaining the persuasion that I had experienced the great change." Such are very commonly the feelings and complaints of real converts, after they have fairly entered into the field of conflict with the world, the flesh, and the devil. But let such learn to know, that we are here renewed but in part, and that the "old man" will struggle as long as any life of sin remains in the soul. Let them learn that this is a scene of conflict; and that the root of sin is deep in the nature of man, and its ramifications extend through his whole constitution of mind and body; that the more the mind is enlightened, the more perspicacious does it become in discovering sin. It is comparable to the case of a person in a dark room, where he is surrounded by disgusting filth, but perceives it not. But let a ray of light into this dark room, and immediately the disgusting scene is apparent; and the clearer the light, the more distinctly are the odious objects by which he is surrounded, perceived. Hence it is, that those men, who have been most eminent for piety, have had the deepest and most humiliating conviction of their own sinfulness.

III. I come now, agreeably to the plan proposed, to exhibit some of the traits of the new creature; and as there is in the language of our text an evident allusion to the creation of the world, it will be proper to bring distinctly into view, the analogy which is obvious between these two works of divine power, the old creation and the new.

1. The first production of almighty power, in the first creation, was light. Before this, indeed, the rough materials of the universe existed, but the substance of our globe was then in a chaotic state. In the language of the inspired historian, "The earth was without form and void, and darkness was upon the face of the deep. And God said, Let there be light, and there was light." So, in the new creation, the first thing of which the rational soul, which is the subject of this work, is conscious, is a new view of spiritual objects. God, who at first commanded light to shine out of darkness, shines into the dark soul with a beam of pure light. "Once," says Paul to the Ephesians, "were ye darkness, but now are ye light in the Lord." And the effect of the gospel, as described in the commission of this chosen vessel to the Gentiles was, " to turn them from darkness to light, and from the power of Satan unto God." He who is the subject of this change is said to be " renewed in knowledge after the image of Him that created him." A man brought up from infancy in a dark cave, might give his full assent to the existence of the sun, moon, and stars, and of the various visible objects on the earth; but how different would be his ideas of these things, if even a feeble ray of light should reveal to him something of the real appearance of these objects! Just so, the man who has heard, all his life, about divine things, has no just conception of them, until his mind is illumined by the Spirit of

God. Then he begins to see these objects in an entirely new light. Now he begins to "discern spiritual things." He beholds something of the glory of God, as it shines in the face of Jesus Christ. Now he begins to perceive that there is a beauty in holiness, which he never saw before. This beauty he sees in the holy law of God, which causes him to delight in it after the inner man. The gospel also appears glorious, as exhibiting the justice and mercy of God; and in the character and life of Christ, he beholds a loveliness, which charms him; and perceiving the love of God to man, manifested by giving up unto the death of the cross, his only begotten Son, he feels himself drawn by the cords of love, so that Christ becomes to him the centre of his warmest affections;—"the chief among ten thousands—One altogether lovely." And as sin is the opposite of holiness, its turpitude and odiousness will be perceived by the same light which reveals the beauties of holiness. He now sees it to be the most abominable of all things. To the soul enlightened by the Spirit, not only do divine things wear an entirely different aspect from what they did before; but even natural objects, the visible heavens, and the earth appear clothed with new attributes. They are now viewed as the works of the great Creator, and as manifesting his wisdom, power, and goodness. To the new convert, the earth is full of the glory of the Lord. To the renewed soul, the Bible appears like a new book. The sacred page seems to be illuminated. The truths of the divine word, are now more precious than gold, and sweeter than honey. The preached gospel has acquired an interest before unknown; and now makes an impression on the renewed heart, which purifies, elevates, and comforts it. And as the people of God bear something of his image, they become the objects of sincere and tender love. Thus, in the new creation, there is to the soul created in Christ Jesus, "new heavens and a new earth."

2. Before the Spirit of God operated on the dark abyss of matter in the first creation, every thing existed in a state of confusion and disorder; but by the divine agency, every thing was made to assume its proper place, and a beautiful order and harmony were produced; the light and air, the sea and dry land, found their proper situation.

Analogous to this, is the moral condition of fallen man. His soul, endowed with noble faculties, and susceptible of various affections and emotions, has by the introduction of sin, been thrown into a state of complete disorder. The higher powers of the mind, reason and conscience, are dethroned, and the inferior passions and carnal appetites have assumed the reins; and instead of harmony, there exists perpetual discord in the rational mind. The regulator of the whole machinery of human agency is wanting. Man was made to love his Creator supremely, but in his fallen state, this principle is wanting; and its place has been usurped by *self*. Self is now the centre of all the affections and pursuits, so that the orderly and harmonious operations of the mind are destroyed. But by the energy of divine power, a new state of things is experienced. God is again placed on the throne of the human heart, and "faith working by love" produces order, by subduing the selfish and earthly affections; and in proportion as these new principles acquire strength and prevail, the disorder of the mind is removed, and harmony restored. The renewed man is no longer a selfish, sensual, and sordid creature. He is now spiritual in his prevailing desires. His affections are set on things above, and not on things on the earth, and he strives to keep a conscience void of offence to God and man, by taking pains to have it truly enlightened as to the rule of duty, and by obeying its dictates uniformly. The course which the renewed man pursues is approved by enlightened reason; and he endeavours more and more to bring all the thoughts and imaginations of his heart into obedience to the gospel of Christ.

3. Another thing manifest in the first creation was the existence of life. At first, the mass of matter was not only dark and confused, but inanimate. Even after the darkness was done away by the creation of light; and after the various substances were separated and reduced to order; and the air, and earth, and water, had found their respective places in creation, there was as yet no sign of life in any part of the creation. Life is of various kinds, but it is the noblest of all the creatures of God. How desolate would the world appear, with all its beauty and order, without living inhabitants! It was to prepare a residence for beings possessed of life, and capable of enjoyment, that the material universe was brought into being. The vegetable creation furnishes the beau-

tiful drapery which renders the world charming and glorious. But the life of animals is far nobler. When the creation was completed, it was in every part, replete with living creatures. And man was made the lord of creation, possessing not only animal passions under the government of reason and conscience, but having the very image of his Creator, delineated on his inmost soul.

The body of man, as first created, will furnish a striking analogy. Though perfect in all its organs and material parts, it was without life, until God animated the artificial frame by breathing into it the breath of life. Then man, under the creating energy of the Almighty, became "a living soul." As the body of Adam, prior to the exertion of divine power, though organized, was but a dead thing; so the soul before the new creation is destitute of life.

Before his regeneration man possesses other kinds of life, but of spiritual life, he is utterly destitute. But when he is quickened by the Spirit of God, he experiences the emotions and desires of a new life. As a new born babe, he desires the sincere milk of the word, that he may grow thereby. He is now alive to God through our Lord Jesus Christ.

And where there is life there is activity and enjoyment. The new creature is an animated, living creature, and manifests the existence of life by action. Out of the heart are the issues of life. There are many kinds of life in the creation of God. Even vegetables possess a wonderful kind of life; but they are unconscious, and unintelligent. Animals possess a much higher kind of life, but in various degrees of excellence, according to the perfection of their organization. Man, possessing an animal body, has many things in common with the inferior animals, as the bodily senses of seeing, hearing, feeling, smelling, and tasting. The appetites are also common to him with them; and also the passions of anger, fear, and the natural affections of parents to their offspring. But man has a higher kind of life. He is endowed with reason and a moral faculty; and by these he is made capable of spiritual life. This he possessed in his original state, which is called "the image and likeness of God." In the new creation this highest kind of life, lost by the fall, is restored. The Christian is said to be "renewed after the image of God;" to be "renewed in knowledge after the image of him that created him." In both which passages, there is an evident allusion to the image of God in which man was created at first. While destitute of this spiritual life, men are said to be dead, and in their regeneration, they are quickened or made alive. They now possess in their souls, the life of God, consisting in knowledge, in holy desires, affections, and purposes. The man who is, by the Spirit of God, thus vivified, though active before, now acts in a new manner. He acts from new principles. He sees spiritual objects in a new light. He has come, as it were, into a new world. His love and his hatred, his joys and his sorrows are changed; they are now different from what they formerly were.

As the natural life in man, and all other creatures, is kept up by suitable nutriment; so this new spiritual life needs to be fed, that it may be preserved and increased in strength; that it may grow up from the imbecillity of infancy, with which it commences, to the maturity and stature of a perfect man in Christ Jesus. And the same efficient power, and the same means are requisite for the preservation and increase of this principle of life, as for its implantation. It is for this purpose that the Spirit of God takes up his residence in the believer, enlightening, purifying, strengthening, and comforting the renewed soul. And as the word was the means of its receiving life; so it is the means of its growth. It is the food by which the believer is nourished. Christ calls himself "the bread of life which came down from heaven," and it is in the word that Christ can now be found. There he is exhibited as our Mediator, our Prophet, Priest, and King. The sacraments are intended to confirm the promises of the word, and to render the truth more impressive on our feelings. This spiritual life, produced in the new creation, manifests itself in external acts of worship and thanksgiving towards God, and in unreserved and universal obedience to his will. Here the new principle finds its highest and noblest expression. Here the renewed heart sends forth its most ardent aspirations, and holiest affections; and here, in the sanctuary, it enjoys in communion with God, its purest, sublimest happiness. For joy is an invariable result of the new creation. And as the sons of God shouted for joy at the creation of the world; so there is joy in the presence of the angels of God over one sinner that repenteth.

This life, bestowed in the new creation, is not in

kind different from the life enjoyed in heaven: the difference is in degree. There the light is perfect, and the affections, purified from every impure mixture, will be exercised to the utmost degree of intensity. There will remain no sinful defect, although there will still be progress; for knowledge will increase; and perhaps the capacities of the soul may be indefinitely enlarged. One comfortable circumstance respecting this new creature is, that he shall never die; that is, his spiritual life shall never be extinct. This certain continuance and perpetuity of the life of the believer, depends not on himself, but on the promises of God. He is able to keep him from falling, and his word is pledged, that he shall never perish. "He that believeth hath everlasting life. He shall never come into condemnation. He that keepeth my sayings, says Christ, shall never taste death." And Paul says, "Being confident of this very thing, that he who hath begun a good work in you, will perform it unto the day of Jesus Christ." (Phil. i. 6.) Again, "For I am persuaded, that neither death, nor life, nor angels, nor principalities, nor powers, nor things present, nor things to come, nor height, nor depth, nor any other creature, shall be able to separate us from the love of God, which is in Christ Jesus, our Lord."

REFLECTIONS.

1. How greatly are they deceived who think that a mere external morality is a sufficient ground on which to build their hopes of eternal life.

This subject, as explained, shows also the fatal

mistake of all who rely on external forms of religion of whatever kind. All external services, where the affections of the heart are not engaged, are rejected by a holy, heart-searching God; whose language to such is, "Who hath required this at your hands, to tread my courts? This people draweth nigh to me with their lips, while their heart is far from me." Again, if in the case of every true Christian, there is "a new creation," then transient impressions and convictions, however deep, furnish no sufficient evidence of genuine piety. Many are like the seed on stony ground, which sprang up quickly, and promised well at first, but which, having no deep root, withered away as soon as the scorching rays of the sun fell upon it. Their faith was temporary, and they fell away in the time of temptation.

The "new creature" is a permanent principle of holiness, which is, indeed, subject to various vicissitudes, but which never entirely faileth. This is a fire which many waters shall not be able to quench.

Those who are created anew, by divine power, are said to be "created unto good works." The performance of good works is, therefore, a necessary evidence of renovation of heart. "Make the tree good, and the fruit good. A good tree cannot bring forth evil fruit." Men, professing repentance, were required by the Baptist, to bring forth "fruits meet for repentance." "Therefore, by their fruits shall ye know them."

Let all those who are conscious that they are yet in their natural state, and have experienced no such change as that concerning which we have been treating, consider the misery and the sinfulness of their condition. You, my unconverted friends, have been long accustomed to hear the gospel, and have enjoyed many precious privileges, of which the majority of our race are destitute; and yet, while others hearing the same sermons and enjoying the same privileges have been savingly converted, and are now new creatures in Christ Jesus, you, alas! have continued in your carelessness and sin; and if at times you have had serious impressions, you have suffered them to be erased from your minds; so that, in all probability a process of hardening has been going on, and you are now further from the kingdom of heaven, than years ago. The gospel is never without effect; when it fails to soften and change the stony heart, it hardens it; just as the sun, while it softens the wax, hardens the clay. "For," says Paul, "we are unto God a sweet savour of Christ in them that are saved, and in them that perish. To the one, we are the savour of death unto death; and to the other, of life unto life." When men have long hardened under the preaching of the gospel, it gives awful reason to fear, lest they are of the number of the reprobate But while we would desire such to take the alarm, we would be far from wishing to drive them to despair. We have no knowledge of the secret purposes of God; and should not wish to pry into them. "Secret things belong unto God, but those which are revealed, to us and to our children." The fountain of life flows freely, and all who will are welcome to come and take of the waters of life freely. And Jesus who cannot deceive has said, "Him that cometh unto me, I will in no wise cast out."

I would earnestly and affectionately warn the impenitent of the danger to which they are exposed. I would entreat them by the awful judgments of God which are impending over their heads, "to flee from the wrath to come." I would say, or rather God says, "Turn ye, turn ye, why will ye die." If the consideration of the terrors of the Almighty and his coming wrath, will not move you, then permit me to turn your attention to his love and mercy, his long-suffering and condescension. Let the goodness of God lead you to repentance. Resist not that love which caused the Saviour to bleed and die on the cross. Reflect on the loving kindness of God to yourselves. While others have been driven away in their wickedness, you have been spared, and while they are beyond the reach of mercy, you are here where God is entreating you to be reconciled. Seize the passing moment. Embrace the gracious offer. Lay hold of eternal life. Flee to the open refuge which is before you Believe and be saved.

SERMON IX.

REPENTANCE AND FORGIVENESS THE GIFT OF AN EXALTED SAVIOUR.

Him hath God exalted with his right hand to be a Prince and a Saviour, for to give repentance to Israel and forgiveness of sins.—ACTS v. 31.

CHRIST said to his disciples, "Nevertheless I tell you the truth. It is expedient for you that I go away; for if I go not away, the Comforter will not come to you; but if I depart, I will send him unto you." (John xvi. 7.) Within ten days after our Lord's ascension, the Holy Spirit was sent, according to his promise, and the disciples, on the day of Pentecost, were enriched, not only with miraculous gifts, but with enlightening and sanctifying grace. The apostles themselves were not only endowed with power to speak with tongues and heal diseases, but received the gift of heavenly wisdom; were made strong in faith and fortitude, and every Christian virtue; so that, henceforth, they did not appear like the same men; and their enemies "took knowledge of them, that they had been with Jesus." But the divine influences, on that auspicious day, were not confined to the apostles and brethren, but extended to the multitude, who had come together;

among whom were many who had been concerned in the crucifixion of our Lord. No less than three thousand souls were on that day brought to repentance, and added to the church. All these spiritual blessings were given in consequence of the ascension and intercession of the Prince of life, the Saviour of the world. And though miraculous powers have long since ceased, as being no longer needed, and peculiarly liable to abuse through the pride and imperfection of men; yet the sanctifying influences of the Holy Spirit are not withdrawn, but have continued in the church unto this day; without which the church could not exist, much less flourish. Every instance of true repentance which has ever occurred, has been produced by the operation of this divine Agent. Christ, exalted to be a Prince and a Saviour, is said, in our text, to give repentance, because in the economy of salvation, it belongs to him to send the Comforter, who is the Holy Spirit.

But what is this gift, called repentance, of which we read so often in the New Testament? It is A CHANGE OF MIND. It is such a sight and sense of the evil of sin, as leads the soul to turn from it with lothing, and self-abhorrence. It is such an ingenuous sorrow for sin, as works a change of mind never to be regretted. But repentance not only is a turning away from all known sin with grief that it ever has been committed, and sincere hatred of the abominable thing, but it is also a turning to God, and laying hold of eternal life It is, therefore, called "repentance toward God," "repentance unto life." It is an internal, moral or spiritual change, evidenced by the fruits of righteousness in the life.

As the soul of every man has an inward monitor, which, according to its light, accuses him of the sin which he commits; and as the word and Spirit of God often give energy to the conscience, impenitent men may, and often do, experience compunction for sin; and their convictions are sometimes very powerful and very painful; so that the sinner cries out in an agony of soul, which is almost insupportable. These awakenings may produce a great change, for a season, in the external conduct, and a diligent attendance on the instituted means of grace. And such convictions from the holy law of God, do commonly precede a true change of heart, and are not to be lightly esteemed; for, to all human appearance, the convinced sinner is much nigher to the kingdom of heaven than the careless sinner. It is well for such as are under these impressions, as they regard their own salvation, to do nothing to quench the Spirit, who is striving with them. And they should assiduously attend on the means of grace; especially on the preaching of the word; for God is pleased to make use of these means for the communication of saving grace; and "faith comes by hearing, and hearing by the word of God." Let the convinced sinner not cease to call mightily on God for his blessing. For those whom God blesses with pardoning grace, he commonly stirs up to great importunity in prayer. And if the result should be a thorough conviction in the mind of a convinced sinner, that he cannot pray aright, and that he can do nothing to obtain the favour of God, it is a state of mind very suitable to receive the free grace of God. Such a soul will never dream of having any merit, or of having laid God under any obligation by his prayers

The point, however, which I wish to bring prominently before your minds, is, that mere legal conviction, however pungent, however long continued, and however great the external reformation which it may produce, is not genuine repentance. And, accordingly, the instances are frequent in which persons are the subjects of this process, and yet after a while lose all their serious impressions, and become worse than before. Or such may get their convictions removed by false comforts, and may be deluded by the arts of Satan into a false confidence of being in a safe state, while they are still in the gall of bitterness and bond of iniquity. Such may remain deceived all their lives, and may occupy a conspicuous place among professors, or even among preachers of the gospel. A true repentance, being not only a turning from sin, but a turning unto God, supposes the soul to be enlightened to understand something of the way in which God can alone be acceptably approached, through a Mediator. No soul ever comes to God, unless it have some apprehension of his mercy in Christ. The exercise of faith in Christ is included in a genuine repentance. It is, therefore, vain to ask whether faith or repentance precedes, when manifestly they both exist together, and the one comprehends the other. But if we would be very accurate as to the order of the exercises of the mind, in conversion, it is not difficult to see, that a saving knowledge of the truth, from the illumination of the Holy Spirit, is necessary to every pious emotion and holy exercise; and that faith cannot be separated from knowledge. If by faith be meant the belief of the truth, and by repentance sorrow for sin and a turning from it, then certainly faith precedes repentance; but if faith be taken in a more restricted sense for coming to Christ, or trusting in him, then repentance as signifying a sense of the evil of sin, and a conviction of its just desert, must precede the receiving of Christ as our Saviour; for to apply to Christ to save us from sin, implies that we have been made to feel the burden of sin, and are sincerely desirous to be delivered from it.

But the Holy Scriptures never deal in metaphysical refinements; although every declaration of Scripture is consistent with the true principles of philosophy; which is the same as to say, that all truths are consistent among themselves. The Christian, however, has no need of philosophy or metaphysics. He has only to receive the truth in its plain, obvious meaning. The Scriptures were written for the use of the ignorant, as well as the learned; and in regard to the great fundamental points of truth, the unlettered Christian does not need the aid of the learned expositor. As it relates to the spiritual character of the truth, the learned and unlearned stand upon a perfect equality. To discern the beauty and glory of divine truth, both are equally dependent on the grace of God. As far as there is a difference, it is in favour of the weak and unlearned, because they are not in danger of being puffed up and blinded by a conceit of their own knowledge, as is too often the case with the wise men of the world; according to that of our Lord, "I thank thee, O Father, Lord of heaven and earth, because thou hast hid these things from the wise and prudent, and hast revealed them unto babes; even so, Father, for so it seemed good in thy sight." And again, "The poor have the gospel preached unto them."

Let it be understood, then, that true repentance is an internal conversion from the love of sin to the love of God; a real change of mind, as the original term properly signifies. In it there are, first, new views of truth and duty; of course new views of God and his holy law, by which means sin is exhibited in its real turpitude. Not only are the views of the understanding changed, but the emotions and affections of the heart are renewed. Sorrow for sin is deeply felt; shame that we have ever had any thing to do with a thing so abominable, fills the soul with confusion of face. An abasing sense of unworthiness prostrates it in the dust; and strong desires after deliverance from the contamination, as well as the guilt of sin, actuate the penitent heart. A sense of ingratitude is among the exercises of the true penitent, of which he is most frequently conscious. But not only has the true penitent new affections and emotions; but his will is also renewed. He now is able to choose that which is good. His heart is fixed on the side of God and his service. He now counts the cost, and yet deliberately chooses the good part which shall never be taken from him. And as the external actions flow from the principles of the inner man, he whose heart is truly changed, will manifest it by a change of life. The subject of gospel repentance will be found endeavouring to walk in all the commandments and ordinances of the Lord, blameless. He hungers and thirsts after righteousness, and delights in the law of God after the inward man. He "esteems all God's precepts concerning all things to be right, and hates every false way." Of course, he will endeavour to grow in grace, and in the knowledge of Jesus Christ. As there is a remainder of sin dwelling in the hearts of true penitents, they will be sensible of its evil and defilement, and will groan under it, and earnestly desire to have it removed. They can, and often do adopt the language of Paul, "O wretched man that I am, who shall deliver me from the body of this death!" And, through the Spirit, they will strive to crucify the flesh, and to mortify the deeds of the body. Thus, their aim and effort is, daily "to die unto sin, and live unto righteousness;" "to put off the old man with his deeds which are corrupt, and to put on the new man, which, after God, is renewed in righteousness and true holiness." Indeed, the man who has experienced this change will be satisfied with nothing short of perfection. If he did not aspire to this, he would not be a genuine penitent; it would be conclusive evidence that he had never seen the odiousness of sin, nor the beauty of holiness. And just as far as he falls short of the mark at which he aims, just so far he blames himself, and is humbled for his sin; and though he not only comes short of the demands of the law, but also of his own purposes and expectations; yet he does not relinquish his efforts, but learns every day to confide less and less in his own strength, and to trust more simply and entirely on the grace of God to enable him to do any thing as he ought. And by slow degrees he learns in practice what he has all along admitted in theory, that his sufficiency is of God. Under this impression he, by waiting on the Lord, endeavours to renew his strength, and thus to mount up as on eagles' wings, to run and not be weary, to walk and not faint. Having from God precious promises of divine aid, he strives "to cleanse himself from all filthiness of flesh and spirit, and to perfect holiness in the fear of God."

From the view which has been taken of the nature of true repentance, we may learn,

1. The great error of those who imagine that they are penitents, because they often feel compunction for their sins, while they have not been persuaded to relinquish them. The worst of men feel compunction, and are sometimes agonized with bitter remorse. But there is no piety in remorse, for the devil, no doubt, has this ingredient strongly mingled in his cup of misery. Who ever manifested more compunction than Saul did for his malevolent and unreasonable persecution of David? and yet, though he desisted from his sin for a season, he soon returned with renewed malice to the pursuit of one who had never injured him, but had always acted faithfully and successfully in his service. And where have we a case of deeper

compunction and remorse, than in Judas Iscariot, who, when he found that his Master was condemned, through his treachery, to be crucified, repented himself, and went and said to the chief priests and scribes, "I have betrayed innocent blood," and threw down the ill-gotten money in the temple, and went and hanged himself? The horrid crime of suicide is commonly owing to the intolerable gnawings of remorse in a soul unacquainted with the efficacy of Christ's blood. It is to be feared, that many are misled by the popular meaning of the English word *repentance*, and suppose that it implies nothing more than regret or sorrow, that they have done what they ought not to have done.

2. And this leads me to point out another grand mistake, into which many of the unconverted fall; and that is, that they can repent by their own will and strength, without any foreign aid. Multitudes are living under this fatal delusion; thinking, that when a convenient season shall arrive, they will then repent; or if such a convenient time does not come before, they will repent of their sins on a death-bed, persuading themselves, and encouraged in the belief by false teachers, that they have the ability to repent whenever they may choose to exert it. Under this delusion it is, that sinners procrastinate attention to the concerns of their souls, until their day of grace is past. If such are permitted to enjoy the exercise of reason on a death-bed, they then find that repentance does not come at their bidding. Alas! in this painful and awful situation, they find that instead of

tender, ingenuous relentings, their hearts are blind and hard, and to save their souls, they cannot command one pious, penitent emotion to arise in their hearts. I would say to those who think they have ability to repent when they please, make the experiment now. "Make to yourselves a new heart." Put your ability to the test. It will certainly do you no harm. But you have no desire to forsake all sin, and herein is the source of your inability; and the same indisposition to turn away from sin will accompany you to the grave, unless the grace of God prevent. No: man never changes his own heart from sin to holiness, until the power of God operates to take away the heart of stone. And then when a heart of flesh is given, the sorrows of repentance begin to gush out; the heart is now yielding to God's will, and is rendered impressible by divine truth. Now, the stony heart is broken and becomes contrite; and on such a heart God looks with favour. "The sacrifices of God are a broken spirit; a broken and a contrite heart, O Lord, thou wilt not despise." (Ps. li. 17.)

3. In the light of this subject we may also see the error of those who take an outward and partial reformation to be repentance. Repentance, we have seen, is an internal change, affecting the understanding, affections, and will, and thus producing the "fruits meet for repentance," namely, a holy life. But men may, and often do, make a partial reformation from some of their evil practices, and yet the root of iniquity remains unsubdued. The man who in his youth was licentious and

indulged his carnal appetites without restraint, when he becomes old, may have abandoned all vices of this class; yet he may be no less wicked than before his reformation; for instead of fleshly lusts, pride, avarice, and malice may have taken deeper root in his soul. It may be with him as with the man of whom our Saviour speaks, from whom one devil went out, but it was only to return with seven others worse than himself. In our day, when so many inebriates have been reclaimed from their degrading and ruinous vice, there is reason to apprehend, that many who have been the subjects of this reformation, may be led to think that such a reformation is all that is necessary to their salvation. Whereas, though such a reformation is exceedingly desirable and important, as it relates to their temporal welfare and respectability, and usefulness; and may be as life from the dead to their mortified and afflicted families; yet they may remain as much under the habitual dominion of sin, and have hearts as much at enmity with God as before. It is not enough to lop off one branch from the evil tree; the axe must be laid at the root. The heart must be changed. The love of God must be implanted. Sin must be forsaken on account of its own turpitude. And not merely one, but all sin must be repented of. If we regard one sin in our hearts, it is a sure sign that our repentance is not genuine. And God has declared, that the prayers of such he will not hear. Often these partial reformations are temporary. The sinner, who for a season curbs his vicious appetites, after a while, weary of this self-denial, gives the reins to his lusts, and rushes down the current of fleshly indulgence with greater licentiousness than before his reformation.

4. We may, moreover, learn from what has been said, that repentance is not a single act, but a great change of moral character; and that as long as men have any sin remaining in them, repentance can never cease. Every day the true penitent is endeavouring to turn away, more and more, from his sins. He never knows a time when the exercise of repentance is not obligatory on him. In every act of devotion, in public or private, he appears before God in the character of a penitent. And the more of godly sorrow and contrition for sin he feels, the more acceptable are his devotional exercises to God, who is graciously pleased to declare, "I dwell in the high and holy place, with him also, that is of a contrite and humble spirit, to revive the spirit of the humble, and to revive the heart of the contrite ones." The more holy a man becomes, the more penitent he is; and as he grows in grace, he increases in his hatred to all sin, and in sorrow that he has ever committed it. And even when the pious man has satisfactory evidence that God has put away his iniquity, and freely forgiven his sins; yet he does not on that account cease to repent of all the evils which he has done. Indeed, the heart is never so completely melted into ingenuous relentings, as when the forgiving love of God is shed abroad within it. The true Christian, then, has this as one of his distinguishing characteristics, that he is a mourner all his days.

But he has the blessedness of those that mourn He shall be comforted.

Finally, we may in the light of this subject, see the miserable imposition which is practised on their ignorant followers by the Romish priests, who teach them, that "to repent" is nothing else but *to do penance*. And what is more to be censured, they have given this as the translation of the original term in the New Testament; so that when their people do read the Bible, which practice is never encouraged among them, they learn nothing of the important doctrine of repentance, as a change of mind; but think that God, in his word, requires them to perform certain acts of self-denial, which may be prescribed by the priest, as a punishment for their sins. When they have submitted to these penances, the priest pronounces them absolved from their sins, although they may give no evidence of a change of heart, and may bring forth in their lives none of the fruits meet for repentance. May the good Lord deliver the people from these woful delusions!

The connexion of the forgiveness of sin with repentance is so certain and indissoluble, that wherever sin is forgiven there is a true penitent; and wherever there is repentance, it is accompanied with the pardon of sin. We should, however, never forget that repentance has no efficacy to atone for sin; nor any merit to deserve the favour of God. This blessing is entirely the fruit of Christ's death, which becomes ours as soon as we sincerely believe in the Lord Jesus Christ.

And as we have shown, true repentance always accompanies a genuine faith, or includes it; therefore repentance is the sure evidence of our pardon. It is, therefore, emphatically denominated "repentance unto life." But though there is no merit in our repentance to deserve forgiveness; yet there is an evident congruity in connecting pardon with repentance. Among men it is customary for an offended person to require some evidence of repentance prior to a reconciliation. These two gifts which our exalted Prince and Saviour bestows, comprehend all that is essential to man's salvation, for they remove the only obstacles which stand in the way of our entering into life. By the one, the corruption of our nature is subdued, and a work of sanctification is commenced, which will be carried on until it is perfected, and the once polluted soul presented before God, without spot or wrinkle, or any blemish whatever. By the other, the curse of the law is removed, and there is no condemnation to them that are in Christ Jesus. For when sin is forgiven, the believing penitent is always adopted into the family of God; and being now a son, becomes, of course, an heir.

Let us, then, never cease to cry to our risen and ascended Saviour, to bestow these rich blessings of his grace upon us and others. His throne is accessible, and we are invited to come with freedom and confidence unto it, that we may attain mercy, and find grace to help in every time of need. As we all need these blessings, let us boldly and importunately ask that we may receive them.

SERMON X.

RECEIVING CHRIST BY FAITH.

But as many as received him, to them gave he power to become the sons of God; even to them that believe on his name.—JOHN i. 12.

IT is a wonderful fact, that though the Jewish nation were looking for their Messiah, yet, when Jesus of Nazareth appeared, and completely answered the predictions of the prophets, the great body of the nation rejected him, persecuted him, and ceased not their malice, until they saw him crucified. "He came to his own, and his own received him not." But while he was contumeliously rejected by the great body of the people, there were a few, even of that wicked and adulterous generation, who received him. "Many were called, but few were chosen." The truth and glory of the Messiah were hidden from the wise and prudent, but were revealed unto babes. The Scribes and Pharisees proudly rejected the Son of God, but publicans and sinners flocked around him and were accepted; so that it was said by way of reproach, "This man receiveth sinners!"

But rich grace was conferred on all those who did receive him. However deeply involved in guilt and crime, they received a free pardon, and acquired the privilege of becoming the sons of God. Let us, then, first inquire what it is to receive Christ; and secondly, what is the exalted privilege conferred on such.

1. What are we to understand by receiving Christ? The Evangelist explains his own meaning in the latter part of the verse, by saying, "even as many as believed on his name." Receiving Christ, and believing on his name, are substantially the same thing. But do not many believe that Christ is the Son of God and Saviour of sinners, who continue in sin and never subject themselves to his easy yoke? We do read of some, in our Saviour's time, who believed in him, yet would not confess him, because they loved the praise of men more than the honour which cometh from God; and of some who received the word with joy, and believed, but their faith was temporary; and of one, who believed and was baptized, and yet was pronounced by an inspired apostle, to be "in the gall of bitterness and bond of iniquity." The apostle James, also, speaks of those whose faith was dead; that is, such a faith as neither worked by love, nor produced the fruits of righteousness and peace.

From all these cases we learn that there is a species of faith which is not connected with salvation. Such believers did never truly receive Christ as their Saviour; and did never believe on him with that faith which is of the operation of the Holy Spirit, which is "not of ourselves, but is the gift of God." It is not strange that there should be in those educated in a Christian country, a common traditionary faith in the Christian religion; for we find a similar faith prevalent among all nations, whatever may be the nature of their religion. They believe in what they have been taught; they believe as their fathers did before them. We may be sure, then, that that faith, among Christians, which has no higher origin than the faith of a Pagan or a Mussulman, is not that faith which is so often declared by our Lord to be connected with salvation.

Let us then inquire what it is to receive Christ, for this is the faith mentioned in our text.

1. And here we may apply the proverb of our Saviour, "They that be whole need not the physician, but they that are sick." Christ came "to seek that which was lost." "He came not to call the righteous, but sinners to repentance." It is plain, therefore, that none will apply to Christ as the Physician of souls, until they become sensible that they are diseased; that none will receive him as a Saviour, but those who feel that they are lost. Men are very averse to being dependent on others for what they imagine they already possess, or can obtain by their own efforts. Even when in some measure convinced of sin, their first effort almost always is to save themselves; and these legal strivings in their own strength, they do not give up until by experience they find that their case grows worse and worse, and that they have no ability to do any thing for their own deliverance.

If Christ is truly received by any, they must view him in his true character, as the only begotten Son of God. If a king should send his own son to negotiate a treaty of peace with subjects in a state of rebellion, and should make it a condition of his pardoning their treason, that they should receive his son as his ambassador; if any, notwithstanding the credentials which he bore, should deny that he was the son of the king; or that he was invested with a plenipotentiary commission to grant pardon to such as submitted, it could not be said, that they received the royal messenger, although they should admit that he had been sent to communicate the will of the sovereign. So, unless men acknowledge Christ to be indeed THE SON OF GOD, "the brightness of his glory, and the express image of his Person," they cannot properly be said to receive the Messiah, or believe to the salvation of their souls; although they may extol him as a perfect man, or even as an exalted angel. We can only be said to receive an ambassador when we acknowledge him in that character, in which he professes to come, and ascribe to him that power and dignity which he claims. They, therefore, who deny the divinity of the Saviour are to be considered as really unbelievers, as if they rejected him altogether. All who truly receive Christ, do believe in him as THE SON OF GOD, who claims equality of knowledge, power, and honour with the Father.

Again, Christ comes as a Prophet, as the prophet concerning whom Moses spoke; or rather the Lord to Moses, "I will raise them up a prophet like unto thee." Christ was demonstrated by his works to be "a Teacher sent from God." When he appeared in glory on the mount of transfiguration, the voice which proceeded from "the excellent glory," said, "This is my beloved Son, hear him." If we receive him, we must receive him as our divine TEACHER, and submit our minds to the instructions which he gives. And as man is not only blind, but indisposed to learn, Christ first convinces him of his extreme ignorance, and next endows him with a teachable disposition. As long as men think highly of their own wisdom, they will not come to Christ, to learn of him. Such are given up to their own blindness, and commonly, become more and more confirmed in their errors. In this sense we must understand what Christ says, "For judgment am I come into this world, that they which see not might see, and that they which see might be made blind." And this is confirmed by the answer which he gave to some of the Pharisees, who, on hearing the words already cited, said, "And are we blind also? Jesus said unto them, if ye were blind, ye should have no sin; but now ye say, We see; therefore your sin remaineth." One of the things which the Holy Spirit is sent to convince men of is, the blindness of their minds, which is not essentially different from unbelief. "And when he is come, he will reprove the world of sin, of righteousness, and of judgment. Of sin, because they believe not in me." This conviction of unbelief goes before the reception of Christ. At first, under the illumination of the Holy Spirit, gross sins, and sins of commission affect the conscience, but as the light increases, the soul is made deeply sensible, that it has not only sinned by positive, external acts, but that there is a corrupt fountain within, and that as much guilt has been contracted by sins of omission, as by overt acts of transgression. And when all hope of justification by the law of works is relinquished, and it begins to turn toward the gospel for relief, it finds in itself no more ability to obey the gospel than the law. Eternal life is offered to every one that believeth; that is, to every one that will come to Christ; and in theory, believing seems to be a very easy thing; so that almost every careless sinner thinks that he can exercise faith whenever he wills to do so. But not so with the convinced sinner. He feels that nothing is more out of his power, than one act of saving faith. He is deeply sensible that he never shall be truly willing to turn to God, until he is made so by divine power. And yet, he does not excuse himself; he is conscious that he is culpable for his unbelief, and for want of a heart to believe. He, therefore, despairs of all help, except from the sovereign mercy of God; and no one can assure him that this will be vouchsafed. He is now in a situation to acknowledge that salvation is altogether of grace. And when God is pleased to reveal himself to such a soul, the blessing comes as a free gift. The object now presented to the believing soul is Christ, as a Mediator, as exhibited in the word of God; for Christ is no where else to be found but in the word. And as he is the lesson to be learned, so he is the great and effectual teacher, by the Spirit whom he sends, not only to convince men of sin, but of righteousness. Henceforth, the humbled sinner desires to sit, like Mary, at Christ's feet, and learn of him. No salutary instruction is expected from any other quarter. The sincere believer continually comes to Christ for instruction, and receives all his words as infallibly true.

But blindness is not the only malady under which the human soul labours; and from which it needs to be delivered. There is a heavy burden of guilt sufficient to sink it to the lowest hell. When this comes to be felt, then, indeed, the condition of the soul is deplorable. All its own exertions and sufferings cannot atone for the smallest sin. "The blood of bulls and goats cannot take away sin." The inquiry may then be, Wherewith shall I come before the Lord, and bow myself before the high God? Shall I come before him with burnt offerings, with calves of a year old? Will the Lord be pleased with thousands of rams, or with ten thousands of rivers of oil? Shall I give my first born for my transgression, the fruit of my body for the sin of my soul?" However careless once, now the cry is extorted, "What must I do to be saved?" Without some conviction of the ill-desert of sin, we are never prepared to view Christ as "the Lamb of God that taketh away the sin of the world." The death of Christ has little or no meaning to a careless sinner. The soul must be deeply wounded by the stroke of the law, before it is ready to appreciate the precious balm intended as a remedy for the pained conscience. But when it is fairly slain by the law, and all hope of satisfying its demands is gone, then to see by the eye of faith, Christ crucified, and to learn that "He was wounded for our transgressions, and bruised for our iniquities," and that he was thus made a curse for us, that we might be redeemed from the curse of the law, new feelings begin to spring up in the soul. Here, indeed, is a fountain opened for sin and uncleanness, a fountain of precious blood. Now it is understood how God can be just, while he justifies the believing sinner. The law, indeed, does not relinquish its demands; this is impossible, but here they are all satisfied. It is more; they are honoured. "Mercy and truth have met together, righteousness and peace have kissed each other." The sword of divine justice has indeed been turned aside from us, but we behold it piercing the heart of our Surety; for when he stepped into our place under the law, there was no remission of the penalty, but the stern demand was laid upon him. Then was fulfilled the word of the prophet, "Awake, O sword, against the man that is my fellow; smite the shepherd and the sheep shall be scattered." According to the covenant engagements of the Son, he assumes our place, and drinks the cup of wrath which the Father put into his hands. When a convicted sinner beholds Christ lifted up, he receives a salvation similar to that which the Israelites, bitten by the fiery serpents, obtained by looking on the brazen serpent, which Moses was directed to elevate upon a pole. For as every one of these received immediate deliverance from his painful and envenomed wound; so, every one who by faith looks to a Saviour exalted on the cross, receives redemption from the guilt of sin. When his faith is strong he is conscious that his deliverance is effected, and that the curse is removed. But faith follows Christ to his exaltation to heaven also, and there sees him still officiating as a great High Priest. Still he appears as "a Lamb that had been slain." Still he exhibits his meritorious propitiation, and sprinkles the blood of the great sin-offering before the mercy-seat in the temple above. "He is able, therefore, to save to the uttermost all who come unto God by him; seeing he ever liveth to make intercession for them." "Such an High Priest becomes us." The believing sinner feels his conscience purified by the sprinkling of this atoning blood. Christ is, therefore, received as a Priest, and the penitent sinner places his whole confidence in him, and cheerfully commits all his eternal interests into his hands, believing that what he thus confides, will be safely kept unto the day of redemption. Thus is Christ received as a Priest.

He is also, at the same time, received as a King. Christ, as God, has an indefeasible right to our allegiance; but he is also King, as our Mediator. All power in heaven and in earth, is committed unto him. To him every knee should bow and every tongue confess. But having purchased a peculiar people, a chosen generation, not with silver and gold, but with his own precious blood, he has a right founded in redemption to rule over them. And though they long resisted his authority, and often said in their hearts, "We will not have this man to reign over us;" yet, by his powerful grace he subdues their proud and rebellious hearts, and in the day of his power, makes them willing to take his yoke upon them. The soul humbled in penitence at the foot of the cross, cries, "Lord, what wouldest thou have me to do?" Other lords have had dominion over it, but now it renounces them all, and voluntarily submits to the authority of the King of Zion, and cheerfully resolves to keep his commandments, and to observe all his ordinances. Christ is now placed on the throne of the affections, and reigns as supreme; and the earnest and continual desire of the believer is, that every thought and imagination may be brought into subjection to the law of Christ. And grief is felt whenever a failure of due obedience is observed. Thus Christ is received in his threefold office of Prophet, Priest, and King; and in these offices he is able to accomplish the salvation of all who put their trust in him. For, "of God he is made unto us wisdom, righteousness, sanctification, and redemption."

Before we proceed to the consideration of the latter part of the text, let us reflect on what has been already said, and endeavour to derive some improvement from it.

1. Let us beware of imitating the ungrateful conduct of the unbelieving Jews. By their unbelief, they forfeited all the rich privileges and blessings which appertained to them, as the covenanted people of God. They gloried in being the children of Abraham; in being of the circumcision; in having the oracles and promises of God among them. But what did all these privileges avail them, when they rejected him in whom Abraham

firmly believed; and refused to receive Him in whom all the predictions and promises concentered? However descended from the father of the faithful according to the flesh; yet they were not the true children of Abraham, according to the promise; "For they are not all Israel who are of Israel. He is not a Jew who is one outwardly; neither is that circumcision which is outward in the flesh; but he is a Jew who is one inwardly, and circumcision is that of the heart, in the spirit and not in the letter, whose praise is not of men but of God." While we are thankful for external privileges, let us beware of trusting in them. They will all avail nothing without "faith, which worketh by love."

2. We learn from what has been said, the true nature of saving faith; it is the "receiving Christ as he is offered in the gospel," as a divine Person, even the well-beloved and only begotten Son of God, who thought it not robbery to be equal with God. It is to receive him as our Prophet, Priest, and King, understandingly and cordially; and renouncing every other foundation of hope, and every other Teacher and Master. It is, in short, to believe firmly all that God has testified of his Son. It is so to apprehend these truths by the illumination of the Spirit, that our supreme affections may be attracted to Christ, and our wills be resolved to follow the Lamb through evil and good report.

SERMON XI.

PRIVILEGES OF THE SONS OF GOD.

To as many as received him, to them gave he power to become the sons of God; even to them that believe on his name; which were born, not of blood, nor of the will of the flesh, nor of the will of man, but of God.—John i. 12, 13.

To be descended from kings and nobles is an honour held in high estimation in the world; but when men are unworthy of their distinguished ancestors, they rather cast a reproach upon them, than inherit any real honour from them. The Jews prided themselves on being descended from Abraham, the friend of God, and the father of the faithful; and many of them rested in their connexion with a pious ancestry, as the ground of their acceptance; but Christ makes a distinction between a natural and spiritual descent. He denies that the Jews, who rejected him, were the children of Abraham; because the works of Abraham they did not do. And John the Baptist, told them not to think within themselves that they had Abraham to their father, for God was able of the stones to raise up children unto Abraham.

Paul also draws a distinct line of division between those who were merely Jews by natural descent and outward privileges, and those who were Israelites in heart. (Rom. ii. 28, 29.) God has one only-begotten Son, generated from his own essence, without being separated from it. The angels also are called "the sons of God," because God is their Father and Creator, and because they bear the image of God. Adam is called "the son of God," because he proceeded immediately from the hand of God, and had no other Father. But believers are the sons of God in virtue of their union to Christ. As he is a Son, in an exalted and ineffable sense, and they are members of his body, his flesh, and his bones, and are "one spirit," they are sons in a peculiar sense, in which no other creatures, however exalted, are sons. The angels have been admitted to no such union with the Son of God, as that with which believers are honoured. Christ, by becoming incarnate, has come very near to human nature. "He took not on him the nature of angels, but the seed of Abraham." He is not ashamed, therefore, to call his people brethren.

Again, believers are sons, because they have been begotten of God. This the evangelist speaks of in our text. He had declared, that all who received Christ, possessed the power or privilege of becoming the sons of God; and lest any one should think that this high privilege was obtained by human descent, or from any external thing, or any human power, he goes on to tell how they became sons. It was by being born. But whence this birth? Was it by blood or natural descent, or from any human origin? No. This would not have made them the sons of God. But they became the sons of God by being "born of God." This fundamental doctrine of Christianity, our Lord treats of fully, in his discourse with Nicodemus, the Jewish ruler, who had come to him by night to learn something of his doctrine. To him, Christ declares, that "except a man be born again, (or from above, as the word should be rendered,) he cannot see the kingdom of God." And when the inquiring Jew marvelled at this, he reiterates what he had said of the necessity of this change; but teaches him that it was a spiritual and not a natural birth of which he spake. The expression, "born of the Spirit," in that passage, is equivalent to being "born of God" in this place. The word "water," which is joined to "spirit," may be merely an external emblem of purification; or it may possibly refer to the ordinance of baptism, which strikingly represents, by an external sign, the work of regeneration; and which is also a duty required of all believers. "The wind bloweth where it listeth, and thou hearest the sound thereof, but canst not tell whence it cometh, nor whither it goeth; so is every one that is born of the Spirit." By these words of our Saviour, we are taught, that the operations of the Spirit are sovereign and free, as the wind bloweth where it listeth. No man can command the wind, or direct its course; "so is every one that is born of the Spirit." Again, we learn from these words, that the operations of the Spirit cannot be traced in the work of regeneration. We can neither explain the manner in which the work commences, the process by which it is carried on, nor its termination; but as in the case of the wind, we can hear its sound, so here we may observe the fruits and effects of the Spirit's operation.

This change is called regeneration, or the new birth, because it is the beginning of a new kind of life. As in the natural birth, we come into the world, and by degrees become acquainted with the objects around us, as they make impressions on our senses; so by being born of God, or born from above, the eyes of our mind are opened upon the spiritual world. We receive by regeneration a susceptibility of taking on lively impressions from objects which affected us not at all before. A new heaven and a new earth seem to be created; for the views of all nature are changed, by the new life which has been communicated. But whence this new light? Does the Lord make a new revelation to every regenerated soul? By no means. This light emanates from the Bible. It is the law contained in the Holy Scriptures which is now seen to be "holy, just, and good," and it is by this law that sin is seen to be "exceeding sinful." It is Christ, as exhibited in the Bible, who becomes the object of the faith and love of the renewed mind. Enthusiasts may undervalue the word, and choose rather to follow their own disordered imaginations; but the soul taught of God is always led to the word, for divine instruction. This is the "lamp to their feet, and the light to their path." By the word the Spirit operates. The reason why the truth, often heard and read, seems to be new, and clothed with beauty and interest unperceived before, is because the films of ignorance and unbelief and prejudice, are removed by the illumination of the Holy Spirit. Something of the glory of God is now seen shining in the face of Jesus Christ; and beholding this, the regenerated soul is transformed into the same likeness from glory to glory, as by the Spirit of the Lord. And it requires Omnipotence to cause the blinded eyes to see. The same power which caused light to shine out of darkness, must shine into our hearts, to give us the light of the knowledge of the glory of God in the face of Jesus Christ. At first, the views of the regenerated soul may be dim and indistinct, like those of the man restored to his natural sight by our Saviour. When asked whether he saw aught, he replied, that he saw "men as trees walking;" but another touch of the Saviour's hand, caused him "to see all things clearly." So, "the path of the just is as the shining light that shineth more and more unto the perfect day." The degrees of light, and the vigour of life, communicated by regeneration, are very different in different converts. The work of grace on the heart, is in kind the same in all, but various in degree, analogous to what is observed in the natural life. The soul born of God, seeks in its most ardent aspirations, to return to God the fountain of life. The affections are now habitually set on things above, and the renewed soul spontaneously goes out in ardent desires after God, desiring to know more of him, and to enjoy the light of his countenance; hungering and thirsting after righteousness, panting after communion with God, and seeking to advance his glory. These, in Scripture, are denominated "seekers of the Lord," and there is a gracious promise, that none of them shall seek in vain. When the Lord says, "Seek ye my face, their heart responds, Thy face, Lord, will we seek."

The tree being now made good, cannot but bring forth good fruit. The regenerated soul loves God above all things, and delights in his law after the inner man. The best evidence of having experienced this change is a habitual purpose and endeavour to keep all the commandments of God, and to oppose and avoid every known sin. Their prevailing motive is love to God; their rule, God's holy law which they cordially approve; and their end, the glory of God. Certainly all who are governed by these principles are, THE SONS OF GOD.

But God not only is the author of regeneration to his children, but of adoption. By adoption, a man takes into his family some poor child, and bestows upon it his affection and care; and treats it, in all respects, as if it were his own child, begotten of his own body. And this little orphan is introduced, it may be, into a rich and honourable family; and instead of penury and disgrace, it is supplied with every thing necessary for its comfort, and becomes the heir of the estate. This practice, very common among some nations, especially the Romans, and not unknown in our own country, is made use of to represent the gracious dealings of our heavenly Father toward poor, lost, and degraded sinners, whom he saw lying in a state of ruin. On these he exercises tender compassion, and rescues them from the miserable condition into which they were sunk; raises them up from their low estate, and makes them sons and daughters. They are brought into his church, and are there nourished and supported with every thing necessary for their spiritual welfare. And that they may be encouraged to come with confidence and freedom into his presence, their heavenly Father bestows on them the spirit of adoption; by which they are disposed to call him their Father, with the fond affection of children. They are no more considered and treated as servants, but as sons; and being sons, they are of course heirs. And as the rich inheritance which is in reversion belongs to the Son of God, who has purchased it, they are made joint heirs with him. While in this world, they are trained by suitable discipline and trials, that they may become meet for the inheritance of the saints in light. But when their time of trial and preparation is ended, they will have an abundant entrance administered unto them into the everlasting kingdom of their Lord and Saviour Jesus Christ; after which they will hunger no more, and thirst no more, and all tears shall be for ever wiped from their eyes. They shall henceforth be ever with the Lord that they may behold his glory. For it is his will, that where he is, there they should be also.

From a consideration of these things we may well adopt the admiring exclamation of the apostle John, "Behold, what manner of love the Father hath bestowed upon us, that we should be called the sons of God. Beloved, it doth not yet appear what we shall be, but when he doth appear, we shall be like him, for we shall see him as he is. And every man that hath this hope in him, purifieth himself, even as he is pure."

The dignity and honour enjoyed by the greatest princes on earth is contemptible when compared with that of the meanest child of God. Soon all earthly glory shall be obscured for ever; and the dust and bones of the greatest monarch will be as loathsome as those of the vilest beggar; but though the bodies of the sons of God, are destined also to return to the earth, yet their very dust is precious in the eyes of the Lord; and though apparently vile while in the grave, yet it is destined to rise again in honour and glory. And in the Father's house there is already a glorious mansion prepared for every one of the sons and daughters of God Almighty.

If believers have made over to them all the privileges of sons of God, they should act as becometh the heirs for whom such an inheritance is provided. We would expect of the son of a king who was heir to a crown, and expected shortly to occupy a throne, to stand aloof from low company and degrading pursuits. We should expect him to live under the constant impression that he was the son of a king. Certainly, then, the sons of God, while detained upon earth, should not be conformed to this world. They should not set their hearts on things below, but should habitually remember that they are heirs to a heavenly inheritance. This object should never be long out of their thoughts, and nothing which they can control should be permitted to draw them off from the contemplation and pursuit of this glorious object. Their citizenship being in heaven they should confess themselves to be strangers and pilgrims on earth.

Finally, the sons of God should be filled with joy in the lively hope of the riches of glory which awaits them. Professing Christians too often go mourning all the day long, and through grief and despondency, hang their heads as the bulrush. And this leads others to think that they are a poor, dejected, miserable set of people, who being cut off by their religious profession from the pleasures and amusements of this world, have found no compensation in religion, and enjoy little or no comfort in the prospect before them. These things ought not so to be. Let saints be joyful in their King. Of all people in the world, they have the best right to be joyful. They have nothing to fear, for all things shall work for their good, and they have every thing to hope for, because heaven is secured to them by two immutable things in which it is impossible for God to lie, that they might have strong consolation who have fled for refuge to lay hold on the hope set before them. A gracious God not only permits, but commands his children to rejoice; yea, to rejoice alway, to rejoice evermore, to rejoice in tribulation, and even in death.

O Christian, think much of the high dignity to which you are exalted by your union to Christ. You are kings and priests unto God. You are the heirs of a heavenly inheritance, joint heirs with Christ. What if here you are a poor and afflicted people; in this respect you resemble your Saviour. If you suffer with him, you shall also reign with him. Though poor and afflicted in this world, in the world to come you will be rich and happy. Your treasures there can never be lost; "Neither moth nor rust doth corrupt, and thieves do not break through and steal." Live, then, by faith, looking "not at the things which are seen, which are temporal, but at the things which are not seen, which are eternal." Live in the lively hope and anticipation of your future bliss. Let this alleviate your burdens, and sweeten the toils of your weary pilgrimage.

SERMON XII.

DECEITFULNESS OF THE HEART.

The heart is deceitful above all things, and desperately wicked.—
Jer. xvii. 9

These words do not describe the moral condition of any particular man, or of any one nation, but are spoken generally of human kind. The meaning is the same as if it had been said, every heart is "deceitful above all things, and desperately wicked." Not that all men are in practice equally wicked; or that, in fact, all hearts are equally deceitful; for there is a progress in sin to which no limits can be assigned. When, therefore, it is asserted that all men are totally depraved, the meaning is not, that all are as depraved as they can be, but that even before moral acts commence, there is in all men an utter destitution of all righteousness. As to original sin, all men stand on the same level. All are destitute of any true love to God. "The carnal mind is enmity against God." By nature we are all "dead in sin," and "children of wrath even as others."

We learn from the example of Paul, in the third chapter of Romans, that the declarations in the Old Testament respecting the character and sinful state of mankind, are applicable to all men, in all ages. And even those traits of moral character, which, when exhibited, had particular reference to the Jewish people, are applicable to other nations. And this rule of interpretation depends on two principles; first, that human nature is essentially the same in all ages and among all people; and secondly, that the sacred Scriptures were written for the instruction of people at all times. The words of our text, however, are free from all objection arising from a special reference to any man or nation; they contain a general proposition, which is as true and as applicable in our age as in another.

There are two qualities here ascribed to the human heart, and both in the superlative degree, viz. *deceitfulness*, exceeding that of every other thing; and *desperate* or deadly *wickedness*—wickedness, incurable by any human means.

In this discourse we propose to treat of the exceeding deceitfulness of the heart; and may treat of its desperate wickedness at another time.

That is properly called deceitful which presents objects in a false light, or leads to a misconception of the nature of things within us and around us. And that is properly called deceitful, which conceals its own true character, and assumes the appearance of what it is not.

1. One of the ways in which the deceitfulness of the heart manifests itself is in its tendency to blind the understanding in regard to religious truth.

It is certainly a matter of primary importance, that our views of the doctrines and precepts of religion be correct. True religion is distinguished from superstition on one side, and enthusiasm on the other, by this, above every other criterion, that it is founded in just intellectual conceptions of the great truths of divine revelation. All pure and holy affections toward God, in which the very essence of religion consists, must be excited by correct views of the divine attributes; and all good conduct proceeds from good motives or pure affections. To have the mind darkened with ignorance, or perverted by error, is inconsistent with the exercise of holiness, or the practice of true virtue. Evidence is always on the side of truth; but that evidence may be overlooked, or so distorted, that the truth may not be perceived, and instead of it error may be embraced and defended as truth The reason why the minds of men reject the truth is, the depravity of the heart. "This is the condemnation, that light is come into the world, and men loved darkness rather than light. A deceived heart hath turned them aside." The grossest errors of idolaters are traced by the apostle Paul, to a wrong state of heart. "When they knew God, they glorified him not as God, but became vain in their imaginations." And it is a principle in the government of God, that men who love not the truth, and deliberately turn away from it, are given up to judicial blindness, and to the dominion of sin. So, when the conduct of the heathen is described by Paul, and their voluntary attachment to idolatry in preference to the worship of the true

God, he adds, "Therefore, God gave them up to uncleanness." And in another place he says, "Because they received not the love of the truth, that they might be saved. And for this cause, God shall send them strong delusion, that they should believe a lie, that they all might be damned, who believed not the truth, but had pleasure in unrighteousness."

Infidelity, and every species of dangerous error, may be traced to the deceitfulness of the heart. If men possessed good and honest hearts, they would search diligently for the truth, and would be disposed to judge impartially of its evidence; and, as was said, evidence being on the side of truth, and the truth congenial with the moral feelings of the upright mind, it would always be embraced. Atheism itself is a disease rather of the heart, than of the head. And idolatry, which darkens with its portentous shadows a large portion of our globe, owes its origin to the deceitfulness and wickedness of the human heart. It was not for want of evidence that men apostatized from the worship of the true God to idolatry; "for the invisible things of him from the creation of the world are clearly seen, being understood by the things that are made, even his eternal power and Godhead; so that they are without excuse. Because that when they knew God, they glorified him not as God, neither were thankful, but became vain in their imaginations, and their foolish heart was darkened."

The influence which the dispositions of the heart have on the judgments of the understanding, to pervert them, is a matter of daily observation.

The connexion between truth and holiness is so intimate, and also between error and sin, that even in minor deviations from the true doctrine, if we could trace it, we should find that every obliquity of this kind produced a corresponding effect on the moral character of the person.

2. Again, the exceeding deceitfulness of the heart appears in the delusive promises of pleasure, which it makes, in the indulgence of sinful desires. This illusion probably arises from an original principle of our constitution. Had man continued upright, this expectation of pleasure would never be disappointed. For then the supreme affections were fixed on God, in whom there is an infinite fulness to satisfy the desires of every creature. But now, when the heart is turned away from God, and the supreme love of the heart placed on the creature, it is no wonder that continual disappointment of our expectations of happiness in the indulgence of our desires is experienced. This is so uniformly the fact, that it is a common remark, that men enjoy more pleasure in the pursuit of the objects of the world, than in their possession. This delusion of pleasure in prospect, particularly affects the young. With them experience is wanting, which serves to correct this error of the imagination; but even experience is insufficient to cure the disease. Men, when disappointed in one pursuit, commonly turn with unabated ardour to another; or they attribute their want of enjoyment to some wrong cause, and still press on in the fond expectation of realizing their hopes in some other pursuit. Vain expectation! They are deluded by an

unsubstantial image which will for ever keep at the same distance before them, and constantly elude their ardent hopes. The experience of all who have gone before, testifying that all results in vanity and vexation of spirit in the possession of earthly good, has no effect to communicate wisdom to those who come after them. The young generation run off in the mad career with as sanguine hopes of happiness, as if no one had ever been disappointed. And in this matter, the world does not become wiser by growing older.

There is another deception of the heart which has relation to the indulgence of natural desires. The person may be apprehensive at first, from former experience, that some evil to soul or body may arise from unlawful indulgence. A pause is produced, and hesitation is felt; but appetite, when strong, pleads for indulgence, and is fruitful in pleas; among which none is more false and deceitful, than that if gratified in this instance, it will never crave indulgence any more. And this false promise often prevails with the vacillating sinner; and he plunges into the gulf, which is open to receive him. For the former deception of the imagination, prior to experience, there seemed to be some plausible pretext; but for this, there is not the shadow of a reason. That any desire or appetite should be eradicated by indulgence, is contrary to all experience. It is a law of our nature, obvious to all, that every affection is strengthened by exercise, and every appetite becomes stronger by being freely gratified. Yet this deceitful plea is made again and again

"Yield but in this one instance, and you shall never be solicited again." After this single indulgence, says the craving appetite, you may be for ever obedient to the dictates of conscience.

Under the influence of an evil heart, every thing appears in false colours. Not only does error assume the garb of truth, but piety itself is made to appear odious. Indeed, there is nothing upon earth, which the carnal mind hates so truly as holiness. But as that which appears good cannot be hated, one art of the deceitful heart is, to misrepresent the true nature of piety and devotion. The fairest face when caricatured, becomes deformed, and appears ludicrous. Wicked men are accustomed always to caricature true religion, that they may laugh at it, and despise it. One thing which assists very much in leading to this result is, the employment of deceptive terms. Men are very much governed by words. Call any man, however dignified and excellent, by some name, associated with the ludicrous and contemptible, and you will never think of him but with ridicule or contempt. Thus men of the world are accustomed to call true religion by the names of enthusiasm, fanaticism, superstition, bigotry, or hypocrisy. Now, as all these are odious things, the application of these names to the best thing in the world, has the effect of blinding the minds of those who use these terms; so that, though in their sober judgment, they cannot but know that religion is necessary and excellent in its nature; yet, by means of this trick of the deceitful heart, they come by degrees to despise or contemn every profession and appearance of religion.

And this result is more effectually produced by false reasoning; as when, from one instance of manifest hypocrisy, the inference is drawn that all professors of religion are hypocrites; or when, from one false step in a good man, it is concluded, that all his actions have proceeded from impure motives. The deceitful heart not only suffers such reasonings to pass, but sanctions them as though these were the legitimate conclusions of the soundest logic.

By the same abuse of words and sophistical reasoning, vice is often dressed up in the habiliments of virtue; and the foulest passions of our nature are dignified with names importing a virtuous or innocent feeling. Thus revenge which prompts a man to imbrue his hands in the heart's blood of a friend, for an inadvertent word, or some other trifling offence, is denominated *honour;* and the guilty murderer reeking with a brother's blood, is received into the society of the world as an honourable, though it may be thought, an unfortunate man. Pride seems now scarcely to seek the disguise of another name. All that is required is some epithet, such as an *honest* pride; such pride as leads a man to respect himself. Sometimes, indeed, bad words are used in a good sense; thus the words *pride* and *ambition*, though properly expressive of evil passions, are frequently employed to signify feelings which are not blamable; but this is a dangerous practice. It brings virtue and vice too near together, and obscures and perplexes the boundaries which separate them. A woe is denounced against those who thus attempt to confound good and evil. "Woe to them that call evil good, and good evil; and put darkness for light, and light for darkness; that put bitter for sweet, and sweet for bitter."

The deceitfulness of the heart is also exceedingly manifest in the false pretensions which it makes, and the delusive appearances which it assumes. And this deceitfulness not only imposes upon others, but upon the person himself. Under this delusion, men persuade themselves that they are not wicked, but that their hearts are good. Their virtues, or semblance of virtues, are magnified, when seen through the false medium of self-love; and their vices are so diminished, that they are either not seen, or appear as mere peccadilloes, scarcely deserving notice. Such persons are also deceived as to their own wisdom. They are described by the pen of inspiration, as "wise in their own conceit." They think that they know much, when in truth "they know nothing yet as they ought to know." And such a blinding influence has the deceitful heart on many, that they imagine that they possess virtues or qualities worthy of admiration, which all their acquaintances know they are utterly destitute of. This is the case with boasters, and vain braggarts. But the most dangerous form of this deceit is, when persons, never converted or renewed, are induced to believe that they are saints. They even esteem themselves superior to those who are truly pious, and make a flaming profession of religion before the world, while pride, covetousness, lust, or envy, are predominant in their hearts, and too manifest in their lives. Evidences of the dominion of sin, which would lead them to entertain a certain opinion that another was still in the gall of bitterness and bond of iniquity, have not the effect to shake their good opinion of their own spiritual condition. This dangerous treachery of the heart, not only misleads the hypocrite to his ruin, but all careless men and women are under its control, as it relates to their future course in regard to religion. They all purpose at some future time to repent and reform, and are fully persuaded, that when a convenient season arrives, they will do so. Now, all these promises and hopes of future repentance and amendment, arise from a deceitful heart. The true cause of the neglect of religion at present, is an aversion to spiritual things, and this disposition will prevent them from attending to religion, at any future time; and with every day will become more inveterate. The deception consists in this, that the person seeing the importance and moral obligations of piety, conceives that that indisposition to God's service, which is now felt, will be diminished by time; or rather that it will not be felt at a future time. Every resolution or promise of any unconverted man or woman, of future repentance and reformation, is an instance of the deceitfulness of the human heart. This is remarkably verified in the case of those persons who are alarmed with the prospect of death, when laid on a bed of sickness. How often do such promise that if God will only spare them, and restore them to health, they will serve him to their dying day. But no sooner is returning health enjoyed, than all these promises are forgotten, or disregarded.

Again, the deceitfulness of the heart is manifest in the good which we promise ourselves that we will do in future. At present there are impediments which stand in the way of doing the good which we intend to do hereafter. When we look back on our past lives, and see many opportunities of doing good, which have been neglected, we feel regret; and when we look forward, we flatter ourselves that we shall be much more active and benevolent, much more watchful and zealous, than we have been. But the true test of character is, what we are actually doing at the present time. Do we now, from day to day, do all the good which is in our power? Do we now improve our time and talents to the utmost? Do we now seek the happiness of all who are near to us, and use every practicable means for their salvation? If we do not, then does our heart deceive us, as to its own real disposition. The apparent penitence for not having done what we ought, in time past, is not genuine; or we should immediately reform, and begin at once to do the good which is now in our power. The confidence that we shall do better hereafter, is a vain self-confidence which will never be realized in fact; for if there was in us a sincere disposition to do the good hereafter, which the heart promises, we would not neglect the opportunities and calls to well-doing, which are present to us every day. The reason of this dangerous mistake is, that when we contemplate duty at a distance, either in the past or future, we view it abstracted from those circumstances which always, in fact, accompany it. We consider the obligation and the goodness of the act, and so its beneficial consequences; but forget the self-denial and pain which may be required in its performance. From the same cause, men are ever deceiving themselves in relation to the conduct which they would pursue, if placed in circumstances entirely different from those by which they are surrounded. The poor man thinks, if he was rich, he would not act as rich men within his knowledge do. He would be bountiful to all around, would aid in every benevolent enterprise, and regard the wants and sufferings of the indigent and distressed. But these are all deceitful thoughts. Thousands of instances are found to prove that men are always deceived in the ideas which they entertain of the course which they would pursue in untried situations. And they might be convinced of this, as before, by the mere examination of themselves, as to the good which they are actually doing with the means in their hands, and the opportunities at present afforded.

Another way in which our hearts deceive us is, by leading us to judge of ourselves, not by a strict scrutiny into our real motives, but by viewing our character through the medium of public opinion; or through the favourable sentiments of our partial friends. When men are aroused by some calumny to come forward and vindicate themselves from the obloquy cast upon them, they commonly make it evident, that they assume as their true character, the estimation in which they have been held by the community. But every man might know, that this is a false and foolish method of judging of his own character. He may be conscious, that the actions which have gained for him a reputation among men, have not proceeded from pure motives. He might know, if he would impartially examine himself, that where good motives have predominated, there has been so much of a sordid and selfish nature mingled, as greatly to detract from their value; and which, if known to the public, would much depreciate the reputation which he has acquired.

The pain of contemplating our moral defects causes us to turn our attention from them, and to seek relief in some more favourable aspect of our character, and this is found in the good opinion of others.

REFLECTIONS.

1. If the heart be so exceedingly deceitful and wicked, we should be deeply humbled before God that we have hearts so evil. Men are prone to boast of the goodness of their *hearts*, even when their *lives* are immoral. But this is a most manifest instance of the deceitfulness of the heart, which leads them to entertain an opinion, not only contrary to the word of God, but contrary to the principles of nature, which teaches that the tree must be judged of by its fruit; and a fountain, by the streams which issue from it. In particular, most men claim to be sincere and free from deceit; but so far is this from being true, that the

heart of every man is by nature deceitful; yea, the most deceitful of all things. Mankind know not their ownselves. They have not proved themselves by the test of God's word; and, therefore, they know not what manner of spirit they are of. If the dark and defiled chambers of their hearts were laid open to the light, it would be like opening a sepulchre. They would begin to see their own vileness, and like Job, would abhor themselves and repent in dust and ashes.

2. If the heart be so deceitful, we should place no confidence in it. "He that trusteth in his own heart," says Solomon, "is a fool." It is a characteristic of the true Christian, to put "no confidence in the flesh." That the heart of a man is not to be trusted, however fairly it may promise, is evident from the thousands of broken vows and promises which men make in sickness and danger, or when urged by the demands of an awakened conscience. Even Christians are often deceived by the fair, but false promises of their own hearts. How often do they resolve and promise that they will live nearer to God, will be more diligent and faithful in the discharge of duty, and make more frequent and vigorous efforts to rescue perishing sinners from the ruin to which they are approaching! But too often these promises and resolutions are forgotten, or only remembered to be neglected.

3. If the heart be so deceitful, it should be watched with care. Even in the sacred duties of religion, it will be prone, like a deceitful bow, to start aside, and the thoughts will wander far away from the object which should engage their attention.

If, then, we would guard against the deceitfulness of the heart, we must give heed to the exhortation of the wise man, "Keep thy heart with all diligence, for out of it are the issues of life." We must watch, as well as pray, and watch unto prayer. Besides, we must endeavour to obtain a more thorough knowledge of our own hearts. In order to do this, we must examine our hearts with assiduity; and not content with this, we must beg of God to search and try us. For, "who can understand his errors?" And in the words following our text, we learn, that God only knows the human heart; for the question is asked, "Who can know it?" And immediately it is added, "I, the Lord, search the heart and try the reins, even to give every man according to his ways, and according to the fruit of his doing." Unless the Lord help us to keep the heart, our own labour will be in vain.

4. From the state and character of the heart here given, we may infer the necessity of a change of heart; and every one should be led to cry to God for renewing grace. "Create in me, O God, a clean heart, and renew a right spirit within me." And as this work of renovation is not perfected at once, we should strive mightily in the use of appointed means "to grow in grace, and in the knowledge of our Lord and Saviour Jesus Christ." As the word is the appropriate means of sanctification, we should be much in reading and hearing the word; and as the word will be ineffectual without the Spirit, we should pray without ceasing for the gift

of the Holy Spirit, that our minds may be enlightened, purified, strengthened, and comforted.

5. We should come often to the fountain which is opened for sin and uncleanness. We need both the purification of blood and of water. And Christ, our crucified Redeemer, emitted from his side a double stream of blood and water, emblematic of the double cleansing needed by the sinful soul; and the means of both which were secured by his death. Let us, then, look to Christ by faith, let us come to "the Mediator of the new covenant, and to the blood of sprinkling which speaketh better things than the blood of Abel."

6. And finally, if any of us have been made sensible of the deceitfulness and wickedness of our hearts, and have, in some degree, been delivered from this great evil of our nature, this change we are sure, has not proceeded from ourselves. A heart deceitful above all things and desperately wicked, can never reform itself. There is in it no principle from which a true reformation can proceed. If, then, there is in any of us a heart which has some good thing in it, it is not from nature, but from God—"from the Father of lights from whom cometh down every good gift, and every perfect gift;" therefore our warmest gratitude is due to him; and our whole lives should be one continuous expression of thankfulness.

SERMON XIII.

WICKEDNESS OF THE HEART.

The heart is deceitful above all things, and desperately wicked.—
JER. xvii. 9.

HAVING in our former discourse treated of the deceitfulness of the heart, I now come, in the second place, to speak of its "desperate wickedness." Indeed, these two qualities of the heart are so intimately connected that they involve each other. If the heart is deceitful above all things, it must be wicked; and if it is "desperately wicked," it must be deceitful; for all sin originates in false views of things. There does not, therefore, seem to be much need to discuss the latter part of the text separately, to produce a conviction of the truth there asserted; but a mere conviction of a truth is not enough. We need to have some truths set before us with much particularity, that by long and patient contemplation of their nature, our hearts may be suitably affected by them. And there is no truth to which this remark is more applicable than to the one now under consideration;

for it is one, the distinct contemplation of which gives pain, and from which the mind turns away with an instinctive aversion. Hence, few persons can be induced patiently and impartially to view their own moral features as portrayed in the Holy Scriptures. And hence, the astonishing ignorance of their own hearts, which prevails among men, and even among church-going people,. Moreover, a distinct knowledge of our own hearts, as to their moral condition and character, is of the utmost importance to our spiritual welfare. In bodily diseases we may have the remedy applied and be healed, without knowing the nature of the malady; but in spiritual diseases this cannot take place, according to the ordinary method of salvation; because the remedy is here applied by faith, which is the act of an intelligent mind, by which we, feeling the malignity of our disease, cannot be satisfied until we apprehend the true and only remedy which the mercy of God has provided in the gospel.

Let us, then, again attempt to remove the covering from the human heart, that we may take a view of its desperate wickedness; and in order to this, I would observe, that the truth contained in this part of the text, will appear more manifest by considering:

1. The universal prevalence of wickedness in the world, in all countries, and in all ages That crimes of every kind have ever abounded, every man who has the least acquaintance with the world, knows by his own observation. No man needs to travel far to obtain the evidence of this

fact; it stares him in the face every where, in town and country, among the rich and the poor, the old and the young. A great part of the business of the world has relation to the existence and prevalence of crimes; either to prevent, to guard against, or to punish them. Our laws, our courts, our prisons and penitentiaries, our locks and bars, our munitions of war on sea and land, are all evidences of the wickedness of man. No nation legislates on the principle, or with the expectation, that men will not be found wicked. Indeed, civil government itself owes its origin to the necessity which exists of guarding against, and coercing the wickedness of the people. We need only look into our criminal courts, or into our newspapers, to be convinced that wickedness is not confined to former ages, or to be witnessed only in heathen countries, but marches with a bold front through every Christian land; often too, in defiance of all laws, human and divine. What crime can be conceived, which the depravity of man has not led him to perpetrate? Yea, crimes which are so abominable as scarcely to have a name, are committed by many. Blasphemies, murders, robberies, thefts, frauds, adulteries, tyranny, oppression, pride, luxury, intemperance, impurity, envy, hatred, deceit, with others too numerous to be mentioned, are common and notorious in every country. And while the beauty and order of society are continually disturbed by open wickedness, the greater part of the foulest actions of men are covered with the veil of darkness. They are committed in secret where no eye but that of the omniscient Jehovah sees the enormity of the crime. At the day of judgment, when all these works of darkness shall be brought to light, the assembled universe will be struck with surprise at the multitude and enormity of the crimes perpetrated by the children of men. Now, whence do all these iniquities proceed but from the human heart? That fountain must, indeed, be corrupt which sends forth such poisonous streams. That tree must be, indeed, evil which produces such fruit. Heathen writers, as well as Christian, give testimony to the fact, that men are desperately wicked. What is history, but a record of the crimes of men? And not only historians, but poets and satirists among the heathen, paint the depravity of man in the most frightful colours. And all modern travellers of veracity, and especially missionaries, unite in testifying that the picture of human nature, drawn by Paul in his epistles, is an accurate delineation of the present condition of the whole Pagan world. And alas! nominal Christians are but little better. Indeed, considering their light and privileges, their guilt is much greater. Although various circumstances make a difference in the moral characters of men, yet all are by nature depraved; all have gone astray like lost sheep. "There is none that doeth good, no, not one. Out of the heart proceed evil thoughts, murders, adulteries, fornications, thefts, false-witness, blasphemies." (Matt. xv. 19.)

2. The desperate wickedness of the heart will appear also, if we consider its aversion to God and holiness. If the heart were not depraved, it would naturally be disposed to reverence and love the

great Creator; for his character is most excellent, and our obligations to him are infinite. We owe every thing to him. We are indebted to him for our existence and all our faculties, and capacities of enjoyment. Every good gift has come down from the Father of lights, and an ingenuous, pure heart would be filled with unceasing gratitude to such a Benefactor, and would continually celebrate his praise. But is this the fact in regard to the majority of men? Is it so in regard to any man, until renewed by the grace of God? Let conscience testify. We need no other witness. This enmity to God is the true cause of all the abominable idolatry of the heathen world. They did not like to retain God in their minds. "And when they knew God, they glorified him not as God." This too, is the true source of the obstinate unbelief of the Jews. The Son of God exhibited the true characteristics of the promised Messiah; but then "he was holy, harmless, undefiled, and separate from sinners;" and showed no indulgence to the pride and hypocrisy of the Pharisees, nor to the infidelity of the Sadducees; but faithfully reproved their vices; therefore they conspired to take away his life. Nothing is so offensive to a depraved heart as a perfect example of holiness; for even when the conscience is compelled to approve it, the heart turns away from it with hatred. If we search also the true grounds of the Mohammedan religion which has subjugated so large a portion of the world, we shall find that it originated in a dislike to the holy character of

Christianity, and a desire to have a religion accommodated to the taste of the depraved heart.

But we need not go to the heathen, to the unbelieving Jew, or to the deluded Mohammedan, for witnesses of this truth, that the heart of man by nature does not love God and holiness. We have proofs enough nearer home. We have them in every congregation, in every family, in every child. Let those who deny the native depravity of man answer this question: Do men, generally, who have the opportunity of knowing the true character of God, love it as the angels do in heaven? Do they love it at all? If they do, would they not all be found zealously engaged in glorifying God by worshipping him in his earthly temples? Would they not be found in constant and cheerful obedience to his will? Alas! alas! the proof is too plain, that men do not naturally love God, or take delight in his service.

Men are not commonly as sensible of the guilt contracted by sins of omission, as of commission; but where the heart is utterly destitute of love to God, it cannot be otherwise than totally depraved, although restraints may have been laid upon it, which have prevented it from acting out the wickedness which is concealed within.

3. Another evidence of the desperate wickedness of the human heart is, that it never grows better, or makes any true reformation of itself; but, on the contrary, grows worse and worse, as long as it is left to the influence of its own corrupt principles. Some diseases of the body have their period and

what may be called their natural course, and when they have spent their force, come to an end; but nothing like this takes place in regard to the wickedness of the heart. The natural period of this awful disease is unlimited—it is eternal. It is a fever which never ceases to burn, and is never extinguished by an accidental cause; but increases continually in its malignity. The young sinner who is just commencing a course of iniquity, will soon grow up to a maturity in vice; but still, unless grace prevent, his course will be onward and downward, in the paths of sinful indulgence. In the former discourse on this text, we have seen, that all the promises which the heart makes of ceasing from sin, and of amendment of life, are deceitful. And for aught that appears, this fearful progression in vice, will not cease with the death of the body; but when those restraints, which, in this world, are laid, more or less, on all men, are removed, then the depraved principle will be acted out, with all the heaven-daring iniquity of devils. Then, indeed, it will be acknowledged by all that the heart of man is deceitful above all things and desperately wicked.

4. But the heart of man, left to itself, not only never grows better, but this disease may well be called "desperate," because it yields not to the most powerful remedies which human wisdom has ever invented; but increases in virulence, under them all. Since men were multiplied upon earth, various remedies have been repeatedly tried; and it is not denied, that under some of them, the symptoms appear in a mitigated form; but the core of

the malady has not been eradicated. Among these, early discipline and careful education have been considered by some sufficient to reach the seat of the disease, and to bring about a radical cure; but the result of impartial examination is, that all the discipline and careful training which have ever been used, can do no more than skin over the foul ulcer of human depravity. A corpse may be so dressed and decorated, that it may appear inviting to a superficial observer; but when it is approached and examined, the cadaverous appearance and stench prove it to be a corpse still. Thus, you may put a gloss on the foul depravity of human nature. You may even paint it with the semblance of true virtue; but, at bottom, it is still selfish, sensual, proud, and at enmity with God.

Philosophy has also tried her power, and has boasted of great achievements; but, while the streams from the fountain of human depravity may have been diverted into a more refined and secret channel, so as to conceal the turpitude of its character, yet its poisonous nature has not been changed. Philosophical pride, ambition, and envy are no better than intemperance and gross sensuality. Morality has been called in to accomplish the reformation of human vice; but while the heart remains unregenerate, morality is a mere appearance of good, a mere shadow without substance, a tree without a root, a superstructure without a foundation. Such morality, though defective in its principles and motives, is nevertheless useful to society, and should, on this account, be encouraged and promoted; but consider as obedience to the holy law of God, it is worthless; and when trusted to as a ground of justification, it is even injurious by engendering and cherishing a delusive hope of heaven.

Further, the desperate wickedness of the heart, not only manifests itself by resisting the influence of all human remedies; but that which exhibits its inveterate malignity in the strongest light is, that it does not even yield to the means of reformation which God has appointed. We might expect that such motives as the word of God presents, would be effectual to produce a change of mind, or to bring the sinner to repentance. But, no: the heart hardens under the bright beams of gospel truth. Indeed, no hearts are so hard and perverse as those which have been often addressed by the solemn, tender, and persuasive exhortations of the divine word. "This," said our Lord, "is the condemnation, that light is come into the world, and men loved darkness rather than light, because their deeds are evil. Ye will not come unto me that ye may have life. If I had not come and spoken unto you, you had not had sin, but now ye have no cloak for your sin." And what is more astonishing still, even the inward strivings of the Spirit are resisted and quenched. "Ye stiffnecked and uncircumcised in heart, ye do always resist the Holy Ghost; as your fathers did, so do ye." Therefore, we have the solemn exhortations, "Quench not the Spirit. Grieve not the Holy Spirit of God."

5. Again, when the heart appears to be converted, and a visible reformation takes place in the life, after a while these promising appearances,

which, like blossoms in the spring, gave ground to hope for abundant fruit, are nipped by the severe frost, or blasted by the chilling wind, and all our hopes are disappointed. The soul was impressed by divine truth, and the affections for a season warmly excited, but the bitter root of iniquity was not eradicated. And though, for a season, under these solemn impressions, the virulence of the sinful principle was not only restrained, but concealed; yet as soon as the day of trial and temptation comes, all these flattering appearances vanish, and the soul, acting agreeably to its true nature, breaks out again into open transgression, or assumes and keeps up the hypocritical garb of religion, while secretly sin is indulged, and the heart is under the government of evil passions. In the sight of an all-seeing God, no hearts appear more desperately wicked, than those which are concealed from men, by the mask of hypocrisy. As our Lord knew what was in man, he could see in the Pharisees of his day, the vilest lusts and passions, covered under the cloak of religion. The people venerated these men for their extraordinary piety; but he tore the mask from their hearts, and revealed to the people the baseness, malignity, envy, and covetousness which reigned within their breasts. This they never could forgive, and therefore sought every opportunity to destroy him; and at last succeeded by means of the treachery of one of his own disciples. Here we have come to the highest conceivable degree of human depravity, in the crime of Judas, and of the chief priests and rulers in "crucifying the Lord of glory." A deeper stain of guilt than that which was here contracted, cannot be imagined. Do you say, that this was the crime of a few; and if you had been situated as they were, you would not have perpetrated such a bloody crime? In this you do but deceive yourselves. Your hearts are as wicked by nature as theirs; and if you have not committed the same crimes or as great, it has not been owing to your own goodness of heart, but to the favour of God's providence, and the inward restraints which he has graciously laid upon you. Left, as they were, to yourselves, and exposed to the same temptations, you would have acted as wickedly as the most wicked. "As face answereth to face in water, so the heart of man to man."

6. No severity nor continuance of pain will ever conquer or remove the depravity of the heart. Many have resorted to self-inflicted tortures, as great as human nature can endure, and have spent their lives in crucifying the desires of the flesh; and they may have, to a certain degree, succeeded in diminishing the ardour of those passions which are connected with the animal frame, by emaciating the body; but this did not reach the real seat of the malady. It lies far deeper than the flesh. When the body shall be put off, then, as was before said, the wickedness of man will come to its maturity, and he will resemble the devils. A mistake respecting the origin of moral evil gave rise to this method of counteracting, and endeavouring to eradicate it. Many ancient philosophers believed matter to be the cause of all evil; and therefore they attempted to destroy sin, by inflict-

ing pain on the body. There is nothing in the mere endurance of pain which has any tendency to eradicate the principle of iniquity in the human heart. Afflictions are, it is true, a purifying furnace to the people of God, but they are only so when accompanied by his effectual grace. We often see, in this world, the deepest depravity accompanied by the most appalling sufferings. The effect of mere pain on the depraved heart is to arouse to fury the angry passions of the soul; and when there is no hope of relief, the guilty wretches, while they gnaw their tongues with anguish, look up and impotently blaspheme the God that punishes them. The pains of hell, therefore, have no tendency to purge away the dross of sin; but the evil rather grows under these unspeakable torments. And thus we see the unreasonableness of the idea of a purgatorial fire to purify those who died unprepared for an immediate entrance into heaven.

7. Another argument of the desperate wickedness of the human heart is the power of indwelling sin in the regenerate. This body of sin caused the apostle Paul to groan, and to cry out, "O wretched man, who shall deliver me from the body of this death!" The working of iniquity in the regenerate soul produces a continual warfare in every renewed heart. "The flesh lusteth against the Spirit, and the Spirit against the flesh; so that ye cannot do the things that ye would;" for, says Paul, "when I would do good, evil is present with me; so that the good that I would, I do not, and the evil that I would not, that I do." I know there are many

who cannot endure the idea, that Paul was here describing his own feelings, or those of any renewed person. But the truly pious, in every age, have had the same sad conviction of inbred corruption; and have experienced the same conflict between the principles of sin and holiness within them. And they have been led by the knowledge which they have obtained of their own hearts, to yield an unqualified assent to the declaration of the prophet in our text. And God, sometimes has permitted the truly pious to be overcome by the strength of indwelling sin, when left to meet temptation without special aid from heaven. A number of falls of this kind are recorded in Scripture, that in all ages, the desperate wickedness of the heart might be made manifest; and that the people of God might learn from these examples, that their standing is not in themselves, but in the grace of God upholding and preserving them in the hour of temptation, when Satan is sifting them as wheat. No man knows how much iniquity still lies concealed in his own heart. Though, by the grace of God, the believer may gain many victories over the old man within him; yet he may expect to experience the violence of his dying struggles, until the hour of his full discharge, when with the body he will put off all the remains of sin; which should reconcile the believer to the necessity of dying; since, as long as he is in the body, the flesh will lust against the Spirit.

Having taken a brief survey of the desperate wickedness of the human heart, let us now, in the conclusion, reflect a little on the awful subject.

The entrance of sin into the world has entailed death on all the posterity of Adam. "As by one man sin entered into the world, and death by sin, so death hath passed on all men, because that all have sinned." Sin is a hereditary disease, which we have derived from our first parents. It is not worth while to dispute against a fact, the evidence of which we have within us and around us continually; neither do we gain any thing by cavilling at the justice of God in bringing us into existence in connexion with an apostate father. We were included in him, and sinned with him, and as he was our covenant head, as well as our natural father, his sin is legally ours, and we are treated accordingly. At any rate we are in a fallen, sinful state, and by nature, children of wrath even as others. Our wisdom is to inquire with all earnestness, whether there is any way of escape from this horrible pit, where every effort of our own only sinks us deeper in the miry clay. If there were no remedy, it would be cruel to torment you before the time, with a representation of the miserable condition into which you are fallen. But there is a glorious and effectual remedy; and although it is not mentioned in the text, yet the same infallible word of God, which shows us our sin and misery, points to the only remedy, which is freely offered to all, and is efficacious in every case in which it has been tried. Though, my hearers, your disease is desperate as it relates to human remedies, it is not so in regard to God's method of recovery. "It is a faithful saying and worthy of all acceptation, that Jesus Christ came into the world to save sinners, of whom, said Paul, I am chief." Hear also the prophet Isaiah, proclaiming to the rebellious house of Israel, "Though your sins were as scarlet they shall be white as snow, and though they were red like crimson they shall be as wool." And the beloved disciple assures us, that we have an advocate with the Father, who is the propitiation for our sins, and not for ours only, but for the sins of the whole world." John also, who saw the double stream flowing from his pierced side, testifies "His blood cleanseth from all sin." "Let us, then, come boldly to the throne of grace, that we may obtain mercy and find grace to help in time of need. We need not despair, for it is written, "He is able to save to the uttermost, all that come unto God by him, seeing he ever liveth to make intercession for them."

But if sin were forgiven, and this desperate wickedness of the heart should remain, there would still be no salvation. The sinner, thus depraved, could enter into no rest, he could enjoy no peace. Sin makes a hell wherever it prevails. The unregenerate sinner would be pleased to have pardon without renovation; but this is a foolish wish. "Except a man be born again, he cannot see the kingdom of God. Without holiness no man shall see the Lord." There must be a remedy for inherent depravity, as well as for guilt; and that remedy is provided in "the sanctification of the Spirit," through the truth. This glorious work of grace is going on in the hearts of all true believers; and he who hath begun this good work will carry it on to the day of redemption. The peculiar people whom Christ hath purchased, he wil' redeem from all iniquity, and make them zealous of good works. By union with Christ, every believer as a scion grafted on the true vine will be enabled to bring forth fruit, and their fruit shall remain. They who are enabled to bring forth much fruit do greatly glorify their Father in heaven, who delights to see these clusters of righteousness on the vine of his own right hand. And by letting their light shine around them, others also seeing their good works are led to glorify our Father in heaven. Let us, then, be truly thankful for the gift of the Spirit as well as the Son, for the work of each is equally necessary, though of a different kind; yet, so intimately connected that he who receives the benefit of the one, is never destitute of the blessing proceeding from the work of the other. Yea, further, we only become partakers of the benefits of Christ's death, when the work of the Spirit has commenced in our hearts; for it is by faith that we are pardoned and justified, and this faith is the fruit of the operation of the Spirit in the regeneration of the soul.

Then, my hearers, though your pollution be deep, and your stain indelible by all human art, yet, behold, the fountain foretold by the prophet, has been opened for sin and uncleanness. Come, wash, and be clean. And this fountain not only cleanses, but refreshes and heals. "Ho! every one that thirsteth, come ye to the waters. If any man thirst, let him come unto me and drink. The

Spirit and the bride say, Come, and let him that heareth say, Come, and whosoever will, let him come and take of the waters of life freely."

The truth contained in our text is not so thoroughly understood by any, as by the growing experienced Christian. As he grows in grace, he grows in knowledge of himself; and every day he has new evidences of the deceitfulness of his own heart, and of the unsearchable depth of his own depravity. On this account it is exceedingly difficult for him to be convinced that he is making any progress in piety; for the sight and sense of his own sinfulness increasing with his increase of grace, he at first naturally concludes, that he is growing worse instead of better; but by reflection he finds, that the deeper his convictions of inherent depravity are, the humbler he feels and the more penitent, and also that his application to Christ for healing always bears an exact proportion to his sense of the evil of sin within him. He learns at length, that what at first he took to be an evidence of backsliding, is really a sure sign of growth in the divine life; and that, when religion declines in his heart, his views of the inbred evils of his heart are more obscure, and his feelings more insensible. The most advanced Christian needs to be constantly on his guard against the treachery of his heart. He must watch and pray lest he enter into temptation. He never arrives, in this world, at a state in which he is in no danger from the deceitfulness and wickedness of his heart.

But the perfect knowledge of the corruption of

the human heart is never obtained by any one. Indeed, we could not bear the full discovery. It would overwhelm us completely, and, perhaps, destroy us. The unsearchable depth of the heart of man is strongly expressed in the words subsequent to our text: "Who can know it? I, the Lord, search the heart and try the reins, even to give to every man according to his ways, and according to the fruit of his doings."

SERMON XIV.

CHRIST OUR WISDOM, RIGHTEOUSNESS, SANCTIFICATION, AND REDEMPTION.

But of him are ye in Christ Jesus, who of God is made unto us wisdom, righteousness, sanctification, and redemption.—1 Cor. i. 30.

THE religion of the gospel is calculated to remove every occasion of glorying from the creature. And as men are prone to value themselves on account of their wisdom and earthly greatness, therefore, it pleased God to select his people from that class of men who are contemptible in the eyes of the world. Paul says to the Corinthians, who dwelt in a city where there was much learning and wealth, "Ye know your calling, brethren, how that not many wise men after the flesh, not many mighty, not many noble are called. But God hath chosen the foolish things of the world to confound the wise; and God hath chosen the weak things of the world to confound the things which are mighty; and base things of the world, and things which are despised, hath God chosen; yea, and things which are not, to bring to nought things that are; that no flesh should glory in his presence." He then proceeds to show, that the salvation of which they were made partakers, was entirely of the Lord. Their union to Christ was a privilege for which they were entirely indebted to God. They did not first love him, but he loved them. "Ye," says Christ, "have not chosen me, but I have chosen you." In all cases, they who truly believe, are those who are "ordained to eternal life." Salvation, from first to last, is all of grace; and it is all through Christ. Whatever we need, in order to our complete deliverance from ruin, and the full attainment of eternal life, is treasured up in Christ; and we are "complete in him."

1. He is made unto us "wisdom." Wisdom is one of the appropriate names of the second Person of the adorable Trinity. Before creation, Wisdom is represented as being with God, as one brought up with him; and even then his thoughts were specially directed to this world; for "he rejoiced in the habitable parts of the earth, and his delights were with the sons of men." The evangelist John seems to have had this passage in his mind, when he penned the beginning of the first chapter of his gospel; for the WORD, of whom he speaks, as being with God, and as being God himself, is the same as WISDOM. "In him was life, and the life was the light of men." Christ is the Sun of righteousness, from whom, and through whom emanate all the rays of divine truth which ever enter the minds of men. "This is the true light which lighteth every man that cometh into the world." "No man knoweth the Father but the Son, and he to whom the

Son will reveal him." Christ is that great Prophet that should come into the world, like unto Moses, whom the Jews expected, but whom they would not receive when he actually made his appearance. He is the great Teacher, by whose instruction all the children of God are brought into the path of life. "All thy children shall be taught of God." There is no interference in the prophetical office of Christ, and the teachings of the Holy Spirit, but a perfect concurrence. Christ furnishes the lesson, and the Holy Spirit renders it effectual. "He shall not speak of himself, but he shall take of mine and show it unto you." "Christ executeth the office of a prophet, in revealing unto us, by his word and Spirit, the will of God for our salvation." In him dwell all the treasures of wisdom and knowledge. Man is endued with reason, but by sin his mind has become blind, and reason itself is perverted. He not only needs external light, but to have the organ of vision rectified, without which the light will shine in darkness, and the darkness comprehend it not. Christ becomes wisdom to the believer, by making him wise to know the way of salvation. He first teaches the sinner something of the depth and malignity of his disease. He wounds that he may heal. When by the law the knowledge of sin is acquired, then he guides the convicted sinner to the cross, and opens his eyes to behold the LAMB OF GOD. He is not only the wisdom of God, as he instructs the ignorant, and opens the eyes of the blind; but as the God-man Mediator, is the most wonderful exhibition of the wisdom of God ever made to the universe. The whole plan of redemption is resplendent with wisdom. The contrivance of a way by which God can be just, while he justifies the ungodly, is so replete with wisdom, that the angels contemplate it with profound astonishment. The gospel, which is the revelation of this plan, is, therefore, called "the wisdom of God." In this there is a depth, which human reason cannot fathom. The apostle Paul, therefore, says, "But we speak the wisdom of God in a mystery, even the hidden wisdom, which God ordained before the world, unto our glory." We may, therefore, in the contemplation of this subject, exclaim with the apostle, "O the depth of the riches, both of the wisdom and knowledge of God!"

Christ is then of God made unto us wisdom, in a twofold respect; first, as he is the brightest display of the infinite wisdom of God; and, secondly, by teaching his people all that is necessary to make them wise unto salvation. He teaches them what they ought to believe, and what they ought to do.

2. Christ is not only made to believers wisdom, but righteousness. By righteousness we should understand conformity to the law of God, and the act of justification which is founded on such obedience. It is much more easy to conceive how Christ should become our wisdom, than our justifying righteousness. The apostle does not mean that he works righteousness in us, for that is clearly expressed in the next particular. God cannot be other than just. He can never view a sinner to be any thing else than a sinner. What is done

can never be undone. And no act or work can render those acts holy which are in their nature sinful. Man being a sinner, the vindicatory justice of God rendered it necessary that his sin should be punished; otherwise, he would deny himself, and make an erroneous impression on the universe as to his own character. How then, it may be asked, is it possible, that a sinner should be justified in the sight of God? This problem could never have been solved by the wisdom of creatures. But by the wisdom of God, the apparent impossibility has been accomplished. With God all things are possible. The method by which this is effected is, by making his own Son the SUBSTITUTE and SURETY for sinners. By imputing their sins unto him, and his righteousness unto them, a foundation is laid for their justification. This is the only ground on which a sinner can be just with God. To suppose that the Judge of all the earth would pronounce a man who is defiled with sin, to be free from all condemnation, and entitled to eternal life, considered in himself, is utterly incompatible with the divine attributes. Sinful man can never be justified but by the righteousness of another, even of that Mediator whom God has provided to meet this very exigence. "By the deeds of the law there shall no flesh be justified in his sight. But now, the righteousness without the law is manifested, being witnessed by the law and the prophets; even the righteousness of God which is by faith of Jesus Christ, unto all and upon all that believe." Sinful man can possibly have no justifying righteousness of his own; for if he was chargeable but with one sin, and that the smallest conceivable, yet could he not be justified by the law, for the language of the law is, " Cursed is every one who continueth not in all things written in the book of the law to do them." Man's only hope of justification is in Christ. And Christ can become the author of his justification in no other way, than by becoming his SURETY, and bearing his sin; and by rendering a full and perfect obedience to the precepts of the law. His righteousness, thus wrought out, by his holy life and meritorious death, can never justify any one, unless it be imputed to him, that is, set down to his account. And it is imputed to none but to those who by faith are united to Christ. Therefore, it is said in our text, " Of him are ye in Christ Jesus, who of God is made unto us wisdom and righteousness. There is, therefore, no condemnation to them that are in Christ Jesus."

3. Christ is also made sanctification to all those who are united to him. He is the author of inherent, as well as of imputed righteousness. It has often been objected to the doctrine of imputed righteousness, that it removes or relaxes the obligation to holy living; as man is justified without respect to his own holiness. That the doctrine, badly understood, has been abused by some, cannot be denied. It was so in the time of the apostle Paul, for he answers precisely this objection, and denies that the doctrine of gratuitous pardon, without regard to our own obedience, has any such tendency. " Do we," says he, " by faith make void the law? nay, we establish the law. How

shall we that are dead to sin, live any longer therein?" As to those antinomians who said, "Let us do evil that good may come," he declares, that "their damnation is just."

But, how is Christ the author of sanctification? The word sanctification has two senses, but so nearly related, that in the end they are virtually the same. The first is consecration to God. Whatever was thus consecrated or devoted, was called *holy*, and the act by which it was done, was termed *sanctification*. But secondly, it means to makes holy, not in a ceremonial, but in a moral sense. The word is more commonly used in the former sense in the Old Testament, and in the latter, in the New Testament. But the latter is very naturally derived from the former; for, when the soul with all its faculties and affections is consecrated to God, it is the same as to be made holy in a moral sense. The important question propounded, how is Christ the author of sanctification? will be properly answered by saying, that the same union by faith to Christ, which makes him our justifying righteousness, also constitutes him the vital head of every one brought into this near relation. In illustration of this, he says, "I am the vine, ye are the branches; he that abideth in me, and I in him, the same bringeth forth much fruit; for without me ye can do nothing." So also, he is the head, and believers are the members, and as he is holy, and the Holy Spirit has been granted to him without measure, the same Spirit by which he is actuated will flow unto every member of the mystical body. Again, he has by his obedience unto death acquired the right and power to send the Holy Spirit, which he has promised to every one who believes in him. The connexion between justification and sanctification is indissoluble; for none but a living faith justifies, as the apostle James has taught; and a living faith works by love and purifies the heart; so that a man cannot be justified by faith without having the work of sanctification begun in him at the same time. So, our blessed Lord, in the commission which he gave to Paul to preach to the Gentiles, sent him, "to open their eyes, and to turn them from darkness to light, and from the power of Satan unto God, that they might receive forgiveness of sins, and inheritance among them who are sanctified by faith that is in me." These two cardinal doctrines of our salvation may be distinguished, but they can never be separated. There are, indeed, important differences between them, which should be well understood; for much evil has arisen from injudiciously confounding them together. Justification is an act of God altering our relation to the law, and pronouncing us free from its curse, and giving a title to eternal life; but sanctification is a work within us, commenced in our regeneration. The one has for its foundation the perfect satisfaction which Christ has rendered to law and justice; the other is a work of the Holy Spirit, who is the Spirit of Christ within us, purifying us from the pollutions of flesh and spirit.

Moreover, justification is perfected at once, and is as complete at the first moment of believing as it ever will be; for "there is no condemnation to them that are in Christ Jesus:" but sanctification is progressive, and is never absolutely perfect in this life; but will be consummated when we leave the body. Although our inherent righteousness is not, in any measure, the ground of our legal justification; yet, sanctification is as necessary to salvation as justification; for "without holiness no man shall see the Lord." Without a renewed nature no man is capable of enjoying the felicity of heaven. The joys of heaven are holy joys, and the exercises of heaven, consisting very much in praise and adoration, are holy exercises. The society in heaven consists of holy persons, and, therefore, none but the sanctified can participate in the happiness of heaven. Heaven is, therefore, called "the inheritance of the saints (sanctified ones) in light."

4. Christ is also said, in our text, to be made unto us redemption. This word, I think, must be here taken to signify deliverance, complete deliverance. Captives were often redeemed by the payment of a ransom-price; and persons of distinction, when made captives in war, were redeemed at a great price. In this strict and proper sense of the term, Christ is truly a Redeemer. He came from heaven to redeem his people from the curse of the law, and from the bondage of sin and Satan. He did not come empty-handed. He came to offer a ransom for every redeemed soul. But silver and gold would answer no purpose in the redemption of the soul and the body of lost man. Nothing would answer as a price for this redemption but blood—and that blood divine—the blood of the Son of God. When his heart's blood was requisite he

did not spare it, but freely poured it out for our redemption. In this view of redemption, Christ was our Redeemer, as obtaining for us deliverance from condemnation, and from the bondage and dominion of sin; but this redemption was virtually treated of in the last two particulars. The word redemption here, then, as was said, is to be taken in a more restricted sense, for our final deliverance from all the evils which sin has entailed upon us. For though the believer is justified, and in part sanctified, yet is he surrounded with evils of various kinds, and his body must return to the dust and see corruption; from which it shall not obtain deliverance, until the glorious morning of the resurrection. For this deliverance, Paul and his fellow Christians groaned within themselves, "waiting for the "adoption," which he calls "the redemption of the body." A captive ransomed and released from bondage in an enemy's country, might have contracted grievous diseases which it would require much time and a painful course of medicine to cure; and he might have a long and difficult journey to perform before he reached his father's house. He might have to pass through a howling wilderness, over rugged mountains, and stormy seas; so that, though fully redeemed, as far as the ransom was concerned, and released actually from his fetters and manacles; yet he might never be so happy as to reach his home, but might miserably perish by the way. The condition of the redeemed of the Lord, is, in many respects, similar. They are free from condemnation, and the power of sin in them is broken; but its remains are, indeed, a deep and inveterate disease, requiring a course of painful discipline, and the Christian pilgrim may be said to be yet far from his heavenly mansion. Before him is a dangerous wilderness, and an exceedingly dark and gloomy valley, called "The shadow of death." His body rendered mortal by sin, must go to the dust, before it can be such a body as will be suited to a purified soul, or be fit for the Jerusalem above. "Many are the afflictions of the righteous." Through much tribulation they must enter into heaven. But in one important respect, their condition differs widely from that of the earthly captive. He is in no danger of perishing eventually. Christ is the Captain of salvation, who has promised to bring him off conqueror, and more than conqueror, through his unchanging love. None shall be able to pluck these feeble sheep from the faithful hands of their Shepherd. No: Christ has declared it: "They shall never perish." Hear Paul's triumphant language: "Who shall separate us from the love of Christ? Shall tribulation or distress, or persecution, or famine, or nakedness, or peril, or sword? Nay, in all these things, we are more than conquerors through him that loved us."

Although death is inevitable, it shall not ultimately triumph, for the body shall be redeemed from the power of death and the grave. The resurrection will be the consummation of the saints' redemption. "It is sown in corruption, it is raised in incorruption. It is sown in dishonour, it is raised in glory. It is sown in weakness, it is raised in power. It is sown a natural body, it is raised a spiritual body. Then, this corruptible shall put on incorruption, and this mortal shall put on immortality. Then shall death be swallowed up in victory," and then shall be sung the conqueror's song, "O death, where is thy sting? O grave, where is thy victory?"

We may remark,

1. The completeness of the plan of salvation which the gospel reveals. Here is provision made for every spiritual want. Wisdom is provided for those who by nature are blind and foolish. They are made wise to know the way of life, and they receive that wisdom which is from above, "which is first pure, then peaceable, gentle, easy to be entreated, full of mercy and good fruits, without partiality and without hypocrisy." Being destitute of any righteousness of their own, which can justify the sinner, they here find in Christ all that the law demands; and, therefore, there is no condemnation to them. "It is God that justifieth, who is he that condemneth?"

Again, being born in sin, and stained with innumerable defilements of actual transgression, they need to be washed and sanctified, as well as justified. By the word and Spirit of Christ, this purification is commenced, and carried on gradually to perfection. All believers are saints, consecrated to God, and delivered from the love and power of sin; and at the appointed time will be made perfect in holiness.

While here, the Christian is subject to manifold afflictions and to the death of the body; but he is permitted to entertain the blessed and assured hope of complete redemption from every evil which sin has introduced. When Christ shall come to gather together his elect, his redemption, even from death itself, will be complete. Death will be swallowed up in victory.

2. And finally, we should never forget that all the blessings of salvation are received through Christ. He is the believer's unfailing treasure, from whom he derives wisdom, righteousness, sanctification, and redemption. He who possesses these cannot fail of eternal life. "He that hath the Son, hath life." "And this is the promise which he hath promised us, ETERNAL LIFE;" and that life they shall for ever enjoy in the presence of, and in communion with Christ.

SERMON XV.

THE ONE THING NEEDFUL.

But one thing is needful; and Mary hath chosen that good part, which shall not be taken away from her.—LUKE x. 42.

OUR blessed Lord, though he seems to have had no place of lodging in the city of Jerusalem, where he spent much time, and laboured much for the benefit of the people; yet, had a friendly family in the neighbouring village of Bethany, on the Mount of Olives, who were glad of the privilege of entertaining so divine a guest. This family consisted of three persons, two sisters and a brother; and they were surely a happy family, for Jesus not only visited them often, but loved every one of them; and on one occasion manifested his friendship by raising the brother from the dead, when he had been four days in the sepulchre. Martha and Mary, the sisters, were both greatly attached to Jesus, but differed in their manner of showing it. Martha was solicitous about giving him the best entertainment in her power. Mary, in order to avail herself of the precious opportunity of obtaining divine knowledge, from him who spake as never man spake, relinquished all care of domestic matters; and as an humble penitent, took her seat at the feet of Jesus, drinking in every word which proceeded from his gracious lips. The whole burden of domestic duties being thus devolved on Martha, her temper became ruffled and her spirit vexed at her sister's neglect of her part of the duties of the family. She, therefore, complained to our Lord of the delinquency of her sister, and solicited his interposition. She said, "Lord, dost thou not care that my sister hath left me to serve alone? Bid her, therefore, that she help me." The answer of Jesus is remarkable for its fidelity and affectionate tenderness: "Martha, Martha, thou art careful and troubled about many things; but one thing is needful, and Mary hath chosen that good part, which shall not be taken away from her." As there is an evident antithesis between the *many things* which occupied the attention of Martha, and the *one thing* pronounced to be alone necessary, several of the ancient interpreters supposed, that the contrast was between many dishes which Martha was engaged in preparing, and a single dish, which, our Lord said, was enough; whereas, the real antithesis was between the many objects of Martha's attention, and the single object which absorbed the attention of Mary; as is evident from the following words, "and Mary hath chosen that good part," that one thing needful, "which shall not be taken away from her." The one thing needful, therefore, is the good part which Mary nad chosen. What then was Mary's choice? We read, "that she sat at Jesus' feet to hear his words." In the general, divine truth, uttered by her Lord was the one thing which engaged her affections, and more particularly the gospel of salvation; or, that plan of redemption by which a sinner can be reconciled to God, and be restored again, not only to his favour, but to his image. As all true religion is founded on a knowledge of truth, and is inseparable from it, the thing needful may be said to be the whole of true religion; which is, indeed, *one thing*, although it consists of many branches; for they all may be fairly traced to the spiritual knowledge of the truth as it is in Jesus. We have, then, from the text, this important instruction, that true religion is needful, and is a good thing, and will never be taken away from those who possess it. We are, moreover, here taught that true religion is a thing of choice; and that possessing this, we need nothing else; that is, our eternal happiness is secure by this alone, though we should be destitute of all other things. Or it may be understood that this blessing comprehends all other good things, as "godliness has the promise of the life that now is, and of that which is to come." In accordance with which, Paul says to the Corinthian Christians, "All things are yours, whether Paul, or Apollos, or Cephas, or the world, or life, or death, or things present, or things to come, all are yours, and ye are Christ's, and Christ is God's."

We shall endeavour to show the excellence and necessity of divine knowledge with its accompaniments, by several considerations:

1. This knowledge is necessary to our reconcilia-

tion with God. The religion of a sinner must necessarily be different from that of an innocent being. He who has sinned, has contracted guilt, which must be removed by an atonement satisfactory to divine justice. While sin remains unpardoned, there can be no peace, nor safety to the sinner. The law, which is inflexible, denounces a curse on every transgressor. "God is angry with the wicked every day," and hath declared, that "He will in no wise clear the guilty." "The wrath of God has been revealed from heaven against all ungodliness and unrighteousness of men." God is a righteous Judge, and hath, in many places of his word, declared that every man shall receive according to his works. Now, as all have sinned and come short of the glory of God, he hath concluded all, both Jews and Gentiles, to be under wrath, and hath declared that the only hope of salvation is in Christ; "whom he hath set forth to be a propitiation for our sins, that he might be just and the justifier of him who believeth in Jesus." There is no other method of reconciliation; "neither is there any other name given under heaven, whereby we must be saved;" "for other foundation can no man lay than that which is laid, which is Jesus Christ." Two things then are necessary to the pardon and justification of a sinner; first, that an adequate atonement be made for sin; and secondly, that the sinner receive the benefit of this atonement by the exercise of a saving faith. The righteousness of Christ justifies no one, until it is set down to his account; and it is appropriated to none, but by faith. Therefore, while we are said to be justified by Christ's blood, and freely by the grace of God through the redemption that is in Christ Jesus; we are also said to be justified by faith. Both these things are equally necessary to the pardon and reconciliation of a sinner; but on very different accounts. Christ's righteousness is the only meritorious ground; and faith is merely the instrument of reception, or the bond which unites the soul to Christ. Now, faith cannot be separated from spiritual knowledge. This last is included in it, as presenting to the mind all the objects of faith. This is saving knowledge. The object of it, or truths known, are all indeed contained in the revelation of God; but the discernment of their true nature—their beauty and their glory—is by the illumination of the Holy Spirit, who takes the things of Christ and shows them unto us. "This is eternal life, to know thee, the only true God, and Jesus Christ whom thou hast sent."

Certainly, then, the one thing needful for man, is the true knowledge of "the way of life." This is to him the *good part* which he has chosen for his heritage, and equally needful for all. Of this knowledge, Christ is the sum and substance. Therefore, the apostle Paul said, "I determined to know nothing among you, save Jesus Christ and him crucified." It is in his face we behold the brightest rays of the divine glory; beholding which, "we are transformed into the same image, from glory to glory, as by the Spirit of the Lord."

II. The second consideration which serves to show the necessity and excellence of the knowledge of divine truth, is, that in this knowledge, and the holy affections which flow from it, consists the highest dignity and supreme excellence and felicity of human nature. With this crown man was adorned in the day of his creation, when he came fresh and beautiful from the hand of his Creator. Deprived of this, the intellect of man was darkened and perverted. All his affections and moral powers became disordered and deformed. In the soul of man, thus deprived of the divine image, all traces of moral beauty were defaced; and man, instead of appearing in the likeness of his Creator in which he was made, took on the likeness of his greatest enemy. No other acquisition or possession can compensate for this radical defect. Knowledge and intellectual power, without being conjoined with the beauties of holiness, only render the human nature more odious. From this deep degradation, no power can deliver us but the power which at first created us. Of all the creatures which God produced, in this world, man was the noblest; and of all the endowments of man, none was so excellent as the image of God. Where this is defaced, to suppose that it could be renewed by any but the omnipotent God, would be to imagine that the most excellent thing which God ever made, could be re-produced by a creature —by a sinful worm of the dust. No: we are born again, or from above, "not of blood, nor of the will of the flesh, nor of the will of man, but of God." "For," says Paul, "God who commanded the light to shine out of darkness, hath shined into our hearts, to give us the light of the knowledge of the glory of God in the face of Jesus Christ." The image of God which is restored in the new creation, is, by the same apostle, in one place, described as "righteousness, and true holiness." "Put on the new man which is created in righteousness and true holiness." But in another place he sums up the effect of this renovation in the single word "knowledge." "And have put on the new man, which is renewed in knowledge after the image of him that created him."

The excellence of holiness is so great, that the apostle Peter describes it as a participation of the divine nature. "According as his divine power hath given unto us all things that pertain unto life and godliness, through the knowledge of him, that hath called us to glory and virtue; whereby are given unto us exceeding great and precious promises, that by these ye might be partakers of the *divine nature.*" When holiness is manifested in the particular virtues of the Christian life, it cannot but win the approbation of every mind, not perverted by error, or blinded by prejudice. Even when moral goodness is calumniated, it is never done as being good, or under the idea of goodness, but it must first be caricatured, and misnamed. Even the devils know that moral excellence is better than sin, for they have experienced the effects of both. Holiness is the glory of God, for this word expresses the sum of all his moral attributes. Holiness is the foundation of heavenly bliss and glory, the golden pavement of the city of God. Without holiness no one can enter into the society of heaven. The knowledge which the best attain nere, is obscure and imperfect; but there the view of divine truth will be perfectly perspicuous. "Here, we see through a glass darkly; there, face to face." In proportion to our knowledge will be our love; and from this perennial fountain will flow uninterrupted happiness.

III. A third consideration which goes fully to justify the choice of Mary is, that the good part on which she had fixed her affections, should never be taken away from her. However excellent a possession may be intrinsically, and however well adapted to promote the happiness of the possessor, yet, if it continue only for a short time, its value would be comparatively small. Or, if it should be liable to be lost by the negligence or misconduct of the owner, this circumstance would greatly diminish its worth. But true religion, when once obtained, is never lost; it abideth for ever. God, after having bestowed on a dead soul, the principle of divine life, will not take it away; for he is of one mind. His purpose of mercy is as unchangeable as his being. "The gifts and calling of God are without repentance;" that is, without change of mind. What he graciously gives, he will not withdraw. And though Satan will exercise all his malicious arts to overcome and destroy the Christian; yet, he shall not be able to prevail; for, "if God be for him, who can be against him?" This sleepless adversary may indeed frighten the timid sheep, and may sometimes be permitted to wound and worry them, but the good Shepherd, who has given his life for them, will not suffer the weakest of them to perish. His word of promise is more stable than the pillars of heaven, and he hath said, "My sheep hear my voice, and I know them, and they follow me. And I give unto them eternal life; and they shall never perish, neither shall any man pluck them out of my hand. My Father which gave them me, is greater than all, and no man is able to pluck them out of my Father's hand."

But, it may be alleged, as religion is a matter of choice, it is obviously possible, that what is chosen to-day, may, with the same freedom, be rejected to-morrow. No doubt, the fall of a pious man is a thing in itself possible. Adam and Eve, though perfectly holy, fell, and a multitude of holy angels fell; and, surely, Christians, who are surrounded with imperfection and exposed to numerous temptations might fall. This cannot be denied. If believers, after their conversion, should be left to depend on their own strength, their fall and utter ruin would be, not only possible, but almost certain. But their standing is not in themselves. And in this we see the wide difference between the covenant of works, and the covenant of grace. In the first, salvation depended on the integrity of a mutable man; in the last, on the faithfulness of God. "We are kept," says the apostle Peter, "by the power of God, through faith unto salvation." The question is not, whether the Christian might not fall away, if left to himself; but whether the grace of God is not sufficient to keep him from falling; and if so, whether the faithfulness of God is not pledged to preserve his sheep from perishing. O! what a triumph would it be to Satan, if he could pluck one of these lambs out of the hands of the Redeemer!

It is true, if the pious man chose to forsake God, he would do it; but, He who at first made him willing to embrace the good part, in the day of his power, can, by the exertion of the same power, influence his will to continue to choose the good part. And in this conservatory influence, there is no constraint or compulsion. God can sweetly and effectually influence the human will, without the least interference with human liberty. Man never acts more freely than when under the operation of divine grace.

It will be argued, however, that many flourishing Christians have entirely fallen away. To which we answer, that many flourishing *professors* have fallen away, we do not doubt; but such may have been mere hypocrites like Judas, or temporary believers, like the seed on stony ground, who had no root in themselves; therefore, in the day of trial, they could not stand, but withered away. "Not every one that saith Lord, Lord," says Christ, "shall enter into the kingdom of heaven, but he that doeth the will of my Father in heaven." The apostle John teaches us what to think of such apostates; "They went out from us, but they were not of us; for if they had been of us, no doubt they would have continued with us." Our Lord, himself, at the last day, when such professors will make a plea of their high standing in the church, will declare that he never knew them: "Depart from me, ye workers of iniquity, for I never knew you."

In conclusion, let all who enjoy the opportunity of seeking divine instruction, feel the importance of not postponing the concerns of the soul and eternity, for the sake of worldly business, or worldly honours and amusements. While Jesus is in the way and accessible, let all come and take his easy yoke, and learn of him, and they shall find rest to their souls.

If a free pardon were offered to a condemned criminal, would he plead for longer time to remain under condemnation? If an effectual remedy were offered to a sick man, would he be guilty of the folly of procrastination, and thus endanger his life? But a greater folly we behold every day, in multitudes, who have the offer of pardon and salvation, if they will repent, and receive Christ as offered in the gospel. Yet, though under the sentence of a law from which none can escape, they neglect the great salvation. They make light of the invitation of the great King, if not in words, yet by their conduct, and go, "one to his merchandise and another to his farm." Or, they make an excuse of their worldly pursuits and avocations. To find examples of such consummate folly, we have no need to go to the pages of ancient history, or to the shores of foreign countries; we have them in large numbers among us, who, though they have been often called, yet still refuse the gracious invitation of the gospel.

But as we know not at what hour, or by what call, God by his Spirit may reach the hearts of careless, delaying sinners, it is our duty still to lift up the voice of warning—still to call sinners to repentance—and to invite all thirsty souls to come to Christ and drink; and all heavy-laden sinners to come to the meek and lowly Redeemer, that they may find rest to their souls. As ambassadors of Christ, it is made our duty to entreat sinners, in Christ's stead, to be reconciled unto God. We are authorized to declare, that "him that cometh, he will in no wise cast out;" but the promise of eternal life is made to every one who receives the Lord Jesus; that is, who cordially believes on his name. Come, then, I beseech you, and seek salvation in Christ. Break off your sins by repentance, and with broken, penitent hearts, approach the cross of Jesus Christ. Come and be sprinkled with his justifying blood. Speedily lay hold on eternal life—let there be no delay. Eternal happiness and eternal misery are at stake—life and death are set before you. "Believe in the Lord Jesus Christ, and thou shalt be saved." But if you continue to neglect the great salvation, there will be no way of escape from wrath.

SERMON XVI.

THE LOVE OF CHRIST.

As Christ also hath loved us, and hath given himself for us, an offering and a sacrifice to God for a sweet smelling savour.—EPHES. v. 2.

As God is incomprehensible in his eternity, his power, his immensity, his knowledge and his wisdom; so is he in his love.

There is a breadth and length, and depth and height, in the love of Christ, which passeth knowledge. But though we cannot comprehend this love; yet we are permitted to know of its existence, and of some of its properties, which will now be the subject of our contemplation.

1. The first thing which strikes us as wonderful in this love of God is, that it should have sinners as its objects. When we consider, that God is infinitely holy—that holiness is his very essence—it cannot but strike us, as an incomprehensible thing, that depraved and guilty creatures should be from eternity the selected objects of divine benevolence. For it should be understood and admitted, that for God to love sinners with the love of complacency

or esteem, is a thing evidently and absolutely repugnant to his nature; and therefore impossible. But a holy being may love those who are unholy, with the love of benevolence; as this consists, not in any delight in their character, but in a desire for their well-being and happiness. Such love contemplates the recovery of its objects, not only from misery, but from depravity; and their restoration to the image and enjoyment of God.

But as the Almighty possessed the power of creating with a word, innumerable intelligent beings, who might become the objects of his love, it is wonderful that he should fix his love on sinful, ruined creatures. It could not be merely as creatures, that men became the objects of this love; for then fallen angels, as being of a nobler nature, had a higher claim. But "Christ took not on him the nature of angels." Devils were not the objects of his love.

2. Another thing which is incomprehensible in the love of Christ to sinners is, that among men, all of whom were equally lost and helpless, it should select a certain number, as its objects, and leave all the rest under condemnation and depravity, as they were before.

If men are the objects of divine favour, why a part only? Why not all? especially, as the means necessary to redeem a part, are sufficient to redeem the whole.

If those elected were uniformly better than those passed by, there would be some small ground of making a difference. But this is not the fact. Some of the elect, we know, were among the greatest sinners upon earth; and, generally, they were no better than others, in heart or life.

This doctrine of sovereign election is so offensive to human reason, or rather to human prejudices, that every evasion which human ingenuity could devise, has been resorted to, in order to avoid it; or so to explain it, that it might be rendered more palatable to the children of men.

The most plausible evasion of the doctrine is, that God, who is omniscient, foresaw that a certain number of the human race would, in the exercise of their free-will, cordially receive the gospel, and persevere in obedience until death; and on this account they were elected unto life. But this is inconsistent with the condition into which the human race are sunk; which is one of entire depravity, or alienation from God. We might as reasonably expect the dead to rise out of their graves, by their own power, as that men dead in trespasses and sins, should of their own accord, put forth any holy act. It is also diametrically opposed to the teaching of Scripture on the subject: where no such reason is ever offered why certain persons were elected unto life, but they are predestinated, that they might be holy. They are not chosen, because it was foreseen, that they would be holy; but they became saints, because God, in his incomprehensible counsel, was pleased to choose them to be heirs of salvation. Their love to God is not the cause of his love to them, but the consequence. "We love him," says John, "because he first loved us." And again, "Not that we loved God, but that he loved us, and sent his Son to be the propitiation for our sins." When Christ rejoiced in spirit, and thanked God that he had hid these things from the wise and prudent, and revealed them unto babes, he ascribes it entirely to divine sovereignty: "Even so, Father, for thus it seemed good in thy sight;" and Paul attributes all to the "good pleasure" of the divine will.

3. A third characteristic of the love of Christ is, its degree of intensity, which is unparalleled. "Greater love hath no man than this," says Christ, "that a man lay down his life for his *friends;*" but Paul says, "God commendeth his love toward us, in that, while we were yet *sinners,* Christ died for us." "God so loved the world," says Christ, "that he gave his only begotten Son, that whosoever believeth in him, should not perish, but have everlasting life." The love of the Father and the Son is the same; but the evidence of the love of the Son strikes us more forcibly, because he it was who became incarnate, and was crucified. He was made of a woman, and made under the law, that he might be capable of suffering, which as God he is not; though some entertain the opinion that the divine nature suffered. This, however, seems to us inconsistent with the immutability, felicity, and absolute perfection of Deity. But the divine and human nature constitute but one Person, and therefore, it may truly be said that the Son of God suffered and died, that is, he suffered and died in that nature which was susceptible of suffering and death. The intensity of Christ's love is manifested by his voluntary giving up his life for the salvation of his people.

He gave himself for us, says our text, *an offering for a sweet smelling savour unto God*. He was, by an oath of the Father, designated to be a priest after the order of Melchisedek; and as our great high Priest, he must needs have something to offer. As Isaac said, My Father, where is the Lamb? so we may say, Here is the Priest, but where is the sacrifice? The answer is, "sacrifice and offering, and burnt-offering, and offering for sin, thou wouldst not, neither hadst pleasure in them. Then said he, Lo, I come, to do thy will, O God. By the which will we are sanctified through the offering of the body of Jesus Christ, once for all." "This man after he had offered one sacrifice for sins, for ever sat down on the right hand of God." "Such a high Priest became us;" and such a sacrifice was necessary for the salvation of one soul, and is in value sufficient for a thousand worlds, for it is infinite.

How exceedingly great was that love, which could induce the Son of God to veil his glory, and leave the riches of heaven, to become a poor, despised, and sorrowful man; yea, to give himself up freely into the hands of wicked men, who maliciously sought his life! He says, "I lay it down of myself, no man taketh it away from me." "He humbled himself and took upon him the form of a servant, and being found in fashion as a man, he was obedient unto death, even the death of the cross."

The efficacy of this sacrifice in procuring reconciliation is signified in the text, by its being called "a sweet smelling savour unto God." God was well pleased with the mediatorial work of his Son. A rich reward was given to him for his humiliation and death. This, we read, he had before him, when "he endured the cross, despising the same."

As the death of the Son was agreed on. in the eternal counsels of Jehovah; and as he perfectly complied with all the stipulations of the covenant; and not only obeyed the law, but endured its curse, his work and his offering could not but be pleasing to God.

4. As this love did not originate in time, but, from eternity, the delights of the Son were with the children of men; so it will never have an end. Many waters cannot extinguish it. Whom Christ loves, he love to the end. It is an everlasting love: "I have loved thee with an everlasting love." If it should be alleged, that the objects of this love may cause it to cease, by wickedly forsaking Christ and becoming reprobates; it may be answered, that his grace is sufficient to save from apostasy, those whom he has effectually called. "They are kept by the power of God through faith unto salvation."

If, indeed, true believers should ever apostatize, they would forfeit the love of Christ; but his promise is express, that such an event shall never take place. "And I will make an everlasting covenant with them, that I will not turn away from them to do them good; but I will put my fear in their hearts, and *they shall not depart from me.*" Christ prays for them, as he prays not for the world: and the Father heareth him always. Again, he says, "Father, I will that those whom thou hast given me, be with me, that they may behold my glory." United to Christ, and members of his body, they cannot perish.

5. The love of Christ to his people is manifested by the revelation which he has made for their instruction; by all the institutions of his church for their edification; and by all the dispensations of his providence, whether afflictive or prosperous. But, especially, the love of Christ toward his chosen people is evinced by the gift of his Spirit, the Comforter, to abide with them for ever. By his effectual agency the soul is renewed, and sanctified, and made meet for the enjoyment of the heavenly inheritance. He takes of the things of Christ, and shows them unto us, and is a Monitor, a Comforter, an Advocate, and a Helper in every time of need and of distress.

6. Finally, the love of Christ to his disciples is a tender, condescending love. He deals with them, as a mother with a child; carries them in his bosom, and gently leads them in the right way; and as they are prone, like lost sheep, to stray far away from his pastures, he goes after them and brings them back. "He restoreth my soul," is language which every disciple has occasion, with gratitude, to use. We see, in the gospel history, clear evidence of the forbearance and condescension of Christ toward his disciples. Now that he is exalted at the right hand of God, he exercises the same tenderness and condescension, as the experience of every true Christian can testify. Even the tenderness of a mother for her suckling is not sufficient, fully to exhibit the tenderness and constancy of the love of Christ to his people. This language, by

the prophet Isaiah, is remarkable: "But Zion said, The Lord hath forsaken me, and my Lord hath forgotten me. Can a woman forget her sucking child, that she should not have compassion on the son of her womb? Yea, they may forget; yet will I not forget thee. Behold, I have graven thee upon the palms of my hands—thy walls are continually before me." The love of God to his people is often, in the Old Testament, called *loving-kindness*. A stronger expression for tender love could not be used.

"The Lord," says the Psalmist, "is merciful and gracious, slow to anger, and plenteous in mercy. He will not always chide, neither will he keep his anger for ever. He hath not dealt with us after our sins, nor rewarded us according to our iniquities. For as the heaven is high above the earth, so great is his mercy toward them that fear him. As far as the east is from the west, so far hath he removed our transgressions from us. Like as a father pitieth his children, so the Lord pitieth them that fear him." But after all, the love of Christ is too great, too wonderful to be comprehended. It passeth knowledge. Paul says, "Who loved me and gave himself for me." He compares the love of Christ to that of a tender husband toward his wife. "Husbands, love your wives, even as Christ also loved the church and gave himself for it. So ought men to love their wives as their own bodies; for no man ever yet hated his own flesh, but nourisheth and cherisheth it; *even as the Lord the Church*. For we are members of his body, of his flesh, and of his bones. This is a great mystery, but I speak concerning Christ and his church."

1. The first inference from this subject is, that if Christ so loved us, we ought to make all the return possible, by loving him supremely, constantly, tenderly. Love to Christ is the only satisfactory evidence we can have that we are the objects of his love. We should love him, because he has manifested such love to us. If we love Christ, we will keep his commandments.

2. The second inference is, that if Christ so loved us as to give himself for us, an offering of a sweet savour unto God, we ought to love one another, and to walk in love; for this is the exhortation of the apostle in our text. To walk in love, our minds should be imbued with this holy affection. Love should be our aliment—love should be our active principle, ever prompting and influencing us. Those whom Christ so intensely and tenderly loves, we ought to love with a pure heart fervently.

3. The love of Christ should be the constant object of our contemplation, and the subject of our continual praises. This will make us meet for heaven; for the everlasting song of the redeemed is, "To him that loved us, and washed us from our sins in his own blood, and hath made us kings and priests unto God, and his Father, to him be glory and dominion, for ever and ever, Amen."

SERMON XVII.

LOVE TO CHRIST.

Simon, son of Jonas, lovest thou me?—JOHN xxi. 17.

JESUS had now appeared the third time to his disciples, when collected together after his resurrection, and had given them the most satisfactory proof, that he was indeed risen from the dead; for, he not only exhibited himself to their eyes in the very form and features, to which they had always been accustomed; but he condescended to permit them to handle him, that they might be certain that it was not a mere apparition, which they beheld; and to remove every shadow of doubt from the most incredulous amongst them, he ate and drank in their presence, as formerly. It was immediately after a repast of which they had partaken, with him, at the sea of Tiberias, that he turned to Peter, and three times proposed the question contained in our text, nearly in the same words; and each time received the same answer, "Lord, thou knowest all things, thou knowest that I love thee."

There was a particular reason why Peter should have been thus interrogated. His conduct had been such as to render his sincerity suspected. He had in the most cowardly and profane manner, denied that he knew the blessed Jesus, when he was upon his trial before the Jewish court. And what added peculiar aggravations to his crime was, that a little before, he had solemnly and publicly professed that he would die sooner than he would forsake his Master. Indeed, at first, when the band of soldiers approached to apprehend Jesus, he did exhibit considerable signs of courage; for he drew his sword, and cut off the ear of one of the high priest's servants; and then went forward to the hall of judgment. But he would have discovered more attachment to his Master, to have run away with his fellows, than to have behaved as he did in his presence. No man is equally bold at all times. Sudden fits of terror will occasionlly unman the greatest hero. Besides, blustering courage is not the most to be depended on. A mild, calm, unassuming temper is commonly the most steadfast, in the hour of danger. Who would have supposed that John, the meek, affectionate, amiable John, would have displayed more fortitude in the face of death, than the bold, intrepid, self-confident Peter? But so it was, and so it commonly will be, that modest firmness will stand the test of real danger, better than confident bravery. John was the first to follow his Master to the iniquitous tribunal where he was condemned; and it was by his influence that Peter was admitted. Well, when introduced, how does he act? Does he, fearless of the consequences, take his stand by his Master, and attempt to soothe him with the tear of sympathy and look of compassion? Does he still express his willingness to die with him, and for his sake? What an opportunity he had now to act the most dignified and pious part! But, instead of this, he hides his face, as it were, from him. He is afraid lest any body should suspect that he had ever had any connexion with him. He skulks among the servants, and sits trembling, lest some unlucky accident should detect him. His cowardly fears were soon realized; for a maid servant recognized him, and charged him with being a disciple of Jesus. O! what a mortifying picture of human nature is now before us! Peter denies his Lord. He is interrogated more sharply a second time. Well, he has had the opportunity for a little reflection. Does he recall his words? No. He denies him again. And, horrible to relate! upon the third charge he affects to be in a mighty passion, and to his denial adds oaths and curses! And all this in the presence and hearing of Jesus himself! But as he turned his face toward his insulted, offended Master, HE looked upon him with a countenance, no doubt, in which indignation and pity, love and displeasure, were blended. He looked upon him, and this look went more directly to his heart, than if a dagger had pierced him. It would be impossible to describe the mingled sensations, which, at this moment, agitated the breast of poor, unfortunate Peter. Honest at heart, but too confident of his own powers, he had been left for a moment to himself; and in his weakness we may see our own.

In his fall, we may learn what a broken reed human strength is! But the principle of piety, though overborne in the moment of trial, is not extinguished. It commonly soon recovers its predominant influence, and frequently exerts itself with unusual energy, like an elastic body after having been bent out of its proper direction. The falls of the pious are, by this, distinguished from those of the wicked; in that, they are soon followed by a deep and thorough repentance, by which they are restored to their former condition; but the latter fall from one grade of wickedness to another, without any experience of that "godly sorrow which worketh a repentance not to be repented of." Peter, overwhelmed with his feelings, and unable to contain himself, went out, and wept bitterly. If he spent the whole night in penitential sighs and groans, and bitter self-reproaches, it need not excite our surprise. Such was probably the fact.

It is a pleasing reflection, that our Saviour knows all things—that he knows the heart. This seems to have been Peter's comfort. If it had been otherwise, he would have found it no easy matter to produce any satisfactory proof of his love. But conscious of the sincerity, and strength of his attachment, and confident that Jesus knew the secret workings of his soul, when asked this pointed question, "Simon, son of Jonas, lovest thou me?" he boldly appealed to his omniscient Saviour, for the sincerity of his attachment; "Lord, thou knowest all things; thou knowest that I love thee."

Love to the Saviour is acknowledged by all, to constitute an essential part of the Christian character. To be destitute of this principle, therefore, is a decisive proof, that we are yet in our sins. To know that we possess it, is the same thing, as to be assured that we are the children of God, the heirs of glory. We cannot, therefore, be too particular, and cautious in examining, whether we are real lovers of Jesus; for if we love the Son, we love the Father, for the Son is the brightness or splendour of the Father's glory, "the express image of his Person."

Permit me, then, to direct your attention exclusively to this subject, which will be the more proper as the service is intended to be preparatory to the reception of the Lord's Supper.

For the sake of presenting my ideas in the most perspicuous form that I am able. I will consider the *foundation, nature, properties, and effects of love to Christ*. And may the Lord enable me so to speak, and you so to hear, that your souls may be edified.

1. In the first place I propose to speak of the foundation of *love to God*. I do not mean the foundation which there is laid for such an affection, in the nature and perfections of the object, but the state and disposition of the mind, which is necessary to make it susceptible of the love of God.

And it may be observed, in the first place, that there must be a foundation for such an affection, in the original and natural structure, or constitution of the soul of man; otherwise it would be absurd to require him to love God. He must have a capacity to know something of the perfections of God, for that cannot be the object of affection, which is utterly unknown : and he must possess the natural susceptibility of being moved by affection or desire; for a purely intellectual being, if we can conceive of such, cannot love, however much it may know. The amount of what I mean by these observations is, that the being, which is required to love God, must be endowed with both intellectual and active powers, such as it is evident man does possess.

But we proceed now to observe, what is of more importance, that the soul of man may become depraved and disordered, so that it shall neither be disposed to know or love its Creator. That this is the actual condition of our whole race, is proved by the testimony of God, and by universal experience. "The natural man receiveth not the things of the Spirit of God; they are foolishness unto him, neither can he know them, because they are spiritually discerned." "The carnal mind is enmity against God; it is not subject to his law, neither indeed can be." Whilst this depravity continues, there can be no love to God, for the idea of a holy God, to an unholy soul, must be extremely disagreeable. The wicked, that is, all unregenerate men, shun the thoughts of a holy God; or, if by any means they are led to contemplate his perfections, they are filled with disgust and horror, instead of love. Their hearts are entirely opposed to such a character, and such a being. This is the reason, that when Christ came into the world, he appeared to men "as a root out of a dry ground;" and still appears to the multitude " without form or comeliness." But it is a maxim in morals that the depravity of the subject does not diminish the authority of the law-giver, nor furnish any kind of excuse for disobedience. For to be depraved is the same thing as to be deserving of blame; and, therefore, the greater the depravity the more inexcusable is the sinner. From this view of human nature, it is evident that the regeneration of the soul, is absolutely necessary, as a foundation for the love of God. "Therefore," said Jesus, "except a man be born again, he cannot see the kingdom of heaven." "He that loveth is born of God." This renewal of the heart is not produced by any human efforts. Not by the man himself, for he can only bring into action such principles as are within him. Nor by any other creature, for another can only address himself to the heart by objectively proposing truth to the understanding; but truth, in order to produce its effect, requires a correspondent state or temper in the mind; so that even the brightest display of God's perfections to the understanding of a sinner, will only excite greater enmity, as in the devils. This change, therefore, is not of "blood, nor of the will of the flesh, nor of man, but of God." The Spirit of God is the agent; and in producing it, is free, sovereign, and incomprehensible. "The wind bloweth where it listeth, and thou hearest the sound thereof, but canst not tell whence it cometh, and whither it goeth: so is every one that is born of the Spirit." The effect of this divine agency is a new principle or new life; or a capacity of being properly affected with truth when proposed. This foundation being laid, the love of God follows as a thing of course. It is easy, it is delightful, to a renewed heart, to love the Lord its God. As this renovation is a necessary foundation for the love of God, so the love of God is a satisfactory evidence of the reality, and genuineness of this change.

2. I proceed, in the second place, to speak of the nature of that affection which we call love to God. Here I would not have you to suppose that any description of an emotion or affection, can convey a clear idea of it, to the mind of a person who has no experience of it. But, as all men are the subjects of love to some object, they may form an idea of the nature of this affection, when it has God for its object. The only reason why any explanation is necessary on this point, is, because frequently, several distinct exercises, or different affections have but one common name, which, in fact, is the case with respect to the love of God, for some have enumerated several distinct exercises as included under this name. But I think the whole may very commodiously be reduced to two heads, benevolence, and esteem or complacency. Both of these are undoubtedly comprehended in love to God, and they are entirely distinct; for the one has for its object the happiness of the being beloved, and the other terminates on his character or moral attributes. Gratitude is only the exercise of one or both of these, mingled with self-love. If it be unconnected with them, it is merely natural, and cannot with any propriety be termed "the love of God." It may be inquired how the Deity can be the object of our benevolence, since his glory and happiness can receive no increase. To this, I

answer, that the very same affection, which seeks the happiness of another, when it is incomplete, rejoices in the happiness of God which is perfect. The pious man delights in the thought, that God is so great, so glorious, so independent, so happy, and so perfectly secure from every danger or possibility of change. When our friend has attained to the object of his and our wishes, our benevolence towards him does not become extinct, because we do not wish him to rise higher; but the affection is, as it were, satisfied. It rejoices in what before was the object of desire.

Complacency, when God is its object, is a most refined, sublime, delightful emotion. It derives value from the superlative excellence of its object; and even assimilates the soul itself to the character of God. Its strength and perfection depend on two principles, viz. the degree of clearness with which the attributes of God are perceived, and the degree of sanctification to which the soul has attained. In heaven, love will be made perfect, and will be the source of that pure, soul-satisfying, eternal joy, which makes heaven such a delightful residence. Faith, hope, prophecy, and every other gift shall fail, but love never faileth.

3. I come, in the third place, to speak of the distinguishing properties of the love of God. It must be sincere, supreme, disinterested, and constant.

1. Sincere love stands opposed to that which is not real, but pretended; and also to that which is not pure, but adulterated.

It is an easy thing to pretend to the love of God.

We may profess with our lips, what our hearts never felt. We may borrow the very language which they use who do love God in sincerity; and put on the same external appearance of sanctity and devotion, which in others proceeds from the love of God; and yet, all this may be hypocrisy. It is the heart which the Lord requires, and not fair words, and a specious profession.

Our love must be rooted in the heart, and not confined to the tongue and the lips. The word sincere means genuine in the Scriptures. Our love to God must be pure, genuine, unadulterated love. I do not mean that sincere love is perfect in its degree, but it must be pure in its kind. It is the more necessary to be particular here, because there is much in the Christian world which bears the name of the love of God, and yet is spurious. The mere stirrings of natural passions, the flights of a heated imagination, and even feelings which belong almost entirely to our animal nature, have been dignified with this name, and many have been deceived; for whilst they have professed themselves to be perfect in love, they have been the willing slaves of sin. In order to the sincerity of love, it must terminate on the true character of God, and not upon an idol of our own imagination. Every one is ready to love such a God as suits his own character. Let the greatest profligate only be persuaded that God is not displeased with sin, and that he will never punish him for it, and he will love him. This is the source of much deception. Multitudes entertain no doubt, but that they love God; yet they have no just conceptions of his true character. They never think of his holiness and justice, but only of his goodness and mercy; and so they continue at ease in Zion, whilst they are "in the gall of bitterness and bond of iniquity."

2. But our love to God must not only be sincere, it must also be supreme. God will admit of no rival in our affections. He is a jealous God, and will not give his glory to another. Unless our love to God be stronger than our affection to all other objects, it will never become a uniform principle of obedience; and it can never entitle us to the denomination of the servants of God. The Lord Jesus Christ constantly required supreme love in those who proposed to become his disciples. If any man love father or mother, wife or children, or even life itself more than him, he is pronounced to be unworthy of him. Many are willing to do much, and go far to obtain a seat in heaven; but they are not willing that Christ should reign in their hearts. A sinful man will give any thing to God, rather than his heart. He has bestowed this already, and is unwilling to change the object of his affections. A young man of high rank, and amiable deportment, came to Christ, and with much earnestness inquired what he should do to inherit eternal life. Jesus, after some conversation, finally told him to go and sell all, and give it to the poor, and to come and follow him, and he should have treasure in heaven. This discovered the true condition of the young ruler's heart, for he went away very sorrowful, because he was very rich. He loved his estate more than he loved his God. Believe me,

there are now very many young men, and old ones too, just in the same situation.

3. Our love to God must be disinterested. It is degrading to religion to suppose that its highest efforts, and noblest affections are merely selfish. To suppose that the desire of our own happiness, is the only principle by which man can be actuated, goes far towards confounding all distinctions between virtue and vice. The greatest sinner, and even Satan himself, possesses this principle, in the utmost perfection. To say, as some eminent writers have said, that virtue consists in the pursuit of our everlasting happiness, but vice leads her votaries to take their portion here below, and that this is the only difference between the two, is much the same as to say, that the sinner's only fault consists in a mistake of the judgment, respecting the best method of securing his happiness. Amongst men it is certainly received as a common principle, that love in order to be praise-worthy, must be disinterested. If a man profess to be my friend, and discover every mark of affection for me, yet if I ascertain that his only motive for this is not any regard for me, but merely a desire to gain some advantage to himself, I despise his professions of love, and will, by no means, agree that he is a sincere friend. That kind of love which we esteem, induces the subject of it to sacrifice his own ease and interest for our good. This deserves the name of benevolence.

Certainly, the pious man, when enjoying a clear manifestation of God's excellence and glory, often forgets himself. He is absorbed in the contemplation of infinite worth; and his soul rests with delight in the object, without looking any further at the time. In pleading for disinterested love, I do not mean to insinuate, that the desire of personal happiness is wrong. It is not the fruit of sin, but belongs to the original constitution of all rational and sentient beings. It has, therefore, simply considered, nothing of a moral nature, good or bad. Very useless and absurd questions have frequently been started, respecting the length to which disinterested benevolence ought to carry us; as whether a holy man should not be willing to be eternally miserable for the glory of God; as if it were possible for God to be glorified by the damnation of one of his own people; or, as if a holy nature could be reconciled to become eternally unholy; or as if it were possible for any creature to divest himself of the first law of his nature, the desire of self-preservation. Cases which can never happen, ought never to be proposed, for they can illustrate nothing. But disinterested love to God will, undoubtedly, lead us to give up any earthly possession, and to endure any temporal affliction to which he may call us. This, indeed, is a most reasonable service; considering the love wherewith he hath loved us; for when we were yet sinners, Christ died for us.

4. The last property of the love of God, which I shall mention is, that it must be constant. It is a constant, steady flame which many waters cannot quench. It is like the fire on God's altar, which burnt day and night without going out. It is not

always equally lively, nor always in actual exercise but the principle is always there. We see many who appear to be inflamed with very ardent religious affections, which the more violent they appear, the sooner they subside. Their zeal blazes out like wild-fire, and their passions are bounded and regulated by no certain limits or principles. Such, for a time, may greatly outshine the real, humble, followers of Jesus, as a meteor does the fixed stars, but their light is not like that of the just, "shining more and more unto the perfect day." Their religion is temporary, founded on sudden impressions and impulses, and consisting in vivid flashes of affection, which soon become extinct. But true religion is permanent. It proceeds with a regular uninterrupted pace, "through evil report and good report." Backslidings there may be, but this cannot be perpetual. It is the characteristic of the wicked to fall and rise no more. It belongs to the Christian to keep himself in the love of God; to hold fast the beginning of his confidence firm unto the end; to renew his strength; to run and not be weary, to walk and not faint. He that endureth to the end shall be saved. The righteous shall grow stronger and stronger.

4. In the last place, we come to speak of the invariable effects of love to God. These will be better understood, and the subject more easily improved in the way of self-examination, if we consider the analogy between the effects of this affection of love, when a creature is its object, and when it is fixed on Christ.

1. One necessary effect of love is a desire to please the person beloved. Love always seeks for a return. The person who loves a friend is ever solicitous to conciliate the esteem of that friend, and cannot be satisfied without a reciprocal affection. "If ye love me," says Jesus, "keep my commandments. He that hath my commandments, and keepeth them, he it is that loveth me. Ye are my friends, if ye do whatsoever I command you." A constant desire to please God, is, therefore, a sure proof that we love him; and an inseparable concomitant of this, will be the fear of offending him. Slavish fear is cast out by perfect love. But the fear of offending him grows with the growth of love; yea, grows out of it. We cannot be at a loss about what course of conduct will be pleasing to God, and what offensive to him, with his word in our hands. Do we then take his word to be the rule of our life? Do we conscientiously aim at universal obedience to all its precepts? Do we sincerely hate every sin? and are we daily striving to mortify the deeds of the body and crucify the flesh, with its lusts and affections? If we can truly answer these interrogatories in the affirmative, it is better evidence that we love God, than if we heard it proclaimed by a voice from heaven.

2. Another effect of love is a desire of the company and conversation of the person beloved, and uneasiness and restlessness when he is absent. These feelings will be in proportion to the strength of our love.

But God is invisible, and Christ is removed far beyond our sight; how then can we enjoy his company or fellowship? This, no doubt, is a great mystery to the natural man; and is one of those things of the Spirit which to him appear foolishness. But, says the apostle, "our fellowship is with the Father and with his Son." Communion and intercourse with the Father, through the Son, and by the Spirit, is a truth clearly taught in the Scriptures; and known by experience to all those who love our Lord Jesus Christ in sincerity. Those who have once tasted the sweetness of the divine presence, and have had "the love of God shed abroad in their hearts by the Holy Ghost," are ever after anxious to enjoy these visitations of their heavenly Father. For this purpose, they frequent the house of God, to inquire after him, and to behold his beauty. With this view, they read, pray, and meditate, in their secret retirements. When the child of God approaches the table of the Lord, if any one should inquire, What is thy request, and what is thy petition? the natural answer would be, I desire the presence of my God; I wish to behold his glory in the face of Jesus Christ. When they are admitted to his presence, they "rejoice with joy unspeakable and full of glory." But when they are disappointed in their views of meeting with their God and Saviour, they go away sorrowful, but still they anxiously seek him, and will not rest until they find him. As the hunted hart panteth after the water brooks, so panteth my soul after thee, O God! O that I knew where I might find him.

3. Another natural effect of love is a desire to be conformed to the character of the person beloved.

Love has an assimilating effect on every mind which is the subject of it.

Then, if we love the Lord Jesus Christ, we shall be seeking conformity to his lovely character. His excellencies will be the object of our habitual imitation. No better evidence can be given of the genuineness of our love, than a constant effort and desire to be like Christ, in his humility and meekness, in his benevolence and compassion, in his zeal and devotional spirit; and so far as we find ourselves wanting in conformity to Christ, we shall be pained and dissatisfied with ourselves.

4. The last effect of love to God is an ardent concern for his glory; which discovers itself in active exertions to promote truth and holiness in ourselves and others; in using our best endeavours to advance the Redeemer's kingdom, by our own exertions, or by aiding and encouraging the exertions of others, and in real joy, when the interests of true religion are promoted, whoever may be the instrument; in grief and sorrow, when piety languishes, when truth is perverted, when iniquity abounds, and the love of many waxes cold. The most care for none of these things. If their own affairs are prosperous, they have no concern whether it goes well or ill with the kingdom of Christ. Many would rejoice at the overthrow of Christianity. If it were in their power, they would utterly abolish this system which so much disturbs their peace. But all the friends of the Lord Jesus rally round his standard, and would rather shed the last drop of their heart's blood, than forsake a cause which is so dear to them.

SERMON XVIII.

KEEPING ALIVE THE LOVE OF GOD.

Keep yourselves in the love of God.—JUDE, verse 21.

THE phrase "love of God," has two significations in the New Testament. First, it imports God's love to us: secondly, our love to God.

In the former sense, it is read in the following passages. Rom. v. 5, "For the love of God is shed abroad in your hearts, by the Holy Ghost sent down from heaven." Rom. viii. 39, "Nor any creature shall be able to separate us from the love of God, which is in Christ Jesus." Tit. iii. 5, "But after that the kindness and love of God to man appeared." 1 John iii. 16, "Hereby perceive we the love of God, because he laid down his life for us." 1 John iv. 9, "In this was manifested the love of God toward us," &c.

It is used in the latter sense in Luke xi. 42, "But pass by judgment and the love of God." John v. 42, "I know you, that ye have not the love of God in you." 2 Thess. iii. 5, "The Lord direct your hearts into the love of God." 1 John ii. 5, "In him, verily the love of God is perfected." iii. 17, "But whoso hath this world's good, and seeth his brother have need, and shutteth up his bowels of compassion from him, how dwelleth the love of God in him?" v. 3, "For this is the love of God, that we keep his commandments." To which may be added the words of our text, "Keep yourselves in the love of God."

Such exhortations do not imply, as some teach, that those addressed possess in themselves a complete ability to perform what is commanded, without divine aid. The maxim that where there is a command, there is always an ability to obey, is a false maxim. The obligation to obedience may remain, when the ability is lost; as is the case with every sinner. The maxim holds good in relation to all creatures, as they proceed from the hands of God. But who would say that the devil is not under obligation to love his Creator; and yet, who would affirm that he has the ability to change his nature from enmity to love? Human agency and divine efficiency are not at war; but sweetly harmonize. God commands what is right, and graciously gives us strength to perform it. It is analogous to what we observe in natural things. It is the duty of the husbandman to plough and sow, and water, but without the genial influences of heaven, the sun, air, and rain, he cannot have a crop. God must "give the increase." The true principle is taught by Paul, Phil. ii. 12, 13. "Work out your own salvation with fear and trembling, for it is God that worketh in you both to will and to do, of his own good pleasure." Our dependence on God is no reason why we should sit still and be idle, but a good reason for our being up and doing. It will be admitted by all, that the love of God is the essence of true religion, under every dispensation. It was the law of Paradise. It was the sum and substance of the ten commandments, uttered in a voice of thunder from Sinai, and written by the finger of God on tables of stone, and it is the soul of gospel obedience. It is unnecessary to attempt any analysis of love. It is too simple for definition, and too well known to all men, to need any explanation of its nature. But as the word includes more than one affection, it may be useful to employ a few words in showing what is usually comprehended under the term. When it is put for all moral obedience, it is used as a generic term, and comprehends all the desires and affections of the heart, which have God for their object, such as admiration, reverence, and confidence. But in its stricter sense, as meaning what is commonly understood by love, it comprehends three affections, which are easily distinguishable. The first terminates on the moral excellence of the divine character, and is termed esteem or complacency. The second has for its object the glory and felicity of God, and ardently seeks the manifestation of his glory, and rejoices in his infinite and unchangeable blessedness. The third is that flow of affection which is excited in the susceptible heart, by the reception of benefits, and is called gratitude. We may exercise benevolence toward one for whom we can feel no esteem; and we may feel esteem and benevolence toward one to whom we owe no debt of gratitude. But in regard to God, all these unite and combine, in that state of heart, in which true holiness or piety consists. We love God for what he is. We rejoice in his glory and felicity, and we feel gratitude for his unnumbered and unspeakable benefits. This is the love of God. The loss of this was the greatest injury sustained by the fall. The recovery of a disposition to love God supremely, is the richest blessing brought to us by the gospel. This is the end of redemption. By regeneration love is implanted again in the human soul, which has a natural capacity for this affection; so that when implanted, it takes deep root. But in the beginning, this affection is commonly feeble: in all, it is imperfect. The spiritual birth is analogous to the natural. All partake of life by this birth, but not all in an equal degree. Some are strong and lively from the moment of their conversion, while others are weak and sickly, and at first give symptoms of vitality so equivocal, that for some time, it may remain doubtful whether they are dead or alive. But these feeble babes, by means of the sincere milk of the word, may outgrow, and come nearer to the stature of a perfect man in Christ Jesus, than those who commenced their spiritual existence under auspices much more favourable. In all, there is room for growth in grace, that is, in love, while they are tenants of these houses of day. The exhortation in the text implies that Christians are liable to lose the fervour of their first love. They are, indeed, prone to declension. The course of the Christian is like that of a man rowing up the stream; if he is remiss for one moment, he loses some part of the distance before gained. All the tendencies of nature within him are downward; and all the influence from the world is in the same direction. There is need, therefore, of constant exertion. We must not be slothful, nor grow weary in well-doing.

In the sequel, some directions for keeping ourselves in the love of God will be given; and some motives presented, to stimulate my hearers to engage heartily in this work.

DIRECTIONS FOR KEEPING THE HEART IN THE LOVE OF GOD.

1. Carefully shun all those circumstances and things which are known to have a tendency to damp the fervours of love, or to extinguish this holy fire. Here a large field opens, but we have not time to occupy it. A few things only, out of many, can be noticed. Above all, avoid every sinful indulgence. Known, allowed sins, of every kind, are as water to the fire. The love of God cannot live in the heart, where any sin is indulged. Fleshly lusts war against this holy principle. Flee youthful lusts. The love of the world is a common and insidious foe. Avarice may be indulged to a great extent, and yet no overt act committed which will alarm the conscience. We should remember that solemn warning, "If any man love the world, the love of the Father is not in him." "Love not the world nor the things that are in the world." Desire of the good opinion of men, often leads even Christians to an undue conformity to the world.

"How can ye believe," says our Lord, "who receive honour one from another?"

The neglect, or careless performance, of the duties of the closet, cannot but have the effect of cooling the ardour of piety in the soul; especially the neglect of reading the word of God which is calculated to furnish fuel to the fire of divine love.

Avoid, also, contention and strife, as exceedingly inimical to the peaceful spirit of piety. "As much as lieth in you, live peaceably with all men."

Every species of pride and vain glory, tends to extinguish the holy fervours of divine love.

In short, whatever thought, feeling, desire, imagination, word, or action has a tendency to grieve the Holy Spirit, should be solicitously avoided.

2. To keep ourselves in the love of God, we should often meditate on the superlative moral excellence of the divine character, as displayed in his works and word. The habit of associating the idea of God with every object of nature, is one of the happiest which can be formed. It brings God near to us wherever we are, or whatever we may be doing. In all our blessings and enjoyments, we should gratefully acknowledge God as the Author, "the Father of lights, from whom cometh down every good gift, and every perfect gift."

God's providential dealings toward us, personally, in giving us so favourable a lot, in the circumstances of our birth and education in a land of churches, Sabbaths, and Bibles, and in preserving our lives in the midst of dangers, or rescuing us from the grave, when in an unprepared state, should have a powerful effect in stirring up our minds to acts of gratitude.

But nothing so powerfully affects the mind which has within it the principles of true piety, as a contemplation of the love of God as manifested in the gift of his only begotten, and well-beloved Son, to die on the cross for our salvation. "Herein is love, not that we loved God, but that he loved us." "We love him because he first loved us." Nothing is so powerful to excite love as the well-grounded persuasion of the love of God to us. This motive so frequently presented in the Scriptures should not be repudiated as unworthy, or selfish. It is a noble trait in any mind to be susceptible of lively gratitude, for benefits received. Much of true piety on earth, and much of the holy exercises of heaven, consist in the flow of grateful affection. "To him who loved us, and gave himself for us, be honour and glory and praise," will be the everlasting song of the redeemed.

3. Every habit and affection is preserved in vigour, and increased by frequent exercise. If we desire to strengthen any member of our body, or to render our senses more acute and susceptible, we find no method more effectual than to exercise incessantly those parts which we wish to improve. Habits and affections of the mind follow the same law, and are strengthened imperceptibly, but powerfully, by exercise. Even in regard to our affection to earthly friends, if we seldom think of them, and do not enjoy their company, our love grows cold. Hence, memorials of absent friends, and correspondence by letters, are so much in use,

for it is found, that the frequent recollection of those whom we love, keeps alive our affection, which otherwise would be apt to die away for want of exercise. Thus it behoves us to keep ourselves in the love of God, by frequently calling up in our minds the idea of his excellence and his ineffable love to us.

The cultivation of other holy affections, and the conscientious discharge of all incumbent duties, will also help to preserve alive our love to God.

4. The greatest hinderance to the exercise and increase of our love to God, is our blindness of mind and unbelief. The objects of sense too much occupy and interest us; while spiritual and invisible objects are obscurely perceived, and make a feeble and transient impression on the mind. Although we know that God is ever present with us, and takes cognizance of all our thoughts and actions; yet how little are we affected, habitually, by this truth!

In order, therefore, to preserve our souls in the lively exercise of the love of God, we must seek an increase of that faith which is "the substance of things hoped for, and the evidence of things not seen"—that faith which "sees him, that is invisible"—which "looks not at the things which are seen and temporal, but at the things which are not seen, which are eternal." The close connexion between faith and love is manifest from the nature of the case; as no object can be loved which is not perceived; and the more vividly an object of love is presented to the mind, the more is the affection increased in vigour. The Scriptures also teach, that it is "faith which works by love." This connexion between faith and love is distinctly and explicitly taught in the context, "Wherefore, building yourselves up in your most holy faith, praying in the Holy Ghost, keep yourselves in the love of God." Let us, then, often present that important petition, "Lord, increase our faith."

5. But in the words just recited, we are admonished that this desirable object cannot be accomplished by mere human effort. It is a solemn truth, that "without Christ we can do nothing." Hence, while we are exhorted to act, and to exert ourselves to exercise faith, and to keep ourselves in the love of God, we are instructed to "pray in the Holy Ghost." Without the efficient aid of this divine agent, all our efforts will be fruitless; but Christ has graciously assured us, that the Holy Spirit will be given to those who ask for this best of gifts. We need this aid that we may pray aright, "praying in the Holy Ghost," and we need the same efficient operation to give exercise to faith and love, and every grace. It is a delightful promise, that the Holy Spirit shall take up his abode in believers; so that their bodies become, as it were, temples of God. "Hereby we know that he abideth in us by the Spirit which he hath given us." "Ask, and it shall be given you; seek and ye shall find; knock, and it shall be opened unto you. For every one that asketh receiveth, and he that seeketh findeth, and to him that knocketh, it shall be opened. If a son shall ask bread of any of you that is a father, will he give him a stone? or, if he ask a fish, will he for a fish give him a serpent? or if

he shall ask an egg, will he offer him a scorpion? If ye, then, being evil know how to give good gifts unto your children, how much more shall your heavenly Father give the Holy Spirit to them that ask him?"

II. The motives which should induce us to use all means to keep our souls in the love of God, are the strongest that can be conceived.

1. By doing this we shall best glorify God upon earth. Every true Christian has this as his chief end, but all do not keep the object sufficiently before their minds; and all do not pursue steadily that course which leads directly to this end. Inferior objects, because they are present and visible, and occupy the attention of those around us, too frequently draw us off from our proper course. Now, to prevent this forgetfulness and unsteadiness, nothing will be so effectual as the lively exercise of the love of God. This holy affection will give a right direction to the thoughts, and elevate the heart from low and groveling, to high and heavenly objects. The love of God will give alacrity and energy in the performance of every duty; will enable us to bear with patience every affliction; and will render our devotional exercises not only pleasant, but profitable. Unless we have the love of God in exercise, we cannot glorify him; and our most painful services will be worthless.

2. The next motive which should influence us to perform faithfully the duty enjoined in the text, is, that this will be the most effectual method of promoting the welfare and salvation of our fellow

creatures. Man is not placed here to live merely for himself. He is bound to love his neighbour as himself—to do good to all men, especially to the household of faith. He should imitate his divine Master, who went about doing good, both to the bodies and souls of men. Christ expects his disciples to abound in good works, to let their light shine, that others seeing their good works may glorify their Father in heaven. And when he comes to collect his sheep into the eternal fold, he will make their affectionate assiduity in ministering to the necessities and comfort of his poor and afflicted brethren, the measure of the reward which he will confer on them. Now, the love of God is the root from which every branch of true piety springs. The love of our neighbour cannot exist in vigour, unless it derive daily strength from the love of God. If, then, you would abound in the fruits of holiness, be careful to water the root. " Keep yourselves in the love of God," and you will not cease to do good, as you may have opportunity, to your fellow men.

3. Lastly, the more we keep ourselves in the love of God, the more meet shall we be for the heavenly inheritance, where perfect love reigns in every heart. Not only so, but the richer reward will be possessed; for notwithstanding the imperfection of our services, God is pleased to make our good works here, the measure of the reward which he will bestow hereafter. All his people are equally justified, but all will not be equally glorified. " In our Father's house, are many mansions," and

some are doubtless much nearer to the celestial throne than others. Some saints will occupy, in heaven, a much higher and more honourable place than others. All will be as happy as they are capable of being; but the capacity of those who loved God most fervently and constantly, will be greater than that of those who loved less.*

---

* The critical reader will find some of the sentiments of the preceding discourse in the introduction of this; and also that there is a slight shade of difference in the description of the affection of love to God. In regard to this, the author would remark, that no less than forty years intervened between the composition of these two discourses; and the first was for many years out of his possession, and what was written in it was nearly forgotten when the latter was composed. And he would further remark, that between some of the discourses in this volume half a century has elapsed; from which it may be seen that the author's religious sentiments have undergone little change in a long life.

SERMON XIX.

STRENGTH RENEWED BY WAITING ON THE LORD.

But they that wait upon the LORD shall renew their strength; they shall mount up with wings as eagles; they shall run and not be weary; and they shall walk and not faint.—ISAIAH xl. 31.

ALMIGHTY power and infinite wisdom belong unto God. The continual exertion of his power in the sustentation of all things, occasions no weariness to him. As he is strong himself, so he is the source of strength to such as trust in him, although they be weak in themselves. But all who rely on their own strength, though they be young and vigorous, will utterly fail; for as human wisdom, in the sight of God, is counted as folly, so human strength in the most vigorous, is but weakness. These ideas are beautifully expressed by the prophet in the context. "Hast thou not known, hast thou not heard, that the everlasting God, the LORD, the Creator of the ends of the earth, fainteth not, neither is weary? there is no searching of his understanding. He giveth power to the faint; and to those that have no might he increaseth strength. Even the youths shall faint and be weary, and the young men shall utterly fall. "But they that wait upon the Lord shall renew their strength; they shall mount up with wings as eagles; they shall run and not be weary; they shall walk and not faint." In considering and applying these words, it is proposed, first, to inquire what are the elements of spiritual strength. Secondly, by what means this strength may be acquired and increased. And thirdly, point out some of the benefits and pleasures of spiritual strength.

1. Wherein consists the strength spoken of by the prophet? and what are its elements? The Philistines were utterly unable to find out in what the amazing strength of Samson consisted, until he revealed it to his espoused wife. It was his religious observance of the laws of the Nazarite which occasioned his extraordinary power. Not that long hair could produce bodily strength; but as long as he was obedient to the Nazarite vow, the Spirit of the Lord was with him, and when there was an occasion to require a great exertion of strength, enabled him to put it forth, to a degree, never observed in any other man. His uncommon bodily strength, therefore, was from the Lord; and when He departed from him, he became weak as another man.

But the strength spoken of in our text is evidently not corporeal strength; it is a power seated in the mind; but neither is it intellectual vigour. It is often found in persons of weak understanding, and in minds not highly cultivated by refined education. The strength spoken of by the prophet is evidently a moral, or more properly, a spiritual quality. As bodily health is only found in a well balanced and healthy state of the corporeal functions; so spiritual strength can only be found in souls into which new life has been infused, and is in vigorous exercise. The elements of this strength are, 1. Faith, genuine faith, founded on divine illumination. This is the mainspring of all spiritual exercises. All men are influenced and governed by some kind of faith; but worldly men have no true faith in things spiritual and invisible. It is not meant, that many, from education or from the convictions of reason, do not give a firm assent to the reality of such things, and thus possess a certain kind of faith; but it does not bring before the mind the true nature of spiritual things; that is, their beauty and glory; and, therefore, they are but little influenced by their belief. "The natural man receiveth not the things of the Spirit of God; they are foolishness unto him, neither can he know them, because they are spiritually discerned. But the spiritual man judgeth all things."

Spiritual strength especially consists in that exercise of faith, called trust or confidence. This is the nature of the mind's full persuasion, when a divine promise is the object. However weak the believer feels himself to be, he possesses all needful strength when his confidence is in God. Yea, when he feels himself most weak, then is he strongest—"strong in the Lord, and in the power of his might."

Again, another element of strength is in the affections. When love to God is ardent and constant in its exercise, then there is real strength. In our present clouded and imperfect state, this affection is more manifested by desire than delight. The soul which pants after the presence of God, and hungers and thirsts after righteousness, is in a state of vigorous health.

But the essence of spiritual strength resides in the will. A fixed purpose is that which more clearly characterizes the genuine Christian than any thing else. When the determination of the will is not only fixed but strong, then the soul is in a vigorous state. Many have raised affections, at times, who never arrive at any fixedness and strength of purpose. Some whose will is inclined to the right side, possess no strength of purpose; their resolution to serve God is easily shaken. Others are continually vacillating between the service of God and the world. These are not strong. They may be babes in Christ, but they have not attained to the maturity and vigour of young men. The apostle John describes such when he says, "I have written unto you, young men, because ye are strong." The royal Psalmist possessed this element of strength, when he exclaimed, "My heart is fixed, O God, my heart is fixed;" and Joshua, when before the whole congregated elders of Israel, he said, "But as for me and my house, we will serve the Lord." Energy properly appertains to the will; indeed, it is nothing else but a strong will; and where this exists there will be active exertion. Where there is strength there will be diligence in well-doing. Indolence is incompatible with spiritual energy; it is its opposite, its most insidious foe.

Humility, meekness, peace, and joy, may not seem, at first view, to contribute any thing to strength, but in truth they are among the necessary elements of this vigour of mind. There may be a vigour which is the effect of a disordered state of the corporeal system—a feverish or spasmodic action, which is much more violent than the strength of a healthy man. So, in religion, there often is observed an unnatural energy and enthusiastic vehemence. This is not genuine strength, but real disease. True piety has no greater enemy than fanaticism, which some are so undiscriminating, as to confound with the fervours of true religion. It is strange fire, which should never be brought into the sanctuary of God. The more powerful any machine, the more it needs a regulator—something to balance, harmonize and direct its action. So in religion, zeal and energy are necessary to strength, but they need something to moderate and guide them. Humility is a just estimation of ourselves, physically and morally. If it is wanting, the soul will be irregular in its religious exercises; and its exertions will be misdirected. Humility is to the Christian what ballast is to the ship; it keeps him in his proper position, and regulates all his thoughts and feelings. A ship, with all its sails expanded to the wind, if it were without ballast, would be capsized by the first violent blast; thus many high professors in the church make speedy shipwreck, because they go forth without humility.

There are also occasions, when the best thing the believer can do is to sit still and cease from his own exertions; when every thing must be looked for from God. Such a case occurred to the Israelites when they arrived at the shore of the Red Sea. They were pursued by the Egyptian army, with whom they were unable to contend. They were hemmed in on the right and left, and the sea was before them. In such circumstances, their own efforts were perfectly useless; their help could come alone from God. Moses, therefore, said to the people, "Stand still, and see the salvation of God." In the thirtieth chapter of Isaiah, we have two remarkable texts pertinent to this point. "Their strength is to sit still." And again, "In quietness and confidence shall be your strength." Often the Christian finds all resources exhausted, and yet there is no deliverance. He finds that his own exertions can accomplish nothing; and all he can do is to wait on God—to stand still and let the Lord do his own work in his own way. Indeed, often our own exertions answer no other purpose than to convince us of our helplessness, and that is the condition of the soul, when the most eminent deliverances are experienced. He says, "Be still, and know that I am God."

That holy joy is an element of strength is evident from the words of the prophet Nahum, "For the joy of the Lord is your strength." Most esteem joy to be a high privilege; but few feel that it is a commanded duty. "Rejoice in the Lord," says Paul, "and again I say rejoice." Joy and peace are mentioned as the fruits of the Spirit, next after love, to which these emotions are nearly allied. Paul also informs us that he not only rejoiced in the glory of God, but in tribulation; and the prophet Habakkuk has left us a lively and beautiful expression of his elevated feelings, where he says, "Though the fig-tree shall not blossom, nor fruit be in the vines; the labour of the olive shall fail, and the fields shall yield no meat; the flock shall be cut off from the fold, and there shall be no herd in the stalls; yet I will rejoice in the Lord; I will joy in the God of my salvation." While grief and dejection debilitate the soul, joy not only animates but nerves the mind with resolution and strength. Christians who hang their heads as a bulrush, and whose spirits are low, and feelings sorrowful, are incapable of much enterprise or vigorous exertion.

The only other ingredient of spiritual strength is zeal, pure zeal, zeal according to knowledge. Zeal to the soul is what animal heat is to the body. Without warmth in our desires and feelings we shall be found feeble and sickly. As was before stated there is a feverish heat which is much more vehement, than that which is healthy. Fanatics and enthusiasts are over heated; but this undue excitement is sure to be followed by a collapse—a cold season, which often is connected with death. But if there be life in the body, there will be heat, and it is one sure symptom of vitality. Zeal gives an impulse to the mind. Zeal fills the soul with courage to encounter enemies and surmount obstacles. Zeal is requisite in every arduous work, and enables the Christian pilgrim to bear adversity, and to achieve works of benevolence and piety, which, without it, would be impracticable.

II. We come in the second place to inquire how spiritual strength may be acquired; and how renewed, when it has been impaired. It has already been shown that the source of this strength is not in ourselves but in God. We are not exhorted, therefore, to be strong in ourselves, but "in the Lord, and in the power of his might." But, in order to obtain aid from on high, we must make use of the appointed and appropriate means. These are all comprehended in one expression; "waiting on the Lord." Let us, then, attentively consider what is included in the duty here recognized. The allusion is probably to the case of persons waiting in the antechamber, or some appointed place, for the entrance of a prince, or other exalted personage, whose aid is sought in some concern of moment. Suppliants cannot command the presence of a king or great man with whom they have business; they must wait his leisure or convenience; and sometimes such petitioners are kept long waiting. The petition may be sent in through the proper medium, and an answer is expected; but the suppliant must wait until it is received. Analogous to this is the condition of those who seek God. They must attend where he has appointed to meet with humble worshippers. If no means of access had been appointed, they could have little encouragement to prosecute their suit; or if they devise means which he has never sanctioned, they need not expect a favourable answer; but the question put to some of old will be applicable to them, "Who hath required this at your hands?" And the words of our Lord show that such seeking will be without fruit, "In vain do they worship me, teaching for doctrines the commandments of men."

Now, it is our happiness to know, that means of access to God have been appointed. The public worship of God in the assemblies of his people, where prayer and praise are offered, and where his word is preached and ordinances dispensed, affords to every sincere seeker an opportunity of drawing nigh to God, and presenting his petitions; for the prayers which are offered are in the name of all who join in the service. And often, through the word, the very information which we need is communicated; and not only do we receive light by the word, but strength and comfort. Therefore, where God has recorded his name; wherever the silver trumpet is sounded, and the people of God are congregated, there God is present in the midst of the assembly; and there should all who desire any blessing of the Lord present themselves. There should they be found waiting to hear what the Lord will speak. Often has he there spoken peace to his waiting people; so that they have said in their hearts, "It is good to be here," and have felt reluctant to depart. Souls oppressed with a load of guilt, have by waiting on the Lord, in his house, often been relieved of their burden, by rolling it on the Lord, according to his gracious invitation; that is, by faith in Christ crucified, they have obtained assurance of the pardon of their sins. And persons, whose minds are clouded and perplexed with doubts and unbelieving suggestions, by going into the sanctuary, like Asaph, experience a speedy relief, and find their faith which was shaken, wonderfully confirmed. This ancient saint, the author of several precious psalms, seems to have been a man of a sorrowful spirit, and much harassed with skeptical thoughts respecting divine providence; especially, when he saw the prosperity of the wicked, and contrasted their thoughtless ease and security with his own daily afflictions, his feet had well nigh slipped. But on entering the sanctuary, he obtained such a view of the dangerous condition of the wicked, as standing on a slippery precipice, that all his doubts were dispelled; and his soul was filled with divine consolation, so that he could exclaim, "Whom have I in heaven but thee? and there is none in all the earth, that I desire besides thee." And from his own delightful experience, he could say, in the conclusion of the psalm, "It is good for me to draw near to God."

But believers are not restricted to public ordinances; they are encouraged to meet with two or three, and Christ promises to be in the midst of them, and to grant any petition which they shall agree to offer. And not only so, but the throne of grace is accessible by individuals, at all times, and in all places. "When thou prayest," says our Lord, "enter into thy closet, and pray to thy Father in secret; and thy Father who seeth in secret, shall reward thee openly." The fervent effectual prayer of one righteous man availeth much, as is proved by the case of Elijah. And greater encouragement to prayer could not be given, than the words of our

Saviour afford, "Ask, and ye shall receive; seek, and ye shall find; knock, and it shall be opened unto you; for he that asketh receiveth, and he that seeketh findeth, and to him that knocketh, it shall be opened." And as the influence of the Holy Spirit is the sum of all spiritual blessings, the promise of this rich and comprehensive gift, is enforced in the most emphatical manner: and we are taught, that in some cases, fasting should accompany our prayers. Three things are plainly implied in the expression, "waiting on the Lord." First, a desire of some benefit, with a petition for the same. Secondly, the exercise of patience. And thirdly, the expectation of receiving what is asked. The desire will be earnest in proportion to our sense of the wants under which we labour. A deep sense of sin and apprehension of the punishment to which it exposes us, will produce importunity in our petitions; and such prayers are effectual. A feeling of unworthiness and entire dependence will cause the soul to wait patiently until it shall please the Lord to show himself favourable, and to return an answer to its earnest petition. We are never more in the way of success in our waiting, than when we are conscious that we deserve nothing, and that a sovereign God, without injustice, might cast us off for ever. Our hope of acceptance in waiting on the Lord is based on nothing else but the mercy of God, the merit and intercession of Christ, and the gracious declarations and promises of God, in which he appears disposed to save the lost, to pardon the sinner, and justify the ungodly, who believeth in Jesus.

And the liveliness of our hope will be in proportion to the strength of our faith. When this is vigorous, the assurance of hope will be enjoyed. Often, in fervent believing supplication, at a throne of grace, for mercy, there is a delightful assurance that our prayer is heard, and that we have the blessing for which we earnestly prayed.

Perseverance is also implied in waiting on the Lord. This, indeed, is included in the patience which has been mentioned. Some seekers, if they meet not with immediate success, are offended, or discouraged, and cease from striving, as believing that it is in vain. Such, although they might promise well at first, yet soon fall away, and not only lose their own souls, but become a stumbling block to others. But souls truly convinced of sin, persevere in waiting. Their determination is, if they perish, to perish at a throne of grace. No consideration will induce them to give over seeking. And all such do find mercy, and obtain from the Lord, the blessings which they seek.

In the third place, let us consider what benefits and aids they receive, who wait upon the Lord. They are said, in our text, " to mount up on wings as eagles." The soul of fallen man naturally grovels on the earth; his face instead of being raised to heaven, is prone toward the ground. But when the Holy Spirit enters into any man, his thoughts and affections are raised to those things which are above, where Christ sitteth on the right hand of God. By the indwelling of the Holy Ghost, faith, love, and hope are brought into lively exercise; and these are as pinions to the soul; under their influence it rises from the earth, and soars on high, like the eagle in its flight; and, like the same, gazes on the sun, not the visible luminary, but the Sun of Righteousness. When, by faith the regenerated soul draws near to God, the earth appears to recede; all its objects are seen to be diminutive; and the realities of the heavenly state are perceived, and operate with power on the susceptible mind. The affections, which may be called the wings of the soul, mount on high; and it is borne upwards and rejoices in the view of the glory of God, and in the lively hope of dwelling with him for ever. But such seasons of elevated devotion, and delightful contemplation, are not constant. Zion's pilgrim experiences night as well as day. He has his nights of weeping, and often fears that the mercy of God is clean gone. But through whatever vicissitudes of feeling he passes, in one thing he is uniform, both in the light and in the shade, on the mount and in the valley, in trouble and in joy; his *purpose* never varies. His determination to continue seeking God never wavers. He can say, under all circumstances, "My heart is fixed, O God, my heart is fixed."

In general, the course of the humble believer, is not an eagle's flight; if he enjoys seasons of this kind, they are few and far between; yet he rejoices in the recollection of them, and the very places where they were experienced, remain fresh in his memory, as we observe in the case of the royal Psalmist. When his soul was cast down within him, he encouraged himself by calling to mind former deliverances. "Therefore," says he, "I will remember thee, from the land of Jordan and the Hermonites—from the hill Mizar."

Our text speaks not only of flying, but of running and walking. There is a race to be run, in which the strong young men utterly fall; but they that renew their strength by waiting on the Lord, are enabled to run in this race without growing weary. Their strength is not in themselves, but in the Lord, and this is the reason why they do not grow weary. Their strength is continually renewed by waiting on the Lord; so that they never grow weary of well-doing. They never become tired of the service of their divine Master; their greatest trouble is, that they are able to do so little for him, who has done so much for them. Though running is necessary in winning a prize in a race; yet a journey or pilgrimage cannot be pursued in this way. Steady walking is the common method of performing a pilgrimage. And when the journey is long and the place to be visited far distant, human strength is apt to fail, and the weary traveller to become faint. In this case the suggestion of prudence is, that he turn aside for a season, and rest his fatigued limbs, and seek some refreshment. This is especially necessary to Zion's traveller. And he knows where refreshment and a recruit of strength can be obtained. The Lord is his strength. By waiting on him, he is enabled to pursue his journey to the end, without fainting by the way.

REFLECTIONS.

1. "The men of this world are wiser in their generation than the children of light." When the body is debilitated and needs to be strengthened, they spare no pains or expense to recover impaired health. If they hear of a medicinal spring, far off in the mountains, they hesitate not to undertake the journey, and undergo the hardships of the rugged way, that they may test the efficacy of the mineral waters. And this is done commonly, in the greatest uncertainty, whether the means will prove effectual. The diseased in body will apply to the most skilful physicians, and be at any expense, which they can afford, to procure the medicines prescribed. But although there is a fountain opened for sin and uncleanness, yet how slow are men to avail themselves of this effectual means of purification! Although a great and infallible Physician offers his services, with all needed remedies to heal the diseases of the soul, and not only so, but to confer immortal life on every one who is willing to come to him, and confide his case entirely to his hands; yet, notwithstanding that multitudes who are perishing are within reach of the great Physician, and hear his kind invitation every week, they refuse to apply to him, and are unwilling to submit to his prescriptions.

2. As our natural life requires to be nourished by suitable food, from day to day, without which it would decline, and death would ensue; so the spiritual life of the Christian needs to be recruited

continually, with the nutriment which is suited to its growth and strength; and if this be withheld, or sparingly partaken of, the soul will lose its healthful vigour, and will languish and fall into dangerous diseases. Of their daily bread men in health are led to partake by the stimulus of appetite; so that there is no occasion to exhort them to attend to this matter: but in regard to spiritual nutriment, there is often in many professors, a manifest defect of both taste and appetite; so that while the means are accessible, and that without expense or trouble, yet they are neglected; and the spiritual life remains languid, exhibiting few symptoms of vitality, and none of strength. Or, as there is too much reason to fear, in many cases, the principle of life is wanting. Having a name to live, they are dead, and no more enjoy the rich provisions of the house of God, than a dead man would the mos savoury and nourishing food. A love to divine ordinances, and a disposition to wait upon God in attendance on them, in private as well as in public, may be given as one test of Christian character.

3. Although every degree of spiritual strength is a precious possession, and we are not permitted "to despise the day of small things," nor to reject from our fellowship those who are weak in the faith; yet it is the duty and privilege of every believer to aim at high attainments in the divine life, and to encourage and aid others in doing the same. They should be covetous of those rich experiences in the divine life, which are represented by mounting up as on wings of an eagle. Such elevated seasons of religious experience are not only inexpressibly

delightful, but exceedingly profitable. One day thus spent, whether in the sanctuary or in the closet, is better than a thousand in worldly business and carnal pleasures. The soul thus favoured possesses an evidence of the truth of the Christian religion, which no other can have. Such elevated views and affections also give an impulse to the soul in its spiritual progress which is like to that which a ship receives from a favourable wind springing up, after the experience of head winds or a calm.

But if we should not be so highly favoured as to be able thus to mount and fly, yet we should certainly not be contented to creep, when, by renewing our strength, we may run and yet not be weary, and walk and not faint. Some who are strong in the Lord, are men of a sorrowful spirit, and subject to fearful conflicts, but God causes them to triumph, and following the Captain of salvation wherever he leads, through evil and through good report, they are made more than conquerors, through his love, through his merit, through his faithfulness, and through his power.

Blessed, then, are all they who continually wait on the Lord; for they will enjoy spiritual health and vigour, while those who rely on their own strength shall utterly fall.

SERMON XX.

THE TRUE ISRAELITE.

Behold, an Israelite, indeed, in whom is no guile.—JOHN i. 47.

NATHANAEL, to whom our text refers, was of Galilee, of the town of Cana; and though a good man, was not without his prejudices; for when Philip, after having seen Jesus, accosted him, saying, "We have found him of whom Moses in the law, and the prophets did write, Jesus of Nazareth, the son of Joseph;" Nathanael replied, "Can there any good thing come out of Nazareth?" Philip persuaded that nothing else was necessary to remove his friend's prejudices than a personal interview with Jesus, invited him to go with him, and see the remarkable person of whom he spake. With this invitation, Nathanael immediately complied. When Jesus saw Nathanael coming, he uttered the words of our text, "Behold, an Israelite, indeed, in whom is no guile." Nathanael, surprized at such a salutation from a stranger, said, "Whence knowest thou me?" Jesus answered, "Before that Philip called thee, when thou wast under the fig-tree, I saw thee." How Nathanael was occupied at the time referred to, must be a matter of conjecture; but it is not improbable that he had been engaged in holding secret communion with God, when alone under the fig-tree. He was, therefore, at once convinced of the omniscience of Jesus, and that he was certainly the true Messiah. His prejudices, arising from the supposed place of our Lord's origin, were for ever dispersed; and the good man exclaimed, "Rabbi, thou art the Son of God, thou art the King of Israel. Jesus answered, and said, Because I said unto thee, I saw thee under the fig-tree, believest thou? thou shalt see greater things than these. Verily, verily, I say unto thee, hereafter ye shall see heaven open, and the angels of God ascending and descending on the Son of man." Whether this promise was fulfilled on the day of our Lord's ascension to heaven, when a multitude of angels came down to accompany him, or at some other time not recorded, we cannot positively determine. It might, for aught we know, have been fulfilled, on several occasions. Most expositors are of opinion, that Nathanael became one of the twelve apostles, and was more commonly known by the name Bartholomew, than by the name here given.

Our object in the sequel of the discourse shall be to delineate the character which Christ ascribes to Nathanael, "an Israelite, indeed, in whom is no guile."

1. It imported that he was a true son of Abraham. From the Holy Scriptures we learn, that the

children of Abraham are of two kinds; "they that are born after the flesh, and they that are born after the promise." And the apostle Paul teaches, that "they are not all Israel who are of Israel." "Neither, because they are the seed of Abraham, are they all children;" that "they which are children of the flesh, these are not the children of God, but the children of the promise—these are counted for the children.' Nathanael was called an "Israelite indeed," not because he was a natural descendant of Abraham; for in this sense the words might have been as properly applied to every individual of the Jewish nation. There is an emphasis on the word *indeed.* It means, that he was a genuine son; one who truly resembled Abraham in his faith and piety. Christ, in his conversation with the Jews, recorded in the eighth chapter of this book, denies that the unbelieving Jews could with propriety be denominated the children of Abraham. "If ye were Abraham's children," says he, "ye would do the works of Abraham." He had admitted, indeed, that as to natural descent, they were the seed of Abraham; but in the more important sense, he denies their claim to this appellation, as their conduct proved them to be of a character entirely opposite to that of the patriarch. Abraham was constituted the father of all true believers; not merely of those descended from him according to the flesh, "For the promise that he should be the heir of the world, was not made to Abraham and his seed, through the law, but through the righteousness of faith, therefore, it is of faith, that it might be by grace, to the end that the promise might be sure to all the seed, not that only which is of the law, but to that also which is of the faith of Abraham, who is the father of us all."

The conclusion which the apostle Paul draws, in another place, is, "If ye be Christ's, then are ye Abraham's seed, and heirs according to the promise." "For he is not a Jew who is one outwardly, but he is a Jew who is one inwardly." "Know ye, therefore, that they who are of faith, are the children of Abraham."

Faith, then, is the characteristic of a true Israelite. This was the trait which was most remarkable in the life of this patriarch. Whatever God promised, he fully believed; whatever God commanded, he hesitated not to do. The testimony given of his faith is, that "he staggered not at the promise through unbelief; but was strong in faith, giving glory to God. Being fully persuaded, that what he promised, he was able to perform."

The same readiness to believe, seems to have been the disposition of Nathanael. It was, therefore, no doubt, on account of his faith that our Lord speaks of him as an "Israelite indeed." And this is the distinguishing feature in the character of every sincere servant of God. Faith is the primary virtue of the Christian life. But the faith of God's elect, must not be confounded with the speculative assent which unsanctified men give to the truth of divine revelation. This is altogether inoperative. It is a dead faith. But the faith of the Christian, is a living and operative principle. It is also fruitful of good works. By its fruits it must be judged. As the apostle James says, "Show me thy faith without thy works, and I will show thee my faith by my works." A genuine faith cannot be unfruitful, for "it works by love and purifies the heart."

2. A true Israelite was one in covenant with God. The nation of Israel were distinguished from all other nations by this circumstance, that God had entered into a solemn covenant with them. Every descendant of Abraham, and every one connected with his family permanently, received the sign of circumcision, which was "a seal of the righteousness of faith." And when God brought his people out of their bondage in Egypt, he entered into covenant with the whole nation, at Sinai, and at Horeb. They thus became a peculiar people, who were favoured with exceeding great and precious privileges; for to them were committed the oracles of God, the covenants of promise, and all the institutions and ordinances of divine worship. But the possession of these external privileges did not interest the people in the spiritual blessings of the covenant of grace, unless they by faith laid hold of the promise, and were thus brought into friendship with God.

The Jews were ever ready to boast of their privileges, and of their being the children of Abraham, and despised all others as being uncircumcised, and out of covenant with God. Both John the Baptist and our Lord took pains to show them that those external privileges would answer them no valuable purpose, unless they became in heart the sincere servants of the most High. The promise, "I will be a God to thee and thy seed," is still in full force, and belongs to every one who has truly entered into covenant with the God of Abraham. Whoever cordially, and unreservedly takes God for his God, Christ for his only Redeemer, and the Holy Spirit for his Sanctifier and Comforter, is in covenant with God. And every such person consents and promises to walk before God uprightly, in obedience to all his commandments and ordinances. To all such, God says, "I will be a father unto you, and ye shall be my sons and daughters." No situation can be so safe and comfortable as to be in covenant with God; for to those who are in this sacred relation, all the promises of the covenant of grace belong. These are exceeding great and precious, and they are all firm and sure. "They are not yea and nay; but are all yea, and amen, in Christ Jesus to the glory of God." Their fulfilment rests on the faithfulness of God, which can never fail. Heaven and earth will pass away, sooner than the least thing which God has promised shall fail of a fulfilment. The true Christian, then, is now the "Israelite indeed," and all things are his, "whether Paul, or Apollos, or Cephas, or life or death, or things present, or things to come, all are yours, and ye are Christ's, and Christ is God's." The covenant of grace is not peculiar to gospel times; pious Israelites were always included in the same covenant of promise, and inherited the same blessings. While the external dispensation of this covenant has been changed, the substance has remained the same. To all true believers, under both the old and new dispensation, God is their reconciled Father; Christ their Prophet, Priest, and King; and the Holy Spirit the source of their spiritual life, and of all their hopes and comforts.

3. A third characteristic of a true Israelite is, that he is a worshipper of the true God. All other nations worshipped idols, and knew not Jehovah the living God. Even of the Samaritans, who professed to worship the God of Israel, our Lord said, "They worship they know not what." The genuine Israelite not only acknowledges Jehovah to be the true and only God, and renders to him external worship, to whom alone all religious worship should be paid; but he worships with the heart—he prays to him with the understanding and with the spirit. Every true Israelite has, as it were, a temple within himself, and God dwells in him. From the altar of his heart he offers daily, morning and evening, and at other times, the incense of a sincere and affectionate heart. To God he gives the best of his services. He brings his whole "body a living sacrifice, holy and acceptable to God, which is his reasonable service." God is a Spirit, and requires those who approach him, to worship him in spirit and in truth. The worship of God, with the true Israelite, is not a mere formal service—a drawing nigh with the mouth, and bowing the knee, but it is a service of the heart, in which its best affections and purposes are consecrated, as first fruits unto God. This service is to him not burdensome, but delightful. He esteems it his highest privilege to draw near to God; and his language is, "One day in thy courts is better than a thousand. I had rather be a door-keeper in the house of God, than to dwell in the tents of sin."

The Israelite indeed shows his sincerity by worshipping God in secret, where his heavenly Father alone witnesses his devotion, as well as in public, where he is seen of men. His family too will attest the constancy and earnestness of his prayers. And, while many around him, may forsake the assembling themselves for the worship of God, the true Israelite will not be found neglecting the prayer-meeting; and on the Lord's day, he rejoices when the doors of the sanctuary are opened; and when his brethren say unto him, "Come, let us go up to the house of the Lord."

4. When giving the character of the true Israelite, we should not omit that circumstance which gave origin to the name Israel. When Jacob was returning with his numerous family from Mesopotamia into Canaan, his native country, from which he had been an exile for more than twenty years, he was thrown into great alarm and consternation, from hearing that his brother Esau, whom he had grievously injured, was coming to meet him with an armed force, of four hundred men. To contend with such an army, he knew that he was not prepared; his only resource was in God. Therefore, after making the best arrangements which he could for the safety of his family, he retired into a private place to pray. And while he was there, a man wrestled with him until the breaking of the day. And he said, Let me go, for the day breaketh; and he (Jacob) said, I will not let thee go unless thou bless me: and he said, What is thy name? and he said, Jacob. And he said, thy name shall no more be called Jacob, but ISRAEL; for, as a prince,

hast thou power with God and with man, and hast prevailed." Thus we see that the import of the name Israel is, "one who has power with God and prevails." Here, then, we have a striking characteristic of the Israelite indeed; he is a mighty wrestler; he wrestles with God, by his fervent desires and importunate prayers. He is one who lays hold of the promises, by a grasp which nothing can loose. He fills his mouth with arguments, and will take no denial.

The exercises of a soul, in offering the prayer of faith with importunity, are well represented by the act of *wrestling;* for in no other case is there a more intense exertion of the mind. We have a remarkable example of that importunity, which would take no denial, in the Syrophenician woman, who applied to our Saviour when he passed near her residence, in behalf of her daughter, who was grievously tormented by a demon. She had no right to lay any claim to the blessings which pertained to Israel, as she was of the accursed race of Canaan which God had doomed to utter destruction. But urged by the necessity of the case, and probably encouraged by a favourable report of Christ's tender compassion to the afflicted, she resolved to make an earnest application. And so repeated and earnest were her cries, that the disciples were annoyed, and requested our Lord to send her away. To this he paid no attention; and the earnest suppliant having pressed through the crowd, approached the person of the Saviour, and falling down before him, said, "Lord, help me." His answer, containing a reference to her alien race, seemed like a complete repulse; for he said, "It is not meet to take the children's bread, and cast it to dogs." But even this, she, in her earnestness, turned into a plea in her favour: "Truth, Lord," said she, "yet the dogs eat of the crumbs which fall from the Master's table." Though of the race of the Canaanites, she was indeed an Israelite, in spirit; for she would not let him go until he blessed her. His final answer to her petition is remarkable; for it evinces, that the answer to believing prayer is not restricted to any nation, nor dependent on any external relations or religious rites. "Jesus answered and said unto her, O woman, great is thy faith; be it unto thee as thou wilt. And her daughter was made whole from that hour."

5. The only other characteristic which I shall mention as distinguishing the true Israelite, is, that he has the promise of an inheritance. To Israel after the flesh, the land of Canaan was promised. First, this promise was made to Abraham, then to Isaac and Jacob; and afterwards, was renewed to the people of Israel, even when they were slaves in a foreign land. To give them possession of the promised land, they were brought out of Egypt, by the hand of Moses and Aaron, and were conducted through a barren and howling wilderness, that they might receive possession of their promised inheritance; and although many failed to enter in because of unbelief, yet Israel, as a nation, were introduced into this land, under the guidance of Joshua; and every Israelite received an allotment in this pleasant land, which is constantly described

as "flowing with milk and honey." So also, the spiritual Israelite, the son of Abraham by a participation of his faith, has received the promise of an inheritance, a heavenly Canaan, where he shall rest from all his conflicts and all his toils and temptations. There already, we know from the infallible word of our Lord himself, are Abraham, Isaac and Jacob; and all the children of Abraham who died in the faith are gathered to their father's bosom; where they shall enjoy eternal peace and consolation, far beyond what they can now conceive. "There remaineth a rest for the people of God." This inheritance is described by the apostle Peter, as "incorruptible, undefiled, and that fadeth not away." And it is reserved for all believers; and is made sure to them, for they are kept by the power of God, through faith unto salvation.

Israel, when all who belong to this holy nation shall be gathered together, will indeed be more numerous than the stars of heaven. They will form a company, which no man can number, and every one of them will possess a true heart, an undissembled love to their Joshua, and a fervent love to one another; and every Israelite shall enjoy his allotted portion.

It may be useful to make a few remarks on this interesting portion of the evangelical history; and

1. The conduct of Philip must be highly approved, and should be imitated. He had found the Saviour, and was fully persuaded, that he was the Messiah, predicted by Moses in the law, and

by all the prophets, and therefore he desires to make his friends also acquainted with the divine Redeemer. This is often observed in genuine converts. One of their first thoughts after experiencng pardoning mercy, is, to bring to the Saviour their friends and acquaintances. Too often, however, not meeting with the success which they expected, they cease their efforts, and give up the hope of their conversion, as desperate; or, at least, as not likely to be accomplished through their instrumentality. In this they do wrong. They should never despair of the salvation of any one; and should never cease to invite and urge them to come to Christ, for there is no other name by which they can be saved.

2. We may learn from the case of Nathanael, that although good men are subject to be prejudiced against the servants of God, yet, when they have the opportunity of being better acquainted with them, these prejudices are sure to be dissipated; and their dislike converted into cordial attachment. It is, therefore, a very desirable thing to bring the people of God, and especially, the ministers of the gospel, into a more intimate acquaintance with each other. By this means, they will find that most of their prejudices were unfounded, and that there is a nearer agreement among the children of God, in all practical matters, and especially, in their religious exercises, than either party apprehended. They may, and do differ in their speculative opinions, and in their external forms of worship; but such a difference is consistent with their being of one heart, and of one spirit. Bigoted sectaries

aim to keep up the walls of separation, but Christian love pants after unity with all the real children of God.

3. Another remark suggested by the history of Nathanael is, that our Lord is the witness of every action of our lives; and especially, of every exercise of devotion. He sees us, when we are concealed from the view of all mortals. He hears the prayer which is offered up, in the recesses of the forest or grove. Nathanael, under the fig-tree, felt himself to be retired from all the world, but there the eye of Christ was upon him. Hannah, when she wrestled with God for her Samuel and was heard, uttered no sound, but only moved her lips. No person present knew what was passing in her mind. Eli, the priest, who observed that she was much agitated by some internal cause, uncharitably attributed it to strong drink; but God, who searcheth the heart, knew the fervent desires of her inmost soul, and immediately returned an answer; in mercy bestowing the very gift for which she so earnestly prayed. The softest whisper of prayer, when prompted by sincere faith enters into the ears of the Lord of Sabaoth. It is not necessary to the efficacy of prayer, that it should be expressed even in a whisper; for our Lord would have all the churches to know that it is he who "searcheth the reins and the hearts." Therefore, the sincere desire which is not expressed by any external sign, is known to him, and is as acceptable as if uttered in a loud voice. We do indeed, read much in the Psalms of crying aloud

unto God; and it is very natural for strong desires to seek for expression by the voice. It is often profitable to employ our voice even in secret prayer, because the sound of our own voice has a tendency to confine the thoughts from wandering, and also to stir up some lively emotion within us. An experienced writer recommends the chanting of the Psalms, in the tone which nature prompts, as serviceable to excite the sluggish feelings. But still, the secret breathing of the heart is real prayer, and is often heard and answered. Through unbelief, we are prone to think of God as removed to a great distance from us, whereas we ought to have the impressive conviction, that we are in his immediate presence, and that he is the witness of all the desires and emotions of our hearts. In nothing, is there a greater difference between our theoretical and practical belief, than in regard to the omnipresence and omniscience of God. No Christian ever hesitates about ascribing these attributes to Jehovah; but alas! how faint is the impression of these truths on our minds; even when professedly engaged in his solemn worship.

4. Finally, we learn from our Lord's address to Nathanael, that sincerity in our religion is essential. He is described as being "without guile." Nothing, not even open impiety, is more odious in the sight of God, than hypocrisy. On account of this vice, our blessed Lord denounced, in the severest language, the Pharisees of his day, who made the loudest professions, and exhibited to the world the greatest show of devotion and strict godliness.

He compares them to whited sepulchres, which although beautiful without, were within full of rottenness and dead men's bones. They made clean the outside of the cup and platter, but altogether neglected to cleanse the inside; whereas, all that is excellent in religion must come from the heart. As out of it proceed evil thoughts and every species of sin; so it is also the seat of every Christian virtue, and of every holy temper. The fear of God, the love of God, faith, penitence, humility, submission, zeal, brotherly love, and every other pious exercise must proceed from the heart. One characteristic of the wisdom which is from above—which is nothing else than true religion—is, that it is " without hypocrisy."

Let us, then, be diligent in searching our own hearts, to ascertain whether indeed we belong to the true Israel of God—whether we are in the faith—whether Christ dwells in us—whether he possesses the throne in our hearts—whether we are divorced from all our former idols—whether we have evidence of having been renewed in the spirit of our minds—whether we are united to Christ as the living branch to the vine—and whether, as an evidence of this union, we are new creatures, old things having passed away, and all things become new.

Sincere religion is not that which a man believes to be right, but it is that which *is* right. In the New Testament sense, sincerity is that which will stand the strictest scrutiny—which will bear to be examined in the clearest light.

Now, as the consequences of being right, and possessing genuine piety, are of infinite moment, we ought to give the subject our utmost attention and never rest, until every doubt is removed; and as our hearts are deceitful above all things, we should most earnestly pray to God, to search and try us; lest at last, we should discover, when it is too late, that we were not of the number of the true, spiritual Israel.

SERMON XXI.

GOD TO BE GLORIFIED BY THOSE BOUGHT WITH A PRICE.

Ye are not your own, for ye are bought with a price; therefore glorify God in your body, and in your spirit which are God's.—1 Cor. vi. 19, 20.

The religion of the Bible relates to the two great branches of human duty, the things to be *believed*, and the things to be *done*. These truths are exhibited in various methods; sometimes in a more general and comprehensive manner, and at other times particular points are distinctly brought into view. The doctrines and precepts of the gospel, though they may be distinguished, must not be separated. There exists an intimate connexion between them. The objects of our faith are not matters of mere speculation; they furnish the motives which should impel the Christian to the performance of duty; and duty cannot be rightly performed, unless under the influence of the belief of these doctrines. Faith and good works have, therefore, an indissoluble connexion, so that where there are no good works, it must be concluded, that, whatever boast may be made of believing the truth, the faith is not genuine and saving.

In the words of the text, we have a doctrine and a duty inculcated in their relation to each other. The duty is so comprehensive, that it includes the whole circle of Christian duties, for it is a command to glorify God with our bodies and spirits; and evidently, this comprehends every duty which God requires of man. The doctrine taught, and presented as a motive for our obedience, is so powerful, that though it cannot be said strictly to embrace every doctrine of the gospel, yet it supersedes the necessity of calling in the aid of any other motive. It is the doctrine of REDEMPTION—redemption from sin and misery by a ransom—a ranson of such inestimable value, that nothing can be added to it. They who are thus redeemed from death, by another, are no longer their own. All their faculties belong to him who has bought them. They are bound by the law of gratitude to conform their conduct, henceforth, to the will of their Redeemer.

In the further prosecution of the subject, we shall first consider the duty; and secondly, the motive offered for its performance.

1. The duty is, "to glorify God, with our bodies and spirits." Let us begin with the latter. How may we glorify God with our spirits, that is, with our rational souls?

This we may do, in the first place, by making use of the reason with which we are endowed, in contemplating the character of God as made known to us in his works and in his word. To enable us to perform this duty was the principal end of our Creator, in making us intelligent beings; and our reason can never be exercised on any subject so noble and excellent. And as our rational faculties were given to enable us to contemplate the divine attributes, so also to search after the knowledge of God. Although "none by searching can find out the Almighty to perfection," yet, by diligent attention to the book of nature, and to the Bible, we may learn much of God that was not apparent at the first view. Every rational creature should, therefore, seek assiduously to know God, as far as he has revealed himself. Things unrevealed, we have no concern with. They do not respect our faith and practice; and it is presumptuous in us to endeavour to pry into them, according to that declaration in the law, "The secret things belong unto the Lord, our God, but those things which are revealed, belong to us and our children for ever, that we may do all the words of this law."

Again, we glorify God when we readily and firmly believe and rely upon all that he has said. God is better pleased with no act of his creatures than faith in his declarations; especially, when they are contrary to the notions which we naturally adopt from our own reason, as probable. Such a faith was conspicuous in Abraham, on account of which he obtained the honourable appellation of "the father of the faithful." "Who, against hope," as says Paul, "believed in hope, that he might become the father of many nations." Though what God promised seemed impossible, according to the course of nature; yet, "he was not weak in faith' —"he staggered not at the promise through unbelief; but was strong in faith, giving glory to God." We may also glorify God in our spirits, by setting our affections supremely on him, and by the constant and lively exercise of pure love. This, indeed, is the essential thing in religion. Without love or charity, Paul assures us, that all knowledge and all faith will profit nothing. Of all excellent gifts and graces, this is the most excellent, and shall abide for ever.

No honour given to any one can be equal to our sincere and supreme love. This, therefore, was the original demand of the law of God; and as that law is immutable, the same thing is now demanded; and, in the same proportion as we love God, in the same we obey the law; and thus we come to the conclusion, that we cannot glorify God so effectually in any other way, as by obeying his law.

We, moreover, glorify God by forming such purposes as are in accordance with the divine will. The character of every man is determined by the habitual bent and purpose of his will. All human actions flow from the will; this is, therefore, the mainspring of all good conduct. Man's depravity consists mainly in the opposition of his will to the will of God. But when the will is renewed, the purposes of the heart are decidedly for God and his service. The stubborn will, naturally so selfish, is now subdued; and the sincere inquiry of the soul is, What is God's will? Now, such a person can truly say, "My heart is fixed, O God, my heart is fixed." "Thy will be done, as in heaven so in earth." And even when the manifestations of the divine will are contrary to the natural affections and inclinations of the person, he learns to acquiesce in the divine will. "It is the Lord, let him do what seemeth him good."

All our duty, however, does not consist in action. In this world the children of God are all subject to various afflictions. These they are taught to consider as paternal chastisements, which are intended to work in them the peaceable fruits of righteousness; and the rod of chastisement is used to correct their faults, and to make them partakers of his holiness. These afflictions are properly called trials, because they bring to the test our submission to the will of God. It is much easier to be thankful for mercies received, than to be cheerfully submissive when our comforts are taken away. Our natural and lawful affections are apt to become inordinate, and it is found hard to resign our possession of objects which have been long enjoyed. The bereavement of dear friends is a sore affliction. None knows the bitterness of soul produced by the loss of such, until he has had some experience of these trials. However well we may be acquainted with the reasons which should have influence to make us submissive to the will of our heavenly Father, and may assent to them all, and acknowledge their weight; yet, when the trial actually comes upon ourselves, we find theory to be very different from practice. At first, even the Christian under severe chastisement is like "a bullock unaccustomed to the yoke;" but after struggling awhile, he learns to submit, and finds resignation the best remedy for every species of trouble. And in proportion as submission is difficult, on account of its crossing the inclinations of the flesh, in the same proportion is it pleasing to God; and by having our wills swallowed up in the divine will, we glorify God as much as in any other way. Afflicted saints, confined to their beds or their houses, often feel as though they were cut off from all opportunity of glorifying their heavenly Father; whereas they are placed in a situation in which they can glorify him more effectually than by active service. Their humble submission to the divine will, and their cheerful resignation of the dearest objects of their earthly affections, at the call of his providence, is a sacrifice with which God is ever well pleased. We may, in this way, glorify God even in death, when with childlike submission we part with life and all its enjoyments, and give up our souls into the hands of him who gave them. "Whether we live, we live unto the Lord; or whether we die, we die unto the Lord."

Finally, under this head, we glorify God with our spirits, when we constantly and deliberately aim at his glory: when, in all that we do, or undertake, we set before our minds the glory of God, as our highest end; and when, in the ardour of our zeal, we call upon every one around us to join in ascribing glory to his name, and not only so, but invite all nature to join in the chorus of praise. Thus the royal Psalmist often invites all creatures to praise the Lord.

But in our text, the apostle speaks of glorifying

God with our bodies, as well as our spirits. Let us, then, inquire how our bodies may become instruments of glorifying God.

In the first place, we glorify God when our bodies are preserved from impurity and intemperance. This was the very idea which the apostle had in his mind, when he introduced the word *bodies;* for he had just said, in the beginning of the nineteenth verse, "What! know ye not that your bodies are the temple of the Holy Ghost, which is in you, and which ye have of God?" As the temple of God must be holy, so it must be preserved from all impurity of the flesh. This is so offensive to God, that in a parallel passage, it is said, "If any man defile the temple of God, him will God destroy." So, also, the body should be kept free from those disorders and insane perturbations produced by inebriating drinks and drugs, and also from all undue repletion of food. The passions and appetites, which have their seat in the body, must be held under a strong restraint. And as a pure and temperate condition of the body is requisite to the performance of any duty, and necessary to the right exercise of the mind itself, it is a duty of high obligation to keep the body under due government, lest fleshly lusts which war against the soul should subdue it, and involve it in ruin. Paul says, "I keep under my body lest while I preach to others, I myself should be a castaway."

Again, as man consists of body and spirit, and as both have been derived from God, it is reasonable that both should be employed in his service. Various duties requiring bodily action are therefore enjoined; and all the institutions of social and public worship demand the employment of bodily organs and members. We are bound to worship God with our bodies, as well as with our minds. We must bow down before him, and by external actions and gestures, manifest our reverence for the divine majesty.

Besides, God is to be praised with our voice in the assembly of his saints, and it is written, "He that offereth praise, glorifieth me." With the tongue then, we should continually glorify the name of the most High. To animate our praise, we need the aid of sacred music. "Praise ye the Lord; for it is good to sing praises unto our God; for it is pleasant, and praise is comely."

Moreover, as God is glorified by acts of beneficence and charity, and indeed, by every species of good works; and all these require the instrumentality of the body; so we may be said to glorify God by every good work which we can perform. We glorify him by the common labours of our hands, whether in the house, or in the field. Those in the most abject circumstances in the world, have it in their power to glorify God, by diligently performing the duties of their station and places. Thus Paul exhorts servants, who were in bondage, "Obey," says he, "in all things your masters according to the flesh, not with eye-service, as men-pleasers, but in singleness of heart, fearing God; and whatsoever ye do, do it heartily as to the Lord, and not unto men, knowing that of the Lord ye shall receive the reward of the inheritance; for ye serve the Lord Christ."

Our hands may be made to glorify God, when they are opened in acts of liberality and beneficence. When, possessed of abundance of the good things of this life, you supply the wants of Christ's poor brethren, it will be openly acknowledged in the day of judgment. Even if you give a cup of cold water to a disciple in the name of a disciple, you shall not lose your reward. Certainly, he who advances the kingdom of Christ by preaching his gospel, or by contributing to the support of those who do; and who makes a pious and liberal use of the wealth which God has bestowed upon him, does thus glorify Him, from whom wealth is received. Rich men labour under some great disadvantages, as it relates to the salvation of their souls; but they possess one means of glorifying God which others want. They have the "mammon of unrighteousness," by the wise use of which they may make themselves friends. Let them, then, "do good and communicate, for with such sacrifices God is well pleased." O rich man, let not the rust of your hoarded gold and silver testify against you. The talents with which you are entrusted must not be buried, but diligently employed for the interest and honour of your Lord.

In short, we are bound to glorify God in all things. "Whether ye eat or drink, or whatever ye do, do all to the glory of God." Good works send forth a shining light, and have a tendency to lead others, who see them, to glorify our Father in heaven, according to that precept of our Lord "Let your light so shine, that others seeing your good works may glorify your Father in heaven." A holy, exemplary life is the most effectual method of glorifying God, before men. If we set before us, daily, the example of Christ, and follow it, we shall not fail to glorify God. "Let the same mind be in you, which was also in Christ Jesus." Imitate his example, "who went about doing good;" and neglect not to ascribe to God the glory due to his august and holy name.

II. We come to consider and urge the motive for our glorifying God, mentioned in our text. "Ye are not your own—ye are bought with a price." When it is said, that we are not our own, the meaning is, that we are the property of the Lord. Every one has a right to the use and benefit of what properly belongs to him. If we are God's, then he may rightfully require all the service and obedience which we are capable of rendering. If he is our Owner, we should employ our faculties of mind and body to glorify him. The apostle might have founded God's right to us on creation. He who makes any thing, among men, has the best title to it; but man can make nothing unless the materials be furnished. God first produced the material, and then fashioned and constituted it, in a very wonderful manner. But the apostle says nothing of this, and why? because his mind was fully occupied with another subject—REDEMPTION. "Ye are," says he, "bought with a price." The redemption of captives was an idea very familiar to the ancient Greeks and Romans

As by the customs of war, every prisoner was made a slave, it often happened, that persons of wealthy and respectable families, would be thus separated from their parents, brothers, and sisters; and from their wives and children, where they had families of their own. It is not surprising, therefore, that it frequently happened, that the relatives of the captive in slavery, would raise a sum sufficient to ransom their friend, and would send a suitable person to find him out, and to pay his redemption price, and bring him home. Suppose a father or brother to go in search of the lost son or brother. He encounters every peril, by land or sea, makes his way over mountains and deserts, until he arrives at the spot where the captive, confined with chains, is labouring under the lash, it may be, of a cruel master. What would be the feelings, do you suppose, of a number of captives confined together, when it should be announced, that a Redeemer had arrived with a large ransom to deliver some one of them? How, in such circumstances, would alternate hope and fear agitate every bosom! But when the fortunate captive heard his own name called, who can describe his exultation? The good news is so unexpected, and the tidings so joyful, that he at first, can scarcely believe the report. But when he sees the face of his father or brother, and sees the ransom paid, and finds himself freed from his fetters, his heart is as full of joy as it can hold. He springs forward and embraces his kind redeemer. He exults, and weeps, and laughs—and knows not how to give expression to his feelings. This is literally what is meant by redemption. Sometimes, indeed, the word is used for any great deliverance; but primarily and properly, it means to buy with a price. And so the apostle says to the Christians of Corinth, "Ye are bought with a price."

The deliverance of sinners from death by the Lord Jesus Christ, bears therefore a striking analogy to the redemption of captives. Men are taken captive by the devil. They are bound fast in the cords of iniquity. They cannot liberate themselves, nor can this redemption be effected by any one but the Son of God. But, though the analogy is striking, yet there are three circumstances in the redemption of the sinner, which distinguish it from that which takes among men.

1. When one went to redeem his brother or friend, though he might have far to go, and many difficulties to encounter, before he found the unhappy captive, still he had not to go out of the world; but when Christ, as our elder brother, undertook the ransom of his people, it was necessary for him to descend from heaven to earth—from the throne of majesty to a stable and a manger.

2. When an earthly redeemer set off in search of an enslaved son, or brother, he had indeed to obtain and take with him a ransom—and it might be a large sum which was requisite, for those who now held the captive in bondage, would raise their demand in proportion to the wealth of the friends. Still the price consisted of silver or gold or precious stones, or some valuable earthly commodity. But when the Son of God came into the world to redeem lost sinners, he must lay down a ransom of

a very different nature. Silver and gold go for nothing in this transaction. All the treasures in the bowels of the earth are insufficient to redeem one soul. The price required is blood—and no other blood will answer, but that of the Redeemer himself. Yes, the Son of God must assume our nature, that he might have blood to offer as a ransom. "Lo, I come, O God," says he, "to do thy will." "A body hast thou prepared me." Having been "made of a woman, and made under the law," he bore the stroke of divine justice due to the sinner, and by becoming a curse for him, redeemed him from the curse of the law. "For," says Peter, "we are redeemed, not with silver or gold, but with the precious blood of Christ, as of a lamb without blemish and without spot." O Christian! behold the blood flowing from the heart of the Lamb of God. This, this was the price paid for your redemption.

3. This redemption is distinguished from the transaction so called among men, by the nature of the bondage and captivity under which the sinner was confined. He was first under a just sentence of condemnation from the law of God. Next, he was held bound in cords of iniquity, which no created arm could loose. And lastly, he was lying under the cruel tyranny of Satan, the worst of masters. From all these our Redeemer came "to save his people." He removed the curse of the law by bearing it in his own body on the tree. He saves his people also from their sins by the washing of regeneration and the renewing of the Holy Ghost, and he dispossesses Satan by

his superior power. "When a strong man armed keepeth his house, his goods are in peace, but when a stronger than he cometh, he taketh away his armour wherein he trusted and divideth the spoils." Christ came "to destroy the works of the devil." Paul was sent "to turn the heathen from darkness to light, and from the power of Satan to God;" and Christians are "translated from the power of darkness to the kingdom of God's dear Son."

Now, those who have been thus redeemed owe a debt of gratitude which, without exaggeration, may be said to be infinite. No wonder Paul judged it unnecessary to urge other motives. If this has not power to influence us to glorify God, no others can possess such a power. Let us, then, cordially and cheerfully spend our lives in glorifying God, with our body and spirit which are his.

REFLECTIONS.

1. Let us reflect penitently on our culpable neglect of this great duty, of glorifying God with our bodies and spirits which are God's. Though we may not be chargeable with a total neglect of duty; though we may have had this as the highest object of pursuit, for years past; though we may be conscious that we have desired and purposed to make every other pursuit subordinate to this chief end; yet, upon a retrospect of his past life, who is not constrained to confess that there has been a great failure in coming up to the requirements of God, all of which are most reasonable? And not only

have we come short of that perfection which the law demands, but we have not reached that degree of perfection at which we fondly anticipated that we should arrive. Deep humility and sincere repentance are the feelings which should possess our minds in looking back on the past.

2. We should endeavour to obtain a lively feeling of our obligations to the Redeemer. We should often remember, that we are redeemed captives, bought off from a cruel servitude, from galling chains; yea, from certain death, not of the body only, but also of the soul—a death of never ending misery. And let us endeavour to excite within our cold hearts, the emotions of lively gratitude, by contemplating the price of our redemption; not silver or gold, or any mundane treasures, but the precious blood of the Lamb of God! And let us meditate not only on the gift, but on the motive which prompted it. There is no greater mystery than the love of God to sinners. In this love there is a depth, and height, and length, and breadth, which passeth knowledge. What shall we render to the Lord? What can we render for such a benefit? The best return we can make is to give ourselves away to our Redeemer. We are not our own; he hath bought us with a price. All our faculties of mind are his, and should be consecrated to his service. All the members of our bodies should be employed, as "instruments of righteousness." All the power or influence which we may possess over others, should be exerted to bring them to join us in this reasonable and exalted work of glorifying God. All our property should be sacredly devoted

to the service of the Lord. He gave it, and he has a right to it; yea, he has bought ourselves with an inestimable price, and this includes all that we possess. Let those, then, that have wealth consider themselves as the stewards of God; and let them prove faithful in dispensing their Lord's goods. His language to such is, "Occupy till I come."

3. Let us esteem it a great privilege to be the redeemed servants of the Lord. It is the highest honour which we can enjoy; and he never requires his servants to be losers by their sacrifices, labours, and privations for his sake. Our highest happiness also is inseparably connected with the performance of this duty. All who forsake God, forsake the fountain of living waters; but they who glorify him, shall enjoy him for ever. All the inhabitants of heaven glorify God with all their powers; and in glorifying him, they find complete blessedness. Their felicity is sweetly conjoined with their duty. If they should cease to glorify God, they would instantly cease to be happy. The servants of God here below, are only truly happy, while they are found glorifying their Father in heaven. The more we lose sight of self the better. The more we are absorbed in the desire to glorify our Redeemer, the more is our true happiness promoted.

Finally, let us remember that the time which remains to many of us, I may say, all of us, is short. We cannot return to live our lives over again, to finish the work which we may now neglect. If we are convinced that we have not improved the time gone by, as we ought to have done, the only way by which we can redeem lost time is by making the best possible use of what remains. Be up and doing—the night comes on apace—the day is far spent. The Master will soon require of us an account of our stewardship. Every day we should act under the deep impression of the account which we must give to Christ when we stand before his tribunal. Let every one endeavour so to improve the talents committed to him, as to be privileged to hear the welcome laudatory, "Well done good and faithful servant, enter into the joy of thy Lord."

SERMON XXII.

THE WAY IN WHICH GOD LEADS HIS PEOPLE.

And I will bring the blind by a way that they knew not; I will lead them in paths that they have not known: I wi'l make darkness light before them, and crooked things straight. These things will I do unto them, and not forsake them.—ISAIAH xlii. 16.

THE person who speaks, in this place, is JEHOVAH, whom the prophet describes in strains of true sublimity. "Thus saith God the LORD, he that created the heavens, and stretched them out: he that spread forth the earth, and that which came out of it: he that giveth breath unto the people upon it, and spirit to them that walk therein. I am JEHOVAH, that is my name, and my glory will I not give to another, nor my praise to graven images."

In the whole of the former part of this chapter, the character of the Messiah and his rich endowments are described and predicted. And in the words of our text, Jehovah speaks of his chosen people, whom he hath determined to bring to Mount Zion, where the throne and kingdom of Messiah is established for ever. "And I will bring the blind," &c. They are called "blind," because in their state of alienation, they know nothing spiritually of the true God, nor of the way of return to Mount Zion. Their condition is often represented by that of Israel in captivity, in a foreign land, who are entirely ignorant of the way in which they can be released, or of the pathway by which they may return to Mount Zion. Spiritual blindness hangs heavy on the eyes of all the true Israel, in their natural state. They are "darkness"—they are "children of wrath even as others."

But Jehovah promises to lead his blind people in the right way to Zion.

Jerusalem and Zion were the established types of the true spiritual church of God; and the way along which they were conducted, in their return from Babylon, or any foreign land of captivity, will represent the way of salvation. Of this way, God's own chosen people are entirely ignorant, until they are led into it by the teaching of the word and Spirit of the Lord; and they are not merely ignorant of this way, but have taken up exceedingly erroneous conceptions of it. The people of God, in their unregenerate state, are involved in the same darkness which enshrouds the minds of others; and when effectually called, are often found wandering in devious paths, at the remotest distance from the right way.

But in Scripture, "darkness" is not only the emblem of ignorance and error, but of misery also. The place of future misery, is always represented as a place of extreme darkness; and the same figure is often employed to set forth the miseries of this mortal life; and, truly, man in his natural state, is subject to all that this expressive emblem imports. He feels a thousand things which he can neither remove nor mitigate: and the burden of his misery increases with his years. Often, too, such reflections and apprehensions enter his mind, as convince him that the thousandth part of the woe to which he is heir, is not yet felt. He dreads the arrival of that day which will fully make known to him how miserable he is. Against these approaching and accumulating evils, he is acquainted with no better refuge than to shut his eyes and refuse to look the danger in the face; as some silly birds are said to do when closely pursued.

By the illumination of the Holy Spirit, however, this darkness is turned into light. The sun of righteousness arises upon the long benighted soul; and the eye which never saw before, is opened to look upon "a new heaven and a new earth." The darkness disappears, and the dawn of a heavenly day is experienced. "If any man be in Christ, he is a new creature; old things are passed away, behold, all things are become new."

But JEHOVAH not only promises to make darkness light before them, but "crooked things straight." The ways of iniquity are called "crooked," because they are deviations from the perfect rule of God's law, which is represented by a straight line; and they may be so called, because of their inconstancy and inconsistency. The sinner first pursues one forbidden object, then another. Continual change seems to be the common lot of transgressors. In childhood, youth, manhood, old age, different objects are pursued. There is a perpetual turning from one pursuit to another; yet every path in which he goes is "crooked." His ways are also inconsistent. There is no harmony in sin. One strong passion impels the sinner in one direction; then another urges him in a different course; and sometimes the one, and sometimes the other, gaining a governing influence over the man, his ways are rendered "crooked." As a ship, without rudder or compass, driven by fierce winds, pursues no steady course; so sinners are driven by every gale, and pursue every course but the right one. But from these crooked paths the sheep of Christ shall be reclaimed, and shall "make straight paths to their feet." They are made to hear the Shepherd's voice and follow him, and shall wander no more; but be led in the highway, which will conduct them through green pastures, and by pleasant streams to Mount Zion, where, collected in the peaceful fold, they "shall go no more out." Finally, JEHOVAH promises that he "will not forsake them." This last promise is essential to their comfort; for if the Great Shepherd should only bring the wandering sheep into the right way, and then forsake them, soon would they be found fatally straying, and would inevitably be lost; or, after leading them along the right way for years, if he, at the last stage of their pilgrimage, should leave his redeemed saints to themselves, the consequence would be, that not one of them would be able to reach the heavenly Jerusalem. So true is that saying of JESUS, "without me ye can do nothing." But our covenant-keeping JEHOVAH pledges his truth, and faithfulness, to his people. He says, "These things will I do unto them, and NOT FORSAKE THEM." Let this sweet promise be as a cordial to our desponding hearts. It is a promise often repeated, as being much needed, for the comfort of God's people. He solemnly declares, "I will never leave thee nor forsake thee:" but lest our timidity and unbelief should suggest that there is still no security, because we may forsake God after all our experience of his love; to render assurance doubly sure, he says, "I will not turn away from them to do them good; but I will put my fear into their hearts, that they shall not depart from me."

Having given a general exposition of the text, our object will now be to show, that from the beginning to the end of their pilgrimage, God leads his people in a way, which previous to experience they know not.

This truth shall be illustrated by the induction of a number of particulars, connected with the leadings of the Spirit and providence of God.

All the acts and operations of the Almighty, in the world of nature, as well as grace, are inscrutable. "There is none by searching can find out God." "The wind bloweth where it listeth, and thou hearest the sound thereof, but canst not tell whence it cometh, or whither it goeth; so is every one that is born of the Spirit."

But to speak of the mysteriousness of these divine operations in nature, providence or grace, is not the object now in view. The nature of the Christian's experience is the subject which will be brought under consideration.

1. The true nature of conviction of sin, is a thing of which the called of God have no distinct knowledge, prior to experience.

There is, no doubt, a great diversity in the exercises and circumstances of souls under conviction. Some are agitated with awful terror, while others are gently led to a view of the aberrations of their hearts and lives from the law of God; but in all that is essential to conviction, there is a precise similarity in the experience of all Christians. The end attained in every case is the same, though the steps, by which it is arrived at, may be exceedingly different.

Every man who is brought under the convictions of the Spirit—for all true conviction is his work—is made serious, and brought to a solemn consideration of his ways. Serious consideration, therefore, may be said, always to be the first step in a religious life. The multitude are destroyed for want of this. They cannot be persuaded to lay aside their frivolity, and their worldly cares; nor to *consider* what they are, and whither they are going. But the first touch of divine influence on the mind, renders the hitherto careless soul deeply serious. An awakened attention to divine things is experienced. The man begins to hear with other ears, to see with other eyes, and to entertain other thoughts and feelings, than he was wont to do. The past, the present, and the future, engage his attention. He asks himself, "What am I? whither am I tending? What have I been doing all my life? and what are my prospects beyond the grave?" Though accustomed to hear the word all his life, it now appears like a new thing—like a message from God to himself; and he can hardly be persuaded that the preacher has not undergone a great change; or has not learned to preach new doctrines; for the truths which now rivet his attention, he never understood; nor did they before make any but a momentary impression on his mind. The awakened soul is often ready to exclaim, "Surely I never heard these awfully solemn, and highly interesting truths before, or I should have been affected by them." Not only the word preached, but read, appears new. He takes down from the shelf the long neglected Bible, which was kept in the house more for the sake of decency, than for use; and shaking off the dust of years, he opens the sacred volume; and whilst he reads, he holds up a faithful mirror, which exhibits to him his own moral features. Here he sees the evil of his past life reflected in a clear, strong light, upon his conscience. Sometimes the truth is so pungent, and penetrates the mind with so much pain, that he is tempted to lay aside the book. The more the awakened sinner reads, meditates, and hears of the truth, the more uneasy he becomes, and the more dangerous does his condition appear to be. At first, gross sins, or palpable neglects of duty, engage his attention, and affect his conscience; and these defects he attempts to reform; but he soon is made to see, that not merely a few, but all his actions have been "evil, and only evil, and that continually, from his youth up." As the light of conviction increases, he becomes conscious that the fountain from which these streams issue, is within him, and is entirely polluted—that "the heart is deceitful above all things and desperately wicked" —and is continually sending forth streams of wicked thoughts and desires. To reform the life, where habits of iniquity have become inveterate, is no easy task; but who can regulate the thoughts, desires, and volitions? Who can command the affections to fix with due intensity on their proper objects? Who is found able to purify the inner man, and restrain all wanderings of thought and desire? Alas! boasted ability turns out to be a mere illusion of an unenlightened mind; and yet the sinner under conviction excuses not himself on account of his inability. He is deeply conscious that it is his own fault. It is the very core of his iniquity. He feels most sensibly that he ought to love God, but his wicked heart refuses. He is convinced that it is his duty to come believingly and penitently to Christ for grace and salvation, but his obstinate will is reluctant; and his heart remains callous and ungrateful under all the representations of God's wonderful love, and Christ's tender compassion, which induced him to endure the cross and despise the shame. This conviction of deep-rooted depravity and helplessness, is a state of mind the most distressing that can well be conceived. The convinced sinner feels as if he could take vengeance on himself, for having acted so shamefully, so foolishly, so wickedly. He groans under the burden of his iniquity, like a slave under hard bondage, and under the lash of a severe taskmaster. But the sinner thus convinced, does not feel tenderly; nor is he sensible of pungent pain

This want of tender feelings, and sensible heart-breaking, is the very thing which gives him most distress. Such an one will often be heard to exclaim, 'I have no conviction of sin—no conviction bearing any proportion to my enormous transgressions—I am quite stupid and insensible—Surely, there never was lodged in any human breast, a heart so impenetrably hard. Nothing moves or softens it in the least. It remains equally unaffected with the joys of paradise, and the pains of hell; even the bitter agonies of Christ in the garden, and on the cross, produce no tender relentings.' Another unexpected conviction which is commonly experienced, is, that the person is growing worse instead of better. Some have strenuously maintained that this is the truth of the fact; concerning which we will not now dispute: that which is asserted is, that to the apprehension of the convinced sinner, it seems to be a truth, that he is growing worse and worse; but this can be accounted for from the increase of light. Just as a man placed in a dark and loathsome dungeon, if he should have the light let in gradually, would see the filth increasing on every side; so the heart when the covering which conceals its turpitude is withdrawn, appears to become more and more vile and abominable.

Now, we say to one under these convictions, if you feel nothing as you say, why do you yet complain? What mean these deep fetched sighs, and these abundant tears? Why are you not contented and at ease, as the multitude are, and as you once were? To such questions and expostulations, he would reply, 'I am distressed because I feel so little distress—I am grieved, because I cannot feel grief. My most earnest desire is, to fall under deep conviction of sin. O, if I could feel my heart sensibly pained, and tenderly affected, I should be in a comfortable state compared with that which I experience.' Now this is real conviction; and it is one of those paths into which the blind are led, of which they knew nothing prior to experience. Before this, indeed, they may have formed a conception of the feelings of a convinced sinner. They imagined that by some flash, like lightning—by some awful stroke, by which their souls should be stunned, as by a thunder-bolt, and shaken to the very centre, and melted as the ice by the rapid heat, conviction of sin would be effected. Very commonly the awakened person strives to produce conviction of the kind conceived, by bringing up to view the most frightful images, by reading the most awful and affecting descriptions of death, judgment, and hell; and frequents that preaching which denounces with the most awful severity the wrath of the Almighty; still hoping and praying to be overwhelmed with such feelings as have been described. But if the convinced sinner could realize all the feelings of which he has conceived, and for which he longs and prays, the end of conviction would not be at all answered; for the end of conviction is to lead the sinner out of himself; to destroy all self-confidence and self-complacency; to show him how evil and how helpless is his condition. But if he could experience such feelings as he wishes, he would think well of himself, as being in the frame in which he ought to be. The views and feelings produced by the conviction of the Spirit, lead the soul to despair—to despair of ever saving itself. Thus self-righteousness, which is so deeply inherent in every man, is cut up by the root. "I through the law, am dead to the law," says Paul, "that I might live unto God." Again, "I was alive without the law once, but when the commandment came, sin revived, and I died." Thus, "the law is a schoolmaster to bring us unto Christ." It is an unexpected thing, of which the blind could form no practical conception, that the nearer the sinner approaches towards deliverance, the further he recedes from hope and comfort, in his own apprehension. That is found true, therefore, in spiritual things, which has been remarked in natural things; that the darkest hour is that which immediately precedes the dawning of the day. When the convinced sinner is brought to the point of fully condemning himself, acknowledging that the sentence which dooms him to misery is perfectly just, then is the time of God's mercy; so that, in the moment when it expected nothing but death, salvation is found. Thus the richness and freeness of the grace of the gospel are magnified, and the saved sinner is prepared to give all the glory to God, and ever afterwards to confess that he deserved nothing but to be cast off for ever.

2. Conversion, also, turns out, in experience, to be a very different thing from what was anticipated. Awakened sinners, having heard of persons being translated from darkness "to the marvellous ligh

of the gospel;" and having, perhaps, heard or read of some remarkable conversions, expect to be brought through the new birth in a way perfectly similar to these extraordinary cases, which, however, are very imperfectly understood. They, therefore, endeavour to place themselves in the same circumstances as those in which others were when they found peace with God; and they continue to look and wait for some sudden and almost miraculous change; and they often endeavour, beforehand, to imagine what their views and exercises will be when their conversion shall take place. These expectations are never realized, and are always erroneous; for when this blessed change actually occurs, the light is commonly like that of the dawn; obscure at first, but shining more and more to the perfect day; and instead of the views being miraculous or strange, they appear to arise in the mind like other thoughts and feelings. The only marked difference is, not in the manner of the views, but in the spiritual beauty and glory of the objects contemplated. Instead of a sudden and violent agitation, there is a sweet exercise of the mind in directing its thoughts to Christ, and to the glorious perfections of God, as exhibited in his works and in his word. The soul reposes with delightful complacency on the truths to which its attention happens to turn; and besides the light afforded by the Spirit shining on the word, there is often a suggestion of precious Scripture promises, or other evangelical truths, suited to the condition and wants of the new born soul. These sometimes come dropping into the mind, successively, as precious morsels on which it feeds. As the recently born infant instinctively thirsts for the nutriment which the mother's milk supplies; so new born souls as naturally thirst for "the sincere, (or pure) milk of the word, that they may grow thereby."

One circumstance, which will appear strange to those who have not learned it by experience, is, that in the first exercises of the new convert, there is frequently no thought or question, whether these are the genuine exercises of one born of God. There is no room, at present, for such reflex acts; the mind is completely occupied with the objects of its contemplation; and often, when these views are clear, forgets itself, and is absorbed in beholding the glory of God in the Mediator, or the wonders of redemption as set forth in the gospel, or the beauty of holiness, as manifested both in the law and the gospel. Thus often Christ is received, true faith is exercised, the heart is humbled in penitence, and exercises sincere love to God, without knowing or even asking what the nature of these exercises may be; and these views and exercises come on so gradually, in many cases, that their origin cannot be traced. So far is it, then, from being true, that every regenerated man knows the precise time of his renovation, that it is a thing exceedingly difficult to be ascertained. It is not difficult to know, that on such a day our minds were thus and thus exercised; but whether those were the exercises of genuine piety, is quite another question; or whether, if they were, they were the first of this kind, is still a different question. Some who speak confidently of the day and the hour of their conversion, never were truly converted, but were imposed on by a mere counterfeit. Others who have the same confidence of knowing the precise time of their conversion, though true Christians, are mistaken as to this matter. They were enabled obscurely to view the truth, and feebly to believe, long before the period at which they date their conversion. Some attain a full assurance of hope, who do not pretend to know when their spiritual life commenced. All they can say is, with the blind man in the gospel, "One thing I know, that whereas I was blind, now I see." As in the dawning of the natural day, we often can know assuredly that the day has commenced, because the objects around us are distinctly visible, when we could not tell the precise moment when the day dawned. Sincere souls, which have the scriptural evidences of piety, need not be distressed because of their ignorance of the day and hour of their vivification. But let not those who have never experienced any change, take comfort from this, as though it were possible that they also may have experienced regeneration, while they knew nothing about it. In regard to such we may truly say, you cannot be converted without knowing something about it; you cannot be the subjects of a series of new views and feelings, without being conscious of these spiritual exercises.

The soul, under the leadings of the Spirit, is often brought near to Christ, when it apprehended he was far off. Their first intercourse with the Redeemer, is like that of the two disciples on the way to Emmaus. Their eyes are, as it were, holden, that they do not know, in very deed, that the person with whom they are conversing is Christ; but afterwards, like those disciples, they can say, "Did not our hearts burn within us, while he opened to us the Scriptures, and while he communed with us by the way?" In such a conference, under such a sermon, while meditating on such a passage of Scripture, did we not feel our minds to be elevated, warmed, enlightened? What could this be but the risen Saviour whispering his love into our hearts? When he thus comes near and we are not aware of his being present, he will not keep the veil long before our eyes, which conceals his true features. He will come nearer still; and in "the breaking of bread," or in some other divine ordinance, he will stand revealed before our eyes, and we shall recognize him as our FRIEND and our BELOVED; and if it should be but a glimpse which he affords us, before he vanishes from our wistful sight, yet even this transient view will be sufficient to convince us, that "He is altogether lovely, the chief among ten thousand."

3. God leads his once blind but chosen people in the way which they know not, as it relates to the means and progress of their sanctification. All the children of God are inspired with an ardent love of holiness; and they are much delighted with the thought of having the power of sin destroyed; and it is often the burden of their prayer, that the very principles of iniquity within them may be eradicated; but little do they know or consider how this is to be effected. They have no idea how slow and

painful will be the process of mortifying the old man with his deeds which are corrupt. Upon their first conversion, they were often filled with comfort, rejoiced in hope, and found sweet satisfaction in attendance on divine ordinances: and they entertained the fond hope that it would always be thus, or better. They were like little children, dandled on the parent's knee, and not exposed to hardship or required to labour; but soon the scene changes. Darkness hangs over them; difficulties perplex; conflicts discourage them. Inbred corruption begins to stir sensibly, and evils appear which were not believed to exist. The power of temptation is felt; and the Christian finds it to be literally true, that he is engaged in a warfare. Pride rises and attempts to regain its former mastery; passion swells and becomes impetuous; the baits which the world presents to avarice, ambition, and the love of ease and pleasure, are found to be far more fascinating than was expected. The pleasures of religion too have subsided, and the lively relish for the service of God is abated. Prayer, meditation, and self-examination, once so delightful, now too often are a burden, and are, therefore, frequently neglected, or hastily and carelessly performed. A distressing reluctance to spiritual duties is experienced; and all the pleasures of religion have vanished. Now the Christian may be compared to a weaned child, from which the mother turns herself away, and refuses it its wonted refreshment; or perhaps is better represented by the child sent off from his father's roof, to shift for himself, in a wide and unfriendly world. To increase his affliction, external troubles often combine with those which are inward and spiritual. Malignant enemies rise up to annoy and persecute; friends die, or become unkind; ministers, on whom perhaps too much dependence was placed, are removed; zealous professors turn back to the world; religion is wounded in the house of her friends; truth lies bleeding in the streets; family comforts decay; and poverty and debt succeed to affluence and comfort; and to crown all, Satan comes forth with a frightful roar, and endeavours to worry whom he knows he cannot devour. Now, indeed, the feeble, timid soul is pressed beyond expression. It groans "being burdened;" almost wishes for death; not because conscious of preparation for a better world, but as a release from trouble. Sometimes, under these afflictions, especially when bodily health is impaired, or a good name blasted by the tongue of calumny, the soul grows pettish and impatient; and the feelings, if expressed in words, would be something like this, "Why am I thus? Why am I left to buffet the storm without help or refuge? Why am I abandoned of God, and made a reproach to my enemies, who daily say, scoffingly, 'Where is now your God, in whom you trusted? There is no help for him in God.'" Or more commonly, the afflicted and heavy-laden soul, sinks into despondency, and concludes that it never has been in the right way; that surely, if it was one of God's dear children, it would never be thus forsaken and left to sink in the horrible pit and miry clay. "Surely," it exclaims, "this cannot be the way in which Jehovah leads his own dear children, whom he hath redeemed." Were it not that now and then there is "a little reviving" in the midst of these years of affliction; unless, after long intervals of thick darkness, some rays of cheerful light gilded the dark scene, and some drops of refreshment fell into the cup of sorrow, the soul would be overwhelmed with a burden which human strength is unable to bear.

But how is this the way of sanctification? It looks more like the path of declension and apostasy. But remember, that before we can ascend we must descend; before we can be filled with the divine fulness, we must be emptied of self and sin. To bring us to feel our weakness and entire dependence, we must be left to try our own strength; and to convince us of the evil of sin, we must, for a season, be left to struggle against its power, and to learn to know the "depths of Satan." To cure us of the undue love of the world, the world must be "crucified to us, and we to it;" and to preserve us from idolizing the creature, the objects of our too fond affections must be snatched away from our embrace. But, doubtless, this is a way which the people of God did not know, until they were led into it. Even when forewarned by experienced Christians, of the difficulties and dangers of the way, they heeded them not; as either not understanding what they meant, or as not giving full credit to their testimony.

4. Another thing in the dispensations of God to his people which, prior to experience, they never distinctly understood, and which cannot easily be explained, is his leaving them for a season to back-

slide; and then recovering them by the exercise of the same sovereign grace which first brought them into the path of life.

The young convert cannot believe that he shall ever grow cold and decline in piety, much less that he may be left to commit some grievous sin, to the sore wounding of his conscience, and perhaps the dishonour of his profession. But, notwithstanding his strong confidence, which leads him to boast, "my mountain standeth strong, I shall never be moved," it will not be a new thing on the earth, or in the church, if he should add one more beacon to the many with which this coast is already strewed, to be a warning to those who come after him. Backsliding begins in the heart, shows itself in the closet first, and soon diffuses its paralyzing influence through the life. The backslider for a while may preserve a fair exterior; his public devotions may appear to be punctual and fervent, while in secret he is cold and careless. The Christian while in this declining state, differs so little from the hypocrite, that it is not easy to discriminate between them. Indeed, to the man himself, this is commonly impossible, and happily so; for when love grows cold, fear must be brought to operate on the natural feelings. If backsliders possess assurance, it is the assurance of delusion. While thus departing from God, they cannot possess satisfactory evidence of his favour, for the exercise of grace is its evidence. The symptoms of backsliding are evident enough. The want of lively faith, and love, and penitence, is the root of the evil. The reality, beauty, and importance of eternal things, are out of view; the world, therefore, rises in magnitude, and seems clothed with new interest, and its objects appear more desirable. Seriousness of spirit is now succeeded by levity, and that tenderness of conscience which shuddered at the mere "appearance of evil," by stupidity. The spirit of the world gains too great ascendency; and conformity to the corrupt maxims and customs of the world becomes manifest. Even lawful objects are sought with too much ardour, and the too anxious desire to be rich has often entangled the souls of professors in many hurtful snares, from which some are never extricated, but their souls are finally pierced through with many sorrows, and drowned in perdition.

When backsliding once begins, there is no knowing how far the declining Christian may depart from God. It cannot be a matter of much surprise, therefore, that in an evil hour, and under the power of temptation, some insidious lust should prevail against him, and should carry him into captivity. Indeed, such is the frailty of the best men, that there is no security for their not falling into gross sins, but in the conservative grace of God; and when Christians begin to backslide they never recover themselves, and return by their own efforts; but by the kind interposition of their faithful Shepherd, whose love to his sheep leads him to leave the ninety and nine, and to go into the wilderness to reclaim one straying lamb. He makes his voice to be heard and recognized. If the common warnings of the word, and gentle suggestions of the Spirit have been neglected, or resisted, it is usual with him to apply the rod. Providence is made to co-operate powerfully with grace; or rather is made a part of that system of gracious means, which God makes use of to preserve and reclaim his erring people; and in the corrective dispensations of Providence, there can often be remarked a connexion between our sin and God's chastisement. Often the objects which have been the occasion of our sin, are some how made the instruments of our punishment; or in some way and by some association observed by us, God points as with a finger, by his dispensations of affliction, to sins long since committed and perhaps almost forgotten. The riches which were too eagerly sought, "make to themselves wings and fly away," as the eagle to heaven; or those for whom these riches were so painfully accumulated, are taken away. If we make an idol of any creature, God will often judge it best to remove the stumbling-block, and make room for himself in our affections. Our heavenly Father knows how to direct the rod so as to produce the desired effect. He knows our frame, and can pierce the point of sensibility, and thus rouse us from our apathy, or from our dreams of worldly pleasure and ambition. The backslider is now arrested in his downward course, is brought to pause and consider his ways. He now sees how far he has departed from the right path. He is convinced of his folly and sin, in forsaking "the fountain of living waters, and hewing out broken cisterns which can hold no water." The convictions of sin in the case of the backslider, are often attended with keener compunction and anguish, than were experienced under his first awakening. Sometimes he almost despairs of mercy; or if he dares to cherish a trembling hope of acceptance, yet he expects no more kind and gracious dealings from his heavenly Father. He calculates, like the returning prodigal, to be placed on the footing of "a hired servant," rather than that of a son. But here again he is led by a path which he knew not; for God not only "heals his backsliding," but graciously forgives all his aggravated sins; receives him as a child, without upbraiding; draws him with loving cords, even the bands of a man, and says, "I will heal their backsliding, I will love them freely, for mine anger is turned away from him."

This abounding of free grace and pardoning mercy to backsliding believers, is one of the most wonderful things in the way in which God leads his blind people. When they were looking for nothing but wrath, behold he shows his reconciled face, and manifests his pardoning mercy with all the tenderness of a kind father. It is by such dispensations of love and mercy, that God proves to us how superior he is to all our highest conceptions. That he is God, and not man, is the reason why his people are not consumed. "For my thoughts are not your thoughts, neither are your ways my ways, saith the LORD. For as the heavens are higher than the earth, so are my ways higher than your ways, and my thoughts than your thoughts."

It should not be inferred from what has been said, that God leads all his people in precisely the same paths; for while there is generally a similari ty, there is a particular diversity. The case of every Christian has probably something peculiar in it; both as it relates to the work of grace within him, and to the dispensations of Providence without him. There are some individuals who are led in a way remarkably different from the common paths of the flock. They are conducted through the world in a gentle, peaceful course; exposed but little to the fierce blasts of adversity, with which others are assailed and almost overwhelmed; and seem to be preserved from those terrific conflicts, and satanic temptations, which others are called to endure; while to others the path is hedged up and full of difficulties throughout. But often, while the first stages of the pilgrimage are smooth, the latter may be rough and painful, or the reverse. During a long season of prosperity and peace, the cup of afflictions is filling up ready to be poured forth at a future day. Indeed, according to the order of natural events, it must be so; for if all the members of a large family are, for many years, spared, there are only so many more marks for the arrows of future adversity; for all these are subject to various misfortunes, and all these must die, sooner or later, as well as others. Those, therefore, who seem for a .while to be exempt from adversity, will in due season have their full share; unless in mercy they are " taken away from the evil to come."

5. Finally, the people of God are often conducted through the " valley and shadow of death" in an unexpected manner. We learn, that anciently there were some " who were all their lives subject to bondage, through fear of death;" whom Christ

came to deliver. Well; that bondage of fear is still experienced by many sincere, but timid Christians; and many anxious thoughts are felt in relation to this awful but inevitable event. Yet when the trying moment arrives—when death appears near, and the evident symptoms of approaching dissolution are experienced, they find themselves supported and comforted, far beyond their highest expectation: and, as this last enemy comes nearer, he appears less formidable: his sting is extracted; and sometimes he seems to assume the face of an angel of light; so that the dying Christian can often say, "O death, where is thy sting?" "For me to die is gain." This peaceful end is not reserved for those alone, who appeared, in life, to possess a strong faith, but doubting, desponding believers are often thus raised above their gloomy fears, and are enabled to triumph in a dying hour. The faithful Shepherd of Israel is always present to guide the sheep of his purchase through this gloomy valley. Although they are blind and know not the way, yet with his rod and his staff will he both guide and protect them. Happy they who have God for their guide.

INFERENCES.

1. We may learn from what has been said, the end to be accomplished by the various dispensations of God to his people is, to humble their pride, to divest them of self-righteousness and self-confidence—to lead them to appreciate the grace and faithfulness of the Saviour; and to give exercise to

the several virtues of the Christian life, and thus to prepare the soul for its heavenly state.

2. Believers, by being led in this way, are instructed in the knowledge of the deep depravity of their nature; the deceitfulness of the heart; the turpitude of sin, in its various forms and aspects; of the malice and subtlety of the grand adversary; and consequently of the riches of divine grace; the wonderful wisdom of the plan of redemption; the tender sympathy, as well as the faithful care, of the Mediator; and of the desirableness of a better rest than this world can afford. Our estimation of heavenly joys will have some relation to our conflicts and afflictions upon earth. No doubt the gratitude of the redeemed, on Mount Zion, is increased exceedingly, by the consideration that they "have come out of great tribulation."

3. Let us learn then to trust implicitly in the providence and in the promises of a covenant-keeping God. His providence extends to the hairs of our head, and his promises are all yea and amen in Christ Jesus, and are "EXCEEDING GREAT AND PRECIOUS." We should learn to live upon the promises, by the exercise of a lively faith and hope, trusting all our interests into the hands of a faithful Redeemer—confidently believing, that whatever he hath promised he will certainly perform. Hath he begun a good work, and will he not accomplish it? None who trust in him shall ever be disappointed; and the more confidently we rely upon his word of promise, the more is he honoured, and the more acceptable are we in his sight.

SERMON XXIII.

NOT SLOTHFUL, BUT FOLLOWERS OF THE SAINTS BY FAITH.

That ye be not slothful, but followers of them, who through faith and patience, inherit the promises.—HEB. vi. 12.

THE Hebrew Christians, to whom this epistle was addressed, appear to have made slow progress in religion, and to have been greatly in danger of apostasy. The apostle, therefore, addresses to them many exhortations and warnings, adapted to their character; and endeavours to arouse them to greater watchfulness, diligence, and exertion, in their spiritual pilgrimage. He tells them, that "when for the time they ought to be teachers, they needed that one teach them again, which be the first principles of the oracles of God, and are become such as have need of milk and not of strong meat; for every one that useth milk is unskilful in the word of righteousness, for he is a babe. But strong meat belongeth to them that are of full age, even those who by reason of use, have their senses exercised to discern both good and evil." And in the beginning of the sixth chapter, whence our text is taken, he exhorts them to advance beyond the first principles of Christianity, and to go on to a more perfect knowledge of the truth. And to stimulate their sluggish souls, he sets before them the awful consequences of apostasy, as well as the unpardonable guilt which, by this conduct, they would bring upon themselves. If after the reception of so many spiritual gifts, and after making such a profession as they had done, they should apostatize, he seems to represent their case as hopeless. It is not necessary hence to conclude, that true believers ever do, in fact, totally and finally fall away; but they are in constant danger of such a fall, and are only kept from it by the word and Spirit of Christ. These warnings, therefore, are not needless to the real children of God: they may be the very means which a faithful Redeemer makes use of to preserve them from apostasy.

We learn from this passage, how far false professors may go in religion. They may not only give their assent to the gospel, but may hear it with joy, as we learn from the case of the seed on stony ground, in the parable of the sower. And they may possess miraculous gifts, as Judas, or even the spirit of prophecy, as Balaam, and yet be destitute of charity, and "love the wages of unrighteousness."

The apostle could not know the hearts of the people to whom he wrote, and, therefore, he addresses them as professors, who, notwithstanding their many gifts and high profession, might possibly be deceived; but he did not wish to be censorious, and says, that although he thus spake, he hoped better things of them and things that accompany salvation. And he gives them credit for the good works which they had performed, which he assures them God would not forget. "For God," says he, "is not unrighteous to forget your work and labour of love, which ye have showed to his name, in that ye have ministered to the saints and do minister." But he would not have them rest satisfied with attainments already made, but to press forward to the highest exercises of piety. "And we desire," says he, "that every one of you do show the same diligence to the full assurance of hope unto the end." And as sloth is one of the most common hinderances to growth in grace, he proceeds to warn the Hebrew Christians, particularly, against this insidious vice, and exhorts them to imitate the conduct of those ancient worthies who had successfully run this race, and had won the prize. "Not slothful, but followers of those who through faith and patience inherit the promises."

Brethren, we have the same race to run, and are beset with the same temptations and dangers from without, and are impeded by the same tendency to forgetfulness and indolence as those to whom those exhortations were originally addressed. They are, therefore, as well suited to us as to them; and they were written for our learning and admonition. Let us, then, endeavour to profit by them, by not only hearing them, but by making a practical application of them to our own souls.

That the truths contained in the text may be

brought distinctly before you, I will endeavour to set before you, 1. The vice against which you are warned. 2. What things in the ancient saints we should imitate. 3. The blessing which we shall by so doing inherit.

1. The evil which we are exhorted to shun is sloth. The bad consequences of this vice, as it relates to worldly concerns, are well understood; and youth are often admonished by parents and teachers, not to indulge a propensity which is inherent in every son and daughter of Adam. But "the children of this world are wiser in their generation, than the children of light." Christians are not commonly so apprehensive of the evils of sloth, in retarding their spiritual progress, as the men of the world are, in relation to earthly pursuits. Great loss is sustained by most who are running the Christian's race, through an undue indulgence of indolence. There is in human nature a natural aversion to exertion. It requires the action of strong motives to arouse the mind from its natural apathy; this is especially true, when mental exertion is requisite. But besides this natural love of ease, there is a sinful aversion to the exercise of holy activity. "The carnal mind is enmity against God; it is not subject to his law, neither indeed can be." Just so far as this depravity of nature prevails, just so far will there be a reluctance to turn the thoughts to spiritual objects. And as conscience condemns according to the light of truth which is in the mind, impenitent men instinctively turn away from the contemplation of their own sins, on account of the pain and remorse which such views

occasion. And, as the pious are renewed but in part, the remains of corruption in their hearts, paralyse their souls, and render them dull and inactive in spiritual concerns. When we feel a secret aversion to any set of objects, we are reluctant to think of them; the soul naturally turns away to such things as are congenial with its present temper. When pious affections are lively, then there is no disposition to indulge in indolence. Love creates alacrity, and sweetens the most toilsome labours. But when love grows cold, in the same proportion the soul moves heavily in the ways of God. Drowsiness benumbs its sensibilities. "I have put off my clothes," said the spouse, "and how shall I put them on?" Prayer, which is so delightful to the lively Christian, becomes a task, and meditation a burden. Closet duties are neglected, or hurried over without any engagedness of spirit. Sloth cuts the nerves of effort. Under its withering influence the most precious means and opportunities of spiritual progress are suffered to pass without improvement. The soul indulges in sleep, when it should be wide awake—sleeps too, on enchanted ground, where many have slept the sleep of death. O Christian, awake to consider your real situation. You are surrounded by enemies, which are ever watchful, ever on the alert. Awake to consider the work which you have to do. The time is far spent. The day in which work can be done for God, and for the soul, will soon be over. "Watch and pray, lest ye enter into temptation." It does not become us "to sleep as do others, but to watch and be sober." Eternity, with all its awful realities is coming on, and will soon be here. Gird up the loins of your mind. "Work while it is called 'to-day,' before the night cometh, when no man can work."

II. But the duty of the Christian is not merely negative: he has positive duties to perform, as well as to shun the evils to which human nature is prone. And the duty enjoined in the text is the imitation of the men distinguished for piety, whose history has been left on record, for this very purpose. "Be ye followers of them who through faith and patience inherit the promises." The apostle evidently refers to those ancient saints, to whom God had made exceeding great and precious promises. And, especially, he seems to have Abraham in his eye; for he goes on, immediately, to speak of the oath and promise of God made to this patriarch, as furnishing a solid ground of consolation to all true believers. The exhortation is, first, to be imitators of the faith of the ancient saints, and no one among them is so conspicuous for constant and extraordinary faith as Abraham. He is, therefore, in many places of the sacred Scriptures, exhibited as a model to believers who should come after him. On account of the strength of his faith, he obtained the honourable title of "the father of the faithful." And when the apostles treat of the nature and efficacy of faith, Abraham is the example commonly selected for illustration. In the eleventh chapter of this epistle, Paul speaks of the faith of this patriarch, in the following strong language. "By faith Abraham, when he was called to go out to a place which he should after receive for an inheritance, obeyed; and he went out, not knowing whither he went. By faith he sojourned in the land of promise as in a strange country, dwelling in tabernacles with Isaac and Jacob, the heirs with him of the same promise. For he looked for a city which hath foundations, whose maker and builder is God." The faith of these ancient worthies of whom the apostle speaks, was strong in death as well as in life; and had respect not merely to temporal blessings, but more especially, to the heavenly inheritance. For, "these all died in faith, not having received the promises," that is, not having seen their fulfilment; "but having seen them afar off," about certainly to be accomplished at a future day. "They were persuaded of them, and embraced them, and confessed that they were strangers and pilgrims on the earth. For they that say such things, declare plainly that they seek a country. And truly if they had been mindful of that country from which they came out, they might have had opportunity to have returned. But now they desire a better country, that is, a heavenly; wherefore, God is not ashamed to be called their God; for he hath prepared for them a city."

In the history of Abraham, there is one transaction which exhibits the strength of his faith, in the clearest manner conceivable. It was his prompt obedience to the command of Jehovah, when directed to sacrifice his son Isaac. The apostle speaks of this extraordinary exercise of unshaken confidence in God, in the following terms. "By faith, Abraham, when he was tried, offered up Isaac; and he that had received the promises, offered up his only begotten son, of whom it was said, In Isaac shall thy seed be called; accounting that God was able to raise him up, even from the dead." This is the kind of faith which we are called upon to imitate; though we may not be able to come up to an equality with it. If we examine more particularly into the nature of Abraham's faith, we shall find in it the following properties.

1. It was prompt. No sooner did he hear the voice of God speaking to him than he obeyed, however repugnant the command might be to human feelings. When God first revealed to him his will, commanding him leave his own country and kindred, he hesitated not, but went out, not knowing as yet, whither God would have him to go. So our faith should be prompt; at once yielding undoubting assent to the truth of what God has in his word declared; and without consulting with flesh and blood, we should be ready, without delay, to obey his commands.

2. Abraham's faith was implicit. He believed the revelations of God, without waiting for an explanation of the difficulties or mysteries involved in the subject. Some of the declarations of the Almighty had the appearance of being, in the nature of things, impossible; as that Sarah when past the age of child-bearing should have a son; and some seemed to be not only unnatural, but contrary to the truth of God's promises, as the command to sacrifice his son Isaac, in whom, it had been promised, all nations should be blessed. But Abraham did not hesitate. Human reason, as well as the fond affections of our nature, often raise up

obstacles in the way of faith in God's revelations; but over all these the faith of Abraham triumphed. He seems to have resorted to no sentiments or reasonings of his own, when God had spoken. His confidence in the divine veracity was such, that what God declared, he implicitly received as true, and acted accordingly. This is the noblest triumph of faith. Reason is no competent judge of divine mysteries. They are not contrary to, but above reason. But how, it may be asked, could Abraham believe in a revelation which seemed to contradict promises already made? Paul explains this. He believed that if he slew his son, God would raise him up again; for he was sure that his promises could not fail. In this respect, we should imitate the faith of Abraham, by implicitly receiving whatever we find clearly revealed in his word, although many of the truths therein contained be in their nature incomprehensible. We should leave it to God to clear up, in due season, mysteries which now baffle human reason; and not trust to our own feeble intellect. Many things we may be unable to reconcile, owing entirely to the imperfection of our knowledge; but there are mysteries which must ever remain such, to all created intelligences; for how can finite ever comprehend that which is infinite? The pride of human reason, which disdains to submit to receive what it cannot understand, has been the fruitful source of innumerable heresies.

3. The third characteristic of Abraham's faith was its strength. Faith may be of very different degrees of strength. We hear our Saviour saying,

"I have not found so great faith, no, not in Israel." Again, "O woman, great is thy faith." On the other hand, he often upbraids his disciples for the weakness of their faith, "O ye of little faith, wherefore did ye doubt?" Now, Abraham received this testimony, that "he believed God, and his faith was counted for righteousness." Paul says, "who, against hope believed in hope, that he might be the father of many nations." That is, when every human appearance, and even the laws of nature stood in the way of the fulfilment of the promise; yet he continued to rely on the faithfulness of him that promised. "For being not weak in faith, he considered not his own body now dead, when he was about a hundred years old, nor yet the deadness of Sarah's womb. He staggered not at the promise of God through unbelief, but was strong in faith, giving glory to God; being fully persuaded, that what he had promised, he was able to perform." The strength of his faith was also remarkably manifest in the transaction already referred to, when he promptly obeyed the command to sacrifice his son, his well beloved son, although the fulfilment of the promises of God was dependent on his life—"accounting that God was able to raise him from the dead." There is no human act more pleasing to God than a strong confidence in his word. Many things which he reveals may be mysterious, and far above our comprehension; but we need no other evidence of their truth than the word of God. So, also, we may be required to perform duties which involve much self-denial; but we should not confer with flesh and blood, but should imitate Abraham, who, without delay or hesitation, obeyed the commandment of the Lord. When he was directed to leave his native country, he immediately went out, not knowing whither he went. And when God commanded him to offer up his well beloved son, Isaac, he demurred not, but saddled his ass, and took his son and went to the place appointed. The path of duty is always the way of safety; and it is the road to happiness. We may hesitate about what is duty, in certain dubious circumstances, but when that point is ascertained, there should be no hesitation about performing what conscience dictates to be right.

4. Another characteristic of Abraham's faith was, that it directed his attention and affections to heaven, as his resting place. The promise of Canaan was of no value to him, individually; for, he owned not a foot of land in the country, while he lived, except a burying ground, which he had purchased, on the death of Sarah. His immediate descendants, Isaac and Jacob, were like himself, strangers and sojourners in the land of promise: and their descendants, for centuries, were in a foreign country, where they suffered great affliction and oppression. All this was made known to Abraham, and yet he lived by faith. He had something in view far better than this earthly possession. "He looked for a city which hath foundations, whose builder and maker is God." Faith was to him the evidence of things not seen, the substance of things hoped for. This, my brethren, is the faith of those who inherited the promises, which the apostle exhorts us to follow.

But those ancient worthies whom we should imitate, are characterised by patience, as well as faith. These two virtues are very fitly joined together, because the good things promised were not immediately received, but were "viewed afar off." "These all died in faith, not having received the promises, but having seen them afar off." Therefore, while they were sojourners and strangers, and exposed to many evils, they had great need of patience, both to wait for the fulfilment of the promises, and to endure the trials, through which they had to pass. All the pious patriarchs possessed both faith and patience; though not all in the same degree. We have selected Abraham, in particular, as a model of faith, which we ought to imitate, and in making this selection we are warranted by the authority of Scripture, where he is called, " the father of the faithful," but whom shall we fix upon to be an example to us in patience? Our thoughts would at first naturally turn to Job, whom, from our infancy, we have been taught to consider the most patient of men. The apostle James says, " Be ye also patient; establish your hearts, for the coming of the Lord draweth nigh. Take, my brethren, the prophets, who have spoken in the name of the Lord, for an example of suffering affliction, and of patience. Behold we count them happy which endure. Ye have heard of the patience of Job, and have seen the end of the Lord; that the Lord is very pitiful and of tender mercy." Among the prophets we might fix upon Jeremiah, as a man of almost unexampled afflictions, from his youth to his death. But though both these ancient saints, Job and Jeremiah were among the greatest sufferers, of whom we have any record; yet they were both, at times, pettish and querulous. The spirits of both of them were so exasperated, on certain occasions, that they cursed the day on which they were born. This certainly is no example for us to follow. They both uttered many things not indicative of a patient, submissive temper. I have, therefore, selected Moses, as the person whose constancy and perfect submission to the will of God, under circumstances of the severest trial, may be held up as a pattern for our imitation, above any other. Though the Scriptures speak of the patience of Job, they no where assert, that he was the most patient of men: and a comparison between him and Moses, will lead to the conclusion, that the latter, in regard to this virtue, is a more perfect model for our imitation than the former.

Moses is declared to have been the meekest man upon earth; and there is a near affinity between meekness and patience Never did mere man endure a more constant pressure on his mind than this servant of God, while he had committed to him the charge and guidance of the people of Israel, in their long journey of forty years, in the wilderness. This people were stiff-necked and rebellious, and left nothing undone which could have a tendency to intimidate, provoke, and render impatient their divinely appointed leader. But, under all these repeated trials and provocations, he remained firm; and never suffered his spirit to be exasperated, except on two occasions. The one was, when he came down from the mount with the two tables of the law, written by the finger of God himself, and beheld the people dancing and shouting around the golden calf, which they had caused Aaron to make, he threw down the tables with violence to the ground, and broke them to pieces. This, however, is no where, in Scripture, represented as a sin; but seems to have been a holy indignation, on account of the sad defection of the people, at the very foot of the mountain, on which God had recently manifested his awful glory, and terrible majesty.

The other instance, in which Moses departed from his characteristic calmness and patience, was at the waters of Meribah. Here he behaved in an improper manner, and "spake unadvisedly with his lips;" on which account, he was debarred from entering the land of Canaan. In all other cases, he seems to have possessed his soul in patience. "He endured," says the Scripture, "as seeing him that is invisible." "He, as a servant, was faithful in all his house." Let us, then, set before us as an example of firmness, meekness, and patience, this eminent servant of the most High, with whom God conversed face to face, as he never did with any other person. His life was made up of vicissitudes. Born under a cruel edict which condemned him to death as soon as born, but concealed by his parents for a while, he was at length exposed in a little ark on the edge of the Nile. Being found by the daughter of the king, and adopted as her own son, he was nursed by his own mother, and when weaned given up to his foster-mother, to be educated in all the learning of the Egyptians. When grown to man's age, he began to visit his brethren in bondage, for he had received an intimation that he was appointed to be their deliverer, and supposed that they would have received him as such; but their minds were blinded. The appointed period of their deliverance had not yet come. The four hundred years predicted to Abraham had not expired, and he had to undergo a long preparatory discipline in a foreign land. Having slain an Egyptian, in defending an Israelite, he was under the necessity of leaving Egypt; and he went into the land of Midian, where he connected himself in marriage with a daughter of Jethro, a wise and good man, and a priest of God. Here he remained, pursuing the occupation of a shepherd, for forty years; at the end of which period, he received a commission from God, to go to the king of Egypt, and demand the release of the children of Israel, and was endowed with the power of working miracles of the most astonishing kind. As the heart of Pharaoh was hardened, he refused to let the people go, until ten heavy judgments were inflicted on the nation; the last of which was one that came home to the bosom of the monarch as keenly as to the meanest of his subjects: all the first-born in every house of the Egyptians were slain by the angel of death. This afflictive dispensation induced him and his people, not only to permit the Israelites to depart, but to drive them out, giving them whatever they demanded, for the people were filled with terror, and apprehended that they were all in danger of perishing. But no sooner had Pharaoh and his people time to recover from the shock of this calamity, than they repented of having let the Israelites go; and they hastily pursued after them, and overtook them at the Red Sea, at a place, where, to all human appearance, escape was impossible. Before them was the sea; behind them the Egyptian army ready to fall upon them; and on the right and left they were completely hemmed in. Great, indeed, was the terror and agitation of the immense multitude, and they charged Moses with the ruin which threatened them. But in these perilous circumstances, how did Moses behave? He was calm and unmoved, trusting in Jehovah. He reposed with unshaken confidence on the power and faithfulness of God "Stand still," said he to the people, "and see the salvation of God." And upon his stretching forth his miracle-working rod, the sea divided, and left a dry path before them, so that they all went safely over; which the Egyptians essaying to do, were all overwhelmed by the returning waters. We might follow Moses, through his whole journey, and should always find him calm, composed, and exercising the most extraordinary forbearance and patience, toward this murmuring and rebellious nation. And yet, when the Almighty proposed to destroy them, and make a greater nation of him, such was his disinterestedness, that he fell on his face, and most earnestly deprecated this judgment, which would have raised him to such an eminence, and made his family illustrious above all the families of the earth. Yea, he prayed, that rather than this should be done, his name might be blotted out of the book of the living. Behold in Moses a model for your imitation! As no man ever lived who was favoured with such near and intimate intercourse with his Maker; so it is probable, that no man ever equalled him in fidelity to his Lord, in every trust committed to him. " Moses was faithful in all his house."

The word rendered *patience* in our text, is more commonly translated *long-suffering;* and is sometimes distinguished from patience. But as these two graces are so nearly the same, it is not necessary to be very critical in distinguishing between them. It may be remarked, however, that no word can better express the prominent trait in the character of Moses, than *long-suffering*. And it is worthy of remark, that this temper is the genuine fruit of faith. If Moses had not had a faith of uncommon strength in the word and promise of God, he never could have possessed his soul in patience, as he did. Be ye then followers of such men as Abraham and Moses, and the other saints of God, whose exemplary lives are recorded for this very purpose, that we might have suitable models for our imitation. These biographical sketches " were written for our learning, that we through patience and comfort of the Scriptures might have hope."

III. In the last place, I am to speak of the inheritance of the saints, which is here mentioned. The saints referred to in the text, are said "to inherit the promises." From the time of the fall, God has been graciously pleased to bind himself by promise and by covenant, to his chosen people. He made promises to Adam, to Noah, to Abraham,

Isaac, and Jacob, and other distinguished saints. And what he promised to them, equally belongs to all who possess the same character. To inherit the promises, is, to have a title to the blessings promised; and these blessings come to us freely as an inheritance, from a father to his children. These blessings, it is true, were dearly purchased, by our elder brother, through whom we have our title; but to us, they are free gifts. We possess them without paying any thing—and such an inheritance suits us, for we had nothing wherewith to buy any of these rich blessings.

"O to grace how great a debtor!"

Most of the early promises to the fathers had relation to the Messiah, that precious "seed of the woman"—that seed in whom all nations should be blessed—that "desire of all nations:" because through him all blessings come to redeemed saints. Indeed, they are all in a sense made to him; or they are made to them in him. The promised Messiah was to believers under the Old Testament the object of faith, and faith then justified, or gave a title to the promises, just as it does now. They, therefore, became heirs of the promises by faith. The apostle Paul demonstrates, that the rich promises made to Abraham are not abrogated, but remain in full force. For the covenant made with Abraham was "confirmed of God in Christ;" and, therefore, he concludes, "if ye be Christ's, ye are Abraham's seed, and heirs according to the promise." And Peter says to the converted Jews, on the day of Pentecost, "the promise is unto you and your children." This apostle, in his second epistle, declares, that "the promises of God are exceeding great and precious." And the apostle John informs us, in a sentence, what is the sum and substance of all the promises, "and this is the promise, that he hath promised us, even eternal life." And this inheritance is not only rich, but sure. The promise of God, according to Paul, is of the nature of an "immutable counsel." "Wherein God willing more abundantly to show unto the heirs of promise, the immutability of his counsel, confirmed it by an oath, that by two immutable things, in which it was impossible for God to lie, we might have a strong consolation, who have fled for refuge, to lay hold on the hope set before us." And in another place he assures us, that the "promises of God are not yea, and nay," that is, not vacillating and uncertain, "but are all yea and amen in Christ Jesus, to the glory of God."

To inherit the promises is to inherit all things. They comprehend all the good which a man is capable of enjoying, and much more than he is capable of imagining. God will do for his people abundantly above what they can think or ask. The promised inheritance is declared to be "incorruptible, undefiled, and which fadeth not away," reserved in the heavens for them. "For all things are yours, whether Paul, or Apollos, or Cephas, or the world, or life, or death, or things present, or things to come, all are yours, and ye are Christ's, and Christ is God's."

1. Since, then, so rich a prize is held up before us, and is promised to him that overcometh, let us lay aside sloth. Let us gird up our loins and

strive, and wait, and hope to the end. Let us not be weary in well-doing, but let us press toward the mark.

2. Let us meditate frequently and profoundly on the characters of the saints, which are left on record, for our imitation. Let it not be supposed, because many of them were inspired, and had supernatural gifts, that they are not proper objects of imitation. They were men of like passions with ourselves, and were supported by supplies of grace from the same fountain from which we are permitted to draw. The same Spirit which wrought powerfully in them still exists in all the plenitude of his power, and is still with the church, and indwelling in every true believer. We are not straitened in God, but we are straitened in our own bowels. But if we cannot attain to the high eminence on which Abraham and Moses stood, can we not make some greater approximation to their character, than we have yet done? Certainly we may derive benefit from imitating them, though at an humble distance. The child who writes after a copper-plate, may not hope to equal its perfection; and yet it is a great advantage to him to have such a copy to follow.

3. Remember that faith is the secret spring which keeps the spiritual life in motion. If you inquire what enabled Abraham to rise so high in the performance of difficult acts of obedience, the answer is, that he was strong in faith. He believed whatever God told him, and therefore he was able to do all that he commanded. And what rendered Moses so firm and faithful in all God's house? The apostle teaches that it was all by faith. And

this has been the secret of the patient and cheerful sufferings of the martyrs. They trusted in God, and his strength was made perfect in their weakness. But if faith becomes weak, all external observances, and all internal strivings will be ineffectual. Let your constant prayer then be, "Lord, increase our faith." It is by faith that we inherit the promises.

4. To faith join patience; for often the fulfilment of the promise is long deferred. Though it tarry, wait for it. The duty of Christians is often, in Scripture, expressed by "waiting"—waiting on the Lord. This implies, that patience is requisite. God may not see fit to appear when we first call. He may wisely intend to put our faith and patience to the test. A hasty, perturbed spirit, however warm the zeal, is not the proper temper of dependent beggars. We must learn to feel that we deserve no favour, and yet earnestly wait upon God, if peradventure he may have compassion on us.

Again, God's people are in this world, an afflicted people. "Many are the afflictions of the righteous." In the world they shall suffer persecution; and through various tribulations must enter the kingdom. Under these various afflictions, the only peace which they can enjoy, is connected with a patient, submissive temper; a willingness to bear whatever their heavenly Father may think proper to lay upon them.

5. Cast anchor on the solid ground of God's promises. Take fast hold, and resolve never to let go, and you will safely outride every storm. No

one has ever been disappointed who relied on the faithfulness of God. "A covenant-keeping God" is one of the titles by which he has made himself known, "His faithfulness reacheth unto the clouds." And he has promised to every one who trusteth in him, "I will never leave thee nor forsake thee." Heaven and earth shall pass away, sooner than one jot or tittle shall fail of all that he has promised. "Hath he said it, and shall he not do it?"

6. Meditate much on the promised inheritance. Think how near it is; only a few days, or at most a few years distant. These will roll round as fast as those which have already gone by. Think how sure it is, resting on the promise of one who cannot lie. Think how rich it is—thought cannot reach it, much less can words describe it.

But it is enough for believers to know that they shall be with Christ, shall behold his glory, and shall be like him, both in soul and body.

SERMON XXIV.

CHRIST THE BELIEVER'S REFUGE AND CONSOLATION.

That we might have a strong consolation, who have fled for refuge, to lay hold upon the hope set before us.—HEB. vi. 18.

GOD would have his people to be comfortable. He has, therefore, laid a solid foundation in the promises of his word, for their consolation. Human faith is weak, and unless well supported, is apt to totter and suffer the soul to sink into deep discouragement. The promises of God, on which the believer leans, are not only rich, but sure: "they are all yea and amen in Christ Jesus to the glory of God."

But as among men, that which is confirmed by a solemn oath is considered more firm than that which rests on a simple promise, therefore, God, in condescension to our infirmity, has been pleased to add an oath to his promise. And because there was none greater by whom he could swear, "he sware by himself, that by two immutable things, in which it was impossible for God to lie, we might have strong consolation who have fled for refuge to lay hold upon the hope set before us."

The form of expression here used, is probably derived from a custom sanctioned by the law of Moses, that when any person killed a man, he had the privilege of fleeing to one of the cities of refuge. Of these, there were three on each side of the Jordan, so situated as to be in reach of the inhabitants of every part of the country. In ancient times, it was usual among most nations, for the nearest of kin to a murdered person, to avenge his death, by slaying the murderer. And the practice still exists among many barbarous tribes. The kinsman, on whom the duty of taking vengeance devolved, was called "the avenger of blood," who was considered bound in honour never to give over the pursuit of the manslayer, until blood was shed for blood. Whether this custom took its rise from what God said to Noah after the flood, "Whoso sheddeth man's blood by man shall his blood be shed;" or whether it originated in the resentful feelings of human nature, it is not necessary to inquire. The Mosaic law certainly did not give rise to this ancient custom, but was intended to modify it, and to prevent the injustice and cruelty which were likely often to be done, in carrying this custom into effect. For, in the case in which a man was slain by another, without the deliberate purpose of taking away life, the kinsman of the slain, while in the heat of passion occasioned by the death of a near relation, would be poorly qualified impartially to judge of the motives from which the act proceeded. There was, therefore, danger lest death should be inflicted on an innocent person, or on one who did not merit so severe a punishment.

By this law of Moses, therefore, an asylum was provided for every manslayer, who chose to avail himself of the privilege, until there was an opportunity of a fair and impartial investigation, that the true character of the act might be ascertained. The gates of these cities of refuge were kept constantly open, that there might be no obstruction to hinder the ingress of the manslayer, by day or by night. The high-ways also, which led to these cities, and the bridges, were required to be kept in good repair.

But although all manslayers were permitted to take refuge in these cities; yet the institution was not intended to screen the malicious murderer from condign punishment; nor could it avail such an one any thing to take refuge in them; for if upon inquiry it was found, that the act was designed, the murderer was immediately delivered up to the avenger of blood to be put to death.

There were, however, other places to which the guilty were accustomed to flee for refuge. We find that Joab when he feared for his life, fled to the altar of burnt-offerings, and laid hold of the horns of the altar, and refused to come away or let go his hold. Solomon, therefore, directed that he should be slain there. As there is nothing in Scripture to sanction this custom, it is probable that it was borrowed from the pagans, among whom temples and altars were always places of refuge for the guilty; and to slay them in these sacred places was looked upon as a sacrilegious violation of the sanctity of the place. Some particular places acquired such a reputation for sanctity, that fugitives from justice might remain securely in them for any length of time. Daphne, near to Antioch, in Syria, was one of the most renowned places of refuge in the whole heathen world. But if the refugees were caught without the precincts of these sacred places, they were liable to be put immediately to death.

It matters not to which of the fore-mentioned customs the allusion is made, in our text: the import is the same, in either case.

The precise meaning of the word *hope*, requires a moment's consideration. By it most understand the object of hope, namely, justification and its consequence, eternal life. Others, however, understand the act or exercise of hope; but it is more probable, that by a common figure of speech, the apostle meant the foundation of hope; that is, the promise of which the apostle had been just speaking, and which generates hope in us. Certainly, this accords best with the preceding context, and with the scope of his argument. God had given a promise and confirmed it by an oath. On this solid foundation faith could firmly rest, and hope is the fruit of faith, and ever rises and falls with it. He who believes the promise, lays hold of hope, for faith in the promises of God, is the pillar and ground of a gospel hope.

Let us, then, contemplate the soul flying for refuge, and laying hold of the sure promise of God. And here it may be remarked, that no one seeks a refuge, unless he is apprehensive of some danger.

The traveller who sees a storm rising, and apprehends some injury from exposure to the wind, rain, hail, and lightning, flies to the nearest shelter, and takes refuge from the gathering storm.

So, he who is pursued by a vindictive enemy, as was the manslayer, bends his course, and hastens his steps, to the city of refuge. Thus, also, the sinner, when awakened to a true sense of his danger, begins to look out for a place of safety. But the person who apprehends no danger will not flee. You may call upon him, and invite him as much and as long as you will, but he heeds you not. He is urged by no motive strong enough to induce him to break off from his worldly pursuits, to seek salvation. Hence, the necessity of conviction of sin, that men may feel their need of a Saviour. "The whole need not a physician, but they that are sick." The first step, then, is, to see and feel that we are in a lost and perishing condition. We learn, in accordance with this, that the first work of the Spirit is, to convince men of sin. And although a mere legal conviction has no tendency to renew the heart; yet, as God deals with sinners as reasonable, accountable creatures, he does not usually bestow grace and pardon on them, until they are made sensible of their wretched and helpless condition. Thus, those convicted on the day of Pentecost, were first pricked in their hearts, and cried out, "Men and brethren, what shall we do?" And the jailor of Philippi, cried out, "What must I do to be saved."

Careless sinners, all who are at ease in Zion, make light of the gospel invitation, and continue to neglect the great salvation. But when, by the law brought home to the conscience, the false peace of the sinner is interrupted; when he begins to open his eyes on his true situation, and finds that he is in reality under a sentence of condemnation, and in a blind and helpless condition—that his whole nature is corrupt, and that he can do nothing to save himself, he begins in good earnest to inquire, whether there is any refuge for one in his wretched condition. He will now be disposed to listen to every report of a refuge whither he may fly and be safe. This subject now occupies his thoughts, and the things of time and sense no longer engross his attention. All earthly things appear trivial, and his only concern is, how he may escape impending wrath, and secure the salvation of his soul. Oppressed with the burden of his iniquities, he groans n anguish. He is filled with compunction for the sins of his youth, which now rise up in fearful array before his conscience. He is ashamed to look up to the throne of a holy God, but cries with the publican, "God be merciful to me a sinner." He takes all the blame to himself, and acknowledges the righteousness of the sentence which condemns him. Sometimes, he is tempted to despair of any relief, but the free offer of salvation to the chief of sinners, in the gospel, encourages him to indulge a feeble hope, that God may intend mercy for his miserable soul. He turns his face, therefore, toward the house of refuge, and resolves that he will never give over seeking, and crying to God, for mercy.

2. The manslayer, pursued by the avenger of blood, might, for a season, persuade himself that

he could be safe in some other place, and might attempt to conceal himself in some refuge nearer home. Such a course would have been exceedingly unwise, for wherever he was, he would still be exposed to danger, and at an unexpected time, his adversary might fall upon him, and take away his life. In all the coasts of Israel, there was no place of security for a manslayer, but in one of the appointed cities of refuge. Here there was legitimate protection, and no where else.

Just such is the case of the awakened sinner. He is convinced that danger impends; and that he must seek some refuge from the coming storm. But he is unwilling to betake himself to the house of safety, to which he is pointed by the gospel. This method of escape is foreign from his thoughts, and uncongenial with his feelings. He naturally turns to the old covenant, under which he was created. The new is strange to him; he does not understand it. He persuades himself that by reforming his life, and forsaking those sins which have particularly affected his conscience, he may be safe without fleeing to the house of refuge, which seems to him to be far off, and of difficult access. And if conscience is still unsatisfied with his reformation, he will add a diligent attendance on religious duties. He will observe the Sabbath, attend the church, pray in his family and in his closet, and manifest much zeal in all that relates to the externals of religion. In the warmth of his zeal, he may even aspire to the holy ministry, and may be a monitor and reprover of other sinners. He fancies himself to be a religious man, and fondly compares himself with the multitude who neglect all attention to religion, and infers that his condition must be safe. He compares his present with his former conduct, and congratulates himself upon the great change in his manner of life. By his fellow-professors he is viewed as an eminent Christian, and his delusion is so complete, that he has no suspicion of himself, but thinks that all is well, and that when he dies, he shall be received into heaven. The awakened sinner has indeed found a refuge, but alas! it is "a refuge of lies." He has no shelter but his own rotten righteousness. He entertains high hopes, but they are built on a sandy foundation. At some future time, he will be convinced that he has taken refuge in an unsafe place, from which he must be driven, or miserably perish. This conviction of danger, may seize him while there is yet an opportunity of escaping to the true city of refuge which God has appointed, where he will still find safety and protection But often the mistake is not detected until it is too late to seek for safety in the true refuge. Some have their eyes opened to see their miserable condition just when they are leaving the world; when it is too late to prepare for eternity; and others apprehend not their danger until the light of eternity reveals it to them. O wretched condition! Let all convinced sinners beware of the danger of resting on a false foundation, or seeking safety in a refuge of lies. Let them never feel at ease, until they have entirely escaped from the plain of destruction, and have taken refuge in the mount of safety. We must be brought to renounce our own righteousness and all dependence on our own works, or on our tears of repentance, and must put our trust solely in the all perfect righteousness of the Lord Jesus Christ.

3. The figure, "flying for refuge," is as well suited to express the act of faith, when Christ is believed on, as any that could be used. And the phrase "laying hold," is strikingly descriptive of the earnestness with which the convinced sinner seizes the gracious promise of God, when his eyes are first opened to understand the freeness and fulness of the offered salvation. As a drowning man, with eagerness seizes a rope thrown to him, and grasps it with a firmness which nothing can loose, so the sinner pursued by the demands of the broken law, flies to the house of refuge which is opened in the gospel, and immediately enjoys the feeling of repose; yea, often, of strong consolation. The expression *lay hold of* would seem to have allusion to the horns of the altar, which the guilty person who sought an asylum, grasped.

Although there is considerable variety in the exercises of sincere converts; yet there are some leading points in which the experience of all true believers agrees. As all are by nature in the same condition of condemnation and depravity; as all are equally helpless; as the same gospel is the object of the faith of all; and as regeneration in all is the work of the same Holy Spirit; there can be no essential difference in the nature of the exercises of genuine converts. All, for example, are convinced of sin, and feel themselves to be in a perishing condition. This conviction may, in some, be attended with a much livelier sense of danger, than in others: but the degree of fear and terror excited, is a mere circumstance which does not determine either the depth or genuineness of the sinner's convictions; for there may be overwhelming terror where there is but little true conviction, and there may be deep and scriptural conviction where there is little terror, and where the mind remains calm. Indeed, it often happens, that when conviction is deepest, the mind is most calm. Even when it seems to be on the borders of despair, and has almost relinquished hope, there is often a calm, but sad serenity, which is not easily accounted for.

There is not only a conviction of sin, in all true converts, but a thorough feeling of utter helplessness; not only a conviction of inability to keep the law, but also to repent of sin or receive the gospel. Unbelief is commonly the last sin of which the Spirit convinces the awakened soul—"of sin, because they believe not in me." But the truly convinced sinner never pleads his inability as his excuse, nor feels less guilty on this account. No, this he is sensible is the very core of his iniquity. Other sins are the branches of the evil tree, but this is the bitter root out of which they grow; and, therefore, every convinced sinner is led clearly to see the justice of God in his condemnation. He may be said to "accept the punishment of his sins;" for he acquiesces in the justice of the sentence which condemns him to eternal misery. He justifies God, and takes all the blame to himself. Indeed, at this point of experience, the goodness, and especially the long-suffering of God toward him, is apt to affect his mind in a very sensible manner; and his feeling is, that if he perish eternally, he never can feel that he has been unjustly treated, but that his gratitude is due to God for his long continued and unmerited kindness. Views and feelings of the kind mentioned, can only be accounted for, on the supposition that a spiritual change has already passed on the soul; though nothing is further from the belief of the subject of these exercises. The sinner is often renewed before he is aware of it. Spiritual life is breathed into the soul, before it is filled with the joy and peace which arises from receiving Christ by faith. There are evident pulsations of life, and vital breathings after God, the effect of renewing grace, before the eyes are opened to behold the reconciled face of God in Christ. One of the earliest sensible feelings of the regenerated soul, is a sense of ingratitude, which breaks the heart hitherto hard, into a melting frame of godly sorrow. Tears flow apace. This sorrow is sweet in the experience, because it is always mingled with a sense of the mercy and goodness of God; and yet there may be no thought of being in a safe state. But, usually, such exercises are soon succeeded by views of Christ as an able and a willing Saviour. These first views of a Saviour are sometimes sudden and overwhelming. The soul feels itself transported, as it were, into a new world. Gross darkness is exchanged for "marvellous light." The "joy is unspeakable and full of glory." The soul exults and glories in the cross of Christ; and all doubt and fear are expelled, and the heart is at once filled with contrition and with love and peace. These first views of a Saviour are often more remarkable, and more sensible in the flow of affection which accompanies them, than any afterwards experienced. The blessed vision of divine truth thus enjoyed, may be repeated twice or thrice, and then the soul is left to what may be called the common encouragements and hopes which the gospel inspires. But it would be unjust and injurious to many sincere Christians, to lay down the preceding, as the uniform experience of all the children of God. So far from it, that I am persuaded, that a large majority of those converted in our day, are led in a different way. Their first views are very obscure, and they can point to no particular time, when all darkness and doubt were banished from their minds. The light, with them, has been like the dawn of day, at first an obscure twilight, but gradually increasing to the clear light of day. They are very sensible of a great change in their views and feelings, from what they once were, but how it came about, they cannot tell. All they can say is, "whereas I was once blind, now I see."

Often, the first views of Christ are very partial. Perhaps, the soul that had considered its case as hopeless, begins to see and understand, that Christ is able to save it, desperate as its condition seemed to be; and even this, which to many would seem as a small matter, is to a convinced soul almost in despair, as life from the dead. O to be assured that salvation is even possible, fills the soul with a delight it never before experienced. Hope now takes place of despondency; and the soul into which this first ray of light is darted, forms the purpose never to give over seeking, until salvation is obtained. And, in its progress, one of its greatest difficulties is to suppress a continually rising thought, that a change has been experienced. As sincere souls are more apprehensive of no danger than of false hope, they become alarmed, when they find themselves insensibly sliding into the opinion that they are already Christians; and yet this persuasion is hard to be resisted, because it is based on the evidences of piety contained in the word of God, and laid down by judicious divines.

4. The blessed effect of flying to this refuge which is set before us is, strong consolation. No feeling with which we have an acquaintance is more delightful, than an assurance of deliverance from a great impending calamity. And as no danger to which we can be exposed is comparable to that of everlasting misery; so no enjoyment is so sweet, as the joy of salvation. It is described as "unspeakable and full of glory." It cannot be otherwise, but that there should be peace and joy in believing; for he who truly believes, must have some view of Christ as an all-sufficient Saviour. He must have some apprehension of the refuge provided for guilty sinners; yea, must have fled to this refuge, which act cannot take place without experiencing something of that repose and comfort, which must necessarily follow from the discovery of a way of escape from the impending wrath of God. But it is evident that though there is ample provision made for strong consolation to all who fly

to this refuge; yet the comfort enjoyed will generally be in proportion to the strength of the faith exercised. Often, faith, in its commencement, is like a grain of mustard-seed, so small, that in the midst of the darkness and corruption of the human heart, it can scarcely be discerned. And there is in many a gloomy, melancholy temperament; or such a degree of suspicion and diffidence of themselves, that they cannot easily be persuaded that they are in a safe state. Their comfort is therefore greatly marred by doubts and fears, which accompany some pious persons through their whole pilgrimage. There are also, often, mistakes entertained, respecting the true nature of conversion. It is assumed as a truth, that this change is in all cases, very great and perceptible; and as they have never experienced any thing of this sort, they suppose that they are still impenitent.

There is, moreover, some degree of perverseness in relation to this matter, in some serious people. They get into the habit of taking part against themselves, and of uttering constantly complaints of their unhappy state; and also of refusing that consolation which the gospel freely offers to persons in their condition. Such persons may be said to deprive themselves of consolation. But it seems wisely orderly, that our spiritual comforts should rise and fall with the degree of strength or weakness in our faith. If we could enjoy strong consolation while faith and love were feeble, it would prevent us from using suitable exertion to rise, and grow in our spiritual attainments. There is, however, in the promises of God a rich fountain, from whence streams of strong consolation may at any time be drawn, by the exercise of a living faith. All other joy fades away in the near prospect of death and eternity. It is earthly in its source, and cannot endure the bright light of eternity to shine upon it. But the consolations which are found in Christ, become richer and stronger, the more we meditate on the awful realities of the future world. Indeed, much of this strong consolation, experienced by the believer, arises from an assured hope of heavenly felicity. It is the anticipation of future blessedness which fills the heart with a joy which cannot be expressed. If, then, we would partake of this "strong consolation," let us be strong in faith; not staggering at the promise through unbelief, but being fully persuaded that what God hath promised, he will surely perform. Let us hold fast the beginning of our confidence, encouraging our hearts to embrace the promises in all their fulness and freeness. Let us come boldly to the throne of grace, that we may obtain mercy.

1. From what has been said, it may be inferred, that there is good reason for the name "gospel"—"good news." For to the sinner, justly condemned by the unalterable law of God, it opens a safe refuge, to which the guiltiest may flee. I would, therefore, now invite, exhort, and entreat every sinner to avail himself, speedily, of this safe retreat. Fly from impending wrath. The storm of divine vengeance lowers over your head, and unless you get into some safe shelter, will soon overtake you, and will surely overwhelm you, and plunge you into endless perdition. Escape then—escape for

your lives. There is no time to be lost. The door of mercy is now open, but none can tell how soon it may be closed, for ever.

2. Let all beware of false refuges. Of these, there are many, into which deluded souls enter in search of safety, but by which they are only exposed to a more dreadful destruction. They can furnish no real shelter from the storm of divine wrath. The most they can do is, to afford a momentary ease, by cherishing false hopes. But when the hope of the hypocrite perishes, as it certainly will, then he is left in a more miserable condition, than if he had never indulged any hope. Among false refuges, we may mention infidelity, or the fond persuasion that there is no danger of future punishment; a trust in a decent, moral life, without any saving knowledge of a crucified Saviour; self-righteousness, or a dependence on the exact performance of religious rites and duties; also the vain self-confidence of fanatics and antinomians, who trust to their own disordered imaginations, or deceitful hearts. Fly not to any of these, for they are all refuges of lies.

3. As long as the Christian is in this world, he needs a refuge to which he may flee in seasons of affliction and danger. In himself, there is no help nor strength. He is like a defenceless, timorous dove, liable to be devoured by every rapacious bird of prey. If he had no place of refuge, he could not escape destruction. But having once entered the house of refuge, he is safe; no enemy dare pursue him within this sacred refuge: or if he should there be assaulted, he has at hand a mighty Redeemer.

4. The believer having found a safe refuge, should be careful to remain within the limits prescribed. The manslayer, though acquitted, could not with safety leave the city of refuge, during the life-time of the high-priest, and that might often be as long as he himself lived. But our High-priest ever lives, and therefore we must ever remain in the refuge to which we have fled. There is safety there, and no where else. And even when we leave this world, we are only transferred to a higher, holier refuge.

5. Let condemned and perishing sinners, who are exposed daily to the wrath of God, avail themselves of the opportunity of escaping to a place of safety. Let there be no delay in fleeing from the wrath to come. While you delay and procrastinate, divine vengeance may suddenly overtake you. Behold, now is the accepted time, and now is the day of salvation. How can you escape, if you neglect so great salvation! Christ, who has provided this refuge, or rather, who is himself the sinner's Refuge, kindly invites you to come to him for rest. And his gracious promise is, that "him that cometh he will in no wise cast out." Be wise, then, O ye sons of men, and know the time of your merciful visitation; for many who once occupied precisely the ground which you now do, have eternally perished. They put off the matter too long, and now must lament their folly through eternity!

SERMON XXV.

RETURNING TO OUR FIRST LOVE.

Nevertheless, I have somewhat against thee, because thou hast left tny first love. Remember therefore from whence thou art fallen, and repent, and do the first works; or else I will come unto thee quickly, and will remove thy candle-stick out of his place, except thou repent.—REV. ii. 4, 5.

ALTHOUGH our blessed Saviour never wrote any thing himself for the church; yet we have in the evangelists many of his discourses in substance, if not entire; and here we have seven epistles, dictated by him, and communicated to his beloved John, after his ascension to glory. The first of these was addressed to the church at Ephesus, the capital of proconsular Asia; and the other churches to which epistles were addressed, were situated in the vicinity. As the apostle John had taken up his abode at Ephesus, these churches would naturally fall under his inspection and care. The angels, through whom these epistles were addressed to the churches, are commonly supposed to have been the pastors; but a late writer of our own country, has an ingenious conjecture, that these angels were, in fact, the messengers of these seven churches who had been sent by them to attend on, and comfort their beloved apostle, in his exile, in the island of Patmos.

Many interpreters, because these epistles are placed as a preface to a book of prophecy, have been of opinion, that they were of a prophetical character, representing seven successive periods of the history of the Christian church. But there is nothing in these letters to the churches of Asia, which has the least appearance of prediction, except the threatenings and blessings which are appended to the epistles, respectively. And the attempts to apply the supposed prophecies to the several periods of the history of the Christian church, have utterly failed; or such force has been necessary to make out any correspondence between the matter of the epistles and the events of history, that every impartial reader must see, that there exists no solid foundation for the opinion, that these seven epistles to the churches of proconsular Asia were intended to be prophetical. It may be satisfactory to some, to mention, that the name *Asia*, as that of *Europe*, was at first confined to a comparatively small district, of which Ephesus was the capital. Most of the cities to which these epistles were addressed are now in a state of utter desolation, and none more so than Ephesus, which was in the days of the apostle, one of the most celebrated cities in the world. The threatening against the church in this place, mentioned in our text, has been most signally fulfilled. Not only has the candlestick been removed, but the city in which the church was situated is a total ruin. There is something fearful, and at the same time, admonitory, in viewing the utter desolation of many ancient cities, which seemed to have as fair a prospect of perpetuity as any which now flourish upon earth. And does the same doom await these also? Will the candlestick be removed from our great cities? Doubtless, these things were recorded for the admonition and warning of all succeeding churches, to the end of the world. There is a greater uniformity in God's government of cities, churches and nations, than most are willing to acknowledge. Without claiming any thing of the spirit of prophecy, it may be predicted, that when the cup of iniquity, in our large cities, is full, (and the filling goes on very rapidly,) they also will become desolate; and the ground now so highly appreciated, will become worthless; and the churches, which have left, or shall leave their first love, and refuse to repent, will be removed; so that no vestige of them shall remain, as is literally the fact, in regard to Ephesus. Already Ichabod may be inscribed on some churches in our land, for the glory is departed. And as it relates to the different denominations of evangelical Christians, it may be predicted that those which decline most from the truth, and from the spirit of genuine piety, will, notwithstanding all their efforts to increase, and although they may, for a while, flourish in numbers and wealth, be cast off, and doomed to become desolate. Let all Christians, therefore, fear the wrath of that august personage, described in the first chapter of this book, out of whose mouth proceeds a sharp two-edged sword.

Before speaking of the declension of these Ephesian Christians, it will be proper to say something of what is here called "first love." The prominent characteristic of every soul truly converted to Christianity, is LOVE to the Saviour. The faith which is the gift of God, and which is wrought in Christians by the Holy Spirit, always works by love. Love is, therefore, set down as the first and principal fruit of the Spirit. Now, there is something peculiar in the exercise of this first love of the young convert. Its exercise is fervent and tender, not founded, indeed, on such accurate views of the character of Christ as are afterwards acquired; and commonly less pure from mere animal excitement, than that of the mature Christian, but accompanied with more joy and exultation. These joyful frames, so common in new converts, may be ascribed to several causes. The first is the recent transition of the soul from a conviction of condemnation, and ruin, and helplessness, to a state of favour and reconciliation. When the views of the way of salvation are clear, and the faith strong, there is commonly a joyful persuasion of safety and pardon; and even the hope of pardon after a dark season of distress and conscious condemnation is like life from the dead. This case is well illustrated by that of a criminal reprieved from death when under the gallows. His first feelings will be extatic, and though his safety is as certain years afterwards, he never will experience the same liveliness of joy.

Another thing which stamps a peculiarity on the first love of the Christian is the novelty of the objects and scenes which are now presented to his enlightened mind. All his life time he has been in darkness respecting the true nature of spiritual things; for " the natural man receiveth not the things of the Spirit of God, for they are foolishness unto him, neither can he know them, because they are spiritually discerned." But now the eyes of his understanding being opened, and the true light shining into them, every thing appears new and attractive; and sometimes, a divine glory is exhibited to the contemplation of the enlightened mind. This light is, therefore, called "marvellous," by an apostle, and the love which accompanies it, partakes of its marvellous nature. " Whom," says the apostle Peter, "not having seen we love; in whom though now ye see him not, yet believing, ye rejoice with joy unspeakable and full of glory."

Again, God deals with his children in the infancy of their spiritual life, as mothers with their children, while they are young. They nurse them with tender affection, and do every thing in their power to render them comfortable. They furnish them with the sweetest nutriment, cherish them in their bosoms, carry them in their arms, and rock them in the cradle. But when they have been weaned, and have grown strong, they are turned out to shift for themselves. They must now learn to work and endure hardships, and are no longer cherished at the breast, or dandled on the mother's knee.

Thus, our heavenly Father, who exercises a warmer and tenderer affection for his children, than the kindest mothers, is pleased to deal very tenderly with young converts; and often pours streams of divine comfort into their susceptible hearts. They are for a season led in smooth and pleasant paths; and, though dark clouds may occasionally come over them, and "weeping may endure for a night; yet joy cometh in the morning." In their prayers and other religious exercises, they enjoy liberty of access to their heavenly Father; and much of their time is spent in grateful songs of praise, for redeeming love and converting grace. The state of the soul at this period, is beautifully expressed by the poet, in the hymn, which begins,

"Sweet was the time when first I felt
The Saviour's pardoning blood," &c.

Earthly things now have little or no attraction. The thoughts and feelings, the conversation and actions are chiefly occupied with religion. These are indeed halcyon days, and will be often afterwards remembered with a mournful pleasure, when the scene is greatly changed; and especially when inbred corruption grows strong, when temptations vex the soul, and when the heart seems to have lost all tenderness; and when, instead of joy, darkness and trouble almost overwhelm the soul. Then is often uttered the exclamation of Job, " O, that it were with me as in months past."

The union of the believer to Christ, is, in Scripture, often compared to marriage; and the joy of the young convert is like the joy experienced in the day of espousals. (Jer. ii. 2.)

The early days of the true Christian may also be well illustrated by the feelings of the newly enlisted soldier. He rejoices in the " pomp and circumstance" of the military life; is animated by the sound of martial music, and by the sight of splendid banners, and the gorgeous costume of his officers; and leads a life of idleness, while his bounty money supplies him with such luxuries as he desires. But how different are the condition and feelings of the same person, when he receives marching orders; and especially, when he is led into battle, when all his energies are put in requisition, and his life is placed in imminent danger!

But the change in the Ephesian church, of which the ascended Saviour complains, and on account of which he brings a charge against them, is not that which naturally occurs by a change of circumstances, which may take place without any real declension in the vigour of piety. When he says, "thou hast left thy first love," he charges them with actual backsliding. And the declension of a church supposes that of the members of which it is composed.

Let us, then, consider the causes and symptoms of backsliding; and the imperative duty of all who may unhappily have fallen into this state.

Declensions in vital piety are owing to a variety of causes, internal and external. Some of these operate in one case, and different ones, in others; the whole, however, may be attributed to the temptations of Satan, the allurements of the world, and the inbred corruptions of the heart. Declensions in religion are very commonly produced by too much intercourse with a careless, money-loving, pleasure-seeking world. Vital religion is a delicate plant, and being surrounded by many unfavourable circumstances, is liable to receive injury from contact with a polluted world. He who is clothed in garments white and clean, will find it difficult to avoid contracting spots which deform and defile his robes, when he is obliged to live in a filthy house. Piety is not the natural state of the heart, but is brought in by a foreign influence, and finds many things inimical to its preservation and growth, in the soul in which it has taken up its abode. For a while, at first, the young convert thinks but little about the business and cares of the world. Perhaps he is culpably inattentive to those duties which are required in making provision for the body. But soon he finds, that he must serve God in a lawful calling—he must make honest provision for his own wants and those of his family. It is hard to pursue the world just as far as duty calls, and then to stop. When the efforts to acquire property are successful, a pleasure is naturally experienced in the acquisition of good things. And, after a while, an undue love of the world is apt to be generated insensibly. The evil creeps in insidiously, and nothing unjust is thought of; but the undue love of the world, whether of its riches, its honours, or its pleasures, will soon injuriously influence the love of the soul to its Saviour. The thoughts are too much drawn off from the contemplation of divine things, and the relish for spiritual duties and enjoyments is sensibly diminished. The duties of the closet are no longer anticipated with delight; and the hours consecrated to private devotion, which were wont to be the pleasantest in the whole day, do not now afford the same comfort as formerly.

The want of enjoyment in religious duties, and the wandering of the thoughts in the midst of them, and the want of lively feeling naturally tend to produce a backwardness to engage in them; so that were not the person forced, as it were, by conscience to enter his closet, he would often omit the duty altogether. But when secret prayer is attended to, the person on whom the world has had an undue influence, hurries over the service; and often the omission would be better than the performance, where the service is merely formal, and the knee is bowed and words uttered, without one devotional emotion.

Worldly company, and too much occupation in secular affairs, are almost sure to deaden our pious affections, and to disqualify us for spiritual exercises. At first, the soul which has in it the "root of the matter," is alarmed at the defect of spiritual enjoyment, and makes, it may be, some inefficient efforts to recover the ground which has been lost; but these not proving successful, it gives itself up to a kind of indifference. It avoids serious reflection on its former state of lively feeling; or perhaps is tempted to think that there was more enthusiasm than real religion in those joyful frames, which were once so highly valued. And this temptation derives strength from the recollection of our ignorance, and the many false impressions to which we were then subject. Just so far as this temptation has influence, the backslider loses all present desire of having his former exercises of religion renewed. This is a fearful and dangerous delusion. In this state of delusion, the person tries to persuade himself, that he has lost nothing; that sober thought and rational feeling have taken the place of enthusiastic fervours. But where there is any spiritual life, there will be seasons of uneasiness, and an irrepressible feeling that all is not right. These, however, are but waking moments in the sleep of carnal security, into which the soul has fallen. For the most part, the conscience is lulled into a false security; and is so little awake, to give warning of danger, that many things now appear to be lawful and innocent, which would have been avoided as highly criminal in the time of its first love. Indeed, while in this state of slumbering, you can perceive very little difference between the declining professor, and the mere moralist who makes no pretensions to religion. And the people of the world are surprised and gratified, to find that those whom they once shunned, on account of their seriousness, are so much like themselves, and can join with them in gay conversation, and participate in their amusements without scruple.

But let a lively Christian attempt to engage such persons in spiritual and experimental conversation on religion, and see what repugnance they will manifest to lay open the state of their hearts. Soon they will contrive to change the subject; and while it continues, they assent with painful feelings, to what may be said. "Out of the abundance of the heart, the mouth speaketh." There is no surer sign of declension from our first love, than an aversion to conversation respecting Christ, and his love, and our great obligations to love, honour and praise him, to the utmost of our power. Many leave their first love to Christ, who never fall into open transgression: but some are not so much favoured. They are "overtaken in a fault," under some sudden temptation, as Peter. Others, gradually sink into a state of carnal security, until like David, they become entangled by some insidious lust. When off their guard, the enemy comes in, and presenting the bait of sensual pleasure, they are overcome, and remain for a season, under the dominion of sin. Often it becomes necessary to exclude such from the communion of the church, for conduct which is dishonourable to their sacred profession. And the judicious exercise of discipline, is sometimes made the effectual means of recovering true Christians from a state of shameful backsliding. Discipline is not intended for the destruction of those on whom it is exercised; but that they may be saved, by destruction of their pride and sinful propensities.

A more common means of restoring backsliders, is the rod of affliction. The reason why God scourgeth every son that he receiveth is, because all have faults and imperfections, which a kind Father aims to correct, by the use of the rod. By affliction, the vanity of the world is seen. The infatuation produced by the love of the world is broken. In the dark day of adversity, when the idols of the backsliding Christian have been snatched away; when sickness has invaded his dwelling, and, either in his own person, or those as dear to him as his own soul, he is excruciated with strong pain, and no earthly resource remains on which he can rely for consolation, he is filled with sorrow for having departed from the fountain of living water, and is driven to seek refuge and comfort in the mercy of our Lord Jesus Christ.

The last thing which we propose to consider, is the return of the soul to its first love. Backsliding Christians might, in justice, be cast off for ever; but God, who has entered into covenant with his people, is faithful; and one of the promises of the new covenant is, that he will "heal their backsliding." The good Shepherd looks after his wandering sheep, and restores them. But this he does by bringing them to a deep conviction of their sin. Their second conversion is, like the first, attended with many painful and anxious feelings, but after many discouragements, they are enabled to come to Christ and cast themselves upon his mercy; and to their astonishment, their reception is most gracious. They are welcomed as though they had never offended, and are restored to the joy of the divine favour.

But let us attend to the directions given in the text, to the Ephesian Christians. And the first is, to remember whence we have fallen. In a state of declension, there is a strange forgetfulness of former experience in the divine life. It is, therefore, very significantly represented by a state of sleep. The very first step towards a return to God, is to be awakened from this spiritual slumber; to remember what we once possessed and enjoyed, and to compare our present condition with our former. This awakened recollection will lead the soul to understand the cause of its departure from God, and to trace all the steps of its retrograde course. Memory is a valuable faculty of our minds, and its exercise is of much avail in religion. "Remember!" My hearers, our exalted Saviour seems to address this word unto us. Let us, then, remember what we once were; what lively feelings of penitence, love, and joy, sweetly mingled their emotions in our early experience in religion. Let us remember what hopes we then cherished, what resolutions we formed—yea, what solemn vows we made and recorded in the house of God. Did we then suppose, that we should ever become so cold and indifferent in our religious feelings as at present? When aged Christians warned us of our danger, we were disposed to think that their solicitude in our behalf was superfluous, for we were confident, that we should never decline from the walk of faith. Our foresight was, indeed, short; by insensible degrees we left our first love, and have wandered like straying sheep. But now, again, the good Shepherd causes us to hear his voice. And his first call to us is to "remember"—to remember whence we have fallen. This is in order to the next step, which is TO REPENT. Be sorry for what you have done. We should be willing to admit the painful, humbling conviction that we have grievously and foolishly sinned, in departing from the living God. Sin is embittered to none, more than to the penitent backslider; especially the sin of ingratitude breaks his heart. He is astonished at his own blindness and unbelief which prevented him from seeing the snare which the enemy spread to entangle his feet. O what infatuation! after having tasted the joy of pardoned sin, and after being favoured with the spirit of adoption, to turn again to folly. This fills him, on the recollection, with astonishment and regret; and he now asks himself, "What fruit had ye in those things whereof ye are now ashamed?" Where now are the promised pleasures of sin? Alas! that which was sweet in the mouth is turned to gall and wormwood in the stomach. Remember, then, from whence thou hast fallen and REPENT.

But our obedience must not be confined to the feelings and affections of the heart, however pious and penitent these may be. A good tree will produce good fruit. Our Lord, therefore, adds, "and do the first works." Immediately, on a sinner's first conversion, he begins to work. "Lord, what wilt thou have me to do?" is the language of every renewed heart. "He that hath my commandments and keepeth them," saith our Lord, "he it is that loveth me." "If ye love me keep my commandments." But in a state of backsliding, the commandments of Christ are neglected, or obeyed in a very imperfect manner. Undue conformity to the world takes the place of self-denial, and formality is substituted for spirituality, in the worship of God. But when the backslider is reclaimed—which is really a new conversion—he is again led to engage cordially in the service of God. He now returns to the performance of his first works, as well as to the exercise of his first love. He again abounds in prayer and praise, makes the Sabbath a delight, and counts it honourable; draws nigh to God in the holy supper; and is found walking in all the commandments of the Lord, blameless. He does justly, loves mercy, and walks humbly with his God. The heart of a reclaimed backslider is sure to be more humble and distrustful of itself than before. There is also, now, more caution and watchfulness, in regard to the heart. It has been found to be "deceitful above all things," and, therefore, ought not to be trusted. The vain self-confidence of such, is now completely cured. The reclaimed penitent knows, experimentally, that his standing is not in himself; that unless he is preserved by the grace of God, he will certainly fall away again.

The penitent backslider is especially on his guard against those sins and temptations by which he was overcome, when he departed from God; so that, in all his after life, he is more secure from these, than from other sins.

Two feelings are predominant in the exercises of a returning backslider; these are shame, and a lively feeling of the baseness of ingratitude. Such a soul is ashamed to look up, and is often so confounded and overwhelmed with this feeling, that it remains silent before God. This frame of mind is vividly described by Ezekiel in the following language: "That thou mayest remember and be confounded, and never open thy mouth any more because of thy shame, when I am pacified toward thee, for all that thou hast done, saith the LORD GOD."

The mercy of God, in graciously receiving the returning backslider, appears to him more wonderful than it did on his first conversion, and his admiration of the long-suffering of the Lord is greatly enhanced. It is true, then, that God in his wisdom, overrules even the falls and declensions of his people, to increase their humility and watchfulness. The reclaimed backslider is also rendered more charitable and forbearing to his brethren, when they appear delinquent in duty, or are overtaken in a fault.

Let all churches make the inquiry seriously and honestly, whether they have not left their first love. With many, the fact is notorious; their departure from God may be said to be visible and great. Where is now that fervent affection and ardent zeal which once characterized them? Where now is that spirit of earnest, wrestling prayer, which seemed as if it would give God no rest until he should cause the righteousness of Zion to go forth as brightness, and the salvation thereof, as a lamp that burneth? Where now is that fruitfulness in works of piety, mercy, and benevolence, which adorned your profession?

"Remember, therefore, from whence ye are fallen and repent, and do your first works." Otherwise, the threatening against Ephesus, so fearfully executed, may be realized in your case. Your candlestick may be removed. Darkness may succeed to light. Error may overspread the church. Faithful ministers may be withdrawn, and false teachers may come in their place. For your own sakes, and that of your posterity, awake out of your sleep. Seek the Lord for the return of his grieved Spirit. Cry mightily to God for his reviving influences.

As every church consists of individuals, I would call upon all professors to consider their ways.

Examine yourselves, whether you be in the faith, and whether you are in a growing, thriving condition; for if not, you are surely in a state of declension. There is no standing still in religion. If you are not pressing forward, you are certainly retrograding. You are, this day, solemnly called upon to remember the times and seasons which are past—to remember the love and joy of your espousals unto Christ, when the candle of the Lord shone upon your tabernacle; and when your chief delight was in the service of God; when the very name of Jesus was as ointment poured forth—when he gave you songs in the night, and in the morning, your first thoughts spontaneously arose to God your Redeemer. Then you could say, "It is good for me to draw near to God." "Whom have I in heaven but thee?" "There is none in the earth that I desire besides thee." "One day in thy courts is better than a thousand, and I had rather be a door-keeper in the house of God, than dwell in the tents of sin." Then you rejoiced, when they said, "Come, let us go up to the house of the Lord."

But how is it with you now? What does conscience testify as to your present condition? What testimony would your closet give, if it could speak? Alas! what a change! Where now are your religious comforts? What has become of that sweet peace you once enjoyed? Perhaps, you even doubt of the reality or genuineness of your former experiences. You have, like the virgins in the parable, fallen into a slumbering state, in which the awful truths of religion are dimly perceived, and make but a slight and transient impression on your mind, when they occur to your thoughts. To you, I would say, "Awake out of sleep, arise from the dead, and Christ shall give thee light." Remember from whence you have fallen; repent and do your first works. Your present situation is one of extreme danger. While in this deadening state, you cannot possess satisfactory evidence of the genuineness of your piety. While in this state you cannot glorify God, nor be useful to men according to your ability and opportunity. And how sad your condition, if death should find you in this unprepared state! "O that they were wise, that they would consider their latter end."

If there should be any present who have been made sensible of their sinful departure from God, and who are sunk in discouragement, and agonized with fear, lest they have sinned beyond the reach of mercy and bounds of forgiveness, and who, by these views are prevented from returning, to such I would say, dishonour not God, by entertaining such hard and unbelieving thoughts. His mercy is infinite. As high as are the heavens above the earth, so high are his thoughts of mercy above our conception. He has left special promises for the encouragement of such as you; and he has never rejected one who came unto him. You cannot gratify the heart of your sympathizing Saviour more, than by exercising confidence in his power and willingness to save you.

I would conclude by addressing you in the language of God by the prophet Hosea: "O Israel, return unto the Lord thy God; for thou hast fallen by thine iniquity. Take with you words and turn to the Lord; say unto him, take away all iniquity and receive us graciously—for in thee the fatherless findeth mercy." To which his gracious answer is, "I will heal their backslidings and love them freely; for my anger is turned away from him. I will be as the dew unto Israel; he shall grow as the lily, and cast forth his roots as Lebanon. His branches shall spread, and his beauty shall be as the olive-tree, and his smell as Lebanon. They that dwell under his shadow shall return, they shall revive as the corn, and grow as the vine. The scent thereof shall be as the cedars of Lebanon; and Ephraim shall say, What have I to do any more with idols?"

SERMON XXVI.

THE BLESSEDNESS OF TRUSTING IN GOD.

Blessed are all they that put their trust in him.—Psa. i. 12.

THAT this psalm relates to the Messiah is admitted by Jews as well as Christians. Whether it has a primary respect to David and the establishment of his kingdom on Mount Zion, or should be entirely referred to Messiah, is a point on which expositors are not agreed; and it is not a matter of so much importance, as to render it necessary for us to discuss it in this place. That it does contain an important prediction of the Lord Jesus Christ, does not rest on the interpretation of fallible men; but is expressly decided by the authority of divine inspiration. "The kings of the earth set themselves, and the rulers took counsel together against the Lord and his anointed." This passage is quoted and expressly applied to Christ by the whole college of apostles, after they had received the plenary inspiration of the Holy Spirit, on the day of Pentecost. For upon hearing the report of Peter and John, who had been arraigned before the sanhedrim, the apostles all broke out in praise to God, saying, "Lord, thou art God, which hast made heaven and earth and the sea, and all that in them is; who by the mouth of thy servant David hast said, Why did the heathen rage, and the people imagine vain things? For of a truth, against thy holy child Jesus whom thou hast anointed, both Herod and Pontius Pilate, with the Gentiles and people of Israel, were gathered together, for to do whatsoever thy hand and thy counsel determined before to be done." (Acts iv. 24—28.)

In regard to the remarkable declaration, "This day have I begotten thee;" the apostle Paul assures us, that such an address was never made to the highest of created angels. There is but one to whom it could with propriety be made; and by orthodox commentators it has, from time immemorial, been supposed to have respect to the eternal generation of the Son; for the expression "this day" is not to be taken as having reference to any particular day, but as relating to a perpetuity of duration.

Paul, in his discourse delivered in Antioch, in Pisidia, applies this declaration to the resurrection of Christ, saying, "We declare unto you glad tidings, how that the promise which was made unto the fathers, God hath fulfilled the same unto us their children, in that he hath raised up Jesus again, as it is written in the second Psalm, "Thou art my Son; this day have I begotten thee." It cannot be supposed by any, that Christ was not truly the Son of God, before his resurrection; therefore the meaning must be that by the resurrection, Jesus was manifested to be the Son of God; just as he was by being born of the Virgin by the power of the Holy Ghost. The exhortation to "kiss the Son"—and the benediction on all who trust in him, can refer to no other but the Son of God. We are never, in Scripture, exhorted to trust in any mere creature, however exalted. On the contrary, a curse is denounced on every one " who trusteth in man, and maketh flesh his arm." This portion of the Psalm, therefore, can have no application to David or Solomon, but must refer solely to the Messiah who is the eternally begotten Son of God.

The act of trust is so familiar to all, that it requires no explanation. Even children know what is meant by trust in any one. Two things are always implied in trusting; the first is a conviction of need, and sense of dependence. He who needs nothing, will, of course, not trust to another for what he has in himself; and he who, though destitute, is not sensible of his need, will never be induced to trust in another

The second thing implied in the act of trust is, a persuasion of the good-will, ability, and fidelity of the person in whom we trust. A child in danger, will fly to the arms of its father with confidence, but will not trust to another child, however affectionate; because it is not persuaded of its ability to protect it. Neither would a child trus to an entire stranger, as having no assurance of hi good-will; nor would it fly to the arms of one, by whom it had often been deceived.

The exercise of a saving faith is not more frely expressed by any term than by *trust*. Indeed, whenever we believe in a promise of any one; that is, when we are fully persuaded of the truth of a promise, that act of faith is properly termed, trust.

Man is so dependent on Providence for the common blessings of this life, that trust in God for these, is the state of mind which is becoming. For, although we procure many temporal blessings by the instrumentality of our own faculties, or the labour of our hands; yet these blessings are as really the gifts of our heavenly Father as if we used no means whatever; for without the blessing of God, all our toil and ingenuity would effect nothing. "Except the Lord build the house, they labour in vain that build it." God is the "Father of lights from whom cometh down every good and perfect gift." This dependence on God, we should eel in relation to all our efforts to procure common blessings; and not only feel it, but openly acknowledge it, when we partake of the common bounties of divine Providence.

But, in regard to spiritual and eternal blessings, our dependence is still greater; for man has already lost the favour of God, and has fallen under his dreadful curse. Man is also sunk deeply into a state of depravity. He has lost all true knowledge of God his Creator; and is not only a miserable, but a helpless creature. He is unable, by any sufferings which he can endure, to expiate the smallest of his sins. He is unable to vivify his dead soul, or to bring back life into his benumbed faculties. If his salvation depended on it, he could not cause his heart to go forth in love to God, or cease the undue exercise of self-love and love to the creature. "The carnal mind is not subject to the law of God, neither indeed can be." But this inability of the heart and will is so far from furnishing any excuse to the sinner, that it is the chief ground of his criminality. What! a heart so depraved that nothing can induce it to reverence and love its Creator! Will any one dare to plead the possession of such a heart, as a reason why he should not be punished when arraigned at the tribunal of God? Man, in his natural state, is also blind and ignorant. Some, like the Pharisees of old, will be ready to ask, "What! are we blind also?" Yes, all are blind, however acute their intellect, however stored with human learning their minds. "The natural man receiveth not the things of the Spirit of God; they are foolishness to him; neither can he know them, because they are spiritually discerned." (1 Cor. ii. 14.)

Here, then, is a threefold misery common to all the children of Adam—blindness, deadness, and guilt; and to qualify himself as a physician to cure the threefold malady, Christ has assumed as Mediator, a threefold office, viz. of a prophet, of a priest, and of a king; and in this threefold office, the sinner must trust in him for salvation. But it may be alleged, that this misery of man is merely imaginary; that the majority of men are in a good moral condition, and behave as well as could be expected in the circumstances in which they are placed. It is admitted that all are not equally abandoned in iniquity. It is admitted, that many maintain a decent outward appearance. It is admitted that many are strict in the observance of rites and forms in religion; and show themselves to be of the same spirit as the Pharisees of old. And it is evident that few among men seem to have any particular conviction of the miseries which have been mentioned. But this blindness and insensibility are rather aggravations of their misery, than alleviations. Indeed, this stupidity respecting spiritual concerns and eternal interests is the very worst symptom of their desperate disease. If they were sensible of their sins, if they lamented their blindness, if they were crying out, "What must I do to be delivered from this dreadful curse?" there would be some hope of them; but as long as this state of blindness and insensibility remains, there is no hope; for they never can be induced, in this state, to apply the only remedy; which remedy is of that nature, that it must be apprehended and appropriated by the rational mind. "They that are whole need not a physician, but they that are sick." Christ says, "I came not to call the righteous, but sinners to repentance."

If you saw, in a public prison, a number of criminals under sentence of condemnation to suffer capital punishment, and should observe some of the number indulging in singing and dancing, and every species of mirth and levity, and using all their influence to bring their companions into the same temper, would you call these happy? Would any man in his senses envy such happiness as this? On the contrary, would not all be shocked at this most unseasonable and reckless levity? And if obliged to choose between this state of mind, and that of those who were cast down and mourning their unhappy lot, who would not prefer the condition of the latter?

All men need a refuge to which they may flee for safety; and happy are they who have been so made sensible of their danger and misery, that they are anxiously seeking a place of safety. Their case is urgent—their danger is imminent—the misery which awaits them is inconceivably great, and they are utterly helpless in themselves, and unable to extricate themselves from their miserable circumstances, or to ward off the threatening danger which is ready to burst on their guilty heads. And as they cannot escape by their own wisdom or power, so no other creature has ability to rescue them from ruin. Whither, then, shall they turn? to whom shall they apply for help and deliverance? The only one who has power to save them is the Person whom they have offended, and whose displeasure they have incurred—the very Person who holds in his hand upraised the sword of vindicatory justice, ready to strike the sinner dead. "The Judge of all the earth will do right." And it is right to inflict condign punishment on impenitent sinners, who have long rejected the gracious offers of reconciliation. Where then is there any hope for the sinner, justly condemned by the law of his God? No where, but in the gospel of salvation. Here, and here alone, is there a door of hope open for the guilty. Sin cannot escape punishment in the just government of a holy God. He says, "I will by no means clear the guilty." "Surely, O Lord, thou wilt slay the wicked." But blessed be

God, sin may be punished in an adequate substitute. It has been punished in our divine SURETY; for "he was wounded for our transgressions; he was bruised for our iniquities." "He was made a curse for us to redeem us from the curse of the law." "Our iniquities were laid upon him." The satisfaction is complete. It is of infinite value. It is impossible that any sins should be of such heinous guilt, that the application of the blood of Jesus will not cleanse it. "Though your sins be as scarlet, they shall be white as snow; though they be red like crimson, they shall be as wool." (Isa. i. 18.)

Jesus of Nazareth is revealed as the true Messiah, God's Anointed, the King of Zion—the only true HIGH PRIEST, after the order of Melchisedec, and the prophet of Israel of whom all God's people are taught. He is the Saviour of the world; and "there is no other name given under heaven, whereby we must be saved." "Kiss the Son lest he be angry, and ye perish from the way, when his wrath is kindled but a little. Blessed are all they that put their trust in him."

Trust in the Redeemer supposes that he has manifested, in some way, a willingness to save us. In order that trust have a firm foundation, it is requisite that there should be, not only a general expression of benevolence and good-will, but explicit promises of relief. And such promises are especially necessary in the case of the sinner; for he can with difficulty be convinced, that there can be any salvation for one so vile as he now sees himself to be. Therefore we find the gospel full of kind invitations and gracious promises to all who will come unto him and receive salvation as a free gift. These are the glad tidings by which so many wounded spirits have been healed and comforted. The convinced sinner, (for no other can trust in the Redeemer,) finding every other refuge to be false, and every other arm to be weak, has, at length, his attention turned to a crucified Saviour. He hears words of mercy and kindness, but at first he cannot believe that they are addressed to him. He thinks this good news is for others less vile than himself. He imagines, if in some way, by prayers, tears, or penances, he could purify his heart, or even get it softened to some degree of tenderness, Christ might receive him; but he cannot easily be persuaded, that he will be welcomed in his present wretched state of mind. He, therefore, is kept back by his unbelieving fears, and by what has the semblance of humility, and sees not the evil of refusing to believe the words of Christ, by which he virtually makes him a liar. He delays—he strives—he prays and fasts—and finally, almost despairs; for these efforts seem to have the effect of driving him further from salvation than before. He concludes, therefore, that he may as well give over seeking, as now he is sensible of his utter impotence. But in this dark, distressful hour, when he nearly depairs of mercy, he is surprised by a view of the way of reconciliation. Christ appears both able and willing to save him; and he sees how God can be just, and yet justify him through the righteousness of Jesus Christ. Every thing appears so plain, that he wonders he never saw it before—so plain, that he feels confident, that he could cause any one to understand it.

But the first views of faith are not always so clear; more commonly, the first light is like that of the dawn of day, which gradually increases. Often the convinced, discouraged sinner is first made to see the fulness of Christ; and whereas before he feared that his sins were too great to be pardoned, he is now brought to believe, "He is able to save—to save to the uttermost, all who come unto God by him." And even this is like life from the dead, to a sinner on the borders of despair. Here is a real exercise of faith, while the believing soul entertains as yet no persuasion of being in the favour of God—an evidence that such a persuasion is not of the essence of faith. But when the view of the way of salvation is at first clear, or whenever it becomes clear, nothing fills the soul with greater wonder, and gratitude at the same time, than that Christ is waiting to receive sinners in all their guilt and vileness—yea, to receive them just as they are; not only without merit, but without preparation; and that he undertakes to do the whole work of their salvation, gratuitously.

Now he begins to know, by experience, what it is to trust in the Lord Jesus Christ. Now he willingly commits his soul into his hands, in confidence that he will keep it safely. He trusts in him for pardon and justification; and this he can do without hesitation, for he sees that he hath borne our sins, and hath become the end of the law for righteousness to every one that believeth. He trusts in him also, for divine teaching; knowing that by his Spirit, his people are all taught of God, and led into the knowledge of all necessary truth. He trusts in him for complete deliverance from inherent corruption, and from the power of the grave. In short, he trusts in him as his complete and eternal Saviour, who, through his love and through his merit, will bring him off conqueror and more than conqueror. He is satisfied with the Redeemer in all his offices, and in all his mediatorial work. The language of his heart is, "He hath done all things well." When the soul, under the influence of the Holy Spirit, is led to view Christ as "the way, the truth, and the life," it is a very common experience, to have precious promises brought successively into view. They come dropping into the soul, as honey from the comb; or rather as the manna from heaven. Sometimes, however, the soul is absorbed in the contemplation of the truth, contained in a single text, for there are incomprehensible riches in the word of God; so that often, the whole plan of salvation is suggested by a single passage of Holy Scripture. All we need is, to have the illumination of the Spirit to accompany the reading or preaching of the word, to cause us to see wonderful things in texts which had often been heard or read without emotion; and in the contemplation of them the mind is filled with unspeakable joy. Now the enlightened soul has no need of arguments to convince it that the Scriptures are indeed the word of God. This is evident from the excellence which is seen in them. And as the light of day reveals to us as the most conspicuous and glorious object in the visible heavens, the sun shining in his strength; so the light of divine truth reveals Christ "the Sun of righteousness," as the most glorious object of contemplation; for it is in his face that the glory of God is manifested. "He is the brightness of his glory, and the express image of his Person." (Heb. i. 3.)

The soul which has thus been raised from the horrible pit and miry clay of natural corruption and condemnation, and is established on the rock of ages, has a new song put into his mouth, even praise for salvation. He can now rejoice in God—in his existence—his attributes—his Providence—his redeeming love in Christ, in all his glorious work of redemption—in the promise of God—in the means of grace, and in the hope of glory!

They who have once found Christ, and trusted in him, however they may be tossed with temptation, or distressed by doubts of their acceptance, never think of any other refuge but Christ—they never attempt to build on any other foundation. They show themselves to be his, by their trusting in him, even when they walk in darkness, and have no light. The more violent the storm by which they are assailed the more tenaciously do they adhere to the rock of their salvation. And when oppressed with a painful conviction of unfaithfulness and short-coming, in the service of Christ, no ease, no peace is experienced, until they come anew to the cross, and by faith obtain a fresh sprinkling of the blood of reconciliation. The blood of Christ is the only balm for a soul wounded with a sense of sin. As to his own best works, instead of pleading them as a ground of pardon, or a reason for acceptance, he is ashamed of them in the sight of God, and continually prays, that their imperfection may not be charged upon him. Still he feels thankful to God that he has given him a heart to delight in his law after the inner man, to hunger and thirst after righteousness, and to aim at the glory of God, and the advancement of the Redeemer's kingdom. He is thankful for every evidence which he has of being renewed in the spirit of his mind; for he knows that if he is a new creature, it is altogether owing to grace. Though the past sins of believers are forgiven, yet he needs fresh forgiveness every day and every hour. But when he sins he has an Advocate with the Father, whose propitiation has merit to take away all iniquity. There is no ground of confidence more satisfactory to the soul than the intercession of Christ. Thousands of trembling souls have trusted in that one declaration, and have found peace—" He is able to save to the uttermost, all that come unto God by him, seeing he ever liveth to make intercession for them." Having a great High Priest to appear in the presence of God for them, they can come with boldness to the throne of grace, that they may obtain mercy and find grace to help in every time of need."

The believer also trusts in Christ for future help and future good. He relies upon him for guidance in the way of truth and duty—he depends on him for strength to enable him to encounter all enemies, to endure all afflictions, and to perform the most arduous duties. And as he must, in his pilgrimage to heaven, pass the valley of the shadow of death, he relies upon the faithful word of the great Shepherd, that he will be present to drive away all fear and all distress. And, in regard to bodily want, there is no ground for anxiety, because he hath said, "I will never leave thee nor forsake thee."

Finally, the true believer trusts in Christ, that when this earthly pilgrimage is finished, he will have administered unto him an abundant entrance into the everlasting kingdom of our Lord and Saviour Jesus Christ. On this point, the promises of God are clear and abundant. Christ says, "In my Father's house are many mansions." "I go," says he, "to prepare a place for you." Again, "Father, it is my will that where I am, there they also may be, that they may behold my glory, which I had with thee before the world began." "Fear not, little flock, it is your Father's good pleasure to give you the kingdom." And at the last day he will say to every one of them, "Come, ye blessed of my Father, inherit the kingdom prepared for you from the foundation of the world." "And these shall go into life eternal."

They trust also, that these mortal bodies shall be raised from the grave, incorruptible and undying, and fashioned like unto Christ's glorious body. Christ is the resurrection and the life, and as in Adam all die, so in Christ shall all believers be made alive.

III. We need not dwell long on the blessedness of those who trust in the Redeemer, for this has been in some measure anticipated in what has already been said. It may, however, be useful to make a distinct mention of the blessings which belong to such.

1. They have received the forgiveness of sin, and have an assurance that they shall never again come into condemnation. "There is no condemnation to them who are in Christ Jesus, who walk not after the flesh, but after the Spirit."

2. They have the indwelling of the Spirit of God, which secures their continuance in a state of grace, and enables them to grow in grace and in the knowledge of our Lord and Saviour Jesus Christ—"to die unto sin and to live unto righteousness." If believers were left to themselves, their conversion would be of little value, for they would soon be overcome by their spiritual enemies, and their last state would be worse than the first.

3. It is a part of the blessedness of believers, that they are the special care of divine Providence. All things work for their good. The very hairs of their head are numbered. Their afflictions are fatherly chastisements, which shall work for them the peaceable fruits of righteousness. Yea, these light afflictions which are but for a moment, work out for them an exceeding great and eternal weight of glory. Even death itself is reckoned in the catalogue of blessings. Not only are Paul and Apollos and Cephas, and things present and things to come, theirs, and life—but death also. The sting of them is extracted, for the sting of death is sin, and the strength of sin is the law; but when the law is satisfied and sin pardoned, then the sting is taken away.

4. They who put their trust in God are blessed,

because they enjoy inward peace. They have peace with God, peace of conscience, peace from the jarring elements of corrupt passions. They look forward to an inheritance incorruptible, unde filed, and that fadeth not away. Hope that maketh not ashamed, is the anchor of their souls in all the storms of life.

5. When they leave the world they shall be blessed in the open vision of God's glory; for they shall see no more darkly as through a glass, but face to face. They shall know as they are known. They shall be perfectly cleansed from the pollutions of sin, and when they shall see the Saviour, they shall be like him, for they shall see him as he is. Glorious state of complete felicity! Blessed indeed are all they who have a part in the inheritance of he saints in light.

SERMON XXVII.

FAITH'S VICTORY OVER THE WORLD.

And this is the victory that overcometh the world, even our faith.—
1 JOHN v. 4.

THE conquest of the world may be considered the highest object of human ambition. In different ages, a few great heroes extended their conquests so far, and brought under their dominion so many countries and nations, that, in the language of eulogy, they have been styled the conquerors of the world. But if it were possible for any man literally to gain possession of the whole world, still he would be poor; the acquisition would be of little real value, and he would remain as unsatisfied as before. Indeed, it is reported of one who came as near the dominion of the known world as any other, that when he had completed his conquests, he sat down and wept, because there was not another world to conquer. It is a truth taught by all experience, that in no form and in no quantity can this world be a satisfying portion to the immortal mind, which was made for enjoyments of a far nobler kind. It would, therefore, be a real benefit to mankind to be cured of their insatiable thirst after worldly possessions, and to have their attention directed to objects of a more excellent and durable nature. Now this is the very design of true religion, which it accomplishes, in some good degree, for all those who sincerely embrace it. But we cannot renounce the world as a portion, without incurring its displeasure. "If ye were of the world, the world would love his own; but because I have chosen you out of the world, therefore the world hateth you." And this enmity is not inoperative. The opposition which exists between the spirit of the world, and the spirit of true religion must produce a conflict; for Christians and men of the world not only mingle together in the same society, but are often connected by the ties of kindred and relationship. Hence it has come to pass, in all ages, that Christianity has been the occasion of enkindling the flames of strife between the members of the same household. And although its natural tendency is to produce peace and good-will among men; yet, agreeably to Christ's prediction, it has brought "a sword." "For I am come," said the Saviour, "to set a man at variance against his father, and the daughter against her mother, and the daughter-in-law against her mother-in-law; and a man's foes shall be they of his own household." The world which lieth in wickedness, is at enmity with God. It is under the usurped authority of the prince of darkness, who is therefore called, "the God of this world." Those, therefore, who come out from the world, and imbibe a different spirit, will be treated as deserters, and will meet with persecution in one form or another. In this contest, if you count the apparent numbers, there is a fearful odds in favour of the world, and against the Christian soldier; but if your eyes should be opened, like those of the servant of the prophet, like him, you will be ready to exclaim, "They that be with us are more than they that be with them." He who has enlisted under the banner of the Captain of salvation, may boldly say, "If God be for us, who can be against us?"

The circumstances of this spiritual warfare vary exceedingly with the condition of the world, and of each individual. Sometimes the battle is fierce and dreadful; while, at other times, there is the appearance of a truce. This, however, is always a deceitful appearance. On the part of the enemy there never is any real cessation of hostility; and on the part of the Christian there should be none. And if, at any time, from the delusive appearance of peace, he should remit his vigilance, and fall into the sleep of carnal security, he will be exposed to the most imminent danger; his spiritual welfare will be placed in the utmost peril.

This contest, though "by poets unsung, and by senators unpraised," is the most important in its results, of any which was ever carried on in this world. It will, therefore, be worth our while to take a nearer view of it, and to inquire how the world opposes the Christian, and how the Christian gains a victory over the world.

A victory implies a conflict, and a conflict supposes an enemy. This enemy, as we have seen, is the world. In the sacred Scriptures, the word *world* is used in various senses. Here, it must be taken to signify that complex idea, made up of the men of the world, with all their sentiments, maxims, plans, and pursuits, and the things of the world, including every object which can, in any way, become a temptation or an obstacle to the Christian pilgrim, in his progress to the land of promise.

The opposition of the world is of two kinds; or it assumes two aspects, of a very opposite nature; and endeavours to stop or retard the believer by addressing two different classes of feelings, which appertain to human nature. The first is, an aspect of terror. It presents to him a formidable array of evils, which he must expect to meet with in the Christian course. It endeavours to alarm him, by holding out the prospect of losses to be sustained of things naturally desirable, of pains to be endured which are abhorrent to our nature, and does not merely threaten these evils, but actually inflicts them, in a very appalling and terrific form. Thus, when Christianity was first propagated in the world, it was met with the most determined and virulent opposition. Its professors were dragged before the judgment-seat of governors and kings. They were insulted and abused by the mob. They were "every where spoken against," and reputed to be "the offscouring of all things"—calumniated not only as the enemies of the human race, but as the enemies of the gods. They were beaten, scourged, imprisoned, tortured, thrown to the wild beasts in the theatre, and put to death by every species of torture which diabolical ingenuity could invent. And these scenes of persecution were not confined to one country or to one age. Wherever Christians were discovered, they were persecuted with unrelenting severity, and punished with death merely because they bore the Christian name. During the greater part of three centuries, were these cruelties practised against the unoffending followers of Christ. Thousands, and tens of thousands, of every age, and of both sexes, were thus put to death; not accepting deliverance, when by uttering a single word, or by a single act of worship to the false deities of the heathen, they could have saved their lives. And this spirit of opposition to the genuine spirit of Christianity has never been more malignant, than when it has been exercised under the name and profession of the religion of Christ. No pagan cruelties and tortures could exceed those practised in the Spanish Inquisition. Infidels have sometimes charged all these upon Christianity itself; but this is most unjust, as the precepts and spirit of this religion are diametrically opposed to all cruelty and to all persecution, on account of religion. When the world assumed the profession of Christianity, with the change of name, there was not, generally, a change of disposition. The two contending parties still existed within the pale of the church; and the spirit of the world is not less malign, for being associated with hypocrisy. Christ's real sheep have ever been a little flock. The multitude, and especially those in power and authority, whatever name they may have assumed, have always been the enemies of the pure, spiritual religion of the gospel.

But the days of fierce and violent persecution have gone by—we hope, for ever. Even those who retain and cherish the spirit of persecution are ashamed to avow their true principles; and find it to be the best policy, in this age, to profess liberality. Christians are, therefore, no longer subjected to imprisonment and death, on account of their adherence to the gospel. But has the offence of the cross really ceased? Is no hostility to true religion felt by the world? Far from it. They that are righteous are still hated by those whose deeds are evil. They that are after the flesh, are still disposed to persecute those that walk after the Spirit. There never can be a sincere peace between the seed of the woman and the seed of the serpent. True godliness is still hated by the world; and they who live godly in Christ Jesus, do still suffer persecution. The spirit of the world is the same as formerly, but the mode of attack is changed. Or rather, the providence of God has put a restraint on the wicked; and they now pursue the righteous with weapons of scorn, ridicule, and calumny. The war is not terminated; the contest is still going on, and will not cease as long as there is a world of carnal men.

There is, indeed, a fashionable kind of religion, against which the world feels no enmity; a religion which makes a compromise with the world, connives at its vices and follies, and shuns all seriousness of spirit, and strictness of behaviour. But this is, in fact, no other than the spirit of the world in disguise. Many professors of religion meet with no opposition from the world, because they are of the world, and the world will love its own. And the men of the world, who are wiser in their generation than the children of light, are sagacious in discovering their friends, under whatever disguise they may appear. Indeed, false professors often manifest a more bitter enmity to true religion, than the openly profane; so that there is no difficulty in discerning what manner of spirit they are of. Such have no contest with the world. Their controversy is with the genuine spirit of Christianity, which they are wont to malign as narrow, illiberal, bigoted, and inimical to human happiness and to elegant improvements in society. These pretend to have discovered an easier way to heaven, than that old thorny path of self-denial and devotion, designated by the example and precepts of Christ. They do, indeed, avoid the offence of the cross, and forsake no earthly honour or enjoyment for the kingdom of heaven. But let any one be in good earnest in matters of religion, and be influenced by its truths, in some proportion to their importance. Let him turn off his affections from the world, and no longer seek his chief happiness in its riches, honours, and pleasures. Let him turn his back on its fashionable amusements and convivial entertainments, and let him lead a life in exact conformity with the precepts of the gospel, however contrary to the fashions and maxims of the world, and he will soon learn from experience, that the world has not become the friend of genuine piety; and that it is still true, that he who will be the friend of the world is the enemy of God. Parents often oppose their own children, and do all they can to hinder them from becoming religious; and husbands throw obstacles in the way of their wives, or wives of their husbands. The old companions of sincere converts treat them with neglect, and soon show that their affections are alienated; and sometimes, manifest their scorn and contempt by signs not to be misinterpreted. And he does not need a long time to learn, that spiritual religion is no favourite with the men of this world.

There is another aspect which the world assumes, in regard to religion. It does not always frown, but sometimes insidiously smiles. The aspect of terror which we have been considering, may produce dismay, but the danger menaced is, in that case, always manifest. But when she comes forth with all the blandishments of pleasure; or when, with the language of friendship, she soothes and caresses, and pours forth her strains of adulation, and heaps favours on the head of her intended victim, and with her syren voice incites to the enjoyment of sensual •pleasure, then is the time of trial. These are the temptations which are more dangerous than fires and gibbets. And the danger is greater because it does not appear to be danger. No apprehensions are awakened. Prosperity and indulgence are naturally agreeable to every one. When the senses and appetites are addressed by baits suited to them, and no gross sins are proposed, but merely a life of elegant—and as they are called—innocent delights, the unsuspicious soul is thrown off its guard, and forgets to watch and pray against temptation; and before she is aware, is ensnared in some forbidden indulgence, or is lulled into a sleep of carnal security. The cup of worldly pleasure is always inebriating. It may be sweet to the taste, and exhilarating to the spirits, but its ultimate effects are deleterious. The soul of the Christian is never in greater jeopardy, than when all things around it wear a smiling aspect. By the deceitfulness of riches, many high professors have been brought low in religion. While they hasted to be rich, they pierced themselves through with many sorrows, and fell into temptation and a snare, and into many foolish and hurtful lusts, which drown men in destruction and perdition. "For the love of money is the root of all evil." Thus fell Judas, Ananias, and Sapphira. Thus fell Demas, a companion of Paul, and a preacher of the gospel. In like manner, the honours of the world and the ambition of power and office, have been a snare to many. They cannot believe, while they prefer the honour that comes from men to that which comes from God. They who love the praise of men more than the praise of God, will be ashamed of the gospel of Christ, and will never confess his name before an ungodly and scoffing world.

But in no way does the world oppose the Christian more successfully, than by alluring him with the prospect of ease and pleasure. On this enchanted ground many have slept, and many have slidden back and fallen, so that ever afterwards, they have limped along on their pilgrimage, with broken bones. On this slippery ground, the "man after God's own heart," met with a sad and disgraceful fall, on account of which the mouths of the enemies of religion were opened to blaspheme and do so to this day. And on this same deceitful ground, thousands besides, have been overcome for a season, and others have fallen to rise no more At this point, the world is powerful, and the best of men left to themselves, are weak. Indeed, few who have set their faces Zionward, have escaped unhurt, in passing over this enchanted ground. Young Christians should take warning from the experience of those who have gone before them, and not foolishly confide in their own wisdom and strength. But all should be strong in the Lord, and in the power of his might, and never cease to watch and pray.

II. Having shown how the world opposes the Christian, we come next to explain how the Christian gains the victory. "And this is the victory that overcometh the world, even our faith." The faith to which this victory is ascribed is not that historical or speculative faith, which nearly all persons in Christian countries possess, and which is the effect of education. This faith, in its origin, does not differ from the faith of heathens and Mohammedans, and in its effects, is powerless. Such a faith never, in any case, overcomes the world; for it is dead and unfruitful. The apostle is careful to let us know, that the faith of which he speaks, is the fruit of regenerating grace, the act of the renewed soul; for in the first clause of the verse, from which our text is taken, he says, "For, whosoever is born of God overcometh the world.' None achieve this great victory, but souls "born of God;" for none beside possess a true faith. Some may allege, that their faith is not the mere prejudice of education, but the result of a thorough and impartial examination of the evidences of divine revelation. To such it is still necessary to insist, that though their faith is rational, as being founded on good and solid reasons, yet it comes far short of a saving faith. The faith under consideration, requires no new birth to produce it; it is merely the offspring of man's reason. But it may be asked, In what respect is it defective? If the reasons on which it is built are sound, and the assent unwavering, what could be added to it? To which it may be briefly answered, that we may have convincing evidence of the truth of a thing, while this evidence does not present the object itself in its true light. But when our faith produces an effect, it arises from the nature of the truth believed. No evidence of gospel truth gives to the mind a discernment of the true quality of spiritual objects, but the illumination of the Spirit. "The natural man receiveth not the things of the Spirit of God; they are foolishness unto him, neither can he know them, because they are spiritually discerned." Genuine faith is a conviction, or full persuasion of the truth, produced by the illumination of the Holy Spirit. The evidence on which this faith is founded, being the beauty and excellence of the truth perceived, cannot but be operative; for it is impossible that the rational mind should see an object to be lovely, and not love it. Such a faith must, therefore, "work by love and purify the heart," and be fruitful of good works. This view of saving faith agrees with Paul's definition " Faith is the substance of things hoped for, the evidence of things not seen." Faith, if I may be allowed the expression, is the eye of the soul by which it looks into the spiritual world, and realizes future and eternal things. The Scriptures constantly testify, that all ungodly men are destitute of the true knowledge of God. They may perceive the mere verity and relative connexion of divine truth, but the beauty and glory of the truth, they see not. Just as a blind man may be convinced by feeling and by testimony of the reality of the existence of the sun, but he can form no idea of this celestial luminary in its glory, as he runs his daily race through the heavens.

There is a wide and real distinction between merely intellectual ideas of divine things and those which are spiritual. The unregenerate man may be endowed with a powerful intellect, and he may exercise his reasoning powers on divine truth, and may draw just conclusions respecting them; but he can never by the mere exercise of reason attain to spiritual ideas, any more than the man born blind can attain to the knowledge of light and colours, by logical reasoning; or the deaf mute attain to the correct idea of sounds in some other way. The weakest Christian, even the mere child, by the illumination of the Spirit, possesses a species of knowledge, to which the philosopher can never attain, by the utmost exertion of unassisted reason. And this knowledge is far more excellent, than that of any human science, however sublime or useful.

From the foregoing view of the nature of faith,

it will not be difficult to understand how it overcomes the world. It will only be necessary to bring to view two principles, to account for the power of faith, by which it achieves this great victory. The first is, that our estimation of the value of objects is always comparative. The child knows nothing which it esteems more valuable than its toys; but when this child rises to maturity, and the interesting objects of real life are presented to it, the trifling baubles which engaged the affections in childhood, are now utterly disregarded, and considered unworthy of a moment's thought.

Again, suppose a person in a low and obscure condition, whose mind has been occupied with small concerns and trivial objects, to have suddenly presented to him the prospect of great wealth and distinction—or say, a kingdom; how quickly would such a man lose all his former estimation of his little cottage and his implements of industry! His mind would now be completely absorbed in the contemplation and pursuit of those more splendid objects, which glitter in his sight. Just so, by means of faith, objects infinitely more valuable and interesting, than any which this world contains, are presented to the mind in their true character. Upon the view of these things, the affections relinquish their hold of earthly things, and however strong the grasp by which they were embraced, they are now voluntarily resigned for the sake of those more excellent things which faith reveals to the soul. With these objects full in view, the glory of this world fades away, and all its grandest objects appear trivial, and little worthy of the pursuit of a rational and immortal mind. The riches, honours, and pleasures of the world, are to the person in the exercise of faith, like the toys of children to the man of mature age. He cannot be persuaded to give his affections to sublunary objects, who is persuaded that an exceeding and eternal weight of glory is within his reach. Such an one will cheerfully part with an earthly portion, for the sake of a heavenly inheritance. The world may frown upon him, may brand with folly his new pursuit, may follow him with its obloquy and contempt, may endeavour to conquer his resolution by every species of torture, but it cannot shake, much less change his purpose. His language still is, "My heart is fixed, O God, my heart is fixed." Even though his enemies kill the body, his faith assures him that they cannot injure his better part. "Fear not," says Christ, "them that kill the body and have no more that they can do." Even while the body is on the rack, or in the flames, by faith he sees "a house not made with hands, eternal in the heavens." He sees his gracious and almighty Redeemer holding out to him a crown of life. He is assured that as soon as his soul leaves the body, it shall be with Christ in Paradise; and that there is in heaven reserved for him "an inheritance among the saints in light, which is incorruptible, undefiled, and fadeth not away." Is it strange then, that with these views which a genuine faith affords, the Christian should be a conqueror over the world, in all the hostile forms which it may assume?

The other principle to which I alluded is this

The true method of expelling from the soul, one set of affections, is to introduce others of a different nature, and of greater strength. The soul of man must have one governing affection, to which all others must yield. It is on this principle that Christ said, "Ye cannot serve two masters. Ye cannot serve God and mammon." Suppose a devotee of sensual pleasure to be suddenly seized with ambition, or avarice, in a very high degree. The effect would immediately be, that he would cease to seek happiness in the indulgence of bodily passions, and he would be led to pursue assiduously the new object, whether honour or wealth, for which he now entertains an affection of paramount strength. Such changes have sometimes been observed in the history of men. But though changes of this kind are real, and great, and are hailed by many as a great reformation; yet there is really no moral change. It is but the substitution of one vicious affection for another. But when faith comes into operation, and love to God becomes the predominant affection, there is not only a great change, but a moral transformation of the soul, from the sinful love of the creature, to the holy love of the Creator. Now the world is conquered. Faith working by love has achieved the victory. The soul is restored to something of its pristine order and beauty. Light has arisen out of darkness, and order out of confusion. Verily, there is "a new creation."

The believer can forsake not only riches and honours, but father and mother, wife and children, and life itself, for the sake of the honour of God his

Saviour. In vain does the world attempt to turn him aside by its terrors and persecutions; by faith he triumphs over all the cruelties and indignities which she can heap upon him. And if she endeavours to subdue him from his allegiance by spreading before him all her charms, her wealth, her honours, and fascinating pleasures, if faith be in lively exercise, all these will be spurned. Like Moses, the believer will prefer the cross of Christ to all the momentary pleasures of sin, and to all the treasures of Egypt. This power of faith to conquer is not a vain boast, but a practical reality. This victory has been achieved by multitudes, yea, by every true believer; and will continue to be achieved, as long as the world stands.

INFERENCES.

1. If what has been said be true, then we must conclude that genuine faith is rare in the world; yea, rare among professors. For when we take a survey of the Christian world, how small the number who seem to have gained a victory over the world! The thirst for riches, honours, and pleasures, is almost universal. By earthly passions the great multitude are subdued and enslaved. Still the words of our Lord are applicable, "Wide is the gate, and broad is the way which leadeth to destruction, and many there be which go in thereat; while strait is the gate and narrow is the way which leadeth unto life, and few there be that find it." O! professing Christian, let go your too eager grasp of the world, or it will sink you to ruin.

Beware of covetousness, and remember that it is written, that covetousness is idolatry, and such shall never enter into the kingdom of heaven. Flee from idolatry, and seek that faith which is the substance of things hoped for, the evidence of things not seen.

2. Let not the poor and afflicted in this world, who believe in Christ, be discouraged. You, my brethren, are placed in the circumstances most favourable to a victory over the world. Those fascinating temptations which have ensnared and ruined so many professors, are removed far from you. You should not repine at your poverty, for riches might have proved ruinous to your souls. And ye, who endure severe affliction, bear it with patience, and even be thankful for it, because "these light afflictions which are for a moment, work out for us a far more exceeding weight of glory." Soon all sense of pain shall cease for ever, and all our feelings of sorrow shall be swallowed up in never ending felicity. "Fight then the good fight of faith; lay hold on eternal life." Henceforth there is laid up for you a crown of life, which God the righteous Judge will give you at that day. "Be faithful unto death," saith the Lord, "and I will give you a crown of life."

SERMON XXVIII.

THE BENEFITS OF AFFLICTION.

It is good for me that I have been afflicted.—Psa. cxix. 71.

"Man is born unto trouble as the sparks fly upward." Manifold are the afflictions incident to humanity; and from these the pious are not exempt. "Many are the afflictions of the righteous." Christ said to his disciples, "In the world ye shall have tribulation." The rich spiritual blessings to which believers have become heirs, are consistent with much suffering; yea, the afflictions of the righteous are a part of their heritage. They are necessary, as a means, to their greatest improvement and happiness. Therefore, it is written, "Blessed is the man whom thou chastenest." "Behold, I have refined thee, but not with silver. I have chosen thee in the furnace of affliction."

Let us, then, inquire what are the benefits which may be derived from affliction.

1. Afflictions have often been made the means of bringing careless and impenitent sinners to serious consideration, which leads them to repent-

ance, and a thorough reformation of life. This effect is produced by cutting off the person from his sinful indulgences. A spell of sickness, or a sore bereavement, interrupts the man in his course of worldly pursuits. It has a tendency to show him the unsubstantial nature of all earthly possessions and enjoyments. Under the pressure of affliction, he feels his dependence. Pain urges him to seek relief; but human help is vain. When sorely distressed he begins to cry unto God. Multitudes now in heaven can say, "It is good for me that I was afflicted; for before I was afflicted, I went astray." We know, indeed, that affliction, like other means of grace, does not of itself produce any beneficial effect on those who are the subjects of it. It requires the influence of the Holy Spirit to render it effectual to the conviction and conversion of sinners. But its tendency is to lead to serious reflection and to a change of life; and often, we believe, the Spirit of God does accompany his chastening rod, so that it is made the means of bringing men and women, not only to consideration, but to a repentance not to be repented of. One instance from Scripture is that of Manasseh. The case is very remarkable on two accounts; first, because he was one of the greatest sinners who ever lived; and secondly, he was an old man, when his conversion took place. The history of this event is found in 2 Chron. xxxiii. 12, 13; "Wherefore the Lord brought upon them the captains of the host of the king of Assyria, who took Manasseh among the thorns, and bound him with fetters, and carried him to Babylon. And when he was in affliction, he besought the Lord his God, and humbled himself greatly before the God of his fathers, and prayed unto him; and he was entreated of him, and heard his supplication, and brought him again to Jerusalem, into his kingdom. Then Manasseh knew that the Lord was God."

2. Afflictions are made eminently beneficial to the pious, by preventing them from fixing their affections unduly on earthly things. There is in all minds too strong a tendency to the things which are present and visible. These worldly objects become a snare to many, and by the too ardent pursuit of riches or honours, they become involved in many embarrassments, and often pierce themselves through with many sorrows. A season of sore affliction, by preventing an inordinate attachment to the world, may be a real blessing. Or, when the affections are already placed too strongly on any earthly object, it is often the method of Providence to remove that object. Even the dearest earthly relatives may become snares to the soul of the pilgrim. Children may be too much loved, in comparison of our Saviour, and if they are snatched away from the tender embrace of their parents, the discipline, though painful, is often salutary, and even necessary. When God thus disciplines his children, he causes them to see why he thus afflicts them; and commonly, they are enabled, after a while, to say, " It was good for me, that I was afflicted." For, although "no chastening for the present seemeth to be joyous, but grievous; yet afterward it yieldeth the peaceable fruit of righteousness unto them who are exercised thereby."

3. As affliction is often employed to prevent the saints from wandering; so, also, it is the usual method by which backsliders are reclaimed. When Christians have considerably declined from the lively exercises of religion, they are but little affected by the warnings of the word. It is to them like a tale often told. They are asleep, and have only a dreamy notion of the realities of eternity. From this sleep of carnal security into which even the pious are liable to fall, they are commonly awakened by the application of the rod. Some severe dispensation of Providence overtakes them, and they are brought to a stand. Serious reflection is, as it were, forced upon them, and their eyes are opened to see how far they have wandered from the right path. By affliction the heart is softened, and the truths of the word now sink deep into the inmost soul. Deep contrition is produced, the soul lies humbled in the dust, under the chastising strokes of its Father in heaven. It mourns in bitterness over its folly and unfaithfulness, and writes bitter things against itself; scarcely believing that God can be reconciled to such an ungrateful wretch. And when he speaks in the language of loving-kindness, Return unto me, ye backsliding children, and I will heal your backslidings; take unto you words and return unto the Lord; say unto him, Take away all iniquity, heal our backslidings and love us freely, and let thine anger be turned away from us, the forgiving mercy of the Lord appears even more wonderful in receiving the backslider on his return, than in his first conversion. At length convinced of the loving-

kindness and tender mercy of the Lord, the penitent backslider responds to the kind invitation of the Lord, "Come, let us return unto the Lord; for he hath torn and he will heal us; he hath smitten, and he will bind us up."

4. Affliction serves as a furnace to purge out the dross which still lurks in the regenerate heart. Just as the precious metals are separated from their dross, by being cast into the furnace heated seven times; so the people of God are purified as by fire. But the furnace not only serves to purge out the dross, but to test the genuineness of the metal. Not every thing which glistens is gold, says the proverb. The ore must be tried in the fire, and if it contain pure gold, while the dross is consumed, the precious metal will shine forth brightly. Thus afflictions also answer the purpose of a test of the genuineness of our piety. If there be nothing in us that will stand the fire, then we may be certain that our religion is no better than a counterfeit. The apostle Peter makes a striking use of this similitude, when he says, "That the trial of your faith being much more precious than of gold that perisheth, though it be tried with fire, might be found unto praise and honour and glory, at the appearing of Jesus Christ."

Affliction not only serves as a test to try the genuineness of our religion, but affords an opportunity of exercising some of the most excellent graces of the pious heart. Faith, before it is tried, cannot certainly be known to be faith; but when the dark cloud of adversity lowers over the soul, faith, when it has existence in the soul, comes forth with vigour, and supports the soul ready to sink, by laying hold of the promises of God. Submission to the will of God has also an opportunity of being manifested. It is easy to say, "Thy will be done," while we bask in the sunshine of prosperity; but when the pressure of affliction is sorely felt, there will be at first a struggle. Self-love makes us restive, and endeavours to throw off the burden; but where there is a principle of piety, the soul after a short conflict bows in submission, and its language is, "It is the Lord, let him do what seemeth him good." Though a spirit of rebellion was felt, it is subdued, and the soul quietly acquiesces in the divine appointment. It even kisses the rod by which it is smitten, saying, "It is good for me that I have been afflicted." And even when it does not see the good to be derived from some bereaving dispensation; like Aaron, when his two oldest sons were smitten dead before his face, held his peace; so the believer is still, knowing from whom the stroke has proceeded.

Patience is another excellent Christian virtue which has no room for exercise, except in a state of suffering. This grace is often and strongly inculcated in the Holy Scriptures; and its exercise tends to exhibit to all observers, the excellency of true religion. The saints never glorify God more, in any circumstances, than when they let patience have its perfect work, while they are suffering in the furnace of affliction. Paul gloried in tribulation, because it wrought patience. "In your patience," says Christ, "possess ye your souls." And Paul exhorts to be "patient in tribulation."

"Be patient," says James, "unto the coming of the Lord. Behold, the husbandman waiteth for the precious fruit of the earth, and hath long patience for it, until he receive the early and latter rain. Be ye also patient."

Affliction being in its nature painful is the opposite of joy, and might seem, at first view, to be inconsistent with this state of mind. But while we suffer tribulation we may rejoice. Paul says, "I glory in tribulation, for tribulation worketh patience, and patience experience, and experience hope, and hope maketh not ashamed, because the love of God is shed abroad in our hearts by the Holy Ghost." Now that heart in which the love of God is shed abroad must be full of joy; and this experience is had in the midst of tribulations. We are commanded to rejoice always, and therefore, we are bound to rejoice in the midst of affliction. Internal peace is often most perfect, when the person is under the pressure of external affliction. The experience of real Christians testifies, that their seasons of richest spiritual enjoyment, are not their days of external prosperity; but the dark and cloudy day of adversity. Indeed, in order to be a proper recipient of spiritual peace, it seems necessary that the heart should be reduced from that state of hardness or indifference which prosperity naturally induces, to a state of sensibility; which effect is often the result of affliction. The joy of the Lord requires a heart deeply sensible of its own weakness and unworthiness, which state of mind, in the truly pious, is produced by having it pierced and wounded, by the shafts of adversity.

One effect of affliction on most men is, that it urges them to seek God, that they may obtain his help. Even the ungodly will often pray earnestly for deliverance from a painful affliction; but in the case of the sincerely pious, this effect of affliction is seldom wanting. Such pray in prosperity, but often their prayers become formal, and their souls are not stirred up from the bottom, and do not go forth in warm desires; but the rod arouses the soul from its apathy, and stimulates it to call upon God with fervent cries and supplications. The spirit of prayer which is excited by adversity, is not merely for deliverance from the pressure of the particular affliction under which it now labours; but by this means, it is brought to a lively feeling of its own sinfulness, and its urgent need of stronger faith, and more perfect patience and submission. It is led to inquire into the reason why it is thus afflicted. It searches for hidden and neglected sins, and can commonly see reason enough for the severity of the divine dispensations; and often can trace the affliction to some particular transgression, or the neglect of some particular duty.

Affliction often opens up to a person's view, a depth of iniquity not before perceived. And thus it serves to humble the soul in deep penitence, which is the very temper suited to prayer. "The sacrifices of God are a broken spirit; a broken and a contrite heart, O Lord, thou wilt not despise." Affliction not only is a powerful means of promoting the knowledge of our own hearts, and of the depth of iniquity which lodges within them; but it furnishes an opportunity for a more experimental knowledge of the wisdom, faithfulness, and mercy of God in his treatment of his children. He brings them into deep waters, that he may manifest the truth of his promises, " which are all yea and amen in Christ Jesus." Man's extremity is God's opportunity, saith the proverb. When hope is nearly extinct, and the distressed soul is sinking as in miry clay, where there is no standing, help from God is experienced. It is delayed, for the purpose of letting the person try his own wisdom and strength to obtain relief, but when all other resources fail, then God is pleased to speak comfortably to the troubled heart. He, as it were, takes him by the hand, and extricates him from the horrible pit and miry clay, sets him upon a rock, establishes his goings, and puts a new song into his mouth, even of praise to God, for delivering mercy. Knowledge of the faithfulness and loving-kindness of our heavenly Father, thus obtained, is far more valuable than the mere theory respecting these truths, without experience. An eminent theologian, on his death-bed, said to those around him, "I have learned more of God in these few days that I have been confined to this bed of sickness, than I ever knew before, with all my laborious study."

Affliction is not always of the nature of chastisement. It is sometimes for trial, and to give a manifestation of the power of faith, to endure with patience the burden which may be laid upon it. Thus, in the case of Job, his overwhelming calamities were sent for the trial of his sincerity and faith. And so, in the case of Abraham, when required to offer up his beloved son Isaac. And we have no right to infer, as the friends of Job did, that, when God sends grievous affliction on any person, it is an evidence that he is a great sinner.

Afflictions—which may seem severe—are often the means of preventing much greater evils. The negative benefits which arise from various means of grace, are incapable of being fully appreciated by us. Yet we may know, by serious reflection on our own experience, that when we have been gradually approaching some dangerous temptation, which would in all probability have overcome and ruined us, Providence has interposed, and prevented the fall, by laying us on a bed of sickness; or by some sore bereavement has broken the snare in which we were entangled, and has opened our eyes to see the danger to which we were exposed. Not only may affliction be the means of preventing the believer's fall into sin, but one affliction may be the occasion of warding off another of much greater magnitude. How often such deliverances occur no mortal can tell, because we cannot know what would have occurred on certain conditions which never took place. God only knows how much we are all indebted to our afflictions for our escape from awful crimes or overwhelming calamities. The children of God would undoubtedly apostatize, were it not for the restraints laid upon them by the external dispensations of his providence, and by the internal operations of his grace.

Once more, afflictions are made use of, in many cases, to prepare the saints for heaven, by causing them to desire rest from their protracted sufferings. Our affections are naturally attached to earthly objects, which are present to our senses; and although grace changes the current of our thoughts, yet still their exists an undue attachment to the objects of sense. Here we have a home, to which we have been long habituated; and every object around us, by association, is prized above its real value. Besides, we are surrounded by dear relatives, with whom we are naturally unwilling to part; a feeble, helpless wife, it may be, and young, dependent children. These also may, as we suppose, need our assistance, and we cannot see how they can be provided for, and rendered comfortable, if we should be taken away from them. We naturally ask, What will become of them? Who will take care of them, when we are gone? In addition, the future is covered with darkness. We cannot comprehend how we shall exist, with what objects and persons we shall be conversant, and what our emotions will be in that untried state. A strong faith will, indeed, counteract these earthly influences; but such a faith is aided by afflictions which show us the emptiness of all worldly possessions and enjoyments; and, under the pressure of long continued disease, the desire of deliverance and rest, becomes strong enough to counteract our attachment to earth, and to make us willing to leave friends and possessions, that we may be free from the pains which we endure.

Some Christians have been distressed because they have been so little afflicted; fearing lest they were not the children of God, as the Scripture says, all sons receive chastisement. Let such not be troubled on this account, for their time of adversity may not have yet arrived. Some families, for many years, appear exempt from the strokes of adversity; numerous children grow up in health, and there is no breach among them. But this cannot last. The longer adversity is in coming, the broader is the mark for its arrows. These children, however healthy for a season, will sicken and die. Be not impatient for affliction, it will come soon enough.

It has already been remarked that there are internal afflictions, which fill the soul with unspeakable anguish, when no external cause exists. These are often among the severest afflictions, and are as real as those which are the effect of external afflictive dispensations.

The use which I would make of what has been said is, to exhort the sons and daughters of affliction,
1. To recognize the hand of God in every affliction. Look not to second causes—look not to the persons who may have been the instruments of your sufferings. If the wicked have reviled and slandered you, follow the example of David, and say, "The Lord hath bidden them," that is, the Lord has permitted this affliction for your chastisement.

2. Never murmur at the dealings of divine Providence. Nothing can befall you without the ordering of God. Repine not, therefore, at what he does, for however dark the dispensation, wisdom and mercy guide the stroke. Say then, "I know that in faithfulness, thou hast afflicted me."

3. Try to improve your afflictions by exercising patience and submission. God has a sovereign right to dispose of you and yours. Rebel not against him. He has promised that all these things

shall work together for your good. More, he has declared that these light afflictions, which are but for a moment, work out for us a far more exceeding and eternal weight of glory.

4. Consider that this is not your state of rest; *that* is to come. Here you are subjected to various trials, but when you have suffered a while, you shall have an abundant entrance administered to you, into the everlasting kingdom of our Lord and Saviour Jesus Christ.

SERMON XXIX.

EXCELLENCY OF THE KNOWLEDGE OF CHRIST.

Yea doubtless, and I count all things but loss for the excellency of the knowledge of Christ.—PHIL. iii. 8.

THE apostle Paul had enjoyed uncommon privileges as a Jew; so that if any man had a right to glory in things of this kind, he more. "Circumcised the eighth day, of the stock of Israel, of the tribe of Benjamin, an Hebrew of the Hebrews, as touching the law a Pharisee, concerning zeal, persecuting the church; touching the righteousness which is in the law blameless." To which we may add what through modesty he would not hint at, that he was a man of extraordinary natural endowments, and had received a finished education, first in the schools of Tarsus, his native place, and afterwards at Jerusalem, under the tuition of the most celebrated doctors. By his birth in Tarsus, he also enjoyed the privilege of being a Roman citizen, which was one of high importance in that day, and of which he sometimes availed himself when in perilous circumstances. It may be proper to mention, also, that he was, prior to his conversion, in high favour with the ruling powers in Judea; and had he continued in the course which he commenced in opposition to Christianity, he would, in all probability, have risen to a high station of honour and power among his countrymen.

But, however great these advantages, he valued them not, when brought into competition with the gospel. A wonderful change had suddenly come over the ardent mind of this aspiring and zealous young man. He had not merely experienced a change, but he had been turned completely round; and from being a raging persecutor of Christianity, he became its most able, zealous, and indefatigable preacher and defender. And the loss which he sustained by becoming a Christian, he counted nothing; yea, he counted it "gain;" and in comparison with the excellency of the knowledge of Christ, he was not only willing to suffer the loss of all other things, but held them in the utmost contempt.

Let us, then, consider the excellency of this knowledge, which had so captivated the mind, and engaged the warmest affections, of such a man as Paul.

1. The excellency of the knowledge of Christ arises from the fact, that in him all divine and human excellence are combined. Whatever beauty and glory resides in the divine attributes, is in Christ; for "in him dwelleth all the fulness of the Godhead bodily." Yea, the brightest display of the moral attributes of God is made in him, which ever has been exhibited. The angels are filled

with profound adoration of the glories revealed in the Son of God, as Mediator. Therefore it is said, "Beholding the glory of God in the face of Jesus Christ." He is called the "only begotten Son, full of grace and truth." And he is declared to be, "The brightness of the Father's glory, and the express image of his Person." He is called the WORD and WISDOM of God, because through him God has revealed himself to man. "No man knoweth the Father but the Son, and he to whom the Son will reveal him." But in Christ, the perfection of human virtues is also exhibited. "He was holy, harmless, undefiled, and separate from sinners." His love to God and compassion for men; his humility, meekness, patience, fortitude, submission, and entire devotion to his heavenly Father's will, and his perfect fulfilment of all righteousness in his life, present an object of affection and veneration, which is above all parallel. We are apt to be dazzled and overwhelmed with the brightness of the divine glory; but when these rays are, as it were, shaded and mitigated by passing through the humanity of our Lord, the object presented is exactly adapted to draw forth the purest and warmest affections of the pious heart. When this beauty is perceived by the light of the Spirit, the believing soul is ready to exclaim, "He is the chief among ten thousands, and altogether lovely."

2. The superlative excellence of the knowledge of Christ is manifest in this, that it has a transforming and assimilating effect on all who believingly contemplate it. This effect is the natural conse-

quence of a spiritual view of the glory of Christ; for the affections of the heart are excited by this view; and our likeness to the moral image of God, consists chiefly in holy affections. "God is love; and he that loveth, dwelleth in God and God in him." Therefore, this apostle says, "Beholding his glory, we are transformed into the same image from glory to glory, as by the Spirit of the Lord." "When we see him," says John, "we shall be like him, for we shall see him as he is."

3. This knowledge is intimately connected with our justification, as well as our renovation; for justifying faith is either included in it, or arises certainly from it. If faith be the belief of the truth, or a full persuasion of the veracity of God speaking in his word, this knowledge includes it. If it be so defined as to comprehend other acts of the mind, they are such as naturally arise from a spiritual knowledge of the truth. He that possesses this knowledge of Christ, most certainly believes in him, and is in a justified state; that is, his sins are freely pardoned, and he is reconciled to God, and adopted as a child to all the invaluable privileges of the sons of God.

4. The superlative excellence of this knowledge is evident from its tendency to generate lively hope and to fill the soul with peace and joy. There is "peace in believing." The very exercise of the mind in contemplating such excellence, is the purest and sublimest pleasure of which we can form any conception. And it is in the atonement of Christ and his intercession for us, in the temple above, that all our highest and most assured hopes

of future blessedness have their origin. He is, therefore, by a common figure of speech, called "*our Hope*." All spiritual comfort flows to us from this fountain. Even in the greatest afflictions, if we possess this knowledge, it not only affords us support and inspires us with patience, but enables us to rejoice; believing that these light afflictions, which are but for a moment, will work out for us a far more exceeding and eternal weight of glory. Thus, we find Paul saying, "We rejoice in hope of the glory of God, and not only so, but we glory in tribulation." The spiritual knowledge of Christ will enable us to obey the exhortation to "rejoice always." If the word of God dwells in us richly, in all wisdom and spiritual understanding, we shall be directed in the way in which we should go. Though the carnal mind is blind to spiritual objects; "he that is spiritual judgeth all things."

5. The knowledge of Christ is excellent above all comparison, because it fits the soul for the enjoyments of heaven. The object of this knowledge is the same to the saint in heaven as to the believer on earth; the difference consists in the clearness of the vision. Here we see through a glass darkly; there, face to face. Here, we know only in part; there we shall know as we are known. Indeed, this knowledge is the commencement of eternal life, according to that declaration of our Lord, "This is eternal life, to know thee, the only true God, and Jesus Christ whom thou hast sent." The noblest life of a rational being must consist in the knowledge of the most

glorious objects, and in supreme love to their excellency.

6. This leads me to remark, in the last place, that this knowledge will be for ever increasing. While here, the believer as he grows in grace, grows in the knowledge of our Lord and Saviour Jesus Christ. To every finite mind the acquisition of knowledge must be gradual. In heaven, though the views of Christ are perfectly clear, they do not comprehend the whole object; this is infinite. It can never be exhausted. In what way knowledge will be communicated in heaven, whether by teachers of our own race, or by angels, or directly by the Spirit of God, it would be presumptuous in us to decide. Still, from the nature of the case, it may be known, that the knowledge of the saints in heaven is progressive; and that this progression is eternal. O delightful prospect! To be for ever learning more and more of the attributes of the infinite God, and more and more of his wonderful works and dispensations! This is a happiness suited to the nature of a rational being. Men in this world are often puffed up on account of the knowledge which they acquire by laborious study; but what is this obscure glimmering, when compared with the knowledge which the least in the kingdom of glory possesses? Believers, who have no opportunity of becoming acquainted with the discoveries of science in this world, need not repine. If they have the knowledge of Christ, and him crucified, all other kinds of useful knowledge will, on their entrance into the clear light of

eternity, be added. The merest babe in Christ, in the future world, will know more of the works of God than all the philosophers upon earth. Knowledge of the laws and phenomena of nature is useful to society, by leading to numerous improvements, which lessen human toil, and minister to the convenience and comfort of this life. But when we view man as an immortal being, whose existence will be commensurate with eternity, all natural knowledge sinks into nothing. Of what account is it now, to those who were distinguished for their scientific knowledge, that they stood above their fellow men, in this respect? Whether they are now in a state of happiness or misery, all their acquirements of that kind, are of no service to them. The knowledge of Christ is the only knowledge which will avail us in another world.

However high the saints may rise in heaven, and however enlarged may be their powers in that world; yet still Christ will be the inexhaustible source of their increase of knowledge. He will be the great Teacher, or rather luminary, from which rays of divine light will radiate and illumine the souls of all his worshippers, to the utmost capacity of their minds. But Christ in heaven as well as upon earth is the object of our knowledge, as he is its source. As he is divine, his perfections are infinite. Probably, new relations of the great work of redemption will be revealed in continual succession. Christ, as seen now by faith, appears to the believing mind, beautiful and glorious; but the glory of his appearance in heaven cannot be conceived by those who dwell in bodies of clay.

The beatific vision cannot be described to mortals; or if described, it could not be understood. It must be experienced before any adequate concep tion can be entertained of it. Paul had a transient view of what was passing in Paradise and in the third heaven; but when he returned, he uttered not a word respecting what he had seen. Indeed, he says, it was "unlawful to utter it," or as the original might be rendered, it was *impossible*. If the knowledge of Christ, seen here darkly through the mists of human weakness and ignorance by faith, is so excellent, we may infer that the unveiled view of this object in heaven must be superlatively glorious. This perfection of divine knowledge is reserved for all the saints, according to their measure of comprehension, in the world to come, where they shall all be collected, and though occupying different mansions in their Father's house, shall enjoy the beatific vision.

Two inferences shall close this discourse.

1. If the knowledge of Christ be so excellent, it should be our constant and vigorous effort to increase in it daily. It is the same as to grow in grace. And to attain this object, two things only are necessary; first, a diligent perusal of the Holy Scriptures, where the character and work of Christ are clearly exhibited; and secondly, prayer to God for the influences of the Holy Spirit, by whose agency alone the mind is enlightened to

behold the glory of God, as it shines in the face of Jesus Christ. And, as we have reason to believe, that our celestial vision of Christ will bear some proportion to our spiritual knowledge of Christ here, this should stimulate our minds to a holy emulation, to rise as high among the ranks of heaven as we can. As such an emulation can injure no one, and may be profitable to ourselves, we should entertain no scruple about indulging it. Fall not below the station to which you may arise. Make the best possible use of your privileges, which are afforded to you for this very purpose.

2. The second inference is, if the knowledge of Christ be so excellent, and so infinitely superior to all other acquisitions, we should endeavour to extend it to as many of our fellow-creatures as we can possibly reach. It is our duty, and should be our delight to spread the gospel over the globe, until the knowledge of God shall cover the earth as the waters cover the sea. And as the Scriptures are the treasure-house of this knowledge, we should do all in our power to circulate the Bible in all languages, and, as faith comes by hearing, we should unite with cordiality, energy, and liberality, in educating pious young men for the ministry, and sending the living preacher to all those nations which are now sitting in darkness and the shadow of death. We should aim at nothing short of the conversion of the whole world; of which there is at this time greater ground of hope than at any former period.

And here again prayer is as necessary as in the former case. Nothing can be effected without divine influence, and this is promised in answer to prayer. Paul may plant, and Apollos water, but it is God who giveth the increase. For that increase let us pray without ceasing.

SERMON XXX.

HOLDING FORTH THE WORD OF LIFE.

Holding forth the word of life.—Phil. ii. 16.

The disciples of Christ are not called to a life of indolence, but to action. As Christ himself came as a light into the world, he would have those who follow him to be lights in their proper sphere. His exhortation to them was, "Let your light so shine that others seeing your good works may glorify your Father in heaven."

In our text there seems to be an allusion to torch-bearers, who in the night went before others to show them the way. The Christians at Philippi, who as yet formed a small proportion of the inhabitants, are reminded of the importance of exhibiting a good example before the heathen multitude by whom they were surrounded; of being blameless and harmless, the sons of God, without rebuke; that is, furnishing no occasion for censure or rebuke, by the holiness of their lives. "Among whom," says he, "ye shine as lights in the world."

But as the verb in the original may with equal propriety be read in the imperative or the indicative mood, it would suit better with what follows, to render it thus, "Shine as lights in the world, holding forth the word of life." Our text will, then, be an exposition of the manner in which they should shine; namely, by "holding forth the word of life." As if he had said, You are bound to shine upon the darkness around you, and this you can readily do, for you are furnished with a lamp or torch, even the word of life, which you ought to hold up to view, that those who are in darkness might be attracted by its light, and might be induced to walk in the light which is shed forth from this radiant point.

Let us then,

I. Inquire why the word is here called the word of life.

II. And, in the second place, consider some of the ways by which this light may be held forth.

And may the Lord afford spiritual illumination to both preacher and hearers this day!

I. No doubt, by the word of life, we are to understand the Holy Scriptures, and they are called the word of life,

1. Because they clearly reveal to us a future life; and teach us the way by which we may obtain it. Nothing certain can be known of a future state of existence without the Scriptures; for even if reason could assure us that we shall exist hereafter, it cannot satisfy us, that we shall enjoy happiness in the world to come. But as we all have a consciousness of sin, the dictate of sober

reason is, that we must expect to be punished for our sins hereafter, since punishment does not always overtake the wicked here. Reason would dictate that the innocent and obedient would of course be happy under the government of a righteous, moral governor; but in regard to pardon and reconciliation for sinners, reason utters not a word; she is dumb; or rather, she speaks a language of terror, saying that every one must be rewarded according to his works. And as we know that we are sinners, what can we expect but to suffer for our sins? To man, thus walking in darkness and terror, the gospel brings a glorious and cheering light. "Life and immortality are brought to light by the gospel." The divine Author of our religion has given us the clearest information which could be desired; not only of the reality of a world of blessedness, but also of the means by which we may reach this happy state. And this revelation being recorded in the word, this is properly called "the word of life."

2. But the word of God contained in the Holy Scriptures, is not only a revelation of a way of life, but it is an authoritative grant of life to condemned sinners, on the condition of faith and repentance. It is one thing to know that there is life, and to be informed of the way in which it may be attained, and another and very different thing, to have an offer by authority of this life to ourselves; yea, a free grant of it, if we will accept the boon. To a prisoner condemned to death it is pleasing to know that the supreme authority is reconcilable; but O how transporting to hear from those appointed

to deliver the message, that he has sent me a sealed pardon! Or to read the document itself, in which he declares in the most solemn manner, that all the sins of every penitent believer are forgiven! The word contains the assurance of eternal life to every true believer; it is, therefore, emphatically "the word of life."

3. But the word is not only an authoritative message from the King of kings, granting life to all who are willing to receive it, but also the appointed instrument of communicating spiritual life to the soul. Though the work of regeneration requires the exertion of the same power which at first caused light to shine out of darkness, yet it has pleased God to ordain that his own truth should be the ordinary means of accomplishing this great work. "Faith comes by hearing, and hearing by the word of God." Christians are said to be begotten by the word of truth, and to be born again by the word. "Being born again, not of corruptible seed, but by the word of God, which liveth and abideth for ever." This metaphor by which the word is compared to a seed, is very appropriate; for though a seed possesses vitality in itself, it will never vegetate unless it is brought under the influence of air, sun, and rain; so, the word of God remains inefficacious until accompanied by the Holy Spirit. And, again, as the word is the instrument by which the Spirit operates, it is called, "the sword of the Spirit." The word is the means by which the sinner is convinced of his sin and danger. While ignorant of the law he remains careless and unconcerned; but

when the commandment comes, sin revives, and he dies. Paul says of himself, "I was alive once, without the law, but when the commandment came, sin revived and I died." "I had not known lust, except the law had said, Thou shalt not covet." By this precept he learned that the law reached the thoughts of the heart. And conversion is produced by the energy of the Holy Spirit under the preaching of the word, as is evident from the texts already cited. The word contains in itself all those objects and qualities which are adapted to excite holy affections in the human soul; and the reason why it does not produce its appropriate effects on the hearts of all who hear or read it is, that there is no capacity in a soul dead in sin to perceive spiritual beauty, and no susceptibility of holy emotions and affections; but when spiritual life is communicated, in proportion to the degree of illumination granted, the truth will appear in its genuine and attractive colours. Its reality, importance, beauty, and glory begin now to be perceived; and the soul, under the influence of the Spirit, is rendered impressible by the truth. Thus every good desire, every holy emotion, every exercise of faith, love, repentance, hope, and joy, are produced by the views of truth which the soul now enjoys. The gospel is, indeed, "the word of life," and the means of spiritual life to every one that is born of God.

4. Again, the word is not only the means of generating spiritual life, but is the nutriment by which this life is sustained, and by which it increases and grows. This progress of the soul

in spiritual strength is what, in Scripture, is called sanctification. The new man, formed in regeneration, though possessing all the members and lineaments of the child of God, is not made perfect in knowledge and strength at once, but, analogous to what takes place in the human body, is first a babe, then a young man, and finally, an old man. Or, like the seed sown in the ground, there is "first the blade, then the ear, and finally, the full corn in the ear." Every kind of life in this world needs nourishment. Man's natural body is in infancy supported by milk, and when grown, by bread and strong meat. So also the spiritual life must have nourishment in order to its continuance and growth. And this nourishment is found only in the word. "Sanctify them through thy truth; thy word is truth." "Grow in grace, and in the knowledge of our Lord and Saviour Jesus Christ."

5. By the word of the Lord the bodies of the saints, at the last day, shall be resuscitated, and inspired with new life. For all that are in their graves shall hear his voice, and come forth, some to everlasting life. Therefore, Christ, whose resurrection is an earnest of that of his people, says, "I am the resurrection and the life," and by his authority and power, all the pious dead shall rise from their graves, and even the sea will give up her dead, in the resurrection day. It is, therefore, said by the apostle Paul, when speaking of the resurrection of the company of true believers, "As in Adam all die, so in Christ shall all be made alive." This doctrine of the resurrection of the dead is peculiar to the gospel, and is an animating

and glorious doctrine. Then, indeed, may it be said that man lives, when "this mortal shall put on immortality." Then, indeed, "Death shall be swallowed up of life."

II. We come, in the second place, as was proposed, to consider the duty of holding forth the word of life.

The allusion is to holding up a light to others who are in darkness. The Philippians, in the preceding verse, are represented as in the midst of a crooked and perverse generation. They were surrounded by heathen idolaters, who were not only shrouded in ignorance, but degraded in their moral conduct. They had no correct knowledge of the true God, and were total strangers to the character and mediatorial work of Jesus Christ. They were at enmity with God, and aliens from the commonwealth of Israel. Now Christians, whose eyes had been opened, and who had been turned from the darkness of idolatry to the marvellous light of the gospel, had a duty to perform to their benighted fellow-citizens. It was incumbent on them to hold forth the lamp of divine truth, to scatter the darkness which surrounded the people; that is, it was their duty to make known to others that word by which their own souls had been quickened and enlightened. Nothing in the material world is more necessary than light. Without it all the beauty of the universe would be obscured. Without it all life, of every kind, would cease. Light is to the bodily eye, what truth is to the mind. Without the knowledge of the truth, the soul of man remains in a state of darkness and disorder. Nothing can supply the place of light in the natural world, and there is no substitute for truth in the spiritual world. But we need not now descant on the preciousness of divine truth, as we have already had the subject fully before us. Our inquiry now is, what can be done to hold it forth, so that others also may be illumined and guided by it, for as to the obligation to communicate the truth to others, there can be no doubt. Our Lord has given us express commands on this subject: "Let your light so shine that others seeing your good works may glorify your Father who is in heaven." And again, "Ye are the light of the world; a city that is set on a hill cannot be hid." And he forbade his disciples to put their light under a bed or a bushel.

Though it is incumbent on all Christians, according to their ability and opportunity, to communicate the truth to their fellow-creatures, there are some on whom this duty rests especially, as occupying stations and filling offices to which instruction appropriately belongs. The preacher of the gospel is by a solemn vow devoted to this very work. His commission extends to every individual of the race to whom he can gain access. "Preach the gospel to every creature." The command of God is, "Be instant in season, out of season, reprove, rebuke, exhort, with all long-suffering and doctrine." By means of the faithful preaching of the gospel, the word of life is held forth to many at once.

But though it is not incumbent on all Christians to preach, it is the duty of all to do what in them lies, to have the gospel preached to all, by lending their aid to prepare young men for the ministry, by obtaining for them such an education as is requisite to qualify them for the ministry. It is undoubtedly the duty of all Christians to give their aid in supporting a faithful ministry in the Church, that all may have the opportunity of hearing the word of life. They may hold forth the word of life by supporting him who is authorized to dispense it; and by freeing him from the necessity of occupying his time in secular business for the support of himself and family. But Christians should hold forth the lamp of life to the heathen world. A large proportion of our race have never heard the gospel, and we know of no way by which they can be saved without it. There is no other word of life. There is no other name given under heaven by which we must be saved—other foundation can no man lay than that which is laid, which is Jesus Christ. Christians are not sufficiently awake to this most important duty. The call is from hundreds of millions for their help. Not that the heathen desire the light of the gospel; but their urgent necessities should sound as a solemn call in our ears continually. And not only the heathen, but the Jews and Mohammedans, a numerous multitude, are also in darkness, to whom the word of life should be held forth, whether they will hear or forbear. Let Christians do what they can to enlighten these millions of men, inhabiting the earth contemporaneously with themselves, and whom they will soon meet at the judgment-seat of Christ.

But "the word of life" may be held forth also by the press, even to a greater extent than by the living preacher. Books and tracts circulate where the sound of the preacher's voice is never heard. The word of God should be translated into all languages, and circulated through the whole world. Within the last half century much has been done in translating and circulating the Bible over the face of the earth. But the work is not yet accomplished; it is just begun. The Chinese and Hindoos will need millions of copies; as also many other heathen nations.

Much may also be done by writing and circulating evangelical tracts and books among the people. This good work has also been commenced and is in progress; but when we contemplate the wide harvest field, we have great reason to pray the Lord of the harvest for more help; for the harvest is great and the labourers few. It is written, that the time will come when many shall run to and fro, and knowledge shall be increased. Does not the enterprise of colportage seem to be an accomplishment of this prediction?

But Christians must let their light shine by example, as well as teaching. The apostle seems to have had this especially in his eye, when he penned these words of the text, for he says, "Be harmless and blameless, the sons of God, without rebuke." Nothing in the power of man is more influential than example. A holy example strikes with force on every mind in which conscience is not seared as with a hot iron. There is something in a holy example which stops the mouths of gainsayers sooner than all arguments.

Let Christians live up to their duty and privileges; let them manifest the true spirit of their holy religion, and exhibit beauty and purity in a consistent Christian example, and even infidelity itself will be abashed, when it has no evil thing to say of them. Even the sneering Gibbon, in attempting to account for the spread of Christianity, was obliged to give the unblamable lives of its professors as one of the causes.

SERMON XXXI.

THE HOUSE OF GOD DESIRABLE.

How amiable are thy tabernacles, O Lord of Hosts! My soul longeth, yea, even fainteth for the courts of the Lord: my heart and my flesh crieth out for the living GOD.—PSA. lxxxiv. 1, 2.

IN the patriarchal ages, the pious had no particular place or consecrated edifice, where they offered up their worship to God; but wherever they happened to reside, there they erected altars, on which they offered sacrifices, agreeably to the original institution; and sometimes consecrated pillars, by anointing them with oil, to be memorials of some remarkable transaction. But in the time of Moses, while Israel remained near Mount Sinai, a command was given to build a tent or tabernacle for the worship of God, of the most precious materials. The quality and workmanship of these were specified with the utmost particularity. The form and dimensions of this sacred structure were also revealed, and it was positively directed that every part of it, even to the loops and pins, should be made in conformity to the pattern shown to Moses in the Mount. Around the sacred tabernacle, a spacious court was enclosed, within which stood the altar of burnt-offerings, and the laver for the purification of the priests. While the Israelites sojourned in the wilderness, the tabernacle moved or remained with them, and the pillar of fire and cloud which rested on it, by night and day, was their constant guide. But when they had conquered the promised land, Shiloh became the permanent residence of the house of God. For several hundred years, even to the time of Samuel the prophet, the tribes were accustomed to assemble for the celebration of divine worship at this place. But in the time of David, the ark of the covenant, after its return from the land of the Philistines, was brought to Jerusalem, where king David had erected for it a new tabernacle on a piece of ground, which, by divine direction, he had purchased from Araunah the Jebusite, at the time of the destructive plague by which so many thousands of the people were cut off.

Here, on Mount Zion, was henceforth the sacred place where God met with his people. But the devout king of Israel was not contented that now, when the nation was rich and powerful, God's worship should be celebrated in a movable tent: he, therefore, by divine permission, resolved to erect a costly and splendid temple, adorned and furnished with the greatest possible magnificence. During the life of David, however, the tabernacle continued to be the place of worship; for, although God approved of his pious purpose to build him a house, yet he chose that the work should be executed, not by him, but by his son and successor, Solomon.

While there was only one place where God recorded his name, and one house where he gave tokens of his presence, it was a precious privilege to enjoy the opportunity of frequent access to the courts and to the tabernacle, where divine worship was daily and periodically celebrated; and where such rites were performed, and such objects exhibited, as were calculated to strengthen the faith, and enkindle the devotion of the pious.

But it was especially desirable and pleasant to enter these courts, and join in the solemn worship of the sanctuary on those sacred festivals, which, by divine appointment, were periodically solemnized: at which times, the scene was rendered peculiarly impressive and interesting, by the number of appropriate and significant ceremonies which were exhibited; and by the eager multitudes of people who attended from every part of the holy land.

On these solemn occasions, it must have been a delightful spectacle to behold the thousands of Israel, of every age and condition, coming up to the house of the Lord, and presenting themselves before the God of Jacob, with their respective gifts and offerings. Who can tell with what rapture the bosom of the devout worshipper swelled, when his eye caught the first glance of that holy and beautiful house which contained so many expressive and mysterious emblems of Jehovah's presence, and of Jehovah's grace! The worship of God in the tabernacle or temple was, doubtless, to the pious Israelite, a most solemn and affecting service. In it the ancient saints took exceeding great delight. Therefore, we find in the Psalm from which our text is taken, and many others, an expression of the most ardent desires to enjoy the privilege of joining with the people of God in the worship of the tabernacle; and the most pathetic lamentations when, by any circumstance, the Psalmist was prevented from attending the public worship of God, celebrated in this sacred edifice. " As the hart panteth for the water-brooks, so panteth my soul after thee, O God; my soul thirsteth for God, for the living God: when shall I come and appear before God?" And the liveliest joy was expressed upon the prospect of entering these sacred courts. " I was glad when they said unto me, Let us go unto the house of the Lord. Our feet shall stand within thy gates, O Jerusalem. Jerusalem is builded as a city that is compact together; whither the tribes go up, the tribes, unto the testimony of Israel, to give thanks unto the name of the Lord." And in our text: "How amiable are thy tabernacles, O Lord of Hosts:" and in verse 10; " For a day in thy courts is better than a thousand. I had rather be a door-keeper in the house of my God than to dwell in the tents of wickedness."

The essence of spiritual worship is the same under all dispensations; the same to the believing Israelite and the devout Christian. They had the same object of worship, for the God of Abraham, Isaac, and Jacob is the Christian's God. They exercised faith on the same Messiah; trusted in the same promises, and hoped for the same reward The devotional exercises of the true worshippers under the old and the new dispensation were not different. Humble penitence, ardent thirsting after God, joy and confidence in his mercy and faithfulness, and fervent gratitude and praise, were common to both of them. Pious Jews and Christians, also, equally delighted in drawing near to God in his house. Here, under both dispensations, much was found to strengthen faith, to encourage hope, to elevate the affections, and to fill the troubled heart with consolation.

And the courts of the Lord are still sought after, and rejoiced in, by all the true Israel. The solemn pomp of ceremonies, it is true, no longer strikes our eyes; the mysterious veil has been rent in twain from the top to the bottom; and the mysteries of the most holy place have been revealed. The mercy-seat is now accessible to all believers; and the spiritual SHECHINAH, *or glory of God*, is seen in the face of Jesus Christ. No longer is it requisite to pour out daily the blood of lambs and bullocks, which is not efficacious for the removal of guilt; but it is ours, to present by faith the sprinkled blood of that Lamb which "cleanseth from all sin."

If the worship of God, under the gospel, has less in it to strike the senses, and affect the imagination, it presents before the mind of the pious worshipper the object of faith much more clearly and strongly. The method of reconciliation is no longer hidden under shadows and types; but the "new and living way" is rendered so manifest, that "the wayfaring men, though fools, shall not err therein."

In the sequel of this discourse, I propose to explain what those considerations are, which have always rendered the House of God so desirable to the pious, both under the old and new covenants or dispensations.

I. The courts of the Lord were highly prized by the pious of old, because, upon entering the sacred enclosure, they were permitted to behold the altar of burnt-offerings, on which, morning and evening, an unblemished lamb was offered unto God, and on which its blood was sprinkled. There is no want which every true penitent feels to be so urgent as his need of pardon; and as it is an unchangeable principle in the divine government that "without the shedding of blood there is no remission," no object of contemplation can be more interesting to such, than an atoning sacrifice. And, although the blood of these sacrificed animals possessed no efficacy to purge the conscience; yet, they served as types to represent, in a lively manner, the real and efficacious atonement which God was about to provide. And a believing Israelite was not only privileged to behold at a distance the blood flowing from the altar, but to be himself the offerer. The scene was still more impressive, and his faith had a more evident ground on which to rest. In this case, the humble penitent was permitted to come near to the altar, and with confession of his sins, to lay his hand on the head of the victim, before it was slaughtered: as much as to say, may my guilt be transferred to my surety, and may he bear the punishment due to my sins. Then, when he beheld the devoted animal sinking under the deadly stroke, and his quivering limbs laid upon the altar to be consumed, and the priest in his sacred garments receiving the shed blood, and sprinkling it on every side of the altar, and pouring it out at its foot, could any other language have taught him more significantly and impressively, that his pardon could in no other way be secured, than by the shedding of blood, and by the infliction of the punishment due to him upon a substitute? Every soul, therefore, which was deeply conscious of guilt, and thirsted for pardon, would ardently desire to enter the courts of the Lord, where he might fix his believing eyes on the sacrifices which exhibited, by anticipation, "the Lamb of God, which taketh away the sin of the world."

And what is it now which renders the house of God desirable and delightful to the pious Christian, but the doctrine of atonement which is there exhibited to his view, in the word and sacraments of the church? This is what causes him to long and faint for the courts of the Lord. Take away all idea of an atoning sacrifice for sin, and what is left that can much interest a soul oppressed with a sense of guilt and deserved punishment? Without the doctrine of an atoning sacrifice, the gospel would be no glad tidings; it would be but an empty sound. The church of God in that case would present no object of ardent desire to convinced sinners: the tabernacles of the Lord would be no longer amiable. The burdened soul would go away unrelieved; the thirsting soul unsatisfied. The sound of joy and thanksgiving would, in that case, be no longer heard in the courts of Zion. O Christian, what is it in the church of God which most enlivens and comforts your heart? Is it not "the Lamb slain"—"the blood of sprinkling"—"the cross"—the Redeemer, wounded for your transgressions, and bearing your sins in his own body on the tree? And what in the preaching of the gospel do you find most attractive and edifying? Is it not "Christ crucified?" Wherever, then, this precious doctrine is plainly and fully inculcated, thither will the sincere seeker of salvation resort. And as long as the world stands, the tabernacles of the Lord will be amiable, when the people can find there a healing balm for a wounded conscience.

2. The next conspicuous object in the court of the Lord's house, was the laver of purifying water. This was a lively figure of the "sanctification of the Spirit." Christ came both by water and by blood. So, when he hung on the cross, and was pierced to the heart with a spear, the disciple who bore witness saw a double stream, of blood and water, issue from his side. Here justification by his blood, and sanctification by his Spirit, were emblematically represented. Every sincere believer earnestly desires to partake of both these rich benefits; and on account of both, the tabernacles of the Lord are amiable and his courts desirable. How delightful is it to those who abhor sin and loathe its pollution, to come to a fountain open for the washing away of sin and uncleanness? The doctrine of regeneration and sanctification by the sovereign and supernatural influences of the Holy Spirit, has ever been precious in the eyes of true Christians. And as these blessings are usually bestowed through

the instrumentality of the word and ordinance of the church, therefore, the house of the Lord is rendered exceedingly desirable. There, the word is like a purifying bath, and the influences of the Spirit descend as the gently distilling rain. "Let us draw near, then, with a true heart, in full assurance of faith, having our hearts sprinkled from an evil conscience, and our bodies washed with pure water."

There is no more decisive evidence of being an Israelite indeed, than a habitual and ardent desire after universal holiness. The "new creature" breathes after complete redemption from the bondage of iniquity; "hungers and thirsts after righteousness," and never can be satisfied until he is filled. The name of Jesus is peculiarly precious to his people, because he saves them from their sins. The antinomian hypocrite desires exemption from punishment, and boasts of his liberty from the law, while sin has dominion over him, and while his pollution is not cleansed. But the truly regenerate knows that Christ came not to be the minister of sin; and that the end of his death was "to purchase a peculiar people," whom he would redeem from all iniquity, and render zealous of good works. God's house is to his people lovely, because it is a holy house. Holiness was, in the tabernacle, inscribed on every person who ministered, and on every utensil used. Every thing which came near to God must be purified; no unclean person or thing was, on any account, permitted to be brought into the sanctuary. And, now, by the grace administered, by means of the word and sacraments, the souls of believers undergo fresh purification from time to time. Here, as in a laver of pure water, they are washed again and again, from the filthiness contracted by too close a contact with the world; and knowing the value of this cleansing, the pious greatly delight in the courts of the Lord; and when prevented from the enjoyment of this privilege, their spirits long and faint, and their very flesh crieth out for the living God. "As the hunted hart panteth after the water-brooks, so panteth my soul after thee, O God. My soul thirsteth for God, for the living God; when shall I come and appear before God?"

3. As the court contained objects of deep interest to the true penitent; so also did the tabernacle itself. On entering this sacred edifice the first thing which would engage the attention of the observer, was the golden candlestick, with its seven branches and lamps, constantly illumining the holy place. This was undoubtedly an emblem of the knowledge of divine truth. The natural light is sweet, and a pleasant thing it is to behold the light of the sun: but blessed above expression, are they who have the light of divine truth continually beaming upon their souls. God is a sun unto those who are privileged to walk in the light. But as the natural sun is too bright for our eyes, with safety and comfort to gaze upon it, without the interposition of some medium to mitigate his burning splendour, so the light of God's glory is too dazzling for the contemplation of human beings: they are overwhelmed and blinded by the exceeding brightness of his countenance. God is said, therefore, "to dwell in

light which is inaccessible and full of glory, whom no man hath seen or can see." But in the church this glorious light is manifested in the face of Jesus Christ, who is "the Sun of righteousness;" and here, without losing any thing of its clearness, its intolerable brightness is mitigated, and accommodated to the weakness of our vision. The divine perfections, by being exhibited in the person of the Mediator, and by being revealed to us through his human nature, are capable of being contemplated by the believing soul, as with open face. This view, however, is transforming; "for we are changed into the same image from glory to glory, as by the Spirit of the Lord." The truth of God revealed in his word, and illustrated by the Holy Spirit, is the light of the soul. All those who know not the truth are in "darkness and walk in darkness, and know not whither they go;" but they who are taught of God are "children of the light and of the day." Christ is to them "the true light,"—"the Sun of righteousness, with healing under his wings." And as in the natural world, the sun itself is the object rendered most brightly conspicuous by his own rays; so Christ is the object most distinctly revealed by the light of divine truth. That is a false light which does not exhibit Christ in his mediatorial work and offices. How pleasing to enter a room which is illumined by a clear but mild light, rendering distinctly visible all objects in the place: such a light radiated from the lamps of the golden candlestick, in the holy place. This light, like the holy fire, there is good reason to think, was never suffered to go out;

for even in the day-time it was needed, as the tabernacle had no window for the reception of the light from without. Thus the lamp of divine truth, since it first began to dawn upon the world has never been extinct, and will go on to shine brighter and brighter, until the earth shall be filled with the knowledge of God, as the waters cover the sea. And as this light still shines in the house of God, the spiritual worshipper rejoices to go thither, that he may be enlightened with its life-giving rays. Therefore, he cries out, "How amiable are thy tabernacles, O Lord!" Here, in the church, are now seen the golden candlesticks, and one walking in the midst of them, who is no other than the Son of man. "One thing," said the royal Psalmist, "have I desired of the Lord, and that will I seek after: that I may dwell in the house of the Lord all the days of my life, that I may behold the beauty of the Lord, and inquire in his holy temple."

4. Another significant emblem in the holy place of the tabernacle, was the table of shew-bread: on which were placed twelve loaves of bread, in two rows, answering to the twelve tribes of Israel. These loaves were covered with frankincense, and were renewed every Sabbath morning; and those which were removed were eaten by the priests within the sacred inclosure.

As food is absolutely necessary to the subsistence of the body, according to the laws which regulate the animal economy; and as bread is the chief article of food, and therefore called, "the staff of life," it furnishes an expressive emblem of that grace and truth by which the soul is nourished in the spiritual life. When the body is in want, hunger impels us to seek for bread, and to go wherever it can be obtained. In vain do we endeavour to satisfy the cravings of hunger with any thing but food. The most precious metals and jewels will be spurned by one perishing with famine, unless they can be made available to procure nourishment. The soul needs nourishment as well as the body. The soul is famished while it has nothing better to feed on than the husks of this world. But a gracious God has made ample provision for our spiritual refreshment. He has prepared "a feast of fat things," and the invitation is gone out, "that all things are ready;" and that there is room and a welcome for all who will come. This feast is exhibited in the courts of the Lord; it is presented to all believers, in the word and sacraments of the church. Here Christ, the true bread, that came down from heaven, may be eaten. The hungry soul may here feast on the hidden manna. Here, the body of Christ, broken for us on the cross, is meat indeed. Here, also, babes in Christ are fed with the pure milk of the word, and grow thereby. Under all dispensations, bread has been an emblem of that grace which nourishes the soul. In the wilderness God prepares a table for his people; and as there is no stint of spiritual provision, his language to them is, "Eat, O friends; drink, O beloved." On every holy Sabbath, the bread is renewed; the ministers of God, by the faithful preaching of his word, bring forth the precious food, and when the table of the Lord is spread, there is a rich feast for God's hungering people. His kind inviting language to them is,

"O taste, and see that God is good. Blessed is every one that trusteth in him." Well, then, might the Psalmist exclaim, when for a season separated from the house of God, "How amiable are thy tabernacles, O Lord! My soul longeth, yea, even fainteth for the courts of the Lord."

5. But in the holy place there was still another interesting object; it was the altar of incense. Every morning and evening sacred perfumes were here burnt, by a coal taken from the altar of burnt offerings. The ascending smoke, the sweet savour, and the officiating priest, exhibited, in an impressive manner, the prayers of the saints, and the intercessions of our great High Priest. How pleasing the assurance, that the prayer of faith enters into the ears of the Lord of Sabaoth! Our sincere petitions rise before him, like the odour of the precious incense from the golden altar. But our imperfect prayers can only be made acceptable through the kind and continual intercession of the High Priest of our profession. In allusion to this altar, the pious Psalmist sings, "Let my prayer be set forth before thee as incense, and the lifting up of my hands, as the evening sacrifice." There is a remarkable passage in the Revelation of John, which seems to have a relation to this subject: "And another angel came and stood before the altar, having a golden censer, and there was given unto him much incense, that he should offer it with the prayers of all saints, upon the golden altar, which was before the throne. And the smoke of the incense which came up with the prayers of the saints, ascended before God, out of the angel's hand."

There is no stronger inducement to bring the pious near to God than the assurance that he is the hearer of prayer. This, in fact, is our only accessible way of approaching our heavenly Father. No greater privilege, therefore, can be enjoyed by the believer, than prayer; and he is so sensible of this, that nothing in the world could induce him to forego this exercise, or to abandon a throne of grace. That house, therefore, which is emphatically called "the house of prayer," is amiable in his eyes. His soul longs to be present with the assemblies of praying people. He loves to mingle his desires, petitions, and praises with theirs. In these social and devotional exercises of the congregation of God's people, he finds unspeakable pleasure. "Blessed is the man whom thou choosest, and causest to approach unto thee, that he may dwell in thy courts. He shall be satisfied with the goodness of thy house, even of thy holy temple." "O thou that hearest prayer, unto thee shall all flesh come."

6. But the tabernacle of the Lord was not only amiable and interesting, on account of what was visible, but more so on account of those sacred objects which were concealed from the eyes of the people, and even of the common priests. Between the holy and the most holy place was suspended a rich, impervious veil, which concealed from view the ark and all the other mysterious emblems of the sacred place. Beyond this veil no one was ever permitted to pass, except the high priest; and he only on one day in the year—the great day of atonement; when, with the blood of the sin-offering, and a censer of incense, he went to make atonement for

his own sins, and those of the people. The worshippers in the court and in the sanctuary well knew, however, what was contained in this most holy place. They well knew that the divine glory visibly rested over the ark, and that there was the propitiatory, or mercy-seat, and the golden cherubim, with their expanded wings and emblematical faces. Their reverence and profound adoration would, therefore, be the more excited by the awful mystery which hung over this part of the tabernacle; and as they approached the house of God, they would be filled with holy exultation, and would be ready to exclaim, "How amiable are thy tabernacles, O Lord!" "I had rather be a door-keeper in the house of my God, than to dwell in the tents of wickedness."

What an awful feeling must have possessed the mind of the Jewish high priest, on the great day of atonement, when his duty required him to enter alone, with the blood of a sin-offering, within the mysterious and sacred veil which concealed the ark and mercy-seat from all mortal eyes, and where the miraculous effulgence of the divine glory was manifest over the cherubim!

But although the Christian, in his worship, has nothing which is so suited to affect the senses, and excite fear; yet, he enjoys a privilege which no pious Israelite could enjoy in the same ample and spiritual manner. He has direct and immediate access to the High Priest, made with a solemn oath of God, after the order of Melchisedek; and who has for him entered into the most holy place not made with hands, not with the blood of goats and calves—which could never take away sin, but with his own blood, which has efficacy to cleanse from all sin. He is, therefore, able to save to the uttermost all who come unto God by him; seeing he ever liveth to make intercession for them. And the Levitical priesthood, and all its accompanying apparatus of types and sacrifices, as being mere shadows of good things to come, have vanished away since the substance has come; just as the shadows of night fly away at the rising of the sun.

The mercy-seat is now accessible to every believer, and it is still sprinkled with the blood of atonement; so that however guilty, we may come boldly to the throne of grace, that we may obtain mercy and find grace to help in time of need. And as the glory of God took up its residence over the mercy-seat, so still, his glory, not visible but spiritual, is beheld in the face of Jesus Christ, who is himself the propitiatory. And as from between the cherubim, God was pleased to utter a gracious response to the petitions of the priest invested with the sacred breast-plate, and the URIM and THUMMIM; so now every true believer is so far made a priest unto God, that he has the privilege of presenting as many petitions as he will, and has the promise of a gracious answer from him who sitteth on the mercy-seat. "Blessed are all they who dwell in thy house."

The inferences from the subject treated, are

1. The benefits and pleasures of public worship being thus great, we ought so highly to prize the house and ordinances of God, as never to be absent from his courts, unless providentially prevented

from attendance. This subject brings a solemn admonition to many who suffer a trifling obstacle to prevent them from appearing in the temple of God when the regular period of public worship comes round. Professing Christians who thus act despise their own mercies. They loathe the children's bread, by which alone they can be nourished. They love darkness rather than light, or they would come to the place where the "true light" shineth. They are insensible of their own pollution, and the value and sweetness of moral purity, or they would frequent the fountain in which their filthiness might be cleansed. They know not the malignity of the disease by which they are infected, and by which their life is threatened, or they would assiduously attend on the great Physician, and make use of the remedies which he prescribes. As to the multitudes who are seldom or never seen in the house of God, it is, perhaps, useless to address an admonition to them, because they are not likely to peruse a discourse of this kind; but if, for a moment, I could gain their attention, I would say, Deluded mortals! you know not what you are doing. You are pursuing happiness, and yet turn your backs upon the only true source of felicity. You neglect preparation for another world, and yet you stand upon its verge. Suffer one word of exhortation from a fellow-traveller to eternity, who seeks your salvation. Turn from the evil, reckless course, which you are pursuing. Turn unto God and live. Turn towards Zion—towards the temple of the most High, where alone safety and happiness can be found. Turn seasonably—that is, *instantly;*

lest, when his wrath is kindled, you perish for ever, with the workers of iniquity. "Behold, now is the accepted time; behold, now is the day of salvation." "Seek the Lord while he may be found, call upon him while he is near. Let the wicked forsake his way, and the unrighteous man his thoughts, and let him return unto the Lord, and he will have mercy upon him, and to our God, for he will abundantly pardon." And that you may receive safe directions into the way of life, go, I beseech you, to the house of God; frequent his courts; listen to his word, and obey his commands. Then you will also join in saying, "How amiable are thy tabernacles, O Lord!"

2. This subject also reproves those, who, for the sake of earthly gain, emigrate from a region where they enjoy the privileges of God's house, and go, with their families, far into the wilderness, where there are no churches, no Sabbath observed, no sound of the gospel, except from some chance itinerant. Here, their children grow up without the beneficial training of the church, and without the salutary and powerful influence of religious society. They grow up nearly as wild as the savages whose places they occupy. There are thousands of families who have thus sacrificed spiritual, for the sake of earthly blessings; who have preferred fat lands and rich crops to the pleasures and benefits of the church of God. They may have obtained for their children a worldly inheritance, while they have put them entirely out of the way of securing for themselves an inheritance among the saints in light. Solemn will be the account which such

persons must give for turning their backs upon the house of God, and removing their children, consecrated to God, perhaps, in holy baptism, from the church into which they were initiated, and from all the means of grace. God may, in some instances, have overruled it for good, by planting germs of gospel churches in the bosom of the wilderness; but this does not lessen the guilt of those who deserted the ordinances of God, without any reason to expect that spiritual good would accrue.

I am not opposed to emigration. In this land, it is the order of Providence to fill up the unoccupied parts of the earth; but I would have Christian people to emigrate with the ark and the priesthood in their midst. Let them first provide for the instruction and spiritual edification of their families, and then let them go forth wherever Providence may direct them. Let them only be careful to follow the leadings of the pillar of fire and cloud, and pitch their tents wherever God may direct.

3. But, finally, I feel my heart moving me to say a word to such as are still, unhappily, far from the tabernacle of God, whether thus separated from the ordinances of public worship by their own fault or not. In such painful circumstances, I know, there are found many of God's dear children. When the Sabbath comes, no church-bell announces the approach of the hour of public worship. No temple of God rears its top towards the skies; yea, no humble tabernacle, of the felled trees of the forest, stands open to receive them. They are doomed to silent Sabbaths. They cannot but reflect with

a mournful pleasure on the privileges and enjoyments of former days.

Dear brethren, I sincerely compassionate your condition, and would suggest a few words of counsel suited to your present destitute circumstances. If you have any pious neighbours, or any near you who have any sense of the importance of religion, however small their number, invite them to meet with you for the social worship of God, and for the reading of his holy word. "Where two or three," says Christ, "are met together in my name, there am I in the midst of them." Be not backward to take a part in these social exercises. Though you may be weak in the gift of prayer, the mere effort will be acceptable in the sight of God; and he often wonderfully strengthens the weak, and aids those who go forward in the performance of duty, in humble dependence on his help. Be not discouraged, although many obstacles should oppose your attempt. Persevere, and God may cause "a little one to become a thousand." From such a beginning, a flourishing church may take its rise. In these social meetings, on the Sabbath, make it a point to catechize the children, and give them good advice. And as a substitute for preaching, let a sermon or a religious tract be read by one of your number. A sermon out of Boston, Burder, Davies, Walker, Scott, Newton, or Witherspoon, will often be found exceedingly refreshing, and will be likely to have a very salutary effect on your children. I have known such social meetings to be eminently blessed, in the absence of public ordinances, in preserving the spirit of piety from becoming extinct.

But I would earnestly beseech you to spare no pains to get the gospel preached among you, by a faithful minister. Go to the nearest presbytery, when met, and supplicate with importunity for aid. Take no denial; but hang upon the skirts of the servants of God, until they consent to visit you. This advice will also apply to many vacant churches. These are often so far removed from settled ministers, that they are seldom supplied with preaching; and often the elders neglect to gather the people together at the house of God. This is a fault to be censured. It is the duty of every ruling elder in the want of a pastor, to do his best in giving the people instruction. He must not preach, but he may exhort the people to the performance of duty. He may instruct the ignorant by familiar conversation; and he may and ought to catechize the children, in the use of the excellent catechisms of our church. And it is his bounden duty to read an edifying sermon to the destitute flock.

Finally, I would say to all Christians, expect not only delight, but profit, from an attendance on the house of God. Prepare diligently for these holy services. Dismiss entirely worldly cares. Endeavour to raise your minds to heaven. Soar above the world in holy contemplation, Guard against formality and wandering thoughts. Exercise a lively faith in the truths which may be presented for your consideration, and let your aspirations to God for his grace be incessant; and may grace, mercy, and peace be upon you, Amen.

SERMON XXXII.

THE MISERY OF IMPENITENT SINNERS.

For I perceive that thou art in the gall of bitterness and bond of iniquity.—Acts viii. 23.

SIMON, the sorcerer, figures greatly in oriental history as the father of many impious and extravagant heresies. A majority of the sects which go under the general name of Gnostics, are, by the early ecclesiastical writers, traced up to this man. His history, however, except what is here given in the Acts of the Apostles, is very obscure and uncertain. We learn from the narrative of Luke, that Simon in his travels had come to the city of Samaria, where he took up his residence for a time; and gained such an influence over the inhabitants by his magical arts, that from the least to the greatest, they gave heed to him, and believed him to be what he professed, "the great power of God." But though the strong man armed seemed to have complete possession of this castle; yet there was one stronger than he, who had power to cast him out.

The gospel is truly *the great power of God.* Wherever it comes it overthrows the kingdom of darkness, and emancipates souls from the tyranny of Satan. As Moses overcame the arts of the magicians of Egypt; so the first ministers of the gospel, armed with the panoply of God, were successful in every contest with the powers of darkness. Their cunning agents and pretended miracles could not bear the light of the everlasting gospel; and all their miracles were found to be only "lying wonders." The gospel was first preached at Samaria by Philip the evangelist, who had at first been a deacon. His preaching being attended with the power of God, produced a wonderful effect on the inhabitants of this city, for both men and women believed the divine testimony delivered by Philip. Simon had no power to prevent the people from turning to the Lord, and submitting to Christian baptism as a sign of their discipleship to Christ; wherefore, artfully and hypocritically, the sorcerer himself professed faith in Christ, and was also baptized; hoping by this means, no doubt, to retain the influence which he had acquired over the minds of the people.

When the apostles, at Jerusalem, heard of the great success of the gospel at Samaria, they deputed two of their number to visit the place; particularly for the purpose of communicating the miraculous gifts of the Holy Ghost, which were at that time bestowed on the churches; but which were only given by the laying on of the hands of the apostles. When Simon saw that through the laying on of the hands of the apostles, the miraculous gifts of the Holy Ghost were given, he thought within himself, what he might accomplish, if possessed of such a power as that exercised by Peter and John. And his covetous heart judging of others by himself, inspired him with the audacity to make an offer of money to the apostles, "Saying, give me also this power, that, on whomsoever I lay hands, he may receive the Holy Ghost." Peter indignantly said unto him, "Thy money perish with thee, because thou hast thought the gift of God may be purchased with money. Thou hast neither part nor lot in this matter; for thine heart is not right in the sight of God. Repent, therefore, of this thy wickedness, and pray God, if perhaps the thought of thy heart may be forgiven thee; for I perceive thou art in the gall of bitterness and the bond of iniquity."

We may learn from the facts here recorded, that men may make a fair profession of faith and be regularly received into the church by baptism, and yet be destitute of a spark of true piety. As far as appears, the sincerity of Simon was not suspected by his fellow-professors, nor by the apostles, until his wickedness was made manifest by his impious proposal.

Churches and church-officers are not to be censured for receiving into the communion such as make a fair profession; and even if they suspect their sincerity, they have no right to exclude them, until by some overt act or speech they clearly discover that their hearts are not right in the sight of God. The power of searching the heart belongs not to men—no, not even to apostles; but is the prerogative of God.

The language of the apostle Peter, in our text, is very strongly expressive of the condition of an unconverted man. For, though some unregenerate men are further from the kingdom of heaven than others, and their condition much more hopeless; yet what is here said of Simon the sorcerer is true of every impenitent sinner in the world. He is in the "gall of bitterness and bond of iniquity." The two prominent ideas of the text are, *bondage* and *misery*; bondage of the worst kind—of *iniquity;* and misery expressed by the "*gall of bitterness.*"

What I propose in the sequel of this discourse is, to show the misery of the state of the unconverted. It would be important, if we had time, first to lay down the marks by which an unregenerate state may be ascertained; but it will be inexpedient, at present, to enter further on that subject, than to observe, that where persons are conscious that they are living habitually in the practice of known sin, or in the neglect of acknowledged duty, the conclusion is undoubted, that the heart has never been renewed.

Again, so great a change as that signified by conversion, or being "born again," cannot take place without the person being conscious of it. It is not meant, that every regenerate person knows certainly that he is renewed; but that every one who has experienced this change must be conscious of new views and new feelings in regard to many things. Every true convert has had his eyes opened to see the exceeding odiousness of sin, and has sincerely repented that he has ever been guilty of that abominable thing which God hates. He has also been convinced of the insufficiency of his own righteousness to justify him, and of the inefficacy of his own efforts to deliver him from the bondage of iniquity, in which he finds himself involved. Every sincere convert has been led to justify God, and to condemn himself by accepting the punishment of his sins as just; and has been led to view Christ as a sufficient, a suitable, and the only Saviour; and has been induced to commit his soul into his hands, by a willing submission and an unreserved surrender of all his faculties to his service.

Now, there are multitudes who are conscious that they never experienced any such change; and are, therefore, still in the state of nature. Others have been the subject of transient religious impressions; but they cannot but know that no radical and permanent change has been wrought upon them. Let no man deceive himself with the deceptive idea, that this change may have been experienced without his being conscious of its effects; and, especially, let no impenitent sinner fall into the soul-destroying delusion that no such change is necessary to salvation; or that it was effected for him in his baptism in infancy. It can be the interest of no one to be deceived in a matter of such momentous interest. Whatever present ease such a deception may afford for a few days, the awful truth must be realized, sooner or later; and if the truth should not be known until it is too late to seek a remedy, the recollection of having foolishly yielded to such a delusion, will enhance the misery of the soul through eternity.

1. The first thing which shows the misery of an unconverted sinner is, that he lies under a sentence of condemnation from the holy law of God. The curse which he has incurred is proportionate to the number and heinousness of his sins. "Cursed is every one that continueth not in all things written in the book of the law to do them." "He that believeth not is condemned already, and the wrath of God abides upon him." "He that believeth not shall be damned."

To be condemned to death by a human tribunal is a state deeply deprecated and earnestly shunned by most men; but what is the sentence of a human law compared with the law of God? What is the sentence of a fallible man upon ourselves, compared with the sentence of the Almighty Judge? What is the transient pang of temporal death, compared with the never-ending agonies of the second death? Remember, O man, that you live daily under a sentence of condemnation, which, if you understood and felt its weight, would destroy all your cheerfulness, and incapacitate you for all your worldly pursuits and pleasures. This bond of the law is one from which you can never extricate yourself. And no creature in heaven or earth can redeem you from this miserable thraldom. Consider, also, that your guilt is accumulating every day. While none of the old scores are wiped out, by your daily sins you are "treasuring up wrath against the day of wrath, and revelation of the righteous judgment of God."

2. While the impenitent man lives in sin, he is miserable. The soul cannot be satisfied with earthly objects—and often great disappointment is experienced by most in regard to the objects on which they place their affections. Their schemes of acquiring wealth utterly fail; or riches, when acquired, make to themselves wings and fly away, as an eagle to heaven. But alas! the great mass of mankind spend all their lives in wretchedness. Vice breeds misery, among the rich and the poor. "The way of transgressors is hard." Crimes committed under the influence of passion, or in thoughtless levity, are bitter in recollection. Remorse, in the time of adversity, is armed with a scorpion sting. Old age to an impenitent sinner is a dreary, desolate period. But a majority of transgressors never arrive at this age. They do not live out half their days. Excesses of every kind undermine the stoutest constitutions; and when avarice or ambition is the governing passion, care and anxiety exhaust the spirits, and wear out the life. Many, also, fear keeps in misery. The dread of death and judgment are thoughts which coming across their minds disturb their gaiety, even in the midst of feasting, like the hand-writing on the wall to Belshazzar. "There is no peace, saith my God, to the wicked."

3. Though it is true that the unconverted are far from being happy in this world; yet statements of the truth on this subject commonly produce very little effect on their minds; for they still labour under the delusion that happiness is attainable in earthly pursuits, or in the possession of earthly

objects. And many, by running a continual round of exciting amusements, try to think that they are living a life of pleasure; while all thoughts of death and eternity are banished from their minds. Others are so completely occupied with the business of the world, that they have no time for serious reflection; and the thought of future judgment is seldom permitted to obtain an hour's consideration. Though this course must soon have an end, and disease or death interrupt their pursuits; yet others follow on in the same track, with as much ardour and with as sanguine hopes, as if all who had gone before them had been successful.

Instead, therefore, of endeavouring to convince the impenitent that they are miserable, I will direct their attention to the future; and especially to the future world. No man can be so infatuated as to expect to escape death. Men may turn away their thoughts from the hated monster; but its reality they cannot doubt. The evidences of man's mortality are clear as the sun light. And every man knows that every passing day brings him nearer to this dreaded event; and no power can retard the rapid speed with which he hastens to eternity. Death, too, is commonly attended with many appalling circumstances. The worldling is snatched away often in the midst of his uncompleted schemes. He must leave all his gains, as well as his prospects, behind; for, "as we brought nothing into the world with us, it is certain we can carry nothing out." The fruits of all his anxious toil are taken away in a moment. What folly and vanity to set the heart on that which must so soon be relinquished for ever! Sickness and bodily pain usually accompany men's departure out of life. The struggle with the last enemy is sometimes long, and, in many cases, the agony great. When the strong man is bowed down with mortal disease, he makes a mighty resistance, but all in vain. The unrelenting foe pursues him through every lane of life, until his conquest is complete. It is wonderful, that living men who have witnessed the last struggles and agonies of the dying, can ever be at rest, or enjoy one moment's ease, until they are prepared for this awful scene. See the sick man on his dying bed, how he writhes in excruciating anguish. See his restless, despairing looks turned every way for relief, but in vain. The physician has exhausted the resources of his art, and has given over the patient. Friend, wife, children, brothers and sisters weep around him; and the parting with these adds to the poignancy of his anguish, and their very tears increase his misery. Wretched man! he has made no preparation for his appearance before the judgment-seat, where all his sins will be sure to meet him. Can nothing be done for his salvation in these last moments? We would not limit the grace or power of God; but surely, the opportunity of accomplishing so great a work in so short a time, and under such adverse circumstances, is small indeed. And often, when the religious teacher is permitted to see him, he finds that it is too late to do any thing effectual. If the dying person has imbibed dangerous errors, there is no time to have them removed by argument. If he is ignorant of the truths of religion, he is in no condition to attend to the lessons of instruction; if hardened in iniquity, sickness and pain and fear have no tendency to soften the heart. And often his reason is clouded or deranged, so that he is physically incapable of receiving any benefit from instruction. In many cases too, the misguided friends and attendants use every art to keep the dying from hearing any thing about religion, lest the awful subject should distress or injure them. What can the minister of God do for such a miserable man at the last hour? Alas! in most cases, he can do nothing with any hope of saving benefit.

It is an unpleasant, as well as an ungrateful duty, to attempt to lift the curtain, and to follow the dying sinner into his future abode; but, however painful, the minister of God, who has the care of souls, and who is commissioned to declare " the whole counsel of God," must not hesitate to present the truth in its solemn reality. The office of the minister is like that of the skilful surgeon, who, when he perceives that unless the gangrened limb be removed, the patient must die, does not hesitate to amputate the diseased member, however painful to the feelings of the person; so, the faithful minister must not consult the taste or feelings of his hearers in administering to them; but must bring forth to their view, and solemnly inculcate on their conscience, those truths needful to be known, however unpleasant to their present feelings. It is better to suffer the pains of compunction now, than to endure the pains of hell for ever. It is necessary to warn impenitent persons of their imminent danger of destruction. They are walking securely upon the very brink of ruin, unaware of their danger. How would we tremble if we saw a blind man approaching the verge of a frightful precipice, without being aware of his danger! And why are we not more affected than we are, with the dangerous condition of unconverted men and women; yea, of the members of our own families; it may be our beloved children; or our brothers or sisters, who, we have reason to fear, are yet out of Christ! This sinful indifference is owing principally to our want of a lively faith in the realities of the invisible world. If the awful truths which the Bible reveals, respecting the future, endless misery of all who die in their sins, without being regenerated and reconciled to God, were firmly believed, we should never cease to entreat sinners to repent, and to beseech the Almighty to awaken them to a sense of their danger. If we could only have a view of the misery of multitudes, who neglected the great salvation, until the day of grace was gone by—could we see their anguish, and hear their groans, we would not be deterred from faithfully warning such as are still within the reach of mercy. Suffer, then, I beseech you, the word of exhortation and warning: "The wicked is driven away in his wickedness." In a moment he is separated from all on which he had set his affections. His wealth, heaped up with so much toil, and often at the expense of a good conscience, he must leave behind him, for he can carry nothing to the grave but his coffin and winding-sheet. He is obliged to bid farewell to all his beloved relatives—torn away, it may be, from the wife of his bosom, and from the children, the offspring of his body. He shuts his eyes, for ever, on all terrestrial things, and launches into an unknown world. And when his spirit has escaped from its clay tenement, what is its condition? Are there any kind friends to meet it on its entrance into eternity? Does the immortal soul find any peaceful retreat—any place of rest after the toil of life? Will such a soul be convoyed by guardian angels to Abraham's bosom? Alas! no; a title to heaven was not sought and secured in the season of mercy; and now the door of mercy is for ever shut. If the glory of heaven is seen, it is at an unapproachable distance. If others, and neighbours, and acquaintances are seen entering those blessed mansions; yet there is no place there for the impenitent. If they should now approach the gates of the celestial city, and beg most importunately for admittance, it will avail nothing. The terrible response to all their petitions will be, "Depart from me, ye workers of iniquity." The assurance that heaven and happiness are for ever lost, will fill the soul with unspeakable anguish. Fell despair, with all its horrid blackness of darkness, from that moment so envelopes the miserable, lost soul, that not a ray of hope is ever permitted to reach it. Yes, the full realization of the eternal loss of the soul is a thing of which we may now talk, but of which all our conceptions are utterly inadequate. But this is not all. The misery of hell is not that of mere loss; there is positive torment to be endured. The lost sinner is cast into the abyss of darkness and fire, "where their worm dieth not, and their fire is not quenched"—"Where there is weeping, wailing, and gnashing of teeth." Who can describe or imagine the horrors of that dismal prison of despair? Who can conceive of the agonies of a soul tormented with remorse and despair, and the pressure of Almighty wrath? Who can dwell with everlasting burnings? One hour of this misery will be an overbalance of all the pleasures of sin. And if an hour of such misery be so intolerable, what will it be for a year? But why speak of hours and years?

Time is ended—eternity has commenced its unchanging, unending duration! Immortality, originally the dignity of man, is now his curse. Conscience, his noblest faculty, is now his chief tormentor. Memory, which brings up the vivid recollection of his sins, is an unceasing source of bitter remorse. Foresight of the future is accompanied with black despair. Passion rages, but all gratification is excluded. Our feelings revolt against the idea of the eternity of such sufferings; but our feelings are no proper judges of what divine justice demands. A child, on seeing a murderer suspended on the gallows, is affected in a similar manner; and if it were in its power would release the culprit. The evil of sin, which is rebellion against a Being of infinite perfection, is not fully understood by us here. It is certainly right to pursue transgression with as much punishment as it deserves; and we may rest assured that a righteous God will not inflict a pang more than is perfectly just. It would, surely, have been infinitely better for those, who shall be doomed to the everlasting punishment of hell, never to have been born. But they will have nobody to blame for their ruin but themselves. The devil and wicked companions may have tempted them, but they could not force them to sin. Their departure from God and rebellion against his government were entirely voluntary, and their rejection of the gospel, which will be reckoned their most heinous transgression, was owing to their love of sin and enmity to God.

Surely every one who stands exposed to such direful torments, and that to all eternity, must be in the "gall of bitterness and bond of iniquity." And their misery is not lessened by their insensibility. In Bedlam you may see a man, who, in his insanity, fancies that he is a king, and that his rags are royal robes, and his straw-bed a gorgeous throne, but does any one envy his imaginary glory? Can any one think his condition the better on account of this strange hallucination? While the house is burning over his head, the owner may be fast asleep in his bed, but the sounder his sleep the greater the danger. He may awake when all opportunity of escape is cut off. Many of the wicked die without any fearful apprehension; their minds are blinded by unbelief, and stupefied by long custom in iniquity. Their consciences are seared; and they have drunk in the opiate of infidelity or universalism; and either think that there is no hereafter, or if there is, that all will be happy in the future world. Can such a delusion be considered any mitigation of the misery, when the moment after death, the irresistible light of eternity shines in upon them with insufferable brightness?

O what a pang of disappointment! What a feeling of intense anguish, when hell is found to be a dreadful reality; when the soul awakes to a full conception of its utterly undone and miserable condition! And what a prospect has the lost soul before it? The day of judgment will indeed make a change; but not for the better. On that day the shame and consternation of the sinner will be great beyond description. His evil doing will be held up to the view of the assembled universe; and all his most secret and abominable sins will be exhibited in the light of that awful day. When the soul is again associated with the risen body, he will endure in both soul and body, agonies and torments which no form of words can fully express. Then will all the unbelieving be congregated in one immense mass, and will all receive according to their deeds. They will be arraigned and condemned out of the books which shall be opened. And at the close of the great assize, the august Judge will pronounce the sentence of eternal banishment upon the whole multitude: "Depart, accursed, into everlasting fire, prepared for the devil and his angels." And no sooner is the sentence pronounced, than execution follows. The vast multitude begin to move off—not to find a secure retreat—not to remain upon earth; but they go away into everlasting punishment. No wonder that the voice of mourning and wailing is heard—no wonder if the shriek of agony pierces the air. It is the voice of despairing millions. It is the commencement of an agonizing cry which shall never cease.

My dear hearers, if these things be so, ought we

not to ask ourselves the solemn question, Are any of us now exposed to the misery which has been faintly described? Are any of us, in this assembly, in the "gall of bitterness and bond of iniquity?" The question suggests another, Are any of you in an unconverted state? Are you living without God in the world? Are you still in love with sin? Is this world your chosen portion? Have you hitherto deferred your repentance? Have you turned a deaf ear to the call of the gospel, in which God has entreated you to be reconciled? And if you should die to-night, does conscience tell you that you are unprepared for heaven? Think then of your sad condition. There may be but a step between you and death; and if you die in your sins, where Christ is, you never can come. And if not prepared for heaven, hell must be your portion. O, stop and consider. Pause before you take another downward step. It is not yet too late to turn and live; yea, the voice of God to you is, "Turn ye, turn ye, why will ye die?" "Behold, now is the accepted time; behold, now is the day of salvation." Seize the present moment. "To-day, if you will hear his voice, harden not your hearts." To-morrow it may be too late.

SERMON XXXIII.

SPIRITUAL WORSHIP.

We are the circumcision which worship God in the Spirit.—
PHIL. iii. 3.

EVERY thing around us shows that there is a God; and that he is wise, and powerful, and good. And, from the sentiments of our own minds, we know that God approves of good conduct, and will punish evil doers. From his word, contained in the holy Scriptures, we learn that God is Almighty, and can do whatever he pleases; that he knows all things, and is perfectly acquainted with our most secret actions, and also with the thoughts and imaginations of our hearts; that he is with us wherever we are, and is a witness of every word which we speak, and of every thing which we do; and we cannot escape from his presence. How strongly and beautifully is this expressed in the 139th Psalm, "O Lord, thou hast searched me and known me. Thou knowest my down-sitting and up-rising; thou understandest my thought afar off. Thou compassest my path, and my lying down, and art acquainted with all my ways. For there is not a word in my tongue, but lo, O Lord, thou knowest it altogether." "Whither shall I go from thy Spirit, and whither shall I flee from thy presence. If I ascend up into heaven, thou art there; if I make my bed in hell, behold, thou art there. If I take the wings of the morning, and dwell in the uttermost parts of the sea, even there shall thy hand lead me, and thy right hand hold me. If I say, surely the darkness shall cover me, even the night shall be light about me. Yea, the darkness hideth not from thee, but the night shineth as the day. The darkness and the light are both alike to thee."

The duty of worshipping God by praising him for his glorious perfections and wonderful works; by thanking him for the blessings, both temporal and spiritual, bestowed on us; and by confessing before him our dependence and sinfulness, and praying to him in humble confidence for such things as we need, is so evident to every serious mind, that it is unnecessary to spend time in proving it. The proper method of performing this duty, and the benefits to be expected from it, will be the subjects of consideration in this discourse.

1. God should be worshipped with a knowledge of his true character. To worship our Creator without knowing what kind of a being he is, is to worship, like the Athenians, an "unknown God." This is the great fault of the heathen in their religion. They are very devout, and take great pains in their worship, but they know not the true

imaginary beings whom they worship, the passions and frailties of men. Yea, they are so sottish as to bow down to stocks and stones, and pay their homage to gods of gold and silver, which their own hands have made. No service can be acceptable to God, which is not founded on a just knowledge of his character. To offer him worship, under a character the opposite of the true, is to offer an insult to the Most High. Hence, the great importance of religious knowledge; and none of you can be at a loss where this knowledge may be obtained. The works of God in creation are set before your eyes. The sun, moon, and stars—the firmament—the light—the changing seasons—day and night—the trees of the forest, and the beasts which roam there—the birds of the air, and the fishes of the sea, all proclaim the power, wisdom, and goodness of the great Creator. But, we need go no further than to our own persons to behold the handiwork of God. If we look at our own bodies, and consider how curiously and wisely they are formed, having so many senses and members, and every thing adapted to a good purpose, and rightly placed, we may well adopt the language of the royal Psalmist in the same Psalm which we have already cited, "I am fearfully and wonderfully made." With such a manifestation of the perfections of God set before our eyes, if we do not learn to know God, it is because we do not like to retain him in our knowledge, and are, therefore, without excuse. This, the apostle Paul assures us, was the true origin of idolatry, with all its vile abominations. And O how stupid, and how inattentive to the works of God are most men, even in Christian lands! Many grow up to manhood, without ever reflecting seriously on these things, or ever raising their admiring thoughts to the great Author of the universe. As men desire not the knowledge of God, nor improve the opportunities of knowing him which they possess, it is just in him to leave them to their own chosen darkness, and to punish them for the enormous sins which they are constantly committing. Verily, "they are without excuse."

But as man is a fallen creature, the mere knowledge which reason can furnish is not sufficient. It does not reveal the mercy of God to sinners. It does not show how man can be reconciled to a holy God—how sin can be pardoned; or how the corrupt nature of man can be purified, and be restored to the image of God which has been lost. Therefore, God in great mercy has made a further revelation of his character in his word. At a very early period of the world, he began to make communications to his chosen servants, and in the time of Moses these were committed to writing, and from time to time, inspired men were directed to add other books to the law given to Moses, until the canon of the Old Testament was finished by Malachi. Then, after four or five hundred years, Christ the promised Deliverer came, and taught the way of salvation much more clearly than any that went before him. And having died for our sins, and having risen again, he gave commmandment to his apostles, to go forth and instruct the world. And these holy men, like the ancient prophets, were inspired to write in books all that was needful for the instruction of the church, for all time to come. The writings of the apostles and their companions are found in the volume of the New Testament. From these two volumes, which make up the Bible, all needful information may be obtained. And so plain are the lessons of instruction here given, that "the wayfaring man, though a fool, need not err therein." They who have access to the Bible, therefore, can have no excuse for not knowing God. Let them come to this sacred volume with an humble, teachable disposition, and they will not go away disappointed. Persons of the weakest understanding may here become wise unto salvation. And if they learn the true character of God, as given by the unerring pen of inspiration, they will be led to worship him with knowledge, and will be delighted to ascribe glory and honour, and praise and blessing to this august Being.

2. God should be worshipped with reverence, or godly fear. It is natural when we come into the presence of one greatly our superior, to feel ourselves overawed. And if this feeling is experienced when we are brought into the presence of a man, how much more reasonable and proper when we draw nigh, in worship, to the great God. There is a slavish dread which leads men to flee from God; and there is a blind superstitious fear which arises from erroneous views of his character; but godly fear is so essential to true worship, that it is often in holy Scripture expressed by this word.

The wicked are described as having no fear of God before their eyes; and the common character of the righteous is, "they that fear God." The fear of the Lord is, by several inspired writers, declared to be the beginning of wisdom. That God should be worshipped with reverence is the dictate of nature. All nations, when they worship, put themselves in an attitude of reverence. They bow their heads, fall upon their knees, or prostrate themselves on the ground. Indeed, the literal meaning of the word *worship* is, to bow down, or to lie prostrate. Every where in Scripture, worship is coupled with fear or reverence, so that where this is wanting, there is no true worship. God is a jealous God, and will not be mocked with the mere external forms of worship; much less will he accept that service which is prompted by pride and levity. "God is greatly to be feared in the assemblies of his saints, and to be had in reverence of all that are about him." "The Lord shall ye fear, and him shall ye worship." Reverence is represented as being most remarkable in the worship of heaven, where the most exalted among creatures veil their faces, and fall prostrate before the throne of the Almighty. The wise preacher has left us this precept: "Keep thy foot when thou goest to the house of God, and be more ready to hear than to offer the sacrifice of fools; for they consider not that they do evil." It seems, then, that a want of serious consideration is the common evil to which men are liable in attending the worship of God. And it is shocking to behold the thoughtless levity with which many enter the place of worship, and the careless indifference which is manifested by the most. This is a great evil, but it is not laid to heart. Many feel that they have performed a meritorious act, when they have spent an hour in the house of God; whereas God, who searcheth the heart, may know that they have not had one solemn impression of the divine presence in their minds during the whole time of their attendance on his worship. Reverence may be considered, therefore, as furnishing a criterion by which true religion may be distinguished from that which is spurious. False religion may have as much fervour as the true, but it is observable that the fear of God is not felt in the raptures of the fanatic or enthusiast. Such often affect a disgusting familiarity with their Maker, and use a liberty with him which would not be allowed towards an equal. Where religious feeling runs into excess and extravagance, there is always a defect of reverence for the presence of the divine Majesty. This feeling would overawe the mind, and preserve it from the indulgence and expression of human passions, in the way which is sometimes observed in worshipping assemblies.

3. Humility is another ingredient in a truly devotional spirit, and it is a temper so essential in the worship of God, that whatever service is destitute of this property, and however costly it may be, and however exact in its conformity with the divine rule in other respects, yet in the sight of God instead of being a sweet savour, it will appear vile and abominable. For, we know, from the word of God, that nothing is more odious in his sight than pride; and of all pride, religious pride is the most

hateful. The parable of the Pharisee and the publican was intended to inculcate this very thing. The Pharisee represents the proud worshipper, who makes a boast of his own performances, and of his superiority to other men; the publican represents the humble penitent, who brings the sacrifice of a broken spirit; and we are taught emphatically, that "a broken and a contrite heart God will not despise." There is no need here of making any distinction between the humble spirit and the penitent disposition They are produced by the very same views; and, indeed, humility is an essential part of true repentance. This is the spirit which is more pleasing to God, than any other which he sees in the human heart; and this is found in no heart but that which is renewed. "The Lord is nigh unto them that are of a broken heart, and saveth such as be of a contrite spirit." "Thus saith the Lord, The heaven is my throne, and the earth my footstool: where is the house that ye build me? For all these things hath my hand made, and all these things have been, saith the Lord; but to this man will I look, even to him that is poor, and of a contrite spirit, and trembleth at my word." And again, "For thus saith the high and lofty one that inhabiteth eternity, whose name is holy: I dwell in the high and holy place, with him also that is of a contrite and humble spirit, to revive the spirit of the humble, and to revive the heart of the contrite ones." "Blessed," says our Saviour, "are the poor in spirit," and "blessed are they that mourn." Thus we find in the Psalms, which furnish us with every variety in the frames of true worshippers, this spirit is strongly expressed in a large portion of them. That worshipper who approaches the throne of God, clothed with the modest robe of genuine humility, always meets with acceptance. Let us, then, worship the Almighty with an humble and contrite spirit; and let us seek after such a frame of mind more earnestly than after extatic delight, or overflowing joys. Set it down as undoubted truth, that in proportion as your views of the character of God are exalted and spiritual, you will be in the same proportion sunk down in deep abasement, from a view of your own vileness and unworthiness. And when you rise to join the worshippers in the courts above, this same sentiment of profound humility will accompany you, and you will feel that you are, in the presence of the Most High, less than nothing and vanity; and you will, with unceasing and unaffected humility, acknowledge your unworthiness of the dignity to which you shall be advanced, and the happiness which there you will for ever enjoy. But the deeper your feelings of self-abasement, the more ardent and constant will be the flow of your gratitude to Him that loved you and washed you in his own blood, and made you kings and priests unto God.

4. But "without faith, it is impossible to please God; for he that cometh unto him must believe that he is, and that he is the rewarder of them who diligently seek him." Indeed, without faith all worship must be a mere empty form, and however decent and proper and orthodox this form may be in itself, in the sight of God it is no better than the

worship of idols. The exercise of faith in prayer is expressly required in many places of Scripture. Our Saviour attributes a mighty efficacy to prayer, offered up in faith. We must rely implicitly on the promises of God, believing assuredly, that what he hath said he will perform. The question is often asked, Ought we to believe, in every case, that what we ask, we shall receive? To which it may be answered, that there was formerly a faith of miracles possessed by him who had the gift of miracles, and also by those, in most cases, in whose behalf the miracle was wrought. This was a full persuasion, that by the power of God the miracle would take place. But since miracles have ceased in the church, there is no room for faith of this kind. The confidence, or faith, which should now accompany prayer, is a full belief that whatever we ask in accordance with the will of God will be granted. The divine promises should be our guide in offering up our petitions. But if we pray for blessings not specifically promised, we have no certain ground of confidence, that the blessing shall be given, for we do not know that it is agreeable to the will of God. But when we pray in humble submission to the will of God, believing that he will grant whatever is best, we may rest assured that our prayers will be answered, and that we shall receive the thing asked, or something as good or better.

The principal exercise of faith in worship has respect to Jesus Christ, the divine Mediator. As guilty sinners, we cannot approach unto a just and holy God, in our own persons. We must draw near in the name of him, whom God has appointed to be our great High Priest. As, under the Old Testament, no person could offer a sacrifice, but by the officiating priest; so all our sacrifices must be offered through the High Priest of our profession. It is only through him, that any of our services can be acceptable. He must offer up our imperfect prayers and praises, giving them efficacy through his own precious merits. In our worship, then, we should eye constantly the Lord Jesus Christ as our Mediator, Advocate, and Intercessor, and expect acceptance only for his name's sake.

It will be found profitable to furnish our minds with such promises of God as it may be proper to rely on, in our petitions, and which we may plead before the throne of grace. We cannot stand on more favourable ground, when we appear before God, than when we rest upon his own word. We should fill our mouths with arguments derived from his faithful promises, and then we shall be sure to prevail. "He cannot deny himself." He will never disappoint the hopes which rest upon his own word.

But we should see to it, that our faith is scriptural in its nature, as well as in its object It must not be a mere speculative assent, which is cold and ineffectual, but a spiritual, cordial persuasion of the truth as it is in Jesus. A true faith may be always known by this mark, that it "works by love and purifies the heart."

5. God should be worshipped with the fixed attention of the mind, and with fervency of spirit. Spiritual worship is interrupted by nothing so

much as the wandering of our thoughts. It is to be feared that the majority of worshippers have not their thoughts steadily directed to the great object of all true worship. They lay no restraint upon their thoughts, ever prone to wander: and when they stray they are not watchful and resolute to bring them back, and place them on the proper object. And even pious people are much to blame for negligence in this respect. They are, indeed, troubled when they seriously reflect upon the matter; but they are apt to forget the sinfulness of professing to worship God, while the heart is far from him. This is one of the accusations which God brings against his ancient people. "This people draw near me with their mouth, and with their lips do honour me, but have removed their heart far from me."

Fervency of spirit is properly joined with fixedness of attention, for they go together, and reciprocally influence each other. If the affections be lively they will carry the train of thought with them, and if the attention be steadily fixed on the object of worship, the affections will commonly be excited, and fervency of spirit enkindled. The offering of the affections of the heart is the soul of devotion. Such offerings alone will God accept. All external services without this, however solemn and decent, are as a smoke in his nostrils; that is, they are abominable in his sight. The crying defect of our worship is the want of *heart;* it is mere formalism, or hypocrisy. We should strive then to worship God in *spirit*, and this we can only do by the aid of the Holy Spirit. We should then be much concerned to have that blessed Monitor dwelling in us, and abiding with us at all times. Keep your hearts with all diligence when you engage in the worship of God, whether in public or private. Let your attention be fixed and your spirit fervent.

6. God must be worshipped according to the Scriptures, by such rites and ceremonies only as he hath appointed, and not by forms and institutions of man's devising. As to the mere external circumstances of worship, as to time and place, and the position and attitude of the worshippers, they should be regulated by the apostle's comprehensive rule, "Let all things be done decently and in order." But as it relates to the worship itself, nothing should be introduced, but what is authorized by the Scriptures, such as prayer, singing the praises of God, reading the Scriptures, and administering the sacraments. "In vain do they worship me, teaching for doctrines the commandments of men."

Appointing rites and ceremonies belongs exclusively to the Head and King of the church. If men may decree one rite or ceremony, they may a thousand; and by adopting this principle the Christian church was from time to time burdened with ceremonies of man's devising, until her ritual was more burdensome than the ceremonial law of the Jews, and the ceremonies introduced often savoured of Paganism, and in fact, were adopted to conciliate Pagans and reconcile them to the church. But in regard to all these the challenge of God, who is jealous of his authority, is, "Who hath required this at your hands?" It is of great importance to the spirituality of our worship that its simplicity and purity be preserved. Striking ceremonies may for a while attract attention, and make an impression on the feelings of the people, but the result will be, that their minds will be occupied with externals, and their confidence will be placed on these rites of human invention; and faith and spirituality in the worship of God will be banished: which we see alas! to be the fact, with those who have pursued this course. There is in human nature a constant tendency to lay much stress on mere externals. Even indifferent actions and signs after a while, acquire, in the view of men, a sacredness which only belongs to divine institutions; and divine institutions themselves may be so observed that the external rite is substituted for the spiritual grace which it was merely intended to represent.

7. Finally, God should be worshipped frequently and constantly. Men are not required to spend their whole time in the worship of God, because they have other duties incumbent on them, which, by the law of God, they are required to perform. But God should be worshipped daily, morning and evening; and the Lord's day should entirely be devoted to his service. In the temple, the daily sacrifices and the offering of incense, which services were accompanied by prayer and praise, by God's appointment took place every day, in the evening and the morning. And on the Sabbath the services were doubled, as this day was by the divine commandment to be sanctified by a rest from all worldly labour and pursuits. We cannot go to an excess

in the worship of God, unless we make this duty exclude others which ought not to be neglected. Some persons may be so situated that they can devote their whole time to prayer, and other devotional exercises, as did the aged Anna, who spent all her time within the precincts of the temple, occupied in fasting and prayer. And some aged widows *now* might pursue a similar course. But all who have families and worldly occupations must attend not merely to one, but to the whole circle of prescribed duties, whether devotional or relative. I have read an anecdote of a woman in England, who took up the opinion that her whole time ought to be spent in prayer, and she therefore entirely neglected her family and her domestic duties. A godly minister having heard of the case, visited the house, and seeing all things lying in filth and confusion, raised his voice and said, in an authoritative tone, "Is there no fear of God in this house, that the care of the family is so neglected?" Which cutting reproof had the effect of reclaiming the misguided matron from her error. But, in our day, there is little occasion to warn men against spending too much time in devotional exercises; especially such as are private. There is more need to excite them to greater diligence in this highest and noblest employment in which a creature can be engaged. We find that the saints, of whom we read in Scripture, were accustomed to be frequent in their prayers. David says in one place, "Seven times a day do I praise thee, because of thy righteous judgments;" and in another place, "Evening and morning and at noon will I pray." It was the custom of Daniel, from which no terrors could induce him to depart, to pray to God three times every day.

Our prayers and praises should not only be frequent, but constant. It is asked, "Will the hypocrite always call on God?" Perseverance in prayer is much inculcated by our Lord and his apostles. Success is especially ascribed to earnest continuance in prayer, in the case of the oppressed widow, and the neighbour seeking a supply of bread to set before his friend. And the exhortations of Paul are frequent and urgent on this point: "Pray without ceasing." "Be instant in prayer." "Pray every where, holding up holy hands." "And he (Christ) spake a parable to this end, that men ought always to pray and not to faint."

1. From what has been said, we may infer, that under all dispensations and in all worlds, the highest duty of all rational creatures is, to WORSHIP GOD; and that all who live in the neglect of divine worship, are living in a state of rebellion against the King of heaven; for they are constantly disobeying one of the fundamental laws of his kingdom, from the obligation of which there can be no dispensation. Such are practical atheists, for they are "without God in the world." They are more inexcusable than the speculative atheist, for he worships not God, because he believes not in his existence; but these believe, and yet refuse to worship. They are more irreligious than the heathen, for all these worship some sort of gods, and generally they are very devout in attendance on their superstitious services.

What an unreasonable thing is it for a creature to refuse to worship his Creator, from whom he derives his being! What base ingratitude is it to be receiving and using the blessings of a bountiful Providence, and yet never acknowledge the hand from which they proceed! How preposterous and vain is the hope which such persons entertain, that when they die they shall go to heaven, since they have no taste for the exercises of heaven! There God is worshipped without ceasing, by all the inhabitants of the place; but what would they do in such a society, who always hated prayer and devotion? Their presence would disturb the harmony of the celestial songs. If by any accident they could enter that high and holy place, it would be necessary immediately to cast them out. And they themselves would wish to depart, for the songs of saints and angels could afford no pleasure to those whose hearts are alienated from God, and who have no relish for devotional exercises.

Again, it may be remarked, that if any are desirous of knowing how they may glorify God most effectually, and most in accordance with his will, they cannot serve God better in any exercise, or in any way, than by sincerely engaging in his worship. In divine worship, the noblest exercises of the soul are elicited. Adoration, veneration, love, gratitude, joy, faith, repentance, humility, confidence, self-dedication, and hope, are all put into requisition. The more frequently, and the more purely we worship God, the more genuine piety is enkindled, and the more constantly will the holy flame be kept alive. And the livelier our spirit of devotion, the stronger will be the impulse which will bear us on in the performance of other good works. And this spirit, like leaven in the mass of meal, will pervade and sanctify all our other doings. If the Christian desires a happy life, let him cultivate a devotional spirit. This is the instrument by which pure joy may be drawn from the fountain of living waters. Certainly, our chief joy should be in God, and this joy of the Lord would be our daily strength. And in the dark and cloudy day of adversity, when thick clouds gather around us, and water-spouts burst upon us, and all his billows go over us, what will be our condition, unless we have a refuge from trouble in God? And we can approach him only by the exercises and ordinances of devotion. If heaven be, as was said, a place of sublime devotion, then what better preparation can we make for an entrance into another world, than by cultivating the spirit of genuine devotion? If we find it to be our highest privilege and sweetest pleasure to draw near to God here in devotional exercises, we shall not be reluctant to be translated to that world, where we shall be able to worship him in perfection.

SERMON XXXIV.

DIFFICULTY OF KNOWING OUR FAULTS.

Who can understand his errors? Cleanse thou me from secret faults.—Psa. xix. 12.

THE truths of the Bible are exactly suited to the mind of man. As soon as he begins seriously to read or hear the word, he experiences its penetrating power. The conscience feels its operation as certainly as the eye perceives the light, or the ear the sound. And as men would know nothing of the appearance of the objects by which they are surrounded, until the light shines upon them, so the soul remains ignorant, in a great degree, of what is in it, until the word of God enters, and enlightens the chamber within. "The entrance of thy word giveth light." "The commandment of the Lord is pure, enlightening the eyes."

A small portion of light, it is said, only serves to render darkness more visible; so, when the light of truth begins to penetrate the mind, it shows that there is within us a dark abyss; and every additional ray discovers more of the intricate windings of the human heart; for there is not only dense darkness, but many false and deceitful appearances which turn out, upon accurate investigation, very different from what they seemed to be. It was some such view as this which caused the royal Psalmist to exclaim, "Who can understand his errors? Cleanse thou me from secret faults."

In the sequel of the discourse, I propose

I. To inquire why it is so difficult to know our own faults.

II. To consider the import of the prayer here uttered.

In the holy Scriptures errors and sins signify the same thing. The very word which commonly is used to express the idea of sin, in both the original languages, literally signifies to miss a mark. It is a deviation from a right line. A law is represented as a straight line, every crook, or departure from which is sin. "Sin is a transgression of the law." Therefore, "by the law is the knowledge of sin." All sin arises from some error or deception of the mind; for it is contrary to the constitutional principles of a rational nature to choose evil as evil. Every choice is necessarily of something which, for the present, has assumed the appearance of good, that is, something agreeable; but sin is intrinsically and wholly evil; and, therefore, in order to be chosen, there must be some deception in regard to it. This might be forcibly illustrated by considering the circumstances of the first sin of man. But every one may be convinced that this is true by referring to his own experience, and recalling to memory the particular exercises of his mind when induced to commit sin.

At any rate, in our text, the word "errors" means sins, for all will admit, that what the Psalmist prays to be cleansed from is sin, but in the original there is no other word to stand for sins; the word *faults* being supplied by the translators.

I. What I have proposed is, to assign some reasons for the difficulty, here implied, in knowing our sins. And it will be proper before going further, to make a distinction between knowing that a particular act is a sin, and perceiving the turpitude or moral evil that is in that act. The true evil of sin can only be known to those who are spiritually enlightened.

1. The first reason which may be assigned for our knowing so little of ourselves is, that few acquire the habit of reflection. It is natural and easy to think on things without, which are the objects of our senses; but to turn our mind in on itself and its operations, requires a painful effort; especially at first. It seems to be an unnatural state of mind, and a running against the natural current of our thoughts. On this account, the number who have acquired the habit of looking within is small.

2. Another cause of difficulty in obtaining the knowledge of our inner man is the fugitive nature of our thoughts, and the ever varying state of our emotions. Indeed, the very effort to inspect these mental exercises changes their nature, so that they are not the same as they were the moment before this effort was commenced.

3. There is in the human mind so great a mingling of different and even opposite feelings, that it is hard to separate things so blended together, and more difficult to ascertain the moral character of every emotion or desire. While some exercises of mind are morally good, and others morally evil, there is a large class which have no moral quality. They are merely natural or constitutional feelings; such as may exist in creatures which have no moral sense, and which are actually found in the inferior animals. But in man, as a moral agent, these animal feelings require to be restrained, directed, and governed; and when this is neglected, or improperly performed, these same feelings, which, considered abstractly, have no moral quality, become an important part of man's moral character. Much of sin consists in the irregularity and excess of these constitutional propensities; and much of virtue in their proper government.

Now, to discriminate between all the variety of emotions and exercises of our minds, and to form a correct estimate of the good and the evil, and to separate these from such as have no moral character, and to ascertain the degree of good or evil in any particular state of mind, is not an easy task.

4. There is another constantly operative cause which prevents men from knowing their own errors. It is that false medium which pride and self-love produce, and through which their sins are either not perceived at all, or are not seen in their true colour and dimensions. Every one has observed how strangely self-conceit blinds the minds of men. And pride itself is nothing else but

an erroneous estimate of ourselves: it is attributing to ourselves what does not belong to us, or forming too high an opinion of the worth of what we do possess. And as it magnifies our virtues, so it diminishes our faults; and thus men practise, habitually, upon themselves a grand deception; thinking themselves to be something, when, in the sight of God, they are nothing. This deception they carry with them into religion, where its consequences are more injurious than any where else. "They justify themselves, and despise others." The language of their hearts is, "Stand by thyself; I am holier than thou." Whole churches, like that of Laodicea, under this delusion of spiritual pride, are found to boast, "We are rich and increased with goods, and have need of nothing; and know not that they are poor and wretched, and miserable, and blind, and naked." The Pharisee described by our Lord, who came up to the temple to pray, boasted of his moral and religious duties, but he made confession of no sin whatever.

This blindness, the effect of pride and self-love, is as common now as ever. Even among those educated under the light of the gospel, it is most manifest. Men will, indeed, acknowledge in the general that they are sinners; but when you come to particulars, they are prone to justify themselves in almost every thing. Even the wickedest boast that their hearts are good. Men may have been taught the doctrine of total depravity, but they are not convinced of it as a practical truth in relation to themselves. The pride of their heart blinds their eyes.

5. There is another consideration, closely allied to the last, which has a powerful tendency to prevent us from knowing our own sins. The discovery of sin produces remorse, which is not only a painful feeling, but a more intolerable pain than any of which the human soul is susceptible, as far as our experience goes. And a sight and sense of sin not only produces remorse, but "a fearful looking for of judgment and fiery indignation." Men naturally avert their eyes from objects which are sure to excite painful feelings. This is one great reason why so many persons neglect the Bible, and never seriously look into their own hearts. It is the constant effort of their lives to keep out the light of divine truth from their minds. The bustle of business, or the round of amusements is kept up to free the mind from the intrusion of unwelcome thoughts, relating to God and to eternity. And if the secret motives which lead to the adoption of soul-destroying error were scrutinized, it would be found that the desire to escape from the uneasy feelings which the truth produces in the mind, has had a chief influence in rendering infidelity, or fundamental error, acceptable to the mind. " Men love darkness rather than light, because their deeds are evil." And when men deliberately reject the truth, they are often abandoned to believe a lie, as a judgment for not loving to retain God in their knowledge.

6. Another cause of erroneous notions respecting our own character is, the habit of looking at ourselves through the medium of the flatteries and praises of others. When persons are in exalted

stations, or called to the performance of public duties, they often excite the admiration of their fellow-men, especially of those who are below them, and, of course, their ears are filled with the commendation of their admirers. Others who wish to gain the favour of their fellow-men make use of base flattery, extolling them for virtues and talents which they do not believe they possess. Now, though a person may be conscious that he does not deserve these praises, yet such is the infatuating influence of self-love, that he is gratified that others entertain so high an opinion of him; and at length he begins to conceit that the qualities ascribed to him by his admirers and flatterers do really belong to his character. This is often clearly manifested when the man is thrown upon his own defence. He then appeals to public opinion, and seems to regard that as the true standard by which his character should be estimated. He comes at length actually to view himself through the medium of other men's opinions.

7. Another reason why men so commonly remain ignorant of themselves is, that they get into the habit of comparing themselves with others around them; and because they observe many addicted to crimes of which they are not guilty, they draw the conclusion that they are better than most; and adopt the opinion that their faults are trivial, and their characters uncommonly excellent. The apostle Paul notices and rebukes this fallacious method of judging. "For," says he, "we dare not make ourselves of the number, or compare ourselves with some that commend themselves; but they measur-

ing themselves by themselves, and comparing themselves among themselves, are not wise." We are very incompetent judges of the real moral character of others. God only knows how to estimate the true character of man. That often which is highly esteemed by men is an abomination in his sight, and whatever others may be, whether better or worse than ourselves, it alters not our character. This remains the same as if no other sinner was in existence.

8. Finally, on this head, the great source of error is not knowing, or not applying to ourselves, the true standard of rectitude. "By the law is the knowledge of sin." Of the extent of the demands of this law, and of the spiritual nature of the obedience which it requires many remain ignorant; or if they theoretically understand the nature of the precepts of the law, they do not apply this standard to their own hearts and lives. This was Paul's case before his conversion; for he says, "I was alive without the law once." In this state of ignorance and carelessness, men remain until the Spirit of God convinces them of sin by the application of the law to the conscience; when new light breaks in upon them, and they who before thought their sins were few and venial, now behold them rising up in dreadful array, an exceeding great multitude and very heinous in their nature. Then the convinced sinner is made to cry out, "Who can understand his errors? Cleanse thou me from secret faults."

Some of the sins of the heart may have taken deep root, and may exist in great force, and yet may not lead to external acts which are manifestly criminal. In such cases the moral turpitude of the mental disposition is often unnoticed; and when such sins have been habitually indulged, constant familiarity with them blinds the mind in regard to their evil.

Thus avarice, pride, envy, and ambition may have predominant influence in the mind, and yet the person under their dominion may, from prudential and selfish considerations, avoid external acts of enormity, and conform externally to the rules of justice and morality. Such are esteemed to be moral men, and maintain a good character in the sight of men. Being restrained from open transgression, they are very apt to entertain a high opinion of their own goodness; and at any rate to remain ignorant of the depraved state of their hearts, which are uniformly under the influence of such affections and principles as the law of God condemns.

If the hearts of many, who boast of their morality, were laid open to public view, how much abominable impurity and iniquity would be seen, even in those who wear externally the garb of modesty and decency!

1. If it be so difficult to know the moral state of our own hearts, we should be led to a more constant watchfulness over our own thoughts and feelings. We should also be in the habit of daily self-examination. And as we cannot judge correctly without having in our minds the true standard to which we ought to be conformed, we must become intimately acquainted with the word of God. We should

be careful to adopt just ideas of the spiritual character of the law, and to view it as extending to the thoughts—to the tempers—to the desires and emotions, and to the most secret motives of our conduct, and to sins of omission as well as of commission.

2. Knowing the treachery of the heart, and the many hindrances which stand in the way of acquiring a knowledge of our sins, we should incessantly and importunately pray to God who alone possesses a perfect knowledge of the heart to search and try us, and see whether any wicked disposition is yet indulged; and so to convince us of our sins, that we may be brought to that state of contrition and humility, which is the temper and state most becoming such imperfect creatures.

II. We come now, in the second place, to consider the import of the prayer here uttered. The prayer is for deliverance, not only from known sins, but also from such as were hidden. There are two kinds of cleansing or purification; the one is from guilt by expiation; the second from inherent pollution by sanctification. As sin is condemned by the law of God, and conscience, as far as it is informed, is an echo of the law, every sinner convinced of his sin must feel a sense of guilt, or which is the same thing, a sentence of condemnation within himself. This burden he can by no means remove, by any acts of new obedience, or by any voluntary sufferings to which he may submit. Rivers of waters may run down his cheeks, but sorrow for his sins cannot cleanse him from the deep stain which sin has left behind it. He may possibly forget that he is lying under a sentence of condemnation. He may even persuade himself that the fact is not so; that the idea of his obligation to obey the law is a mere fiction. Or he may adopt the opinion that pardon is easily obtained, and, therefore, he need give himself no concern about the penalty of the divine law. But all these false notions, being in direct opposition to the clearest dictates of his own conscience, are not accompanied with complete assurance; and he is still liable to be disturbed and alarmed by the voice of conscience; especially when overtaken by sickness, or some other calamity. Nothing can produce permanent peace of conscience but that which provides an atonement which will be a complete satisfaction to law and justice. On this account the conscience can be cleansed from guilt by nothing but the blood of Christ.

Here is the expiatory fountain in which the house of David and the inhabitants of Jerusalem may be washed from all their uncleanness. And such is the efficacy of this fountain of blood, that the greatest sinner may here be cleansed from all his guilt. The most heinous sins are perfectly cleansed by the application of the blood of Jesus. "His blood cleanseth from all sin." No greater sin can easily be conceived of than the murder of our Lord, but many involved in the guilt of this crime were pardoned on the day of Pentecost. And when the risen Saviour gave instructions to his apostles to preach repentance and remission of sins to all nations, they were directed to begin their ministry at Jerusalem. Paul reckons himself to be the chief of sinners; yet he was assured that he had found mercy. And in writing to the Corinthian converts, he gives a black catalogue of crimes, and says, "Such were some of you, but ye are washed, ye are sanctified, ye are justified in the name of the Lord Jesus, and by the Spirit of the Lord."

There is, indeed, one sin which is declared unpardonable; but not, as we suppose, on account of any want of efficacy in the blood of Christ to remove its guilt, but because those guilty of it are never brought to repentance. This cleansing from guilt in Scripture is called justification; and this blessing is received no otherwise than by faith. This doctrine is most clearly set forth by Paul, in the following words: "Being justified freely by his grace through the redemption that is in Christ Jesus; whom God has set forth to be a propitiation through faith in his blood, to declare his righteousness for the remission of sins that are past, through the forbearance of God. To declare, I say, at this time his righteousness, that he might be just, and the justifier of him who believeth in Jesus."

This blessing David most earnestly prayed for in the time of his deep penitence and humiliation, or account of his great sin in the case of Uriah. He cries, "Wash me throughly from mine iniquity, and cleanse me from my sin"—"Purge me with hyssop, and I shall be clean; wash me, and I shall be whiter than snow."

As it is said, "Cursed is every one that continueth not in all things written in the book of the law to do them;" and as God has repeatedly declared, that he will render to every man according to his works, it is plain that the guilt of every man must be very great. And as many of our sins are secret, unknown to our fellow-men, and many hidden from our own view, the petition to be cleansed from such sins is one which it behoves every person continually to offer. Our sins are compared in number to the hairs of our head, and to the sand on the sea-shore, and there is not one of this great multitude which, if it should remain unpardoned, would not be sufficient to shut the soul out of heaven and sink it to hell. How great, then, is the need of pardon! How many are the sins both known and unknown, for which pardon must be received, or the sinner perish! Besides, every day we are committing sins which are prevented from bringing us again into condemnation by nothing else but the sprinkling of atoning blood. "Let us," says Paul, "draw near with a true heart, in full assurance of faith, having our hearts sprinkled from an evil conscience, and our bodies washed with pure water." Here we have the two identical blessings prayed for in the text, brought fully into view.

The cleansing for which the Psalmist so earnestly prayed, includes substantially all that the sinner needs in order to his salvation; all the rich blessings of the new covenant. If he is cleansed from guilt by the blood of sprinkling, and from pollution by the washing of regeneration and renewing of the Holy Ghost, there is nothing to hinder his entrance into heaven, and his enjoying the blessedness of that holy place. For those who are cleansed by the process which the gospel prescribes are free from every stain. Though their sins were as scarlet, they are made white as snow; though they were red like crimson, they are as wool. Christ, the great Purifier, will present them before his Father's throne without spot or wrinkle, or any such thing. Certainly, then, our prayers for this double cleansing should be fervent and incessant. And unless we receive this cleansing of our souls from secret sins, and all manner of sin, our condition through eternity will be one of extreme misery and degradation. That burden of guilt which the forbearance of God alone keeps from crushing the impenitent sinner, will fall with all its dreadful weight on the gospel rejecter, and will sink him to the lowest hell. It will be more tolerable for Sodom and Gomorrah in the day of judgment, than for him. Let him, then, fly speedily from the wrath to come. Let him make his escape to the appointed house of refuge, where he will find shelter from every storm, and safety from every danger. Let him come near to the cross, and direct his eyes to the Saviour, lifted up for his salvation.

But the soul not only needs to be cleansed by the blood of Christ from the stain of guilt, but being internally polluted, must be washed with the washing of regeneration, and renewed by the renewing of the Holy Ghost. Pollution has defiled all the powers of the soul, and for this there is no remedy but in the "sanctification of the Spirit." This cleansing is begun when the first ray of divine light is let in to the dark mind of the sinner. Before, he knew not the turpitude of his sins. Indeed, until this time, he took little notice of the moral state of his heart. If he could keep up a decent external behaviour, he was satisfied with himself

But now his eye is turned inward, and the heart which he had often boasted to be pure, he finds to be corrupt, "deceitful above all things, and desperately wicked." In his first concern, he hoped to be able to do something to cleanse himself. By prayers, by penances, and external reformation, many have, as it were, cleansed the outside of the cup and platter; but their inward part was still full of the pollution of sin. And even when the evil of the heart begins to be discerned, the whole depth of the evil is not seen. There are still many hidden iniquities, "secret faults," which conceal themselves in the deep recesses and intricate windings of the deceitful heart. Sin often assumes the guise of virtue and innocence, or presents such palliations and excuses as seem to lessen its turpitude. The more spiritual light any man enjoys, the more sensible is he of the wickedness of his own heart. It may be compared to a dark chamber, full of abominations. Until light is let in these odious objects are not seen, but as soon as a single ray is darted in upon them, they begin to be seen in their deformity. While the light is partial, the whole will not be perceived; every new ray of light reveals something not before discovered. Thus it is with the renewed man: the further he advances in piety, the deeper is his sense of the want of purity in his heart. So far is he from entertaining the vain conceit that he is already perfect or approaching near perfection, that it is difficult for him to conclude that he is not, every day, growing worse. And it is on this account especially, that the pious are so often mistaken in regard to their real progress in piety. But the more we see of our own sinfulness, the more intense will be our desires for cleansing. Indeed, all spiritual exercises will bear an exact proportion to our sense of the "exceeding sinfulness of sin." This conviction fills the soul with penitence, and humbles it in the dust before God; and at the same time drives it to the fountain opened for sin and uncleanness. Though the efficient power by which the soul is purified is the Holy Spirit, yet means are not on this account rendered superfluous. God works commonly by appropriate means, both in the world of nature and of grace. The word of God, or divine truth, is necessary in this operation. The rational soul to act right must have the knowledge of the truth, and God's word contains the truth. If we hope for cleansing, we must look for it by means of the divine word. The intercessory prayer of our Saviour was, and no doubt still is, "sanctify them through thy truth, thy word is truth." The ordinance of baptism is a visible representation of the purification of the soul. Therefore, it is said, "Except a man be born of water and the Spirit, he cannot enter into the kingdom of heaven." The washing of the body in the baptismal water is, therefore, referred to when the internal cleansing of the soul is meant; as in the text already quoted, in which the double cleansing by blood and water is mentioned—"Having our hearts sprinkled from an evil conscience, and our bodies washed with pure water." The connexion between the word and the sanctification of the soul is clearly manifest from the exhortation of Paul to the Corinthians:

"Having, therefore, these promises, dearly beloved, let us cleanse ourselves from all filthiness of flesh and spirit, perfecting holiness in the fear of God." And more clearly still in Ephes. v. 25, 26, "Even as Christ loved the church, and gave himself for it, that he might sanctify and cleanse it with the washing of water by the word." Peter also connects increase of holiness with the knowledge of the truth, when he says, "Grow in grace, and in the knowledge of our Lord Jesus Christ." The importance of prayer for the aids of the Holy Spirit is evident from the earnest petition in our text, and from many other similar prayers in the Psalms: "Wash me throughly from my iniquity, and cleanse me from my sin." "Purge me with hyssop, and I shall be clean; wash me, and I shall be whiter than snow."

In conclusion, it may be remarked,

1. That the best evidence of the existence of a holy nature, is the sincere and prevailing desire of perfect holiness. "Blessed are they that hunger and thirst after righteousness, for they shall be filled." The love of holiness is the same as the love of the law. Says the royal Psalmist, "O how love I thy law." "I esteem all thy precepts, concerning all things to be right, and hate every false way." The language of Paul, and of every renewed heart is, "I delight in the law of God after the inner man."

2. The evidence of a gracious state is not the persuasion that the object sought is fully attained, but an ardent, habitual desire to reach it. "Not as though I had already attained, or were already

perfect," says Paul; "but this one thing I do; forgetting those things which are behind, I press forward to those things which are before, for the prize of the high calling of God in Christ Jesus;" endeavouring, through the Spirit, "to mortify the deeds of the body," and "to perfect holiness in the fear of God."

3. When, on account of sin, the conscience is again burdened and wounded, recourse must be had to the same "blood of sprinkling" which afforded relief at first. No peace can be found any where else. Penances, and pilgrimages, and multiplied religious ceremonies and works can do nothing toward procuring true peace of conscience. Faith in Christ, a believing view of the cross, is the only remedy for guilt. "My little children," says John, "sin not; but if any man sin, we have an Advocate with the Father, who is the propitiation for our sins, and not for ours only, but for the sins of the whole world." Let the believer, then, learn to live near the cross, and often look by faith on the bleeding sacrifice of "the Lamb of God, which taketh away the sin of the world."

4. We must not forget that many of our sins are hidden from ourselves. For these we should seek for pardon and purification. Though we cannot repent of these in detail, we can in the general. We can repent of the sin of our nature, commonly called original sin, from which all actual transgressions proceed. But it behoves us to be diligent and faithful in searching for our secret sins, that when discovered we may apply to the mercy of God for pardon and cleansing.

5. The neglect of secret sins often leads to the commission of presumptuous sins. By degrees the concealed poison gathers strength, until at last, on some favourable occasion, it exerts its power and breaks out into overt acts, and for a season, at least, gains dominion over the man. Such falls in professors open the mouths of the wicked, and give them occasion to blaspheme that holy religion which they profess.

SERMON XXXV.

GOD'S GRACE SUFFICIENT.

My grace is sufficient for thee.—2 Cor. xii. 9.

The apostle Paul, though not inferior to the other apostles in gifts and plenary inspiration, and in labours and success more abundant than them all, was nevertheless subject to like infirmities, passions, and temptations as other men. He had, indeed, received larger supplies of grace than most others, but this did not render him in any degree independent and self-sufficient, nor exempt him at all from those conflicts and temptations which are commonly experienced in the Christian warfare; nor from the need of those means of improvement which a gracious God has appointed for the preservation and edification of his people while sojourning upon earth. We find him, therefore, much given to prayer, and often requesting the prayers of others in his behalf; also observing a rigid discipline toward himself, in keeping his body under, lest while he preached to others, he himself should be a castaway.

Paul was favoured with very full revelations of gospel truth, without being dependent on the teaching of men. In this respect his preparation for the work of the ministry was peculiar; the ascended Saviour himself condescended to become his Teacher. He was also favoured with frequent visions, and with the knowledge of the future destinies of the church. On one occasion he was caught up to Paradise and to the third heavens, where he heard things which it was not lawful for a man to utter. By this heavenly rapture, the faith of the apostle must have been greatly strengthened, and his desire of a constant participation of the joys of heaven, rendered very intense. But such is the infirmity of even the holiest men, and such the tendency to self-exaltation, that the enjoyment of any high privilege, or the reception of any distinguishing honour, is apt to puff up the mind, and produce a degree of self-exaltation; or, at any rate, of self-complacency. Paul the apostle was not exempt from the danger of being exalted above measure by his abundant revelations, therefore his divine Master put him, by way of prevention, upon a course of painful discipline. He sent him "a thorn in the flesh, a messenger of Satan, to buffet him." Whatever might be the precise nature of the apostle's affliction, we know that it gave him much uneasiness; for he prayed, not merely once or twice, but thrice that it might be removed. His prayer was heard and answered, but not in the way which he desired; but in one which seemed better to infinite wisdom. The thorn was not removed, but God said, "My grace is sufficient for thee." By which answer he was assured, that he should be supported under the severe trial which he felt to be so grievous; and, doubtless, he might infer from this answer, that benefit might be derived from the affliction laid upon him.

There is not a word in the whole vocabulary, of richer import than the word GRACE. It expresses the beginning, the middle, and the end of man's salvation. It was grace, that is, undeserved love or favour which moved the eternal mind to devise the plan of redemption. It was grace which designated the persons who should be made partakers of salvation. It was grace which induced the Son of God to condescend to become man, and to become "obedient unto death"—thus offering himself an expiatory sacrifice for our sins. "Ye know the grace of our Lord Jesus Christ, that though he was rich, yet for our sakes he became poor, that we through his poverty might be made rich." It was grace which caused the church to be founded, means of salvation to be established, and the gospel to be preached. It is grace which brings down the Holy Spirit to enlighten to regenerate, to sanctify, to comfort, and to conduct triumphantly to heaven the redeemed heirs of glory. And it will be grace which will crown with everlasting felicity, all those who have "an abundant entrance administered to them, into the everlasting kingdom of our Lord and Saviour Jesus Christ." As the foundation of the spiritual temple of the Lord was laid in grace, or the love of God; so the top stone shall be brought forth with the shouting, "Grace, grace unto it."

Although the words of our text were primarily addressed to Paul for his support and encouragement; yet they were recorded in the sacred volume, that we also might derive consolation from them; for they are equally suited to the case of every believer; and " those things that were written aforetime were written for our learning, that we through patience and comfort of the Scriptures, might have hope." It will not, therefore, be a departure from the spirit of the text to consider these words as containing a promise from God to all believers, that God will never leave them nor forsake them; but that in all exigencies, and under all trials, his grace shall be afforded in sufficient measure to enable them to perform the duties which may devolve upon them; or to sustain with patience and fortitude the burdens which they may, under the dispensations of Providence, be called to bear.

Our object in the remainder of this discourse, therefore, shall be to apply the promise to believers in those circumstances in which they specially need comfort and encouragement.

1. In the first place, then, the words may be applied to such as are labouring under a conviction of sin, and are oppressed with a sense of guilt. Whether such have already believed or not, there is encouragement in these words to induce them to embrace the promise; for the fountain of grace is so rich, that there is no possibility of its being exhausted; and so free, that all are invited to come and take of the waters of life. To an awakened conscience, the recollection of past sins, with all their aggravations, is exceedingly painful and

terrifying. To them the judgment day presents a scene awfully alarming. And the language of their hearts is, "What must I do to be saved?" To all who are thus pursued by the demands of the law, and the upbraidings of conscience, I would say, You need not despair. There is hope in your case. The gospel brings you glad tidings. The burden of its message is, salvation by grace—"grace abounding to the chief of sinners"—"grace reigning through righteousness, unto eternal life." "Believe in the Lord Jesus Christ, and thou shall be saved." To all who are bowed down under the burden of their sins, I am authorized to preach the sufficiency of divine grace for their complete pardon, and perfect justification from all the demands of the law. Sinners who are at ease in Zion, and "alive without the law," persuade themselves that it is an easy thing to obtain pardon and reconciliation with God; not from any exalted estimation which they entertain of the grace of the gospel, but from their very low estimate of the evil and ill-desert of their sins; and of the spirituality and binding obligation of the law. But when the light of conviction breaks in upon their minds, and they are made to see the exceeding sinfulness of sin, and the infinite holiness of God; and that "the law is holy, and the commandment holy and just and good," the humbled and contrite sinner can with difficulty be induced to believe that a holy God can, consistently, extend favour to such a guilty creature; or that such sins as his can be forgiven by a God of infinite holiness. They, who are thus convinced of the demerit of their sins, are precisely in the situation most favourable to the reception of the gospel. They are the sick who need the Physician. All who ever believed have been placed in similar circumstances. God condescends kindly to reason with such, "Though your sins be as scarlet, they shall be white as snow; though they be red like crimson, they shall be as wool." "It is a faithful saying, and worthy of all acceptation, that Jesus Christ came into the world to save sinners, of whom (says Paul) I am chief." "The blood of Christ cleanseth from all sin." And "He is able to save to the uttermost all who come unto God by him; seeing he ever liveth to make intercession for them."

2. Again, these words are calculated to afford comfort and encouragement to such as are struggling with the inbred corruptions of their own hearts, and with the temptations of the wicked one; who feel "another law in their members, warring against the law of their mind;" "the flesh lusting against the spirit;" "so that when they would do good, evil is present with them"—tending to bring them again into captivity to the law of sin and death; so that their feelings are expressed by groanings, which cannot be uttered. And when they cry, their language is, "O wretched man that I am, who shall deliver me from the body of this death!"

Now, although in this conflict between the old and new man, human strength is weakness, yet, when we feel our weakness most, we are strong in the Lord, for "His strength is perfected in our weakness." What Christ said to Peter, in the view of his temptation and fall, may be applied to every humble penitent; "I have prayed for thee, that thy faith fail not." Were it not for his intercessory prayers in our behalf, we could not hold out in opposition to any powerful temptation. That he does thus intercede for all believers, in all ages, we know from the prayer which he offered for for them while upon earth : "I pray not that thou shouldst take them out of the world, but that thou shouldst keep them from the evil which is in the world."

3. The grace of our Lord Jesus Christ will be sufficient to support and comfort believers under the severest trials, the heaviest afflictions, and most violent temptations, to which they may be subjected. Afflictions are the lot of the people of God in this world. It is written, "Many are the afflictions of the righteous;" "they who live godly in Christ Jesus shall suffer persecution;" and, "through much tribulation we must enter the kingdom." As Christ was, all his life, a sufferer, "a man of sorrows, and acquainted with grief," his disciples should calculate upon having the same lot in the world as their Master. Indeed, this seems to be made a condition of our participating of his glory. "If we suffer with him, we shall also reign with him. If we deny him, he also will deny us." But human strength cannot bear up under these calamities. We need help. We must have an almighty arm on which to lean. Christians have suffered inconceivable agonies in the times of persecution; which they endured even unto death, and that too in the most cruel forms But they were

sustained by an unseen hand. Christ never forsakes his followers in the time of their distress; and the Holy Spirit will not leave them comfortless. Their richest joys are sometimes experienced in the midst of the furnace of affliction. When the three children were seen walking unhurt in the midst of the fiery furnace, there was seen one like to the Son of man in their company. It was verily the Son of man himself; and this was written for our learning, that we might trust to his presence and aid in the hottest fire of persecution. His promise is, "My grace is sufficient for thee." Even in death we need not fear; for "precious in the sight of the Lord, is the death of his saints." And a royal saint of old sweetly sang, in the view of this termination of human life, "Though I walk through the valley and shadow of death, I will fear no evil; thy rod and thy staff they comfort me."

A lively faith in the realities and glories of the heavenly inheritance will disarm death of all its terrors, and cause us to think all our afflictions light and of momentary duration. Thus the matter appeared to Paul: "These light afflictions which are but for a moment, work out for us a far more exceeding and eternal weight of glory. While we look not at the things which are seen, but at the things which are unseen; for the things which are seen are temporal, but the things that are not seen are eternal." It is faith that gives the victory over the world, whether it assails the Christian by its blandishments or by its terrors. And this victory it achieves, through the grace of Christ, by bringing the unseen world into view.

4. But grace is requisite to enable us to act, as well as to suffer. Arduous duties are incumbent on the Christian. He is placed and continued here to glorify his Maker and Redeemer, to benefit his fellow-creatures, and to secure the salvation of his own soul. The performance of duty often requires strong resolution, and much painful self-denial in the disciple of a crucified Redeemer. Some are called of God to the arduous work of the gospel ministry, for which no human wisdom, or human power is sufficient. "Who is sufficient for these things?" But Christ has promised to be with his ministers "always to the end of the world." We are commanded, indeed, "to be strong," but not in our own might, but "in the power of the Lord."

Some are called in the Providence and by the Spirit of God to forsake father, mother, brothers and sisters, and to bid adieu to their own native land, and beloved country, to spend their days among the uncivilized heathen, subjected to many privations, and exposed to numerous dangers from a savage people, and from a deleterious climate. But they need not be dismayed; their Master will accompany them, and he says, "My grace is sufficient for thee."

REFLECTIONS.

1. How truly blessed are they who have obtained an interest in the grace of the Lord Jesus Christ; and how solicitous should we all be to have this matter placed on a secure foundation. All his

people may confidently say, "The Lord is my Shepherd, I shall not want."

2. Christians should habituate themselves to confide implicitly, under all circumstances of affliction, and in the performance of all arduous duties, on the all-sufficient grace of Christ. It will ever be to them according to their faith. But if they are doubtful of his aid, and distrust his promises, the consequences will be unfavourable. What Christ, above all things, demands of his followers is, that they trust him.

3. All who have been made partakers of the grace of God, are bound to exercise unceasing gratitude for such unmerited favour. If you have been chosen unto life eternal, it was to magnify his glorious grace. If your sins are pardoned, and your persons accepted and justified, it is by the grace of God in Christ. If you have been regenerated and made partakers of the divine nature, it is not by works of righteousness which you have done, but by his grace that you are saved. Even the chief of sinners, who believe in Christ, may exult in the unsearchable riches of his grace. Where sin abounded, grace shall much more abound. Thanks be unto God for the unspeakable gift of his grace! Amen.

SERMON XXXVI.

THE DYING MARTYR'S PRAYER.

Lord Jesus, receive my spirit.—Acts vii. 59.

As death is inevitable, and as none who die return to give us any account of their condition in a future world, and as reason cannot penetrate the gloom which hangs over the grave, it is a matter of rejoicing that we are in possession of a well-attested revelation, which contains all the information which we need, in regard to the future destiny of man. Even under the old dispensation, although believers enjoyed a glimmering light respecting a future state, yet the light was by no means clear; a mysterious darkness enshrouded the state of the dead. But since the coming of Christ, that which was before obscure has become bright. "Life and immortality are brought to light by the gospel." The resurrection of Jesus Christ sealed the instructions which he had given on this point. We know that as surely as he lives, in another world, so surely his disciples will live also, and be with him where he now is. His immediate followers, therefore, had no fears of the future; they contemplated death as a kind friend, sent to release them from a world of sin and sorrow. The curse was taken away; the sting was plucked out; the victory was wrested from this universal conqueror.

To illustrate these remarks, I would refer you to the example of the first death which occurred among Christ's sincere disciples after his resurrection. I mean that of Stephen, the proto-martyr; for although we read of the awful end of two professed disciples, Ananias and Sapphira, before the martyrdom of Stephen, yet we know that their profession was hypocritical. They were numbered with the disciples, but were destitute of true faith, and stand on the sacred page as an awful warning to professors in all future ages to beware of hypocrisy, and to take heed of trifling with the sacred profession of Christianity.

Concerning the conversion of Stephen, the Scriptures furnish no account; whether he was one of the seventy disciples, or of the one hundred and twenty who consorted together before the remarkable increase of the church at Pentecost; or whether he was one of those who, on that memorable day, was pricked in the heart, and brought to repentance by the effusion of the Holy Spirit, attending the preaching of Peter, we cannot now ascertain; nor is it important. It is enough to know from the unerring word of inspiration that he was an eminent Christian; although that name was not yet given to the disciples. When it became necessary to select seven men of honest report, full of the Holy Ghost and wisdom, to take charge of the distribution of the charitable funds of the primitive church, Stephen was the first on the catalogue; and was particularly characterized as a man " full of faith and the Holy Ghost." He seems to have been, in a very peculiar manner, endowed with miraculous gifts which had been so copiously shed on the disciples on the day of Pentecost; and to have stood forth as a conspicuous instrument in extending the knowledge of the truth; for we read, that " Stephen, full of faith and power, did great wonders and miracles among the people." But it was then, as it has been ever since, the more useful and conspicuous any servant of God is, the more certainly does he become the object of some kind of persecution. The infant church at Jerusalem was a type of all Christian churches ever since. No sooner did she exist, than her destruction was threatened. And whence did this opposition arise? First, from the rulers, who imprisoned and beat the apostles, and forbade them to speak in the name of Jesus; and then from the synagogues, which ought to have been the first to receive, and foremost to defend the truth. And as Stephen was a leading man in the church, these opposers entered into controversy with him. As long as error and sin exist in the world, there must be conflict. Light and darkness —Christ and Belial, can have no concord. But " they were not able to resist the wisdom and spirit by which he spake." They resorted to the usual weapons of the enemies of the truth. They endeavoured to destroy his usefulness by malicious slanders; yea, they suborned men, who said, " We have heard him speak blasphemous words against Moses and against God. And they stirred up the people, and the elders, and the scribes, and came upon him, and caught him, and brought him to the council, and set up false witnesses, who said, This man ceaseth not to speak blasphemous words against this holy place and the law. For we have heard him say, that Jesus of Nazareth shall destroy this place, and shall change the customs which Moses delivered unto us."

Stephen was now arraigned before the Sanhedrim, the highest court in the Jewish nation. He seems to have stood alone in the midst of his persecutors; but that Jesus whom he preached, and who had said, before his ascension to heaven, " Lo, I am with you always," did not forsake him at this moment of trial. The Holy Ghost, with whose influence he was endowed, did not now leave him. And to confound his adversaries the more, and to render their conduct the more inexcusable, Stephen was so illumined with the rays of celestial glory, that his very countenance became radiant, as did that of Moses, on another occasion. " And all that sat in the council looking steadfastly on him, saw his face as it had been the face of an angel."

The high priest, who presided in this grand council, now said, Are these things so? Upon which Stephen delivered that remarkable discourse, the substance of which is recorded in this chapter. When he came to the application of his discourse he addressed his persecutors with a directness and pungency of reproof, which produced a powerful impression. He said, " Ye stiff-necked and uncircumcised in heart and ears, ye do always resist the

Holy Ghost as your fathers did, so do ye. Which of the prophets have not your fathers persecuted? And they have slain them which showed before of the coming of the just One, of whom ye have been now the betrayers and murderers; who have received the law by disposition of angels and have not kept it." "When they heard these things, they gnashed on him with their teeth; but he being full of the Holy Ghost, looked up steadfastly into heaven and saw the glory of God, and Jesus Christ standing at the right hand of God. And he said, Behold, I see the heavens opened, and the Son of man standing at the right hand of God. Then they cried out with a loud voice, and stopped their ears, and ran upon him with one accord; and cast him out of the city, and stoned him. And the witnesses laid down their clothes at a young man's feet, whose name was Saul. And they stoned Stephen, calling upon God, and saying, Lord Jesus, receive my spirit! And he kneeled down, and cried with a loud voice, Lay not this sin to their charge."

This prayer, which closed the martyr's course, may have been heard in regard to many; but in regard to one, it certainly was. I refer to the young man at whose feet the witnesses laid their clothes. This young man, a person of extraordinary talent, was a strict Pharisee, well educated, and zealous for the law. He seems to have taken an active part in this prosecution, for he gave his vote against Stephen in the council, when he was condemned, and was forward to assist in the execution. But is it not astonishing that this scene could be witnessed by this person, and others, without conviction? The truth is, that such is the blindness and perverseness of men, that no external means, however striking, or even miraculous, ever did or ever will convert a sinner from the error of his ways, without the internal efficacy of divine grace.

But our present subject is especially Stephen's dying prayer to Christ, "Lord Jesus, receive my spirit." These few words convey much precious instruction, to which I would now call your attention.

1. Stephen addressed his prayer to the Lord Jesus. He had just been favoured with a vision of this divine Person in his glory. He saw him standing on the right hand of God. He would never have thought of addressing himself to any of the saints or angels, who also stood round the throne of God. What should we think, if he had died calling on Gabriel or Moses, and saying, Gabriel, receive my spirit—or, Moses, receive my spirit? No example of any such prayer is found in the Bible. But here, "a man full of faith and the Holy Ghost," in his dying moments prays to Jesus Christ, and this is recorded for our example and encouragement. And if we may call upon this name when dying, we may also at all times. Indeed, this is given as one characteristic of true worshippers, for the Scripture saith, "Whosoever believeth on him shall not be ashamed—for the same Lord is rich unto all that call upon him. For whosoever shall call on the name of the Lord, shall be saved."

2. The second truth which we may learn from

this text is, that the soul exists separate from the body in an intermediate state between death and the resurrection; and that in this state it is with Jesus. When we look at the dead body of a fellow-creature, and attend merely to the suggestions of sense and reason, we are tempted to suppose that the thinking principle which recently actuated this body, has become extinct, or has ceased to be active; but sense and reason are not to be trusted in this case. Divine revelation, which is the word of God, teaches no such gloomy doctrine. It opens to our view another state of being—another world, where Christ is gone, and gives us assurance that believers, while their bodies rest in the grave, are with Christ. So our Lord, when on the cross, said to the penitent malefactor, "This day shalt thou be with me in Paradise." And Paul, who had been caught up into the third heaven, had such a sense of the excellency and glory of the place, that he "had a desire to depart and be with Christ." He knew "that if our earthly house of this tabernacle were dissolved, we have a building of God, an house not made with hands, eternal in the heavens;" and that to be "absent from the body" is to be "present with the Lord." And are not Moses and Elias in the heavens? The latter, indeed, has his body with him; but the former died and was buried.

Stephen undoubtedly asked and expected to be received at once into the presence of Christ. He does not say, Receive me at the resurrection. "Lord Jesus, receive my spirit." The idea of the sleep of the soul, or of some other place than heaven being its residence till the resurrection, is unscriptural Surely Christ has ascended into the highest heavens—and where he is, there also it is his will that his disciples should be with him. He has gone to prepare a place for them—and when he comes, he will bring with him all who have died in the Lord. Is he the Head, and are they members of his body, and will he not gather all those who are united to him around him, as fast as they leave the world?

3. Every believer, when called to die, should consider it his high privilege, cheerfully and confidently, to commit his departing spirit into the hands of Jesus, his Lord. He who acts the part of a kind Shepherd, while we are passing up through this wilderness, guiding, protecting, and feeding his little flock, and even carrying the lambs affectionately in his bosom, will not forsake the sheep of his pasture, whom he loves, and for whom he has laid down his life, when called to pass through the last gloomy valley. There are many shadows of death through which he leads them safely, but in their passage over one which is pre-eminently deep and dark, he has enabled one of old, as an example to the flock, to say, "Though I walk through the valley of the shadow of death, I will fear no evil, for thou art with me. Thy rod and thy staff, they comfort me."

Death is abhorrent to nature; and many are, all their life, subjected to bondage through fear of death; but Christ came to deliver us from those appalling terrors; and he does it by enabling us to exercise faith in his name. The soul that so believes in the day of adversity, and in the last hour, as to be able to commit itself unto Christ by an act of unwavering confidence—that soul need fear no evil. If the great High Priest, and the ark of the covenant lead the way, the swelling waters of Jordan shall be driven back, and a free passage to Canaan be secured. Death has no power to harm the true believer, since Christ, the Captain of salvation, received his envenomed shaft into his own vitals. He has extracted the venomous sting, and trode the monster under his feet; so that he makes his people conquerors, and more than conquerors, through his love. "O death, where is thy sting! O grave, where is thy victory!"

4. No doubt the martyr's prayer was heard. No doubt the every where present Redeemer would willingly receive the precious deposit, now with confidence committed to him. None that trust in him shall ever be confounded or disappointed in their hopes. There is some reason to think that every believer when he dies will be conducted to Paradise by angels commissioned for that purpose. In the account of the rich man and Lazarus, we read that no sooner had the soul of this pious beggar departed from the body, than it "was carried by angels into Abraham's bosom." Now this representation of the state after death, does not seem so much to have been intended to teach what happened to a single individual, as to furnish us with a general view of the different circumstances of the righteous and wicked, when they enter into the invisible

world. And, therefore, we may conclude that all true saints, as well as Lazarus, will be provided with a convoy of angels. And would it be considered an extravagant thought, that those angels which act as guardians to the people of God here, keeping watch around their dwellings, and holding them up in their hands, should be the ones commissioned to perform this kind office; for no doubt they contract an affection for those committed to their charge, and would be prompted to engage in such a service in behalf of those souls whom they watched over, during their painful pilgrimage through the world. And for aught that we know, the departed saints will need some persons to be their guide in the new regions into which they at once enter, and where they are entire strangers.

But, however, pleasing may be the thought of being met at the very entrance into the future world by angels, the true believer finds no prospect of the future state so pleasing, as that which promises to bring him into the presence of his Saviour. That which reconciles him in an absence from the body is, the expectation of the presence of the Lord. And as he is not only ever present to render effectual aid in time of need, and has especially signified that he will comfort and sustain his friends in their last conflict, the disembodied spirit desires to be received into his kind embrace. And as he has a body, and therefore is visible in heaven, it will above all things pant for an admission into his immediate presence. For this, Stephen prayed, and for this thousands have since prayed; and their suit has not been denied. How happy they are who are thus present with the Lord, no human heart can conceive, or tongue express. Truly, their joy is now full.

REFLECTIONS.

1. As we must take this journey—as there is no discharge in this warfare—and as we have no experimental knowledge of the country to which we are going, and have no opportunity of conversing with any who have experience in this matter, it is obviously of the first importance to secure a guide who will both have power to protect and wisdom to conduct us safely through this gloomy valley Such a guide is the great Shepherd of Israel.

2. Our sensitive souls naturally shrink with dread from the thought of plunging into an unknown state of existence. If we feel no dread of the misery of hell, yet we cannot easily divest ourselves of the fear of appearing in the immediate presence of God; and even the idea of the sudden blaze of celestial light and glory, creates a degree of dread entering the invisible world. As the appearance of a single departed spirit, however much beloved, would throw us into consternation, we are prone to transfer these feelings to a future world. But the true remedy for every kind of fear is to cast ourselves into the hands of our divine Redeemer. He has loved us, and died for us, and

will receive our departing spirit, and introduce them to the seats of the blessed in that way which wisdom and goodness will direct.

3. But what shall the dying sinner do? Who will receive his spirit in that awful moment? He rejected the Saviour, and now the door of mercy is closed for ever. Now he may cry and not be heard. Alas! alas! alas! what will become of the impenitent sinner when God requires his soul?

SERMON XXXVII.

CHRIST'S GRACIOUS INVITATION.

Come unto me, all ye that labour and are heavy-laden, and I will give you rest.—MATT. xi. 28.

As a stream of living water to a traveller perishing with thirst, as a skilful physician to one sick with a dangerous disease, as a reprieve to a condemned criminal, such is the voice of mercy to the miserable, self-condemned sinner—such, in ten thousand instances, have been these blessed words to heavy-laden, weary souls. These are words which can never lose their interest by age or repetition. As food is equally relished by the hungry appetite after having been eaten a thousand times as at first, so the precious promises of God bring the same refreshment to the soul, however often they may have been received by faith. The Christian does not desire novelties; all he wants is a heart to embrace and relish the same truths which have stood on the sacred page from the beginning There is no penury in the divine word. All fulness and riches are included in this treasure, if we are only in possession of the key of faith to unlock the ark in which it is contained. One great excellence of the sacred Scriptures is, that they never lose their power and sweetness. After the lapse of ages, God's promises to believers are as firm and consolatory as when first made; and Christ's invitations to sinners are as full and as free to those who now hear the gospel, as when first uttered.

If Christ, while upon earth, had spoken no more than these few words, they ought to be esteemed infinitely more precious than all the golden sayings of all the heathen sages. Let us, then, be truly thankful for such a gracious invitation, proceeding from the lips of him who always spake as never man spake; and let us lift up our hearts to the Father of lights, to open our eyes and prepare our hearts to understand and appreciate the grace which is exhibited in these divine words of our Redeemer.

But who are the persons here addressed by the Saviour? What class of persons are designated by the "labouring and heavy-laden?" As the gospel is directed to be preached to "every creature," and as this call contains the essence of the gospel, there is no reason why we should not consider all who hear the invitation, as included; especially as our Lord complains of the conduct of the most proud and unbelieving of his hearers for refusing to come to him; "Ye will not come unto me, that ye may have life." All men are miserable; all men are "by nature children of wrath;" all men are labouring in the vain pursuit of earthly happiness; all, therefore, may consider themselves invited. None need feel themselves excluded from Christ's invitation. And the giving this universal latitude to the call, harmonizes with parallel passages of Scripture, especially with that remarkable invitation in Isaiah lv. 1—3. "Ho, every one that thirsteth, come ye to the waters, and he that hath no money: come ye, buy and eat; yea, come, buy wine and milk without money, and without price. Wherefore do ye spend money for that which is not bread, and your labour for that which satisfieth not? Hearken diligently unto me, and eat ye that which is good, and let your soul delight itself in fatness. Incline your ear and come unto me; hear, and your soul shall live." And the gracious invitation of the Spirit, in Rev. xxii. 17, is equally free and universal: "And the Spirit and the bride say, Come. And let him that heareth say, Come. And let him that is athirst come; and whosoever will, let him take the water of life freely." And the same extent ought to be given to Christ's public invitation at Jerusalem, on the last day of the feast of tabernacles; "In the last day, that great day of the feast, Jesus stood and cried, saying, If any man thirst, let him come unto me and drink." John vii. 37.

But while we think that this kind invitation ought not to be restricted, we readily admit that it is more applicable to some of our race than others. The poor, the oppressed, the diseased, the persecuted, the halt, the blind, the friendless among men, may have been more particularly in the eye of the blessed Redeemer; for it was given as one characteristic of his being the Messiah that was to come, that "the blind receive their sight, and the lame walk, the lepers are cleansed, and the deaf hear, the dead are raised up, and the poor have the gospel preached to them." Matt. xi. 5.

But there is another class to whom the Saviour's address may be considered as still more appropriate; I mean convinced sinners labouring under a sense of guilt, and almost sinking under a burden too grievous to be borne. Surely Christ had respect to these, for he came not " to call the righteous, but sinners to repentance ;" " to seek and save the lost ;" to heal those that are sick, namely, such as are sensible of their mortal maladies. And even they who are groaning under the burden of a blind mind and hard heart, and think that they have no conviction; even these, who are so prone to exclude themselves, are of the number invited. Yes, Christ speaks to you—he speaks to you more particularly than unto others. Do not, therefore, put away from you the gracious call, as if it were intended only for others; do not any longer ingeniously argue against your own souls; do not by unbelief shut the door of mercy, which the Redeemer has graciously opened.

Neither should penitent believers, who are burdened with a deep sense of their own defilements, and continual imperfections, be omitted when the several classes of heavy-laden sinners are designated. The great Shepherd of the sheep has always especial regard to the tender and weak of his own flock. "He carries the lambs in his bosom, and gently leads those that are with young." The kind condescension of the Son of God to the humble penitent is, in many parts of Scripture, set forth in remarkable words. He was described in prophecy, as one who would "comfort all that mourn;" and who would give unto them "who mourn in Zion, beauty for ashes, the oil of joy for mourning, and the garment of praise for the spirit of heaviness." "Thus saith the Lord, Heaven is my throne, and the earth is my footstool; but to this man will I look, even to him that is poor and of a contrite spirit, and trembleth at my word." "The bruised reed will he not break, nor quench the smoking flax." Let those, then, who are walking in darkness, and troubled in spirit—let all those who are harassed and cast down with manifold temptations and sore inward conflicts, which cause them to express their feelings in groanings which cannot be uttered in words, attend to the gentle accents of mercy which proceed from the lips of Jesus. Unworthy and wretched as you feel yourselves to be, he passes you not by. He addresses you, not in the language of reproach or condemnation, but in that of tender affection. Yes, he calls you also to come unto him.

II. Having considered the objects of the invitation, let us now contemplate the character of Him from whom it proceeds.

Though we need to know more than the name of this divine Person, yet even this is "as ointment poured forth." His name is Emanuel, "God with us." Said the angel to Joseph, "Thou shalt call his name Jesus, for he shall save his people from their sins." When our Lord put it to his disciples to say who he was, Peter, in the name of his brethren, answered, "Thou art the Christ, the Son of the living God." And because he was born of a woman, and made flesh, he often speaks of himself as "the Son of man." The prophet Isaiah, when he speaks of the child that should be born, and of the Son that should be given, adds, "And his name shall be called Wonderful, Counsellor, the mighty God, the everlasting Father, (or rather, the Father of Eternity,) the Prince of Peace." And in the sublime vision which John had of the white horse, "he that sat upon him was called Faithful and True. His eyes were as a flame of fire, and on his head were many crowns, and he had a name written that no man knew but he himself. He was clothed in a vesture dipped in blood, and his name is called the Word of God." He is also styled "King of kings, and Lord of lords." And as his names indicate the dignity of his person, so they do the benign offices which he executes. He is the Redeemer—the Saviour—the one Mediator—the great High Priest—the Advocate—the great Shepherd of the sheep—the Judge of quick and dead. Immediately before he uttered the gracious invitation which we are considering, he had declared his divine knowledge and power: "All things are delivered to me of my Father; and no man knoweth the Son but the Father; neither knoweth any man the Father, save the Son, and he to whomsoever the Son will reveal him." None but he who was God with God, in the beginning, could utter these words without the highest blasphemy. But he who was in the "form of God, thought it not robbery to be equal with God." And if our Redeemer was not omnipotent, his people could not trust in him; if he was not omniscient, it would be vain to call upon him. In Christ there is the most wonderful union of majesty and condescension; of heavenly glory and human sympathy and tenderness. While he claims to be " God over all," he is not ashamed to call us brethren. He took not on him the nature of angels, but the seed of Abraham. And the reason why we may come boldly to the throne of grace is, because " we have not an high priest which cannot be touched with the feeling of our infirmities." And the reason which he assigns here, to induce us to come to him without hesitation, is, that he is " meek and lowly in heart."

III. How must we come? Not by a bodily approach, for this is impossible. Where Christ now is we cannot come: and a local approach, if it were practicable, would be useless. Many came near to the Saviour, when he sojourned on earth, who never derived any benefit from him. His worst enemies and murderers came in contact with him, when they seized, bound, buffeted, scourged, and crucified the Lord; and the traitor Judas lived in his family, and travelled in his company for years, and kissed him in Gethsemane; but this will only serve to render his doom the more intolerable. It had been better for that man never to have seen Jesus—yea, never to have been born.

Coming to Christ is undoubtedly an act of the rational soul, irrespective of the body. It is a spiritual approach, in which the Saviour is apprehended by the enlightened mind in his true character. It is a full persuasion that he is indeed the

Son of God, and Saviour of the lost. It is the act of a convinced, distressed soul, flying from the coming wrath, to take shelter under the outstretched wings of his mercy. It is an exercise of humble confidence in the Redeemer of sinners, that he will deliver it from all the evils which are felt or feared. There is nothing difficult in this act to the soul under the influence of the Holy Spirit; nor does it require a long time. It is executed as quick as thought. It is nothing else but the soul's cordial consent to receive Christ as a complete and only Saviour. The weary and heavy-laden sinner, when almost overwhelmed with the burden of his guilt, having sought relief from other quarters, at length hears the kind invitation of Jesus, "Come unto me;" and being enabled to give full credit to the truth and sincerity of the call, and to see the excellence and suitableness of Christ as a divine Saviour; and being persuaded, that every blessing needed to secure eternal salvation, is treasured up in him, receives him, as he is freely offered in the gospel, and willingly commits all its immortal interests into his hands; and resolves to submit to him and obey him, in all time to come. In all this, the soul, though operated on by an Almighty power, is conscious of no restraint, unless it be the sweet constraint of the love of Christ. There is, indeed, an irresistible drawing towards Christ, but the more powerful it is, the more freely does the soul seem to act. Under the sweet influence of grace, the affections spontaneously go forth to him, who now appears altogether lovely; and the weary soul experiences a sweet rest by casting all its burdens on the Lord. The principal act of faith is an act of trust. "Blessed are all they that trust in him." And having once tasted this blessedness of confiding in Christ, we never think of seeking any other refuge. The believer is not only persuaded that he is the way, but the only way. On this account he is prized above all price. "To you who believe, he is precious." Well may the name of Jesus sound sweet to the believer's ear, because there is "no other name under heaven by which we must be saved." No wonder that he values above rubies, or kingdoms, that elect and precious corner-stone—though rejected by the proud and self-righteous—which God has laid in Zion, because he is sure that it is a safe foundation on which to build for eternity; and because he is persuaded "that other foundation can no man lay than that which is laid, which is Christ Jesus."

Coming to Christ is not an act to be performed only once, but is to be continually repeated. Every day we need his aid; and every hour we should have recourse to him by some confiding or grateful act. This access once obtained, the intercourse should be continually kept open. He allows his disciples the privilege of friends, to come as often as they will; and he invites them to come with freedom and confidence to his throne of grace, "to obtain mercy and find grace to help in time of need." So intimate and endearing is the intercourse between Christ and believers, that there is a mutual indwelling; Christ in them, the hope of glory—and they in Christ as members of his body, or as branches engrafted into him, the true vine.

But, perhaps, the anxious inquirer still asks, "How must I come?" To which I answer—come poor and naked, and helpless, and unworthy—come renouncing all dependence on your own righteousness. If you attempt to come with a price in your hand, you will be rejected. Christ must be acknowledged and received as our only Saviour. He will have nothing to do with those who place any confidence in their own works, or in their religious privileges. He will not save you on account of your natural amiableness; or on account of your moral honesty, or diligent attention to external duties. You cannot in these respects go beyond the rich young ruler in the gospel, and yet he "lacked one thing," and that was the main thing. In the punctilious observance of external duties and rites, you cannot exceed the Scribes and Pharisees, and yet your righteousness must exceed theirs, or you can never enter the kingdom of heaven. You must come to Christ for wisdom, righteousness, sanctification, and redemption. As long as sinners think that they are "rich and increased with goods, and have need of nothing," they will not come to Christ; but when they are convinced that they are "poor, and wretched, and blind and naked," they will be inclined to hear his counsel, and come unto him, "to buy gold tried in the fire that they may be rich, eye salve that they may see, and white raiment that they may be clothed, and that the shame of their nakedness appear not." In short, delay not, that you may make yourselves better, or prepare your hearts for the reception of Christ, but come at once—come as you are. If you are sick, apply at once to the Physician. If you are defiled, come to the fountain opened for sin and uncleanness. If you are burdened with guilt, come to a crucified Saviour, whose blood cleanses from all sin. If you are miserable, Christ promises you rest if you will come to him. Are you kept back by a deep sense of unworthiness? this is the very reason why you should come. Christ came to save *sinners*. The deeper your guilt, the greater your need of just such a Saviour. He saves none because their sins are small; he will reject none because their sins are great. He is as willing to receive the penitent who is the chief of sinners, as the amiable youth whose life has been stained with no acts of gross transgression. Where sin has abounded, grace shall much more abound. "This is a faithful saying, and worthy of all acceptation, that Jesus Christ came into the world to save sinners, of whom," says Paul, "I am chief." Come, then, with confidence, trusting in that great assurance, " Him that cometh, I will in no wise cast out."

But as your case is urgent and dangerous, let me intreat you to come speedily. Make no delay. In such a case, delays are dangerous. *Now* is the accepted time. *Now* is the day of salvation. Enter while the door of mercy is open. Work out your salvation while it is day, before the night cometh when no work can be done. And the work which you are required to perform, is to believe on him whom God hath sent. You have no need to leave your seat to perform this act. "Believe in the Lord Jesus Christ, and thou shalt be saved." Help is near. The Deliverer is present. Application to him is as easy now as it ever can be. Take words and return unto him. Fall down before him with confession and humble supplication; "for he that calleth on the name of the Lord shall be saved." Venture on him, for you are perishing where you are, and you will but perish if he should slay you. But if you are rejected and spurned from his feet, you will be the first that has thus perished; for God cannot lie, and he hath promised to receive the soul that comes.

IV. What will be gained by coming to Christ? One thing only is promised. "Come unto me, all ye that labour and are heavy-laden, and I will give you rest." But in this one thing, every thing good is included. They only can be said to be at rest, who are in a state of happiness; and true happiness can only be found in the favour and love of God. Can that man be said to be at rest, whose sins are unpardoned, whose passions are unsubdued, and on whom the wrath of God abides? "There is no peace, saith my God, to the wicked." "The wicked are like the troubled sea, which cannot rest, whose waters cast up mire and dirt." Wicked men are like the evil spirit which went through dry places, seeking rest and finding none. They are in constant pursuit of a phantom, which for ever eludes their grasp. There is in this world no foundation of solid rest. To be preserved from perpetual agitation, our anchor must be cast within the veil. Noah's dove, which found no rest even for the sole of her foot, is an emblem of the restless condition of men. But the same dove, returning to the ark, is an emblem of the distressed soul flying to Christ from the deluge of deserved and coming wrath. And, O how kind is that hand which is stretched out of the ark, to take in the fluttering weary soul! Then, indeed, rest is enjoyed. "I will give you rest," says the gracious Redeemer. And when he gives this precious blessing, it is found in experience to be a solid, undisturbed, sweet, and permanent rest. It is in no respect different from that peace which Christ so often and so emphatically promised: "Peace I leave with you, my peace I give unto you; not as the world giveth, give I unto you. Let not your heart be troubled, neither let it be afraid." It is the declared will of the blessed Jesus, that the joy of his people should be full; therefore he says to his disciples, "Your sorrow shall be turned into joy" —"your heart shall rejoice, and your joy no man taketh from you." Delightful, indeed, is that peace which Jesus not only speaks, but breathes into the soul, and sweet is that rest which the weary soul experiences, when it takes refuge under the outstretched wings of his mercy, from the gathering storms of wrath. In that auspicious moment, the troubled spirit not only rests from fear and remorse, but also from its own fruitless struggles of self-exertion. It rests from the unprofitable works of self-righteousness, and finds complete repose in the perfect righteousness of Jesus Christ. A believing view of the cross causes the heavy burden of guilt to fall off; and, although the coming soul bows to the yoke of Christ, and takes up his burden, yet love makes "his yoke easy," and his "burden light." How sweet is the calm which the first lively exercise of faith in Christ produces! The cheerful light of day is not so pleasant to the eyes of one long immured in a dark dungeon, as the light of his Father's reconciled face to a prodigal just returned from his wanderings. It is, indeed, "a marvellous light" which the gospel beams on the renewed soul. It is justly a day of feasting and rejoicing, when one that was lost is found, and when he that was dead is alive again. How affectionately and confidentially does the believing soul repose on the bosom of Jesus! and when his love is shed abroad in the heart, how intimate, how precious is the communion which it enjoys! Here, truly, it has found rest. But while in the body, these bright views and pleasing prospects are often obscured. While the Bridegroom is present, the bride rejoices, but when he is absent, she mourns, and often inquires, "saw ye him, whom my soul loveth?" If we lose sight of the objects of faith; and, especially if sin be indulged, and the Spirit grieved, darkness and sorrow will again visit the soul; and rest can only be found by coming again to Jesus, from whom it was first received; and as often as we come to him, we find his promise verified; rest is obtained.

But whatever is experienced here—whatever seasons of calm repose may be enjoyed—whatever moments of extatic joy—yea, "unspeakable and full of glory," may transport us, these are but drops from the fountain above—a mere foretaste of the river of pleasure which flows from the throne of God. Here our pilgrimage is through a wilderness. But soon all our sorrow shall cease, and we shall enter into that rest which remains for the people of God.

The last conflict of the believing soul is in death; for this is the last enemy. The last darkness which will ever be experienced, is that of "the valley and shadow of death." The last bitterness which will ever be tasted is the "bitterness of death." The last waves of sorrow which shall ever roll over such a soul, are the swellings of Jordan. The last fiery dart which the enemy shall ever be permitted to aim at the friend of Christ, will here be cast. Yea, better than all, the last consciousness of indwelling sin is experienced in this hour. Pain will no more be known but in the joyful consciousness that it is gone for ever. Admitting then that this is a dark passage—an appalling scene—an unnatural separation—a painful agony—a direful conflict; yet even here, the Shepherd of Israel can give us rest. Even here, the Captain of salvation can make us "conquerors, and more than conquerors." In the midst of the darkness of death, a celestial beam often shines to guide and cheer the heavy-laden traveller. Even the sting of death may be absent; and all fear and all doubt removed. Rest may be—has been, enjoyed on a dying-bed. The pious dead sweetly rest in the bosom of Jesus. How calm—how serene—how confident—how abstracted from earth—how heavenly they sometimes appear, before they forsake their clay tabernacle: knowing that they have a house not made with hands eternal in the heavens.

> "Jesus can make a dying-bed
> Feel soft as downy pillows are,
> While on his breast I lean my head,
> And breathe my life out sweetly there."

But we should not make too much of the comforts of a dying hour. Some of God's dear children pass through this gloomy way, with scarce a twinkling ray to animate or guide them; yea, some who in life enjoyed pleasing prospects of future bliss, have had their day turned into night, and the death-scene to them has indeed been a tremendous conflict. The powers of darkness have been let loose to assault them; the sweet light of divine favour has been withdrawn, and added to this, the confusion of physical derangement has contributed to spread over the pious mind a dense cloud, even in the departing hour. But still, Christ is in the cloud; Christ has not forgotten his promise—"I will never leave thee, never, never, never, forsake thee." He will shield his own from real evil; and will speedily grant a rich recompense for every pang He especially knows how to sympathize with those dying in agony and under darkness. It was his own sore experience. O how bitter was that cry above all others: "My God, my God, why hast thou forsaken me?" And in proportion as the agony is severe, will be his promptitude to grant deliverance. It may be, that desertion at such a time is permitted, that the soul may know something of the intensity of the suffering of the dear Redeemer at that moment. But it is soon over. The passage, though dark, is short, and the transition is glorious. The sweetness of the promised rest, when first enjoyed, will bear some proportion to the bitterness of the death just escaped. At any rate, Heaven will be as truly a rest to such as die under a cloud, as those who experienced an anticipation of heaven on their death-bed. We need make no distinction; rest is promised to all, and the joy of all shall be full. If some experience a delight superior to that of other believers, it will be because they are capable of taking in more of the bliss and glory of that boundless ocean in which all swim. There indeed is rest—rest from labour —rest from trouble—rest from persecution—rest from sickness—rest from conflict and temptation— rest from doubt and fear—rest from sin—in short, rest from every evil, and the enjoyment of every good, of which a purified, glorified, immortal soul is capable.

This, then, is the motive to induce you to come to Christ, for all this, and much more is included, when he says, "Come unto me, all ye that labour and are heavy-laden, and I will give you rest."

THE END

Other SGCB Classic Reprints

In addition to *Evangelical Truth* which you now hold in your hands, Solid Ground Christian Books is honored to present the following titles, many for the first time in more than a century:

THEOLOGY ON FIRE: *Sermons from the Heart of J.A. Alexander*
A SHEPHERD'S HEART: *Sermons from the Ministry of J.W. Alexander*
A GENTLEMAN & A SCHOLAR: *Memoir of James Petigru Boyce* by *John Albert Broadus*
OPENING SCRIPTURE: A Hermeneutical Manual by *Patrick Fairbairn*
THE ASSURANCE OF FAITH by *Louis Berkhof*
THE PASTOR IN THE SICK ROOM by *John D. Wells*
THE NATIONAL PREACHER: Sermons from the 2nd **Great Awakening**
THE POOR MAN'S OT COMMENTARY by *Robert Hawker* **(6 vols)**
THE POOR MAN'S NT COMMENTARY by *Robert Hawker* **(3 vols)**
FIRST THINGS: *The First Lessons God Taught Mankind* by *Gardiner Spring*
BIBLICAL & THEOLOGICAL STUDIES by *the 1912 Faculty of Princeton*
THE POWER OF GOD UNTO SALVATION by *B.B. Warfield*
THE LORD OF GLORY by *B.B. Warfield*
CHRIST ON THE CROSS & THE LORD OUR SHEPHERD by *John Stevenson*
SERMONS TO THE NATURAL MAN by *W.G.T. Shedd*
SERMONS TO THE SPIRITUAL MAN by *W.G.T. Shedd*
HOMILETICS AND PASTORAL THEOLOGY by *W.G.T. Shedd*
A PASTOR'S SKETCHES 1 & 2 by *Ichabod S. Spencer*
THE PREACHER AND HIS MODELS by *James Stalker*
IMAGO CHRISTI by *James Stalker*
A HISTORY OF PREACHING by *Edwin C. Dargan*
LECTURES ON THE HISTORY OF PREACHING by *John A. Broadus*
THE SCOTTISH PULPIT by *William Taylor*
THE SHORTER CATECHISM ILLUSTRATED by *John Whitecross*
THE CHURCH MEMBER'S GUIDE by *John Angell James*
THE SUNDAY SCHOOL TEACHER'S GUIDE by *John Angell James*
CHRIST IN SONG: *Hymns of Immanuel from All Ages* by *Philip Schaff*
COME YE APART: *Daily Words from the Four Gospels* by *J.R. Miller*
DEVOTIONAL LIFE OF THE SUNDAY SCHOOL TEACHER by *J.R. Miller*

Call us Toll Free at 1-877-666-9469
Send us an e-mail at sgcb@charter.net
Visit us on line at solid-ground-books.com

"Uncovering Buried Treasure to the Glory of God"

www.ingramcontent.com/pod-product-compliance
Lightning Source LLC
Chambersburg PA
CBHW021823220426
43663CB00005B/109